Reimagining Civic Education

Reimagining Civic Education

How Diverse Societies Form Democratic Citizens

E. Doyle Stevick and Bradley A.U. Levinson

ROWMAN & LITTLEFIELD PUBLISHERS, INC.
Lanham • Boulder • New York • Toronto • Plymouth, UK

ROWMAN & LITTLEFIELD PUBLISHERS, INC.

Published in the United States of America
by Rowman & Littlefield Publishers, Inc.
A wholly owned subsidary of The Rowman & Littlefield Publishing Group, Inc.
4501 Forbes Boulevard, Suite 200, Lanham, Maryland 20706
www.rowmanlittlefield.com

Estover Road
Plymouth PL6 7PY
United Kingdom

British Library Cataloguing in Publication Information Available

Library of Congress Cataloging-in-Publication Data

Reimagining Civic Education : how diverse societies form democratic citizens /
E. Doyle Stevick And Bradley A.U. Levinson [editors].
p.   cm.
ISBN-13: 978-0-7425-4755-1 (cloth : alk. paper)
ISBN-10: 0-7425-4755-8 (cloth : alk. paper)
ISBN-13: 978-0-7425-4756-8 (pbk : alk. paper)
ISBN-10: 0-7425-4756-6 (pbk : alk. paper)
1. Civics—Study and teaching. 2. Citizenship—Study and teaching. I. Stevick,
E. Doyle, 1969–   II. Levinson, Bradley A.U., 1963–
LC1091.T46 2006
321.8071—dc22   2006023268

Printed in the United States of America

For my parents, Eugene and Emily Stevick, who made this book—and so much more—possible

—Doyle Stevick

For Jorge Baxter, Pablo Zúñiga, and the Organization of American States

—Bradley Levinson

Contents

Acknowledgments

First and foremost, we thank Judith Torney-Purta for her supportive participation in this project and her patience and flexibility throughout the publication process. We are also grateful to the editors at Rowman & Littlefield who saw promise in this volume. In particular, Alex Masulis embraced the concept for the volume and saw it through its evolution, promptly fielding questions large and small without complaint. Marian Haggard saw us through the initial edits. Elaine McGarraugh provided us with a smooth transition when Marian left, and has been delightfully responsive and helpful in guiding us through the final stages of the process.

We also thank the authors of this volume, as well as all those who expressed interest in contributing chapters to this book. We know now as well as anyone that the confines of a solitary tome cannot contain all of the exciting work being done in this growing field. It has been a delight to work with the authors as their chapters and the volume as a whole came together. Their receptiveness to constructive suggestions has been a happy surprise, and was quite gratifying professionally. We would like to single out Kathleen Staudt for her helpful feedback on multiple versions of our introduction.

Bradley thanks his wife, Debra, and his children, Ella and Kira, for their understanding and support. Whatever civic virtue Bradley can muster is made possible by the domestic virtues of his family! Bradley also gives particular thanks to Jorge Baxter, Pablo Zúñiga, David Edwards, Sofialeticia Morales, Lenore García, and other staff members of the Organization of American States. Their work on behalf of "reimagining civic education" for democracy across the Americas has been singularly inspiring.

Doyle thanks all those who helped to make this book possible. In particular, his co-editor, (tor)mentor, and (now) colleague Bradley Levinson, who showed him the ropes of book publication. He served double duty as co-editor and expert consultant, and played yet another important role in Doyle's professional development. There is no question that this book would not have happened without Bradley's timely and intensive efforts on a number of fronts. These efforts have been deeply appreciated and will be rewarded with a lifetime supply of PITA.

Doyle also thanks the University of South Carolina and its College of Education for their support as this project was completed. Their policy of offering a course release for new faculty has been critical to creating the time necessary to complete this volume. In particular, Ken Stevenson and Zach Kelehear have carefully guarded the time so that Doyle could get off to a good start in the Department of Educational Leadership and Policies. Their support has been greatly appreciated.

In the big picture, whether it is a book or a baby—and sometimes the differences are smaller than anticipated—it takes a village. Or at least an extended family. Doyle's parents, Emily and Eugene Stevick, have been unflagging in their support throughout his life, and have contributed in countless ways, materially, temporally, conceptually, spiritually. Professional conventions may not place their names on the spine, but this book is to no small extent an indirect outcome of their efforts throughout the years. Spending time on a book means time away from the children, and so Doyle's sister's, Chris Stevick, insatiable infatuation with her niece and nephew has also allowed Doyle to shift attention from one to the other.

Doyle's wife Kara's family, the Brown clan, has also contributed so much. Kara's sister Erika—with her family, Pete Blackshaw, Liam and Layla—has been one of our biggest supporters. Beverly and Walter Brown were positively relentless with their generosity and support throughout the completion of Doyle and Kara's doctoral programs, as they tried to balance work, academics, and a small family. Walter in particular had a clear message that was reinforced with regularity: eyes on the prize, just get it done. Throughout the summer of 2005, when much of the editing for this volume took place in the Adirondacks, Walter looked after baby Calvin and read stories for Lucia. It is wished he could be here to see this.

Finally, Kara, Lucia, and Calvin make every day a great day. Kara's support has been indispensable throughout this process, even taking the children out of town for the weekend as Doyle dotted the t's and crossed his eyes. As these final words are written, they are arriving at the airport; now he can turn his attention back to them.

Introduction: Cultural Context and Diversity in the Study of Democratic Citizenship Education

E. Doyle Stevick and Bradley A. U. Levinson

> I know of no safe repository for the ultimate powers of society but the people themselves; and if we think them not enlightened enough to exercise their control with wholesome discretion, the remedy is not to take it from them, but to inform their discretion.
>
> —Thomas Jefferson

THE LONG CONVERSATION: THEORY AND PRACTICE IN DEMOCRATIC CULTURE AND POLITICS

Jefferson's "safe repository" for the power (*kratos*) of the people (*demos*) is democracy itself. Since the Athenians first coined the term more than 2,500 years ago, democracies have taken remarkably diverse forms, even while debates over democracy's essential and ideal characteristics continue. What constitutes a democratic society? The mechanisms of voting? The alternation of power, freedom to assemble, and to speak as one wishes? Meaningful participation for all citizens? Sets of rights—political, civil, cultural, human? Social safety nets or unencumbered markets? Openness to newcomers?

Although debates over democracy's forms are spirited and ongoing, no less dynamic are the debates about the education of democratic citizens. What should citizens know, believe, and be able to do? How can schools and society best convey the knowledge, develop the skills, and cultivate the attitudes and dispositions required for democratic citizenship? In much the same way as debates over democracy itself, these questions are contested and complex, and they play out in such diverse forums as classrooms, government, the media, and popular culture. A dynamic tension exists between these issues—how to foster citizenship and how to practice democracy—propelling them forward in tandem. Their trajectories must further be understood in relation to the dizzying evolution of the world itself—its technological change and economic integration, conflicts and cultures, migrations and ideologies, its transnational institutions and local practices.

Democracy is not an abstract system that can be dropped into any new context and be expected to function, nor is it a set of institutional arrangements that can be evaluated satisfactorily simply by examining a flowchart in a document. Democracy is rather the product of interaction, the interaction of a system and its institutions with the cultural context and the people who make them real. Institutions and practices are infused with culture. And so are schools, educational practices, and the debates that surround them. Richard Holbrooke, then a U.S. Assistant Secretary of State, captured this dual nature of democracy well when the 1996 elections in Bosnia were imminent. "Suppose the election was declared free and fair," he said, and those elected are "racists, fascists, separatists, who are publicly opposed to [peace and reintegration]. That is the dilemma" (Zakaria 1997).

A purely procedural or minimal definition of democracy, such as the existence of free, fair, open, regular, and contested elections (Patrick 1996), may be a sine qua non but still be insufficient to characterize democracy. Beyond such narrowly framed institutional definitions, more is needed. But what? As Joseph de Maistre expressed it, "A constitution that is made for all nations is made for none." There must be a fit between a society's governing institutions and the peoples and cultures it serves. To answer the question, then, "What beyond minimal definitions of democracy is needed?" we must include *democratic cultures*, complex and diverse configurations of shared understandings that do not lend themselves easily to minimal definitions or universal characterization.

If culture is a murky realm, resistant to both quantification and macro-level study and subject to diverse interpretations, it becomes no less critical to explore and to understand. If a minimal yet sufficient definition of the criteria for democracy is difficult to establish, then the question of what constitutes democratic culture is even more difficult. Long-standing democracies and free societies may retain strands of authoritarianism or patriarchy that undermine democratic freedoms. And societies that have endured tyranny may have funds of knowledge, traditional practices, or cultural capital that can provide a solid foundation for the construction of a democratic society.

We are not so bold as to venture a single, universal definition of what democratic culture might be; rather, by exploring questions about the education of democratic citizens in diverse contexts around the globe, we hope to shed light on the many disparate practices, debates, challenges, and understandings that currently mold the democratic citizens of tomorrow.

The volume before you consists of sociocultural studies of democratic citizenship education—conceived broadly as the many formal and informal practices that shape the creation of democratic citizens. The studies apply the manifold tools of qualitative and interpretive research to explore the development of citizenship for democracy in diverse cultural contexts around the globe.

If democracy cannot flourish amid widespread racism or other antidemocratic sentiment, neither can authoritarian pedagogy foster democratic citizenship. This sentiment was perfectly distilled by the Mexican administrator who was exasperated that many teachers did not grasp the dialogical focus of Mexico's new civics program. She declared to Bradley Levinson, "*Ya pasó el tiempo de los dictadores, pues*" ("The time of the dictators is over, come on!"). Her dictators were not political leaders, however; she meant the teachers who stand over the class, dictating content to be faithfully reproduced in students' notebooks. Her choice of words suggests that in order to rid themselves of dictators at the political level, Mexicans would also have to eventually rid themselves of classroom dictators. In other words, the way to create a more active, participatory Mexican citizen who would no longer accept undemocratic regimes was through a more active, participatory pedagogy. Only teachers who could develop such a pedagogical style would be appropriate for modeling and thereby encouraging democratic conduct.

Such a perspective is by no means confined to Mexico: indeed, the democratic citizen's prospects around the globe are evolving in ways not imagined even two decades ago. The fifteen years spanning the collapse of the Soviet bloc, the end of authoritarian rule in much of Latin America and Asia, and the end of South African apartheid have spawned great hopes for billions of people. Yet emerging global developments, from the rapid growth of international migration to September 11, 2001, and its fallout, pose grave new challenges. Narratives of "transition to democracy" and "democratization" heralded the dawning of a progressive era throughout the world, and new and revived forms of democratic governance have been developed in countries that had previously experienced long periods of authoritarian or totalitarian rule. Still, for many residents in the "new" or "multicultural" democracies, the full promise of democracy is yet unrealized. The rights and responsibilities of democratic citizenship continue to be eclipsed by old cultural habits or the specter of economic injustice. Citizenship itself has become a contested terrain.

In this book, we delve into the messy, conflicting struggles over the creation of democratic citizens in real societies and institutions. We examine the cultural particularities and the striking multiplicity of local practices that today constitute our attempts at democratic political socialization. We explore practices whose variety and diversity are both consonant with and enriching of core conceptions of democracy. Through these explorations, we hope that this volume can contribute to the many conversations taking place around the globe about what education for democratic citizenship can and should entail, in specific places, in specific cultures, at specific times.

We are pleased to enter this enduring and distinguished conversation. From the time the Athenians adopted democracy in 508 B.C., millennia before schools would be charged with the task of crafting citizens, wildly diverse cultural practices performed this function. The great playwrights Aeschylus, Euripides, and Sophocles continually reworked and retold the shared Greek mythical narratives, from the Trojan War to the fall of Oedipus, in ways that resonated with contemporary debates and inspired citizens to reflect once again on war, justice, or the conduct of the Athenian empire. If musical tragedies seem an unusual venue for citizenship education, one can only imagine the diversity of practices that preceded the advent of the public school and its broad dissemination and near-universal adoption around the world. Even while Homer's epics brought a shared frame of reference to children and adults alike across the city-states of the ancient Greeks, historians and philosophers were debating whether such poets were to be trusted (Herodotus) or even banned outright (Plato). In other words, the long conversation has been carried on next to, often in tension with, the actual cultural practices of political socialization.

Whether democratic political socialization occurs primarily through the classroom practice of citizenship education or in other venues from talk circles to saunas, culture continues to mold the particular social relations and practices of democratic citizenship education. To the long conversation about what kind of citizenry is necessary to sustain democratic institutions and a democratic society, and what kind of education is necessary to create such a citizenry, these chapters contribute some of the concepts and findings of the many fields of qualitative research, particularly those centered on culture. The authors assembled here apply different concepts and methods to the task of understanding the dynamics of democratic citizenship education in different contexts around the world. We believe that these concepts and approaches, in tandem with the concrete data that demonstrate their salience, will bring valuable perspectives to one of humanity's most important and longest-running discussions.

This particular conversation may never have had so many thoughtful participants as it does today. Even beyond the rich literature examining the role of education in democratization generally, recent qualitative research into the actual practices and meanings of civic education has boomed, both with individual case studies and innovative comparative work. We note a few of the most outstanding contributions of the last decade. Carole Hahn's seminal *Becoming Political* compared the civic education practices of predominately middle-class suburban students in four wealthy countries of Western Europe plus the United States. Noel McGinn and Erwin Epstein's notable two-volume collection of the role of education in democratization, *Comparative Perspectives on the Role of Education in Democratization*, pulled together much valuable work concerning identity, socialization, and education in transitional societies. The epic International Association for the Evaluation of Educational Achievement (IEA) Civic Education study, which featured qualitative and quantitative stages, has already produced four indispensable volumes, including the initial collection of twenty-four qualitative country case studies that were designed around a common set of questions and methodology to produce data that could be used in comparisons (Torney-Purta, Schwille, and Amadeo 1999) as well as a volume of essays that sought innovative ways to compare that data (Steiner-Khamsi, Torney-Purta, and Schwille 1999). We are delighted that Torney-Purta, a prime architect of these volumes, provides a commentary at the conclusion of this volume.

Although the IEA study found the majority of its participants in Europe and North America, W. O. Lee, David Grossman, Kerry Kennedy, and Gregory Fairbrother helped to expand our knowledge of civic education practices around the globe by producing *Citizenship Education in Asia and the Pacific*, a volume whose contributors frequently move beyond the traditional focus on the country level and develop promising new lines of inquiry, particularly the examinations of how religious traditions relate to citizenship education. Although the world's most populous democracy, India, was absent from this book—and any volume may lack an important topic because a relevant contributor was not available—James Banks's *Diversity and Citizenship Education* features India and several other prominent countries around the world, in addition to essays from some of civic education's most prominent scholars from across disciplines. Finally, one of the most exciting contributions to the field has come from Werner Schiffauer, Gerd Baumann, Riva Kastoryano, and Steven Vertovec in *Civic Enculturation: Nation-State, School and Ethnic Difference in the Netherlands, Britain, Germany and France*, the finest volume of comparative anthropological research into political socialization to date.

To this rich stock of scholarship, we hope to contribute a few more elements. While most previous studies have highlighted what is universal or what is comparable, we venture out into the peripheral, unique, divergent, border-crossing, contested, cosmopolitan, and ever-changing realms that constitute democratic citizenship education. While prior research has emphasized the effectiveness of classroom practice, children's knowledge outcomes, and the individual country as the level of analysis, and it has also focused most frequently on suburban, middle-class schools in advanced liberal democracies, dominant cultures, and powerful states, the reader will find less explored areas in this volume: dynamics between distinct institutional and policy levels; education in smaller and lesser studied countries and societies, and rural, urban and impoverished areas; third sector activities and private and religious schools; and especially the question of culture and meaning in the lives of teachers, policymakers, and students. Prior research has laid the groundwork for these productive forays into areas still ripe for additional exploration, and we intend no indictment of the choices made by those who have come before. Rather, we believe that these chapters can shed new light on earlier research, and this volume is richer for the scholarly context it enters.

The first element we aim to contribute further advances the work of the contributors to Lee et al. in moving away from the focus on individual countries as a unit of analysis. In the essays here, flows of money, meaning, and material, and processes of adaptation and interpretation take center stage. The analytic lens opens to many angles of vision, not a single frame. Although the country-level retains an important position, the microlevel processes of individual schools, classrooms, and institutions—the level at which ethnographic research often focuses—play a central role in constituting macroprocesses and policies (Burawoy and Verdery, 1999). In addition, increasing attention is being paid to the diverse groups within established democracies, whether indigenous populations of Australia and the United States, as explored in the essays by Joan DeJaeghere and Robert Whitman, or to immigrants and their reception in France and Cyprus, which Deborah Reed-Danahay and Stavroula Philippou address.

A focus on culture also allows a shift from such norm-laden questions as "Is this teaching practice effective?" to the more interpretive question "What does this practice mean to the people who are engaged in it?" Indeed, many of our essays put the focus on the teachers themselves, the primary agents who mediate between education policies, official curriculum, textbooks, and student learning in their classrooms. The increased attention to teachers is warranted particularly in contexts of rapid political change—in countries emerging from Soviet occupation, for example, or in other places trying to move beyond authoritarian legacies. Many teachers were brought up with traditional pedagogies, were compelled to teach propagandistic courses such as Leninism, and have seen reductions in their personal authority and economic security. Do they have misgivings about some of the changes? Does their prior work teaching Marxism or other pro-paganda still shape the way they interpret the changes going on around them? And how do radical societal changes, coupled with teachers' shifting ideologies and life circumstances, shape their classroom practice of civic education? In this volume, Audra Skukauskaite provides an especially poignant answer to some of these questions, based on her research in Lithuania.

We hope that this volume will be of interest and of use to the broad range of people who are involved with democratic citizenship education around the world, whether they are adult educators, schoolteachers, curriculum developers, policymakers, textbook authors, or simply concerned citizens. To that end, we have sought to avoid unnecessary jargon while acknowledging that researchers often develop new terminology for a reason. We draw attention to—and try to explain cogently—the ideas, theories, terms, and concepts that help researchers make sense of the data they collect and the dynamics of culture they encounter in their work.

NEW FORMS OF CITIZENSHIP EDUCATION FOR A CHANGING WORLD

As the world's integration and complexity increase, and as its many societies respond to these changes and to each other in new ways, we find dynamic tensions in their political expressions and in their distinctive models of citizenship. Such tensions drive debates and new practices in the explicit curriculum, particularly in emerging school-based programs for democratic citizenship education. But they also affect how citizenship can be learned in other diverse institutional and cultural contexts, such as the adult learning circles that Souto-Manning studies in Brazil or the media debates about Holocaust education that Stevick explores in Estonia (both in this volume). Furthermore, global and local transformations mean that we cannot rely on a good secondary school–level civics course to sustain lifelong democratic citizenship. Democratic citizenship education does not conclude with compulsory schooling: adults and teachers in democracies new and old continue learning, not just to stay informed and to vote responsibly, but to shape and to fulfill the evolving conceptions of citizenship in their changing worlds. This book explores the many facets of the democratic citizen, the learning experiences that form them, and wider debates about the formative learning that societies should provide for them.

In a famous joke, a ship is sinking, and one sailor asks the other, "Do you know how to swim?" The second replies, "Well, I read about it in school, and I think I get the theory of it." There is an ever-growing sense around the world that democracy, like swimming, cannot be learned through rote classroom practice alone. Democratic citizenship requires real experience in democratic practices. Yet executing this vision can be difficult within the constraints of traditional instruction, a crowded curriculum, and standardized tests. The discrepancy between the ideals democracies hope to instill and the manner in which they are transmitted by teachers is often stark. The chapters in this volume by Wendy Gaylord, James Huff, and Bradley Levinson explore these discrepancies in Indonesia, El Salvador, and Mexico, respectively.

Still, it may be easier for many to fall into the traditional habits of an authoritarian classroom than to envision forms in which a democratic ethos pervades education. While authoritarian classrooms concentrate power and absolute knowledge in the hands of the teacher, more democratic classrooms often acknowledge the possibility of divergent interpretations and encourage students to come to their own conclusions.

The ancient Greek historian Herodotus, one of history's great civic educators, understood very well the political nature of knowledge and the danger of conflating political power with authority in the realm of knowledge. In his voluminous histories, Herodotus both celebrates the role of democratic Athens in fending off the invasion of the mighty Persian empire and emphasizes the importance of dissent through dozens of stories in which societies suffer because they fail to pay heed to the one person who had the courage to speak the truth. Herodotus, whose literary voice and storytelling skills place him on an even plane with those who heard his stories, repeatedly draws attention to the flawed knowledge of claims authority figures (Christ 1994). Their claims, which are so difficult for their subjects to contradict due to their power, were often wrong: political authority conferred neither omniscience nor intellectual authority. In fact, a regular person like Herodotus's narrator could see through the kings' problematic claims, and throughout the text the reader also learns this skill.

Herodotus's attempts to distinguish leaders' political authority from their authority as experts did not particularly take hold in later teaching and schooling. Teachers, parents, and rulers have quite often conflated authoritarianism and authoritativeness as if they were intrinsically linked or were in fact equivalent. In democratizing countries or postauthoritarian societies, democratic education for democratic citizenship—in which the manner of learning is consistent with the content—often trails behind replacement of the ideological textbooks and other teaching materials. Constitutional civics may take the place of Marxism/Leninism in the curriculum without a profound change in teaching style, and democracy can remain distant from the experience of teachers and students—no more than another concept to be learned from a textbook. Robert Everhart's classic American ethnography, *Reading, Writing, and Resistance*, shows how artificial the combination of authority and expertise often becomes in schools. He demonstrates how schoolchildren are confronted with lists of reified, immutable, categorical, and absolute knowledge over which they have no meaningful control. For Everhart, "reified knowledge" is "knowledge that while abstract, tenuous and problematical, is treated as if it is concrete and 'real' . . . [and] is treated unequivocally as a fact. . . . It is, stated somewhat crudely, 'recipe' knowledge. . . . The world of education is that which supplies objective facts, concrete and agreed upon, that are to be learned, manipulated, and applied in an empirical fashion towards predefined ends" (86).

Doyle Stevick witnessed such an episode in the first day of the civic education course for final-year students (age eighteen to nineteen) in a small town of about ten thousand in a rural corner of Estonia, not far from the Russian border. The students, all ethnic Estonians in courses that were taught in the Estonian language, were given a textbook's list of the "seven civilizations of the world," starting with Western (presumably secular) civilization and continuing on with others that were often defined by religion (Islamic, Confucian). When "Orthodox" was read, a student piped up, "Oh. Like us." The door was opened for a profound discussion of identity, history, culture, minority rights. But the teacher quickly shut the door. Her response was unequivocal: "No! We are part of Western civilization," she exclaimed, and then paused for a moment. Estonia had at times been under the rule of the Russian empire and has historically had a Russian minority, one that today constitutes about one-third of Estonia's population. This particular town was founded by the Russian empress Catherine the Great. From the school's windows it was possible to see the Orthodox church established in her honor (St. Catherine's), which was a stone's throw from the Lutheran church, also St. Catherine's. When the teacher resumed, she implicitly acknowledged these facts in this way: "We have *traces* of Orthodox culture here." Just as the boundary that had trapped Estonia inside the Soviet Union had recently disappeared, so too the border between civilizations could shift to the east or west; yet, the tidy boundaries of the categories separating us and them, Orthodox and West, Russian and Estonian, remained inviolate.

A related and equally important consideration for the teaching of democratic citizenship is the attitude toward social and cultural difference modeled in curriculum, textbooks, and teachers' practice. Around the globe, the unitary models of national citizenship that required strong assimilation are now mostly in retreat. Pluralist discourses, championed by indigenous and ethnic minority social movements, have created greater democratic inclusiveness in the conception of citizenship. It is increasingly common to find positive representations of cultural diversity in nationalist civics textbooks and classrooms. Yet most liberal states still retain the prerogative to define the cultural features of democratic citizenship, and there is an active debate about the extent to which diversity can and ought to be encouraged. In their interpretive studies of policy and curriculum change in Japan and Australia, respectively, Yoko Motani and Joan DeJaeghere (in this volume) discuss the ways that new understandings of democratic citizenship can be promoted through recognition of internal diversity and promotion of external solidarity (cosmopolitanism, or global citizenship). Meanwhile, Stavroula Philippou's work in Cyprus demonstrates how a particular curriculum intervention can have significant impacts on children's perceptions of difference and sense of civic identity.

CONTEXT AND CULTURE IN DEMOCRATIC CITIZENSHIP

This volume works from a few key premises. First, it is assumed that there must be a fit between a political system and the people who operate within it. Without democrats, there is no democracy. Countries that overcome authoritarian rule to create or to restore democratic rule must quickly produce (or reproduce) democratic citizens. It becomes imperative to cultivate their cultures' democratic tendencies and to develop traditions of democratic citizenship for their youth. Formal citizenship education in schools becomes a central focus because it marks the deliberate attempt by a state to instill the dispositions and behaviors needed for democracy to take hold and to endure. Education is a primary means to develop the fit between citizens and their system of governance.

The failure of the United States to fulfill the promise of *Brown v. the Board of Education* provides a good illustration of this problem of "fit." The 1954 Supreme Court ruling, which formally outlawed the segregation of black children into separate and unequal schools, constituted a profound transformation of the legal and political institutions of the time. That systemic transformation stood alone, however, because no parallel transformation of individual and societal attitudes toward race and racism was undertaken. We know the answer in this case to Richard Holbrooke's question—there were free and fair elections, the democratic system worked and reflected the desires of the electorate, putting racists in office, and many southern politicians aggressively resisted attempts to desegregate schools, often with great success. Northern cities like Chicago and Boston fared little better, with strong resistance to bussing children in order to integrate schools. The full potential of the *Brown* decision was squandered.

The second key premise of this volume builds on the first: because there must be a fit between a system and its people, culture plays an important role. Francis Fukuyama captures the importance of the fit between institutions and local cultures in a discussion of development assistance and best practices:

> There's enough ambiguity in the design of institutions . . . that you don't have a technical set of blueprints that you can actually give to developing countries. And I think that if you think sensibly about public sector reform, one of the big enemies is actually best-practices mentality, and unfortunately, this is something the World Bank tends to do a lot of. A program will work in Peru for the delivery of vaccines or, let's say, a certain kind of public education and they immediately say, "a-ha, that's a best practice, let's universalize it and do it in Botswana or Morocco," or other places that the Bank operates. There has to be a sufficient degree of local knowledge that is built into the design of these institutions that is really critical to make them work, which means that you need contextual judgment in the applicability of foreign models. That's not to say that foreign models won't work, but you won't even know where they'll work unless you know a great deal about the local society. (Fukuyama 2004)

Such knowledge, he says, is "entirely local, contextual, historical, cultural and the like." While we are leery of top-down approaches that install foreign models in development contexts, his observations—about transferability, about the importance of local knowledge in making institutions function well, and about the types of knowledge that are needed—are consonant with our own.

The concept of "transferability" and the type of knowledge it requires are crucial both to the practice Fukuyama cites and to the traditions of ethnographic, sociocultural, and qualitative research that this volume features. For qualitative researchers, transferability often provides a way to think about meaningful comparisons within research paradigms that are focused on what is local, specific, and contingent. The first stage of the IEA research serves as a useful contrast: its qualitative case studies of separate countries were organized around a shared set of questions that were developed collectively through an iterative process. The qualitative stage of the IEA study was thus designed to create sets of data that were comparable and could be analyzed accordingly.

This volume brings together qualitative inquirers who have been pursuing independent qualitative research. It is not explicitly comparative (although a case can be made that case studies are inherently comparative). While some researchers use individual cases to generate grand social theory at a high level of abstraction, the authors in this volume tend to adopt one of two main approaches to questions of comparison or generalization (what is often called external validity). These two approaches, often implicit, are analytic generalization and case-to-case transfer (Schwandt 1997: 58). Analytic generalization uses the particulars of a given case to "test, refine or modify some theory or theoretical idea, concept or model"

(Schwandt 1997: 58). For such researchers, a case can "provide the context-specific stuff or material that makes it possible to think 'realistically and concretely about' social scientific concepts and theories . . . and to work 'creatively and imaginatively with them'" (Geertz, cited in Schwandt 1997: 58). Finally, in qualitative inquiry that has a constructivist epistemology, case-to-case transfer asks the researcher to provide enough information about a particular case and its context that readers could make a reasonable, informed judgment about whether certain conclusions or practices would apply in another setting (Schwandt 1997: 58–59).

Macrolevel statistics and theorizing in fields such as economics and political science do not provide the local, cultural, historical, and contextual information that is necessary to evaluate transferability. It is rather the product of qualitative research, particularly those approaches that investigate culture, meanings, local practices, and institutional arrangements through interviews, observation, document analysis, and the like. This volume offers a sampling of the rich and various traditions of qualitative inquiry that can be applied to obtain such knowledge and understanding. Additionally, our authors are either sufficiently knowledgeable in the languages of their research sites to have relatively unmediated access to the events unfolding there, or insiders who know the places they study intimately. Their disciplinary training in qualitative research methods affords them an original view. Their language ability permits an engagement with issues of culture that is otherwise difficult to achieve.

The question of "what kinds of knowledge are needed," however, is not just a question for researchers but is also a central concern for the education of citizens anywhere. Just as the free, fair, open, regular, and contested elections constitute a minimal conception of democracy, a minimal conception of responsible citizenship requires "the capacity for informed, reasonable, deliberative and freely made choices in response to competitive public elections and contested public policy issues" (Patrick 2002: 17). In all states, mass public education is charged with substantially forming the citizen (Boli, Ramirez, and Meyer 1985). Yet this minimal definition is also culturally rooted. More recently scholars have begun to articulate citizenship in cultural terms (Rosaldo 1997), with an emphasis on the typically unwritten yet vitally present assumptions about who "counts" in a democracy: who is licensed or privileged to speak in the public sphere, what kinds of cultural traits are most valued and recognized, and so forth.

The model political citizen of constitutionalist democracy, legitimated by Western political theory and exported now around the world, actually promotes a number of particular cultural values which, pace Kagan and Harrison (2006), are not the only ones that support what they call "progress." Moreover, when this model of political citizenship meets the embedded cultural definitions of citizenship present in national and regional cultures, unique adaptations are likely to take place. We align ourselves with the stance recently articulated by Anderson-Levitt (2003)—that the expansion of Western institutional forms such as modern schooling does not so much impose a new regime of meanings as provide a new template for making meaning.

THE STUDIES AND THE SECTIONS

The contributors to this volume were selected for "maximum diversity," with the broad theme of democratic citizenship education serving as a unifying thread. But even though the studies range across national curricula to classroom practice, from El Salvador to Estonia, and Cypriot children to South African adult citizens, a surprising number of common elements emerged from the collection as a whole. Even in explorations of our diversity, new signs of our shared experiences and concerns reveal themselves. We have organized the book into three sections, which build from the ground-level practice of citizenship education for children in schools, to the ongoing citizenship education of adults and teachers in societies that have undergone dramatic political change, to the larger policy and curriculum debates that interpret the changing world and envision citizens' roles within it.

REFERENCES

Anderson-Levitt, K., ed. 2003. *Local Meanings, Global Schooling.* New York: Palgrave.

Banks, J. 2004. *Diversity and Citizenship Education.* San Francisco: Jossey-Bass.

Boli, J., F. Ramirez, and J. Meyer. 1985. "Explaining the Origins and Expansion of Mass Education." *Comparative Education Review* 29, no. 2: 145–70.

Burawoy, M., and K. Verdery, eds. 1999. *Uncertain Transitions: Ethnographies of Change in the Postsocialist World.* Lanham, Md.: Rowman & Littlefield.

Christ, M. R. 1994. "Herodotean Kings and Historical Inquiry." *Classical Antiquity* 13, no. 2: 167–202.

Fukuyama, F. 2004. "State-Building: Governance and World Order in the 21st Century." A lecture given at the Woodrow Wilson Center, December 12, Washington, D.C.

Hahn, C. 1998. *Becoming Political.* Albany: State University of New York Press.

Harrison, L. E., and J. Kagan, eds. 2006. *Developing Cultures: Essays on Cultural Change.* New York: Routledge.

Lee, W. O., D. Grossman, K. Kennedy, and G. Fairbrother, eds. 2004. *Citizenship Education in Asia and the Pacific.* Hong Kong: Kluwer Academic.

McGinn, N. F., and E. H. Epstein. 1999. *Comparative Perspectives on the Role of Education in Democratization.* Berlin: Lang.

Patrick, J. 1996. "Principles of Democracy for the Education of Citizens in Former

Communist Countries of Central and Eastern Europe." In *Building Civic Education for Democracy in Poland*, ed. R. Remy and J. Strzemieczny. Washington, D.C.: National Council for the Social Studies.

Patrick, J. J. 2002. "Defining, Delivering, and Defending a Common Education for Citizenship in a Democracy." In *"Civis Americanus sum (I am an American citizen)": Proceedings of the First Massachusetts Summit on Civic Learning in Teacher Preparation and Professional Development*, www.civiced.org/civamericanus, pp. 16–31.

Remy, R., and J. Strzemieczny, eds. 1996. *Building Civic Education for Democracy in Poland*. Washington, D.C.: National Council for the Social Studies.

Rosaldo, R. 1997. "Cultural Citizenship, Inequality and Multiculturalism." In *Latino Cultural Citizenship: Claiming Identity, Space, and Rights*, ed. W. V. Flores and R. Benmayor. Boston: Beacon.

Schiffauer, W., G. Baumann, R. Kastoryano, and S. Vertovec. 2004. *Civic Enculturation: Nation-State, School and Ethnic Difference in the Netherlands, Britain, Germany and France* New York: Berghahn Books.

Schwandt, T. A. 1997. *Dictionary of Qualitative Inquiry*. Thousand Oaks, Calif.: Sage.

Steiner-Khamsi, G., J. Torney-Purta, and J. Schwille, eds. 2002. *New Paradigms and Recurring Paradoxes in Education for Citizenship*. Vol. 5. Oxford: Elsevier Science.

Torney-Purta, J. 2000. "Comparative Perspectives on Political Socialization and Civic Education." *Comparative Education Review* 44, no. 1 (February): 88–95.

Torney-Purta, J., R. Lehmann, H. Oswald, and W. Schulz. 2001. *Citizenship and Education in Twenty-Eight Countries: Civic Knowledge and Engagement at Age Fourteen*. Amsterdam: International Association for the Evaluation of Educational Achievement.

Torney-Purta, J., J. Schwille, and J. A. Amadeo, eds. 1999. *Civic Education across Countries: Twenty-four National Case Studies from the IEA Civic Education Project*. Amsterdam: International Association for the Evaluation of Educational Achievement.

Zakaria, F. 1997. "The Rise of Illiberal Democracy." *Foreign Affairs* (November), www.fareedzakaria.com/articles/other/democracy.html.

I

THE VIEW FROM THE SCHOOL: STUDENTS AND TEACHERS NEGOTIATING DEMOCRATIC CITIZENSHIP

Despite the importance of other venues and means for democratic citizenship education, "we cannot ignore the school" (Torney-Purta 2000: 94). It is no surprise that newly democratizing states most often turn to schools to advance the project of democratic citizenship. Usually compulsory, public schools have the added benefit of gathering children for several hours a day and exposing children to forms of social and cultural diversity they might not ordinarily experience elsewhere. They also have long experience in the tradition of civic education that has accompanied identity and nation formation. In Part I, the authors focus their analysis on life in schools, with particular attention to the role played by teachers in negotiating the meanings of democracy in programs and curriculum for citizenship education.

In this section, Rob Whitman's work with the Spokane Indians of Washington State reveals the conflict in purposes between the globally oriented goals of the school and curriculum, and the cultural practices of the Spokane. While the materials and policies of the school seek to lure students into productive roles—off the reservation—in the global economy, Indian teachers try to foster a spirit of identity linked to place and to accommodate the notably egalitarian cultural practices that characterize the larger community. Students feel a binary choice between worlds, local and global, even while the schools function as a kind of hybrid or gateway between them. Whitman shows specific cultural differences that collide in the hybrid environment of the school. He also explores the ways that teachers have found to transcend differences, notably in the role of the Wellpinit Warrior. The Warrior encompasses Indians who fought for the tribe in times past and the veterans of American wars abroad, thus creating a historical and cultural continuity. As the "real world" is constructed around conceptions of global capitalism, and success is equated with departure for the real world, community teachers persist in making spaces for traditional community practices, whether through nonconfrontational techniques to uphold requirements or in keeping alive traditions of gathering and narrative.

Wendy Gaylord's research in secondary school classrooms explores how two teachers at an academically accomplished public secondary school in the province of West Sumatra, Indonesia, taught civics and government during *reformasi*, a time of national political and administrative change. Gaylord provides an overview of civic education in Indonesia since independence, and then she considers how teachers respond to the decentralization of education and to the deregulation of the civic education curriculum during the country's rapid political change. She considers teaching methods and classroom management, the use of resources and textbooks, and the civic environment of school. Her work documents both how change at this school is a complex matter and how teacher decisions are as much about meeting administrative demands as they are about educating students. One teacher works with students to ensure that they master the required material for exams, using active methods to help them understand and recall on demand. The other teacher makes an effort to try new methods, activities, and technology (the overhead projector) to engage students' interest and stimulate their thinking about how the civic values they must learn for exams can be applied to their daily lives. The civic context of their classrooms and of the school plays a major part in shaping the teachers' roles, and the teachers respond in unique ways.

American anthropologist James Huff takes us into the classroom of a Salvadoran high school teacher to show us how new national civic education reforms for the teaching of democratic "values" are unfolding. Huff argues that El Salvador's secondary education system offers a unique vantage point from which to consider how religious change, privatization, and education reform are shaping the contexts of action within which Salvadoran teachers are forming their pedagogies of citizenship education. Starting with a broad historical sketch, Huff shows how the various national administrations in power during the postwar period have steadily advanced a so-called modernization project of the public education system through far-reaching education reforms. One of the results of such reforms has been extensive privatization, especially in the capital city of San Salvador, where nearly three-quarters of the high schools are private—and many of these belong to Pentecostal orders. Yet these schools, too, must implement the Ministry of Education's guidelines for the new civic education. By way of illustration, Huff details some of the educational practices developed by Daniel Ariaza, a social studies teacher with whom he worked closely while carrying out fieldwork at a large private, Pentecostal high school. He describes those classroom practices associated with certain aspects of civic education policy, including the use of so-called participatory instructional methods and the allotment of instructional time to address students' "social problems" in class. By delineating the varied ideas and propositions that Daniel brought from other social and historical contexts to his educational work with the students, Huff explores how policies associated with the new civic education program are being mediated by teachers at the classroom level. The result is a fascinating cautionary tale about the latitude teachers have to make broad interpretations of civic education reform.

Stavroula Philippou, a Greek-Cypriot educational scholar, presents the results of an "intervention curriculum" in Greek-Cypriot elementary classrooms designed to create a more inclusive sense of European citizenship. One of the points that stands out in Philippou's chapter is the degree to which "foreigners," potential immigrants, are imagined by schoolchildren to be beyond the pale of Cypriot citizenship. This resonates with an important point made later in the volume: Deborah Reed-Danahay shows that the construction of European citizenship would not seem to incorporate those who currently are not conventionally recognized citizens in the EU member states. The imagined Muslims, no matter how diverse—whether in the films analyzed by Reed-Danahay or the Turks on the other side of divided Cyprus—pose a persistent challenge for more expansive and inclusive forms of identity and conceptions of citizenship. Philippou's experience implementing curricular materials that directly challenge the xenophobic nationalism and sense of religious superiority reveals that curriculum can contribute to increased openness to difference and a greater understanding of others in the language of human rights.

1

Civic Education in Two Worlds: Contestation and Conflict over the Civic in School and Community on the Spokane Indian Reservation

Robert Whitman

> If I don't move away, then I'm nobody.
>
> —Galina W., ninth-grade Spokane high school student,
> shortly before quitting school

> They've got to learn to live in the real world.
>
> —Superintendent's oral response to tribal language
> and culture curriculum for the school

> We as parents, students, and community members will pay the highest price if our children are not educated to live equally well in both worlds.
>
> —*Spokane Tribe of Indians Language and
> Culture Program Resource Guide*

Indigenous communities in North America are a salient site to explore questions of the social production of democratic citizens, for in educating this particular citizenry in the U.S. context there has simultaneously been a mission to destroy. This destroy/create binary in terms of citizenry was captured in the words of Richard Henry Pratt, who first as an army officer in the American Civil War (1860–1866), then later in the nineteenth-century as a reformer, took indigenous peoples away from reservations to educate them into Euro-American culture and practice. Pratt would often point out that he differed with those who believed that the only good Indian was a dead Indian. Instead he believed that, through education, we should "kill the Indian in him and save the man" (Pratt 1892: 42). On the Spokane Indian reservation in northeastern Washington where I have been conducting fieldwork for three years, community members often perceive civic education as part of a larger colonial assimilation process that seeks to destroy family, community, and tribal relationships, making it less likely that some form of "tribal culture" will survive into the next generation.

In this chapter, I explore the idea that civic education for democracy, often in the name of empowering and creating democratic engagement, is inextricably bound up with historical and ongoing colonizing relationships. When civic education in the United States is embedded in a set of larger macroeconomic relationships that foreground the production of global citizens, then, for many students on the reservation, embracing identities offered through schooling destroys social ties that make *local* civic culture, empowerment, and democracy possible.

As I meant to indicate in the quotes that open the chapter, for many indigenous students on the reservation embracing a global citizen identity means moving away and going to college, getting a job, joining what the public school superintendent often calls "the real world." If they choose not to do this, at some level the message from the school is that they are "nobody." When we implement a civic education curriculum in schools, the stated goal is to ensure that "new generations are inducted into political culture, learning the knowledge, values, and attitudes that contribute to the support of the political system" (Gimpel, Lay, and Schuknecht 2003: 13). But this assumption has to be questioned. Following the introductory quotes from stakeholders in a public school on an Indian reservation, I ask, What kinds of citizens do students have to become to enter into this "real world"? Do classroom learning contexts around civic education create opportunities for these children to actually "live equally well in both worlds"? Finally, if indeed "nobodies" are being produced, what mechanisms in the interaction of school and community create these identities?

This chapter presents ethnographic, oral, and written discursive data from three distinctive places that are inextricably linked with creating civic culture, broadly construed, on the Spokane reservation. To make explicit links between macrolevel processes and microlevel practice I present data from the level of nation-state, from school classrooms, and from community talk. I discuss processes of education as they are embedded in the new millennial drive toward the creation of a "global citizen," achieved through excellence, high test scores, "globalized" classrooms, individuated technology users, and college attendance mandates. These governmental and institutional mandates recruit students to particular meanings of civic democracy and of becoming a citizen.

Presentation of ethnographic data from individual classrooms, teachers, and students illustrates a set of mixed or hybrid practices where the civic embodies, not without contradiction, both traditional Spokane values and global citizen practices. Finally, oral speech from the community's members gives clarity to what it means to "be Spokane" and what "success" means in terms of being a good community member. These conversations reveal that civic education in the community practice is largely implicit and apprenticeship oriented, with no discussion of democracy or institutions of government that a formal civic democracy school classroom might have. If we are to make sense of explicit civic curriculum in the school, we need to embed that practice within the implicit civic education of the family and community. On the Spokane reservation, implicit apprenticeship constitutes a powerful hidden curriculum through which many community members continue to reproduce a civic culture and social capital that strongly contradicts messages emanating from state and school. While presenting this contradiction might imply a simple dichotomy between a local traditional culture and a global modern capitalist one, the picture on the ground reveals much greater complexity. The dichotomy of a "two worlds" picture is itself a social construction, and the contexts of teaching and learning reveal multiple local and globalized "worlds."

Ethnographic description and the analysis of oral and written discursive forms illustrate several points about civic education that are not captured in large-scale quantitative studies to date (Owen 2004; Prinzing 2004; Torney-Purta et al. 2001). For one, they show civic democracy practice as it is closely connected with the idea of social capital (Putnam 2000). Robert Putnam, for example, in his book *Bowling Alone*, argues that establishing social relationships builds social capital. This kind of capital, the relationships we build to groups and organizations, is the web that creates civic culture. Using this concept of capital one could argue that the early building of social relationships provide a base for people's notion of what civic democracy *is*. They constitute something like "structures of feeling" (Williams 1979) or, to draw from Bourdieu (Bourdieu 1991; Bourdieu and Passeron 1991), a kind of *habitus*, a structure of largely unconscious dispositions and associated practices, that students then take into school. Part of what a study of this kind uncovers is the importance of different kinds of capital, including locally constituted, ground-up capital. Putnam argues that early social relationships build social capital for individuals, who then use that capital to build webs of community relationships, helping to create the structures of civic life. Civic ties constituted through relationships create a kind of capital, a resource that community members can draw on as they engage in everyday life practices in the community. But what happens if, when one gets into school, those social relationships, that civic life, that *capital*, is seen as making you a "nobody"? It is the interplay of these relationships, made real through practical activity, discourse and texts, which this chapter reveals.

This chapter also shows local traditional practice as it is necessarily embedded in a "broader cultural and discursive struggle against the ideological hegemony of mainstream American culture" (Foley 1996: 80). In addition to Foley, I frame my discussion of struggle with the work of Colin Lankshear on New Capitalism (Lankshear 1998; Lankshear and Knobel 2003), where hegemonic school practice is tied to the processes and needs of a globalizing capitalist economy. State institutional and local practice at school have often given at least a tacit nod to American Indian activism, local control, and indigenous curriculum during the last forty years. But, an examination of the Spokane context shows a much more complex picture. Students are simultaneously being recruited to *multiple* global and local communities, rejected by some, recruited again by others, constantly cycling through several possible "worlds." This picture undermines any simplistic dichotomy of local/global, colonizer/colonized, and Indian/non-Indian. Indians have access to multiple local worlds, and there are many iterations of the "global" citizen in addition to the one that Wellpinit students find coming at them through school.

WALKING IN TWO WORLDS

In the title of the chapter and in one of the opening quotes, the idea of "two worlds" is explicitly invoked. Walking in two worlds as a metaphor is often used unproblematically to "describe the goals of education for indigenous groups in the United States" (Henze and Vanett 1993: 116). It finds its way into tribal documents as it has in the Spokane Tribe Language and Culture Resource Guide cited at the beginning of this chapter. I saw it recently cited in a television program produced in Montana when a voiceover said, "Walking in two worlds shows how students can balance their two worlds when they're equipped with skills necessary to be contributing members of American society while still retaining their rich culture and heritage."

Regional educational institutions use the metaphor constantly. Examples can be found in the literature of the Northwest Regional Educational Laboratory in Oregon, the Bureau of Indian Affairs sponsored Indian Education Outreach Program at the University of Idaho, and an extensive coastal tribe curriculum that was recently developed through Evergreen College in Washington State. The idea of walking and balance between cultures illustrates problematic assumptions that underlie this metaphor, many of which have been explicated elsewhere (Henze and Vanett 1993; Henze and Davis 1999). For the purposes of this chapter, I am interested in what worlds students are being recruited into through explicit and implicit civic practices in school and community. Such an examination leads one to question to what extent "balance" and "walking between" are likely or even possible for the majority of the students in this community. Also called into question is the notion of two worlds at all. Ethnographers who work with indigenous communities on reservations have observed that there are many "worlds" on the reservation and off, and that the simple dichotomizing of two worlds hides not only the complexities of community both within Indian country and off, but also their complex interaction (Bauman and Briggs 2003; Collins and Blot 2003; Foley 1996; Levinson and Holland 1996; Philips 1983; Sarris 1993). I argue here for a critical appraisal of a simple "two worlds" dichotomy with traditional tribal culture on one hand and the global citizen on the other. It is in the spaces between these two socially constructed worlds that many students live and where social constructions of the "nobodies" are often found.

HISTORICAL PRODUCTION OF THE CIVIC INDIAN—THE SPOKANE STORY

The Spokanes, a Salishan tribe of the inland Northwest, have had a history that many other North American indigenous communities would recognize. Their history has followed a pattern of trading posts as first contact in the early nineteenth century, followed shortly by Catholic and Presbyterian missionaries by the mid–nineteenth century, violent military intervention, and the creation of reservations shortly thereafter. Coerced schooling through the Bureau of Indian Affairs and forced agriculture in the latter half of the nineteenth century substituted for direct military interventions as the Euro-American settlement grew. Forced expropriation of arable land was institutionalized through federal and state legislation by the early 1900s.

In the late nineteenth to middle twentieth centuries, the pattern of land expropriation continued through federal legislation, along with reduction of water rights and destruction of salmon access through damming. Resource extraction centered around timber and, later, the mining of uranium. Assimilation through schooling continued during this time through local boarding schools just off the reservations where Spokane language and customs were forbidden. In the late twentieth century like many indigenous groups in North America, a rejuvenation of language and culture has been taken up largely by a traditional-practice-oriented segment of the tribe. Generally tribes in Washington State have been winning back some political and economic sovereignty through the courts and have created new revenues through gaming and tourism. The Spokane reservation has a casino, and some funds from gaming went toward helping build a new K–12 school in the mid-1990s. The school committee is made up of tribal members who are elected and report to an elected tribal council. As on many reservations, the tribal council governs but an informal system of elders provides a strong traditional voice in decision-making.

More recently, tribes have experienced the forced imposition of newer education norms, particularly state-mandated standardized tests that stigmatize students out of the mainstream, and coercive standards in reading and math achievement. In this climate, schools are "taken over" if they fail to meet adequate yearly progress, known as AYP. These directives come from federal intervention into schooling through the Elementary and Secondary Education Act of 2002, a reauthorization of the federal presence in primarily state-funded U.S. education that began in 1965. The popular title for this legislation is No Child Left Behind.

Throughout the history of the Spokane tribe, there has been intermarriage between Euro-Americans and Indians. While the school is designated 95 percent "Indian," a visitor would think that over half the students were "white." Families typically have both Indian names used for gatherings and Euro-American names used in day-to-day transactions: Fletts (Scotch-Irish), Wynecoops (Polish), Seylers (German), Peones (French), and Andrews (Scottish) all belong to extended families that are found on the Spokane reservation and within the geographic region of the American inland Northwest. "Traditional" Spokanes, those practicing, preserving, and reconstituting the culture of their ancestors, tend to be concentrated in those families that have kept a line of strong spiritual leaders and make up perhaps 10 to 15 percent of tribal membership. Here one finds drummers, dancers, medicine leaders, and families that tend to specialize in particular areas of knowledge. Seylers are very conversant with local history, Fletts with language, Abrahamsons with historical sites.

College-educated Spokanes, some traditional and some not, are increasingly concentrated in tribal government. Many of these extended families continue to live on allotment sites where several generations often reside on one fifty- to hundred-acre parcel of land. Many Spokanes will also leave these large extended family sites. There are two subsidized housing sites where young couples, kids who have left school, and poorer Spokanes tend to gather. These are seen within the community as problem spots where lots of "drugging and drinking" take place. And, of course, large numbers of non-Indians are living on Indian land. Half of the estimated five thousand residents living on the reservation are non-Indian. This complicated sociohistorical context means that any simple glossing of the Indian "world" as a culturally coherent whole would be ridiculous.

Civic education for democracy takes place in a community of many local "worlds," worlds where certain memories tend to be shared. Memory works to recount processes of genocide, forced assimilation, expropriation of land, water, and cultural resources, and schooling as a place that took children away from their families. There are also those who see school as a force for good or as at least a necessity, despite its many problems. Spokanes will often quietly avow their identity as Indians and wonder aloud about the extent to which school might allow for that. Inland Northwest cultures neither developed a strong village culture like those on the coast nor had strong tribal affiliations like those of the plains tribes (Roy 1961; Ruby 1976). Instead, inland Northwest cultures are said to have a highly flexible family and clan structure with individual egalitarianism as a key identity marker. This is relevant today as Spokanes will insist that they are "different" from tribes to the east and west, pointing toward distinctive ways of what it means to be "Spokane." These highly egalitarian and flexible family structures are vehicles through which families and communities build civic relationships and social capital. Spokanes generally, and traditional Spokanes in particular, are very conscious of this.

"EXCELLENCE AT WELLPINIT": INSTITUTIONAL DISCOURSE

The drive from the regional city of Spokane to the small town of Wellpinit and the Spokane Tribe of Indians reservation is about forty-five miles. It lies northwest of the city and is bounded on the south by the Spokane River, on the east by Tshimmican Creek, and on the west by the Columbia River. Two main communities, Wellpinit and the "West end," reflect a historical pattern of family settlement from the period when the reservation was originally defined by treaty. Wellpinit, on the southeastern end of the reservation, is set in the southern part of the Okanagan highlands, a mountainous region of north-central Washington with a dry climate, conifer pines and grasslands, and lakes that are highly dependent on snowmelt in the summer. Wellpinit is the seat of tribal government with a post office, a trading post, some subsidized housing, and, down the road another quarter mile, the K–12 school.

A visitor crosses a cattle guard leaving the small town to get there on the road going west. The superintendent famously, I learned later, says "when they (children) cross that cattle guard, they belong to me." The school's executive summary of 2004 reads, "The school's support staff proudly maintains one of the cleanest facilities in Washington State," and in walking into the school, this is certainly one of the first impressions. As an ethnographer, I did not originally go into the Wellpinit school looking for an ideology of the global citizen. However, the physical spaces of the school itself, conversations with the superintendent, principal, and support staff, and official texts through which the school presents itself to the real world, captured my attention from the beginning. In my field notes from my first visit I wrote:

> On entering the school I was struck by the whiteness of the walls, large glass windows, large potted plants in the corners of the hall, artifacts displayed on the walls, a half-moon round reception area with two, very nicely dressed women wearing headsets asking to direct me to the "boardroom." When I was ushered into the meeting room it had a 25-foot long table, a dozen high-backed leather chairs, and more tasteful indigenous art on the walls.

Some locals do jokingly refer to the school as Wellpinit, Inc. During my first year of fieldwork, school spaces, community spaces, and local talk provided entries to thinking about what kinds of citizens this school was engaged in educating, and eventually, to asking what meanings of "civic" would be valued in this setting.

Two school documents, the "2004 Wellpinit School Executive Summary," a mission statement, and the "Superintendents Goals of 2004," provide a picture of what "excellence" entails at the Wellpinit school. Discourse in these texts set the table; they point toward the beliefs, values, and practices that students are being recruited to through school and society. In linguistic terms, one says that these words are *indexical*—they are pointers—when it comes to the production of student citizen identities. The superintendent's goals for the school, listed here, provide a graphic example of what I mean.

1. Individualized learning plan for each student.
2. Core knowledge curriculum implemented in grades K–8.
3. International baccalaureate program candidacy initiated.
4. JROTC program established 9–12.
5. Early college and career selection in grades K–12.
6. College applications and FAF completed in grades 9–12.
7. Graduation rate at 100%.
8. Zero drops and zero out-of-school suspensions.
9. Attendance rate at 95% for all students.
10. Travel to China for all senior students.
11. Life goals plan for all students 9–12.
12. New middle school in operation.
13. 25 year comprehensive plan initiated.
14. 20 technology skills completed for all students and staff.
15. Full time foreign language teacher on staff.
16. 12 full scholarships awarded to high school seniors.

17. School board is Washington State school board of the year.
18. Community technology center instituted.
19. Funding reserve at one year of budget.
20. Field house construction started.
21. Multi-track learning system established for each student.
22. Merit salary increase tied to student achievement.
23. Population of alliance high school at 100 student FTE.
24. Global classrooms established in China, Jordan, and Africa.
25. Three teleportec teaching sites established.

Close analytical attention to documents such as this help establish and connect macro processes of a society to micro processes of school practice. Institutional documents often provide these connecting points and are amenable to discourse analysis and critical scrutiny (Fairclough 1995; Lankshear 1998). They are texts that tell stories about those they talk about, in this case students and staff (Mehan 1996). Goal statements are also about imagining and staging futures (Beck 2000). Grammatically, those who are indexed, like students and staff, are pointed in particular directions to particular places that they will inhabit in an imagined "future." Much of this pointing is obscure in terms of how these actions will be accomplished and who acts to accomplish them. For example, the "missing" verb phrase in the goals listed earlier is "will be," as in *"There will be an* individualized learning plan for each student" in goal 1. While those who will be acted on is stated (students, staff), those who act to make these initiatives happen are not. Individualized plans, core knowledge curriculum, technology skills, and global classrooms appear as if out of thin air. This kind of omniscient and obscured voice is often present in institutional goal pronouncements and sets the stage for a place where things just happen.

The items on this list, taken individually, are not surprising, and might be found listed on many high school websites around the United States. But taken as a group, they point toward the social production of citizens who will have certain identity markers; students shall become highly individuated learners (goals 1–3, 11, 21, 23), they shall master the latest technology (14, 18, 24, 25), they shall successfully complete a highly academic curriculum and successfully attend college (2–9, 16), and they shall join a global citizenry (10, 15, 24, 25). The goals on this list frame what defines school success but also echo larger societal beliefs about what it means to be successful members of a global society.

Framing documents set the boundaries for many of our understandings (Lankshear 1998; Lakoff 1996; Mehan 1996), and in this instance, our understanding of school success and/or the successful global citizen. They signal the recruitment of students to particular epistemologies, and an explicit civic curriculum would be powerfully impacted were the epistemologies behind these goal statements embedded in day-to-day school practice.

Lankshear (1998) calls the production of these kinds of documents and the associated practices part of the "new basics," a term derived from his work on literacy, the social organization of the workplaces, and "New Capitalism" (Lankshear and Gee 1996; Gee, Hull, and Lankshear 1997). The new basics derive from a change in social relationships associated with a shift from a heavy industry, Fordist economy to an information/services economy. In moving from a hierarchical Fordist factory-line economy to a highly decentralized service-based and communications technology–driven society, social relationships within the whole society will be transformed. This includes school, family, work, major institutions—in short, everything. In such a working world there will be both more face-to-face interaction through teaming *and* more impersonal communicative communities based on computer technologies. Work will require greater self-sufficiency, more abstract and symbolic logical capacities, and an emphasis on higher-order thinking skills. New economy work will be heavy on information technology, demand teamwork, oral communication skills, self-direction, just-in-time learning, and problem-solving skills.

The categories in the goals documents are derived from and consistent with the brave new world of new capitalism. These categories are supported and extended through an executive summary from 2004. The summary is full of language on individualized plans, early college and career selection, life goals plans, and multitrack learning systems where the self-regulating individual learns flexibility and problem solving. "Highly effective interactional students engage in academically intensified science and mathematics curriculum . . . pursuing advanced studies at an early age." New curriculum structures such as core knowledge and international baccalaureate are in their initial phases of development. Both are generally seen as highly academic. Students develop "state of the art technology skills" with support from "guest lecturers" from "the University of Washington and the NASA Ames Research Center." This language denotes not just any old "real world" but a very particular future world. Thus, futures are framed at the site of a school mission and goals. But these goals and documents do not simply determine classroom practice, and the classrooms presented here show three different places where civic education curriculum interacts with these directives in multiple ways.

SCHOOL SITES OF CIVIC EDUCATION—
ANGIE, JERI, AND PAT

In most of the classes that I have observed in more than two years of fieldwork, it is clear that the goals cited earlier have become deeply embedded in day-to-day practice. The need to meet "adequate yearly progress," a term and process defined through the national legislation of the Elementary and Secondary Education Act, is one vector through which these practices enter into schooling at Wellpinit. The reading and math curriculum uses an individuated skills-based approach in the primary grades and a computerized comprehension-intensive program for middle and high school students. A similar math curriculum, Saxon Math, is in place. Much of the curriculum is becoming computerized and students work individually at three-sided computer consoles where they won't be distracted by others. Core knowledge and international baccalaureate curriculum, both highly academic and lacking in local indigenous content material, are in the early stages of implementation as well. A Spanish teacher was brought onboard, and students are now all enrolled in Spanish class, with a reduction in the time that they learn the tribal language justified through the argument that the tribal language does not "qualify as a global language." Overall, the official curriculum of the school is coming into close articulation with the goals as stated by the superintendent and the mission statement; it is becoming highly individuated, with an emphasis on high test scores, college attendance, foreign language acquisition, all pointing students toward the "real world."

Typically, in the Wellpinit school as in other schools around Washington State, civics education is introduced in fourth grade with an emphasis on state history and governance, then followed up in middle school with an emphasis on U.S. national governance, and tenth grade with an emphasis on U.S. history. These are also the years when the state has two weeks of testing for academic proficiency on the tests mandated by No Child Left Behind. Between test preparation and test taking, teachers in these grades told me that far less civic curriculum could be covered than they would wish. In the fourth grade, the teacher said to me, "We haven't even opened the book. It's been reading and math, reading and math."

When students have a chance to open the fourth-grade Washington State book, the eighth-grade civics book, or a secondary U.S. or Pacific Northwest history book, they rarely see anything that connects directly to their day-to-day life on an Indian reservation or to the oral history tradition of the Spokane tribe. The newest Washington State history book, at 256 pages, devotes just 8 pages to native peoples in the state. The eighth-grade American civics textbook is entirely about national government. A Pacific Northwest history book, used in the American history class, has a twenty-five-page chapter on native peoples generally. However, making an evaluation of civic democracy education based on what I have described so far would be premature. The picture became more complicated when I observed the teachers in fourth, eighth, and tenth–eleventh grade, where a civic education curriculum is officially in place.

Angie teaches fourth grade. She is a white, middle-class teacher who married a tribal member, Ben, when the two of them met at a regional university. She is twenty-five, had her first child in 2003, and during 2004 was expecting a second. Her husband, she said, "wants lots of kids!" She is tall, with long blonde hair, and typically dresses in professional skirt and blouse. She has an M.Ed. in literacy education and was in her first year as a teacher when I spent time in her class in 2003–2004. I began observing late in the fall, a few months after she had begun her first year as a teacher.

Angie would very faithfully follow the script for the Open Court Reading Program, then the script for the Saxon Math program. In reading, this involved reading a scripted story in a small group, working on some comprehension questions, memorizing some vocabulary, and then moving on to another group while the first group "read" independently or worked with an aide. Reading and math would usually take all morning. In the afternoon, many students would be pulled out for additional computerized tutoring in a reading program that was "guaranteed" to raise test scores. After observing this pattern for several weeks I asked her about fourth-grade civic education. Angie replied, "I don't have time. It's reading and math, reading and math."

Later we spoke about the reading curriculum, where she has an advanced degree and a great deal of professional knowledge. She said:

> When I first took this job, I knew I wanted to do a lot of oral reading with this group.
> I thought I could enrich the Open Court with lots of *good* books. Books about the Spokanes. I spoke to Ben about it and he agreed. "Read stories out loud, let the kids listen," he said. So that's what I started doing. But Mr. R. [the superintendent] and Tammy [the principal] came in. Then they called me in and told me to "stick with the curriculum." And the way they said it, well, it was a threat, and Mr. R., he said, "No fluff. Reading stories is fluff. We are building excellence here."

Angie clearly feared for this, her first job, and she also is, in a sense, iconic. By this I mean that the majority of classes that I observed, taught mostly by white middle-class women, looked very similar to Angie's class.

An interesting complement to Angie was Jeri, a Spokane tribal member who teaches seventh- and eighth-grade social studies at the middle school. Jeri and I had gotten to know one another during a summer encampment on the Spokane River that brought together teachers, teacher aides, tribal elders, and language teachers to talk about culturally inclusive curriculum. Jeri was in her midforties, had served in military intelligence as an officer in the first Gulf War, lived in Washington, D.C., and San Francisco, and had come back to the reservation to be close to family. Jeri was the one teacher who had already consistently brought the local culture into her teaching. She commented that she had the latitude to do what she wanted to in the classroom, ignoring the official curriculum and connecting to the students and their own lives. I asked how it was possible for her to do that, and she replied:

> Well, I'm a member of the tribe, and like a lot of these kids, I'm a white Indian. Kids can relate to that 'cause a lot of them are white Indians, too. I see myself as a community member and not as a teacher. In the classes that I teach I'm related to two-thirds of the kids. Also, Mr. R. can't fire me cause the community wouldn't stand for it.

During the course of the 2004–2005 school year, I was able to spend a lot of time in Jeri's class and see firsthand what it meant to know the kids and their families as a community member. One unit she did with the kids was on war veterans from World War I to the war in Iraq. Kids planned and carried out interviews with a war veteran in the community. They then wrote up a brief biography of that person, what they did in the war, and shared stories that they heard during the interview process. Students then constructed a "Wellpinit Warriors" book where all the stories were recorded. Community members, elders, veterans, and family members were then invited to class for a sharing of the book. Community members cried as students recounted stories of warriors from the tribe. A sense of pride was palpable. Jeri noted how powerful the final sharing was—that this community had so many heroes.

Not only was the curriculum relevant to students and community, but Jeri's activity structures were relevant to the local community. Jeri's kids started out by brainstorming in groups what the words *veteran* and *warrior* meant to them. Jeri said, "Asking questions of these kids to start out will shut them down. In our community kids aren't asked direct questions and when they're learning from elders they aren't supposed to have answers to questions until they really know that what they say will be right. So they stay quiet if I start by questioning. Brainstorming works better." The word choices linking veteran to warrior were also important. Kids could make a connection between national service in a U.S. war with local connotations of what it means to be a "warrior." Jeri acknowledged the importance of this with the title of the book, "Wellpinit Warriors," where a warrior was someone, as one veteran put it, "who goes off to fight to protect the people, then comes home to be a father, husband, and provider."

Jeri also didn't test in the typical sense. Instead, students produced a group product that became a part of the community. Jeri says, "I evaluate by watching, listening, and interacting with them. When we assess and give a grade, I sit down and we discuss what was learned. I do this with them as a group and individually."

Jeri often makes the point that to be an effective teacher at the Wellpinit school, you have to join the community. She says, "You go to a basketball game, and how many teachers do you see? Maybe one. I took time off for state B [the state basketball tournament]. I mean, state B is part of the culture, the tribe and basketball, and it's all nonexcused absence. Parents are forced to tell a lie about a doctor's appointment so that kids can go to the tournament. And how many teachers are there? None."

Jeri constructed culturally relevant curriculum that tapped into local culture and civic understandings through interviews and group sharing where the sharing and not the book became the focal point of the activity. Use of the word *warrior*, and its eventual presence in the title, focused attention on local understandings of what it means to fight for your community and also pointed children to narratives of warriors from the past (although the Spokanes explicitly reject the idea that they are a warrior culture akin to some Plains tribes). The community was brought into the school and the oral tradition was used as it is in other community gatherings.

Pat is a tribal elder and community member who teaches in the high school. I visited with two classes that Pat had: one with tenth graders and one with ninth graders. Pat is a quiet man, like many Spokanes, and he avoids confrontation. He is a deeply traditional man, invoking elders, grandparents, storytelling, and the language as a way to talk about history and social science. He has a quiet, even tone, a rare but heartfelt smile, and never directly confronts students either through facial expression or body language.

Pat's class at first glance looks like a typical social sciences classroom; posters of the world, a map of the United States, a line of computers, white boards on opposite sides of the room, and a teacher desk facing rows of student tables in four rows. However, there are a lot of small indications that Pat is native, has lived much of his life on the reservation, is an elder of the tribe, and a war veteran. For one, there is dress. Pat's hair is long and braided into two strands that run down either side of his face. Rather than wearing the school's yellow vest that says "Wellpinit School," Pat wears a dark blue one that says "Spokane Tribe of Indians" with a Spokane bonnet image done by one of the tribal artists. He wears a string tie with a locally made choker, black jeans, a silver-inlaid belt, and cowboy boots.

The class has lots of touches that also are not a part of the typical classroom. The ubiquitous classroom round clock with black numbers is covered with paper. Pat doesn't want students to pay too much attention to what he calls "little bits of time." Underneath a world map is a map of tribes and nations in North America. On one side of the white board a powwow poster with a dancer drawn by a local artist sits next to the world map, and below that is a map of the reservation lands. Above one of the white boards are eight-by-twelve pictures of two tribal elders from the early part of the twentieth century. "Most of these kids are related to one or both of them," Pat remarked.

On one of the days that I observed Pat, his class curriculum consisted of a worksheet that asked students to find facts and figures from the chapter they had been assigned to read. The first class completed a worksheet on Canada, and the second class did one from a chapter on Indians from the Pacific Northwest. The activity is a typical "find the answer in the book and fill in the worksheet" task. Students fill in sentences that say "The capital of Alberta is _____" or "Indians on the coast relied on fishing for _____."Pat says that a read-and-discuss approach doesn't work because students won't read so they can't discuss. He also says many of the students will not and cannot take on the text at its level of difficulty. Pat talks about the schoolwide concern for the ninth graders as they will have to pass the state achievement test next year in order to graduate. The majority of the students either cannot or will not decode a ninth-grade social studies text.

In the following excerpt, Jeanelle, a ninth grader with long black hair and a tattoo of Jesus on her shoulder, is moving back and forth between two groups. She moves to a group other than the one she starts with and helps them read a graph and calculate the output of wheat production for a Canadian province. Billy and Jimmy are working together in one group. Jeanelle is part of a larger group comprising at this moment five students: Jeanelle, Bob, John, Jean, and Mandy. They have already worked out their answer to the question. Braces indicate overlapping speech.

Billy:	Hey, Je-, Hey, hey we need you.
Jeanelle:	OK, OK. What, what is it that you guys need
Billy:	Number 7. The output is, we think {that it's}
Jeanelle:	{You have to} (walks over) You have to look at the output in tons and change it change it to pounds
Billy:	OK, then how do we {do that}
Jeanelle:	{Multiply by} by 2,200.
Jimmy:	But then, what's the {answer?}
Billy:	{can do it} (doing calculations)
Jeanelle:	{I'll help if} you need it.
Bob:	Jeanelle! We need you.

While this exchange on the face of it appears unremarkable, close examination illustrates several aspects of a particular kind of activity structure that is common in some indigenous communities and *uncommon* in school. First, there is no teacher direction in terms of how to do the activity; that is, there is no highly directive leader. Students work in self-organized groups, not teacher-organized groups. In addition, these groups are fluid in that students move back and forth from one group to another as the task progresses. This constant movement is a way to share resources to solve the particular problem of the moment, be it a geography question, a history question, or, as illustrated, a question that requires some calculating ability. There is talk across groups, and answers are found both within groups and across groups. Pat is silent during the entire activity time, walking around the class, never admonishing or making direct eye contact, speaking in a low and quiet voice. The work is egalitarian in the sense that answers are shared within and across groups. Particular students like Jeanelle are called to perform because they are good at different aspects of the activity. One student who is good at reading graphs is in demand by all groups for two questions. Jeanelle, who is good at doing math, came into demand as students get to the seventh question that requires reading a graph *and* doing some calculations. Students are also moving in and out of the classroom. Reasons vary: to get a book, get tissues, see a parent, go to the bathroom, and respond to a summons to the office were all reasons that I observed in one fifty-minute class. Pat never denies permission. Even when a student sits in his chair and peruses the grade book, which most Euro-American teachers would see as a direct challenge to their authority, Pat responds nonconfrontationally and engagingly:

> *Pat:* What'cha doin' there, Lyle? You shouldn't be looking at that.
> *Lyle:* I wanted to see how many days I'd missed.
> *Pat:* Well, that stuff is supposed to be confidential. Just ask me and I'll tell you.

It is worth considering how a "typical" teacher might respond to such behavior. Pat and other tribal members recognize in this context and this culture that authority is highly distributed and *acting* to find out days missed is not a challenge to their authority. It is the action of an apprenticing member in a highly egalitarian culture where how many school days one has missed is of central importance to students. Students in Wellpinit, and on many reservations, typically miss a lot of days due to community activities such as births, marriages, sickness within the family, wakes, birthdays, naming days, basketball tournaments, and pow-wows. In the year 2004–2005 when my observation took place, there were two tragic deaths in the high school when both school and community came to a complete halt. For many months the community was in mourning for the two young people, and in that context, students were often not at school. Yet these absences are deemed unacceptable by the school, so that students, responding to the civic requirements of the local community, find themselves in conflict with official school requirements for attending. Pat, as a local community member, would know that the question of days missed would be of importance not just to Lyle but to many students in his class.

At the end of Pat's class, we talked about Spokane culture and how kids learn to be Spokane—my question about where civic culture would be learned and of what it could be said to consist. Pat said that grandparents would have fulfilled this role and did up until the end of World War II. They would have been around and told stories about their parent's grandparents, how things were, and kids would have learned Spokane ways in this manner. Pat said, "Kids now don't have much contact with their grandparents and there aren't as many old people around for them to listen to. Fred Wynn [an elder] is someone who still does that, but there aren't many left who do." It was striking that Pat does not identify himself as someone who shows kids how to be "Spokane," highlighting the implicit character of this kind of civic identity building.

Many classrooms in the Wellpinit school provide details of how the school is tied up in practices that in one way or another begin to represent new capitalism. This dynamic includes an emphasis on testing, processes of individuation, and the mastering of the technologies of the information age. Angie's class provides, as I said, an iconic example of this. Both Jeri's and Pat's classes also provide counter examples—two classrooms where there exists an interweaving of civic education with local community practice and nation-state recruitment to economic structures. Pat's class works with community activity structures of egalitarianism to complete what Lankshear (1998) calls "lingering basics" tasks of filling out worksheets. Jeri's class, using elders and parents, actually undermines calls for individuation, but it uses technology to create community artifacts. At the same time this activity is reproducing a constituent component of the American civic ideal—patriotism (Owen 2004). It is also hybridizing the classic American patriotism and a war civic curriculum, co-opting both to build local civic relationships and social capital structures.

COMMUNITY TALK AND CIVIC PRACTICE—"WE GATHER"

This final section comes primarily from conversations that took place during and after a summer gathering on the Spokane reservation in July 2004. At that gathering were teachers and teacher aides from the school, tribal elders and Salish language teachers, community children, and tribal council members. While the official purpose of the meeting was to develop culturally appropriate math and science curriculum, many conversations were about the divide between school and community, and the often implicit social construction of identities (Levinson, Foley, and Holland 1996) that takes place through community civic events. During one of these conversations, an elder named Pauline said, "It's collide and bounce off between native and *suyapi* [white, literally "upside-down faces"] cultures." The summer gathering director, who is a member of the neighboring Colville reservation, said, "I think it's because we have culturally different ideas of *success*. Pauline, how would you say culturally that our people define success. And how does school define success?" Pauline replied,

> P: I guess mostly
> Happiness and contentment
> Food and milk for your family
> Enough money to give a dinner for the community every so often
>
> I think that's one thing
> We don't realize
> We haven't imparted to the white culture
> We *gather*."

Articulated in this conversation during the gathering, community members evoked an implicit understanding of what it means to be Spokane from a traditional perspective. Under the rubric of talking about how "our people culturally define success," speakers made clear through discourse that in their perception many of the characteristics of civic activity in the community were in direct contradiction to those mandated in the school.

In discussion, four major themes came up again and again with respect to how Spokane practices conflict with school practice. First, heart and head cannot be separated when thinking and speaking: they are at the core of social relationships that embody the sacred. Second, places, family, and home are organized around practices of gathering, in contrast to things that are "out there" where the purpose and practices associated with gathering are undermined and degraded. Third, practices of the body, gaze, and time in school and community spaces conflict with one another. Finally, narrative knowledge and a narrative universe are threads that connects these points all together. As one elder put it, "naming the place brings you back to that place, to your body and heart." Elders and community members at this gathering agreed that while most students did not grow up anymore in "traditional" ways, that these four areas were still a significant part of the childhood experiences of many, affecting how they "came to the school." Much as Susan Philips (1983) found more than twenty years ago, the embodied communicative practices of many children were unlikely to articulate well with those required for school excellence.

"I want them to be able to look at themselves in the mirror. Looking in the mirror is where you see your heart" was one comment that reechoed throughout the week as members of this community talked about what it meant to construct culturally relevant curriculum. "Learning in the heart," said one elder, "means teaching by example, learning by doing." "Speaking from the heart, head" illustrates traditional tribal ways of thinking about communicative competence—what counts as face-to-face interaction. There can be no knowing without the heart and without connection between objects and subjects. Salish is a fundamentally relational language and despite the fact that few members actually speak it, these relationships live on in tribal practice. Words for *like* and *love* in Salish are *active* verbs, like *going* in English. They have no passive aspect. This grammatical construction illustrates that objects and subjects are always connected by processual verbs. Relationships cannot be disconnected from processes and places in Salish. As Basso (1990) made clear in his work on Apache place names, they cannot easily be decontextualized as they can in English. Many Euro-American teachers at the gathering, particularly in science and math, struggled with this idea. "Aren't some things just true?" they asked. "What about facts?"

Social relationships, social capital, and social facts are of the heart. Many Spokanes see the practices of school as eradicating that connection and set of relationships. Highly individuated curriculum, teaching, and learning the core knowledge curriculum, and technology skills constitute knowledge of the world as universal, disconnected, and decontextualized. The superintendent's goals are not of the local world; they point students to membership in a globalized United States, to what teachers and administrators call the "real world."

During the week of gathering, community and school members had a great many conversations about the world of the local in its relationship to the "real world." One commentary came from a Salish language teacher, Marsha, regarding her daughter's experiences in the school.

M: these kids
They're dropping out *now*
And he adds higher academic expectations   (*he* is the superintendent)
But doesn't change the curriculum.
Then these kids are going to be even higher dropouts

It's not culturally relevant to *any* of those kids
So it's gonna cause a higher dropout. (rate)

My daughter that's there
She dropped out in 8th grade
And I was telling R   (R is the superintendent)
Way back then

She says that
'Nothing in the school has anything to do with me"
and he's all
"Unfortunately that's not the real world."

Here Marsha, in heart-rending terms, is discursively constructing a two-worlds dichotomy, with herself as an "Indian person" in one world and the "real world" and superintendent in the other. While Marsha and her child are more complicated than that, it is important to note the important work that the dichotomy does—it creates her daughter as a dropout, on the road to being the nobody. Place, meaning family, home, and the purposes for coming together are differently constructed in these two arenas. School is "out there" because of the things that happen to kids in the school. Grades, which are seen as degrading, are not a part of community places where people are evaluated in noncompetitive ways. Evaluation in the community is also not highly individuated; indeed, it is seen in terms of what one can eventually give back to and share with others. School is also a place where how much money one has becomes important, how one looks and dresses is central, and both of these come from "out there." Family and local spaces are constructed as "where you belong." Again, with respect to school goals, it is the purpose of education for students to leave the reservation. College education requires students to leave. Global classrooms in China, Jordan, and Africa, the *international* baccalaureate curriculum, and bringing in a full-time Spanish language teacher are all pathways that point kids toward living off the reservation. It reproduces a traditional Anglo-American ideal where young people will "go out and make their way."

Community members consistently talked about the interrelationships among body, gaze, space, and time to talk about the disconnect between school and community as well. They explicitly connected this discussion to the "success" metaphor introduced at the beginning of this section, again indicating how Spokanes do things. For example, in a world where direct interaction is the norm, Spokanes say "we turn away." Spokanes turn away in terms of both body and gaze as a sign of respect to others, but teachers insist on having the kids face them. "Look me in the eye so I know you're telling me the truth," is a common teacher direction. One teacher, who was also a tribal member said, "To our kids direct gaze means dominance, violence, even anger." School norms for discipline involve direct and constant surveillance that requires teachers and disciplinary officers to confront students in the halls between class if they are transgressing school rules. Tribal teachers like Pat never gaze directly at or turn their bodies toward them when asking them to change their behavior. However, Pat is in the minority.

Time is a huge issue for kids in school. Time is always being parsed for them into incrementally smaller bits in the forms of individualized learning plans, life goal plans, early college and career plans, and daily school practice. Plans also imagine a future where "learning to get ahead" is the metaphor that is central to the school culture and, through curriculum such as core knowledge or the international baccalaureate, students learn that to be a global citizen means to engage in "just in time" learning.

Creating a narrative universe where people learn through listening to and inhabiting story is also a central place where community members identified the creation of local civic culture. People in the community consistently say, "Our elders are our books," or identify elders as the repository of particular kinds of knowledge and stories as the primary mode for passing on that knowledge. Again, a question was asked about what some of the ways were that Indian students could be successful. One elder replied,

> I think telling kids the stories
> (for) their behavior within the community
> that's really important
> As far as being successful

Community members also discussed how stories, even in English, could capture some of the cadences of the language, where it's the "language of the heart and it teaches us about the sacredness of relationships." Stories about place did this for some, as one tribal member recounted the story of where her tribe came from, the village of Inchelium. In that story, Inchelium, which means "Singing Waters," was a place where one really did grow up with waters that sing and that, for her, exemplified the necessary relationship between head and heart, between knowledge and memory. Others spoke about the many coyote (*Spilya*) stories in the tribe. Spilya stories have been historically used to instruct the young about what happens to those who transgress the social norms. One teacher from the school asked, "There's a lot of teachings about that isn't there? A lot of stories? Aren't there rules about relationships, about generosity, about not being stingy and hoarding things?" Pauline responded with this story:

> If someone admires what you have
> you give it to them.
> Mom says, if you don't
> Something's going to happen to that.

> I admired a big bone necklace she made for dancing.
> She said, "I'm taking it to Omak this week
> And I hope I can sell it so
> I can have some stick game money."

> I says, "Oh, OK." (1.0)
> Somebody stole it   (groans)

> And it just so happened
> That the police seen him
> Somebody with that necklace
> And he went and got it back to her . . . (1.0)
> She gave it to me   (much laughter)

DISCUSSION

Civic education for democracy is usually portrayed as a program of citizenship education, created in governmental and educational institutions, practiced in schools and classrooms, that leads to a set of skills, knowledge, and attitude outcomes that students will practice as citizens of a state. This chapter has shown that to capture the complexity of civic education on the ground, we have to look at the changing landscape and social relations of a global capitalist culture as well as a local construction of civic culture that may or may not align with school-based citizenship programs. By looking at three contexts, the global, the school based, and the community, we can see that they all impinge on civic education and the production of school-situated identities.

At a macrolevel, through school-created spaces and school documents written for public consumption, many of the purposes for education are being recruited to an economic imperative of global capitalism. This is at the core of the "real world," which is reflected in both school spaces that mimic corporate spaces and school goals that focus on individuated workers who go to college, perform well on tests, master technology, and work in the global workplace. Through the core knowledge and international baccalaureate curricula, some students are recruited to move toward a high level of mastery in subject or discipline areas, developing expertise in the respective languages or literatures of these fields. These students are learning what Lankshear (1998: 260; Lankshear and Gee 1997) calls "elite literacies," the abilities to critique, innovate, and manage organizational practices and people, mastering these areas to become leaders in new capitalist workplaces. Most Wellpinit students, though, through reading and math interventions, are placed in learning contexts where abstract and higher-order thinking skills are learned through repetition. Reading comprehension or mathematical problem solving becomes a skill learned by rote and students presumably will be able to take on independent roles in post-Fordist information services companies. Formal civic education in this context, for most of the classrooms at the Wellpinit school, is becoming largely moribund, falling into the category of music instruction, art, or recess. It is disappearing particularly for schools that perform poorly on state-mandated tests.

The fourth-grade civic education curriculum, Washington State history, was not taught in 2004–2005. The entire year was spent on reading and math skills using the Open Court system, Saxon Math, and ReadRight as a pull-out program for twelve of the fifteen fourth graders. Angie's class was an example of this approach. When she used her university training, supported by advice from her husband and community members to read stories aloud, both superintendent and principal intervened to discipline her and require that she implement the Open Court curriculum. Fearing for her job, she acquiesced.

In Jeri's class, students connect with community members, creating social capital and civic culture embedded both in the local and the national. They also bridge the oral/literate dichotomy in the production of a book that gets used in oral reading and listening contexts. In other words, the purpose of book production is the use in sharing with an emphasis on listening. The actual use of the book in a culminating activity privileges the *aural* over the oral, the close listening that is a part of sharing and gathering in Spokane culture (Collins and Blot 2004). Jeri uses the nominative terms *veteran* and *warrior* as a way to bridge tribal and national civic cultures, while she herself would not say she was a "traditional" Spokane. Jeri describes herself as a "white" Indian. However, both the creation of local civic social capital and the privileging of listening over speaking, which are themselves both part of what it means to "be Spokane," are not seen as desirable in school-based constructions of the global worker-citizen. By taking on these qualities of being, students make it less likely that they will gain entry into highly indi-viduated global economic structures where communication is face-to-face, eye-to-eye, and highly oral. Here we begin to see the outlines of how a "nobody" gets constructed.

In Pat's class, students use highly egalitarian activity structures that might well be prized in global capitalist culture. But it is important to remember that the use of distributed understanding in Pat's class, the use of particular members who have particular skills to complete the task, depends on local knowledge. Because these students know each other very well, they can draw on each other. Pat's class is also an example of students using basic decoding and numeracy skills, what Lankshear (1998) would call the lin-gering or "old basics." They are still mastering the building blocks for breaking the code in alphabetic literacy and numeracy. The emphasis in Pat's class is on accuracy; correct spelling; self-correction in spelling, add-ing, and subtracting; and the ability to copy accurately. Most of the ninth-grade cohort will not pass state-mandated tests, will not get a high school diploma, and will not go on to college. Access to positions in the global economy, should they choose that path, has been effectively denied to them. In both contexts, when we think of building social capital, the hybrid capital that students would take away from such activities would serve them well in the local community. It would not give them access to higher education and global workplaces.

For the Spokanes, gathering together is a tool for creating social capital and local civic culture. In gathering, people reconnect with tribal knowl-edge and practice, learn the epistemologies of heart and head, the local forms of communicative practice, and the narrative universe through which Spokane identity is produced and reproduced. They build forms of civic culture that are not strictly of some idealized indigenous world or strictly of a globalized world—they are hybrid and multiplex. These practices, encouraging people to connect to place, emphasizing shared distributed knowledge across groups, eschewing highly individuated forms of competition, valuing narrative knowledge over procedural or factual knowledge, often will not fit well with what is portrayed as valuable in school. The dynamic social capital and civic life of a community is devalued and disallowed in school even while providing great strength and comfort as families and groups gather in a myriad of ways.

The picture portrayed here lays out an important aspect of exploring civic education processes around the globe: the interplay between the explicit and the implicit. While many of the chapters in this book give attention to the formal civic democracy programs, in many communities civic education will primarily take place under the rubric of what it means to "be" somebody. The explicit role of family and community in providing social capital to children is of particular importance when it is devalued in the context of perceived economic needs of a larger nation-state. In those cases we get such statements as "Unfortunately, that's not the real world" and students who see themselves as "nobody." This illustrates the struggle of balance and "walking between worlds." The real world, through the power of the schooling, reproduces a set of colonial relationships—natives as lazy, incapable, primitive, uncaring—while at the same time holding out a meager promise of educating citizens for democracy. And even this promise is being undermined for poorer schools in the United States. As we place a greater emphasis on economically instrumental curricula in reading and mathematics, programs for civic democracy are given less play in indigenous schools. Balance and walking between worlds will remain difficult for students at the Wellpinit school and for many other similar schools around the country.

REFERENCES

Basso, K. 1990. *Western Apache Language and Culture: Essays in Linguistic Anthropology.* Tucson: University of Arizona Press.

Bauman, R., and C. L. Briggs. 2003. *Voices of Modernity: Language Ideology and The Politics of Inequality.* Cambridge: Cambridge University Press.

Beck, U. 2000. *What Is Globalization?* Malden, Mass.: Polity.

Bourdieu, P. 1991. *Language and Symbolic Power.* Cambridge, Mass.: Harvard University Press.

Bourdieu, P., and J. C. Passeron. 1990. *Reproduction in Education, Society, and Culture.* London: Sage.

Collins, J., and R. K. Blot. 2003. *Literacy and Literacies: Texts, Identity, and Power.* Cambridge: Cambridge University Press.

Fairclough, N. 1995. *Critical Discourse Analysis: The Critical Study of Language.* London: Longman.

Foley, D. 1996. "The Cultural Production of the Silent Indian." In *The Cultural Production of the Educated Person*, ed. B. Levinson, D. Foley, and D. Holland. Albany: State University of New York Press.

Gee, J. P., G. Hull, and C. Lankshear. 1996. *The New Work Order: Behind the Language of the New Capitalism.* Boulder, Colo.: Westview.

Gimpel, J. G., C. Lay, and J. Schuknecht. 2004. *Cultivating Democracy.* Washington, D.C.: Brookings Institute.

Henze, R., and L. Vanett. 1993. "To Walk in Two Worlds—Or More? Challenging a Common Metaphor of Native Education." *Anthropology and Education Quarterly* 24, no. 2: 116–24.

Henze, R., and K. Davis, K. 1999. "Authenticity and Identity: Lessons from Indigenous Language Education." *Anthropology and Education Quarterly* 30, no. 1: 3–21.

Lakoff, G. 1996. *Moral Politics.* Chicago: University of Chicago Press.

Lankshear, C. 1998. "Meanings of Literacy in Contemporary Educational Reform Proposals." *Educational Theory* 48, no. 3: 351–72.

Lankshear, C., and J. P. Gee. 1997. "Language and the New Capitalism." Paper presented at the AERA annual meeting. Chicago.

Lankshear, C., and M. Knobel. 2003. *New Literacies: Changing Knowledge and Classroom Learning.* New York: McGraw-Hill.

Levinson, B., D. Foley, and D. Holland, eds. 1996. *The Cultural Production of the Educated Person.* Albany: State University of New York Press.

Levinson, B., and D. Holland. 1996. "The Cultural Production of the Educated Person: An Introduction." In *The Cultural Production of the Educated Person*, ed. B. Levinson, D. Foley, and D. Holland. Albany: State University of New York Press.

Mehan, H. 1996. "The Construction of an LD Student: A Case Study in the Politics of Representation." In *Natural Histories of Discourse*, ed. M. Silverstein and G. Urban. Chicago: University of Chicago Press.

Owen, D. 2004. "Citizenship Identity and Civic Education in the United States." Paper presented at the Conference on Civic Education and Politics in Democracies: Comparing International Approaches to Educating New Citizens, sponsored by the Center for Civic Education and the Bundeszentrale für Politische Bildung, San Diego, California, September 26–October 1.

Philips, S. U. 1983. *The Invisible Culture.* New York: Longman.

Pratt, Richard H. 1892. "The Advantages of Mingling Indians and Whites." *Proceedings of the National Conference on Charities and Corrections* 46.

Prinzing, D. 2004. "Americanization, Immigration, and Civic Education: The Education of the 'Ignorant and Free.'" Paper presented at the Conference on Civic Education and Politics in Democracies: Comparing International Approaches to Educating New Citizens, sponsored by the Center for Civic Education and the Bundeszentrale für Politische Bildung, San Diego, California, September 26–October 1.

Putnam, Robert. 2000. *Bowling Alone: The Collapse and Revival of American Community.* New York: Simon & Schuster.

Roy, P. 1961. *Assimilation of the Spokane Indians.* Pullman: Washington State University Press.

Ruby, R. 1976. *Children of the Sun*. Norman: University of Oklahoma Press.

Sarris, G. 1993. "Keeping Slug Woman Alive." In *The Ethnography of Reading*, ed. J. Boyarin. Berkeley: University of California Press.

Torney-Purta, J., Ranier Lehmann, Hans Oswald, and Wolfram Schultz. 2001. *Citizenship in Twenty-eight Countries: Civic Knowledge and Engagement at Age Fourteen*. Amsterdam: International Association for the Evaluation of Educational Achievement.

Williams, R. 1977. *Marxism and Literature*. Oxford: Oxford University Press.

2

Reformasi, Civic Education, and Indonesian Secondary School Teachers

Wendy Gaylord

> If we have a class discussion and the students learn one thing in civic education class and see another in real life they protest nowadays. For example, if we teach about democracy, "Democracy is an institution," then discuss, for example, in the family, what should be the rights and responsibilities of children? The students [go home and] complain. Whoa, this can become a problem, a problem for society, so teachers who encourage this are considered not [good].
>
> —Secondary school civic education teacher,
> Padang, West Sumatra, 2002

How do teachers in secondary school civics and government classrooms respond to democratization efforts in national political life and to uncertainty in curriculum content? How do they organize their practice according to what they think democracy means? With the stated aim of Indonesian education being the production of "good Indonesian citizens," the role of the teacher is crucial, although in reality by senior secondary school Indonesian students pay attention to those aspects of schooling that they are most interested in and merely do what they need to get by in the rest. Education is compulsory for nine years, and only about 40 percent of the school-age population continues on to senior secondary school. What do government and civic education teachers do in classrooms of secondary

45

school students who will be voting and working under changing political and social conditions? This chapter will explore how two teachers at an academically good public school in the province of West Sumatra taught civics and government during *reformasi*, a time of national political and administrative change.

Teaching occurs within the broader social and political context whereby government policy sets the curriculum and exams, provides guidance on implementation, and reflects broad national political trends. Indonesia has been undergoing political reform, *reformasi*, since the 1998 resignation of President Suharto after thirty years in power. At the same time as political change, it has been undertaking decentralization of many aspects of government authority from the national to the district level (the level below province). Laws No. 22, of 1999, and Laws 25 and 28, of 2000, established the policy on decentralization, providing limits on what authority was handed over to local authority and how funding was allocated between local and central governments. Levinson and Sutton (forthcoming) provide an overview of the national policy context of *reformasi* and decentralization.

Prior to the 1999 decentralization law, national policy was already moving in the direction of more local control of education. The Ministry of National Education had regional branches in each province that worked for and reported to the central ministry. Each district or city also has a local education office, and with decentralization these local education offices now report directly to the national level and have no official relationship with the provincial office.

A BRIEF HISTORY OF CIVIC
EDUCATION IN INDONESIA

Indonesia has had explicit citizenship education since 1950, a year after the nation finally gained independence from the Dutch. Teachers used a 1933 Dutch textbook until 1956, when the first Indonesian text was published, and its aim was "to raise and sustain awareness and consciousness that Indonesian citizens have a responsibility to themselves, to society and to the nation." The course topics included "Indonesia, My Country"; the national anthem; the flag and national symbol; citizenship rights and responsibilities; government; finance; taxation; and the economy and cooperatives.

The official state philosophy of Pancasila first entered the civic education curriculum after a presidential decree in 1959, and the official teachers' civics book, *The New Indonesian Person and Society (Civics)*, covered the topics of Pancasila, the history of the Indonesian struggle, rights and responsibilities of citizens, and the state speeches of President Soekarno. However, after an attempted coup in 1965, this textbook was banned, and in 1968 the Ministry of Education and Culture issued an instruction that the new civics program would cover Pancasila, the 1945 constitution, parliamentary decrees, and the United Nations. Later, topics on the New Order government, Indonesian history and geography were added.

However, it was only in 1972 that a national seminar on civic education issued an official definition of civics and of citizenship education. *Civics* was defined as "a discipline with the object of study being the role of citizens in spiritual, social, economic, political, judicial, and cultural matters in accordance with and as far as is regulated by the Preamble and Body of the 1945 Constitution." *Citizenship education* was defined as

a program of education with the main aim of guiding citizens to be better according to the requirements, criteria and measures of the Preamble and Body of the 1945 Constitution. Materials will include: Civics, including national defense, Pancasila philosophy, Pancasila mentality and the philosophy of national education.

In 1975, citizenship education was replaced with a subject called *Pancasila moral education*, as stipulated by a 1973 Parliamentary decree that stated, "To achieve desirable personal qualities, the curriculum at all levels of education, from pre-school through tertiary education, both public and private, must include Pancasila Moral Education sufficient to pass on the spirit and values of 1945 to the younger generation."

And in 1983, a Parliamentary decree on the Broad Outlines of State Policy (GBHN) included the following:

a. In carrying out National Education steps must be taken to make all parts of society familiar with and believe in Pancasila.
b. Pancasila Education includes Pancasila training (P–4) and other measures to improve efforts to pass on the spirit and values of 1945 to the younger generation through increased attention in the curriculum from pre-school through tertiary education, public and private. (Noer 2001)

Thus, Pancasila civic education began in 1976 and continued through the 1994 curriculum that was still in effect in 2003, renamed Pancasila and Citizenship Education as stipulated by the first National Education Law (No. 2, 1989).

Pancasila, the state philosophy of Indonesia, consists of five principles outlined in the preamble to the 1945 constitution as "belief in One, Supreme God; a just and civilized humanity; the unity of Indonesia; democracy that is guided by unanimity in decisions made through deliberation amongst representatives; . . . creating a condition of social justice for the whole of the people of Indonesia." Leaders have used this national ideology to maintain stability and moderation and to quell both extremist ideologies and ethnic and religious particularism throughout the history of the nation since 1945.

Nationally, Pancasila training (P–4) was a one-week intensive program taken by all civil servants, employees of large companies, community and youth groups, teachers, and secondary- and tertiary-level students. In 1998 the Parliament abolished the Pancasila training (P–4) requirement, leaving schoolteachers at a loss because the 1994 civic education curriculum was organized strictly according to the list of values presented in the national P–4 curriculum. In 1999, a supplement to the 1994 curriculum was issued, with no changes in content but an elimination of some topics in the civics curriculum and a combining of others that were overlapping.[1]

Because Pancasila has been the basis of all civic education, in and out of school, for so long, its five principles have been the referents and justification for much public policy, including the school curriculum. Thus, religion as a belief in one God, social justice, national unity, and Pancasila democracy are well-known ideas. It is the attempt to imbue these terms with new meanings that has been the challenge for Indonesia under *reformasi* and decentralization. Current debates on religious freedom, human rights, corruption, local control of government and resources, participation in public life, and questions of freedom versus responsibility have represented attempts to give new meanings to these old terms.

CIVIC EDUCATION IN THE CLASSROOM

It was within this national context that in 2002–2003 I spent a school year at one of the top urban public high schools in Padang, West Sumatra, where I observed classes, talked to teachers and administrators, and sat in the teachers' room listening and watching. The school was one of fourteen public senior secondary schools in the city. The school had a competitive admissions policy, and there were about 1,200 students in grades 10–12, with an average class size of over forty students. The city was the provincial capital with a predominantly moderate Muslim population of about seven hundred thousand, and although the vast majority of people were ethnic Minangkabau, there was a sizable Chinese population and smaller populations of indigenous people from local islands as well as members of other ethnic groups. Mosques were ubiquitous, and there were also a few churches and at least one Chinese temple. Many people, including Muslims, sent their children to the local, private, Catholic schools that had a good academic reputation.

My aim in this chapter is to show how two of the teachers I observed while at this school implemented the national civics and government curricula in senior secondary classrooms. One taught nine Pancasila civics classes that met once a week for two class hours, and the other taught three government classes for the twelfth grade social sciences stream that met six class hours per week.

The three aspects I discuss are some of those frequently identified as problems for teachers dealing with civic education during *reformasi*. First, I look at teaching methods and classroom management and see how these teachers structured student learning activities that reflected their views of democratic classrooms. Second, I examine curricular implementation—how teachers taught civics and government in the face of a changing national curriculum and national political scene, with awareness that semester exams were set at the district, not school, level. Next, I consider how teachers selected and used textbooks and other resources to further their goal of developing their students as good citizens. I conclude with a look at some ways that the civic environment of the school structured student roles and aimed to form good citizens.

TEACHING METHODS AND CLASSROOM MANAGEMENT

Lecturing, sometimes accompanied by question-and-answer exchanges, was by far the most common method of teaching that I observed in classes at this and other schools. Students in civics and government classes were at various times interested, relatively engaged, bored, or actively engaged in other activities such as doodling or completing homework for another class. Lectures generally began with a review of the previous class and a preview of the topic for the day. Teachers would pause at appropriate places throughout the day's lecture to ask if the students had any questions, and then continue lecturing. When I compared the content of the textbooks with the content of many teachers' lectures, there was often little difference. Therefore, students knew that they did not need to read the textbook, and they were rarely asked questions other than "Do you understand?" or to give examples of something the teacher presented. When they were asked to recall facts or information from the textbook, they would often be silent until the teacher gave the answer.

One observer of Indonesian education (Coleman 1987) characterizes these large lecture classes as "teaching spectacles and learning festivals" where students were present but not paying attention to the teacher. Presence, not attending to the content, was important. He notes the similarity between the endless ceremonies that civil servants often had to attend, but not attend to, as their presence was sufficient evidence of loyalty and obedience. Thus, he posits that school was a good preparation for someone to become a civil servant. I found both this type of civic education and a more thoughtful version, where teachers thought about how to make students active partners in learning, rather than spectators, in the West Sumatran schools that I studied.

Teachers who varied teaching methods and expected qualitatively different student participation in class found that the initial class reaction was confusion, sometimes resulting in total silence and sometimes in noisy chaos. The two teachers I observed organized their classrooms for teaching and learning to occur while trying new methods and introducing new content to their students. Each had a clear individual style and used it effectively. Both were very concerned with student learning and with student performance on exams, and both used the lecture method for some portion of their teaching. And, while both understood the importance of covering the curriculum as presented in the Ministry of National Education documents, they had somewhat different approaches to teaching related to their views of democracy and citizenship, which led to different teaching methods and techniques.

In Ibu Satu's government classroom, the teacher's means of working was to keep the students focused on the subject matter. She did this by being, alternately, a performer, and a master of ceremonies while the students performed, a role that reflected her background as a singer and master of ceremonies. She responded quickly to the level of student interest in the classroom, changing the tempo and type of activity in the classroom when necessary. For example, during a lecture on important events around the time of the Proclamation of Independence, she suddenly stopped and called a female student to the front of the class: "Please come up and recite the Youth Pledge! Everyone applaud her! [Students clap, and the student recites it]. OK, though it was mixed up. Y, please come up and correct it! [Students clap again]."

She continued her lecture, stopping to quiz students on dates and names of key people throughout the well-paced presentation. All the students were paying attention as they might be called on next, and because most of them already knew the dates and names well from repeated civics and history lessons over the years. Later in the same lecture, she sensed students were losing interest, so stopped and said, "Now I will test you." She dramatically introduced another student and asked her to recite the Proclamation of Independence, again calling for applause (Padang notes, September 2002).

While adhering closely to the curriculum, particularly important in government class with its heavy load of factual information to be learned, the teacher had identified areas that students found difficult and had devised ways to help them learn particular things. So, for example, she had quiz games, had groups of students prepare and teach specific topics, gave oral tests, and had debates where students presented various sides of an issue as outlined in their textbooks. She lectured when appropriate and did not expect students to have read the textbook unless she had given them responsibility to do something with the information, such as presenting or teaching it to others. She only occasionally asked students to evaluate information, give opinions, or compare or contrast differing opinions on issues outside the textbook. She did require memorization but was able to quickly check on student mastery and not spend a lot of class time on it.

> When I asked her how students prepared for the discussion today, she told me that she required all students to prepare individually and then chose some to sit in front as a panel to lead the discussion. She said, "I get angry when some students do not participate. So the students teach and I add when necessary." She said her aim was to get students to think about the material and not just memorize it (Padang notes, October 2002).

Her classroom management of group work was businesslike and efficient. At the beginning of the year, she got the students in the habit of moving quickly into groups, and she would announce at the end of class that the next day the tables should be arranged for the group or panel discussions she had scheduled. When she arrived in class, the students would be organized already, allowing for more time on task. After class she would give an evaluation of the day's discussion and list what students needed to know from the day's work.

The teacher stood at the back of the classroom and spoke to the students.

> "I evaluate that the discussion was done well. But there is one group of boys that did not participate. So there is no progress if only the same students are active. So I want to change the system. I am not going to refer to this material again. If you are just memorizing it you do not need to understand it deeply. (But) for discussion these are very good questions—you have to understand, not just memorize." She went through the 3 questions, saying, "I am going to summarize. You need to know the following on this topic, in accordance with the curriculum." (Padang notes, October 2002)

In Ibu Dua's civic education classroom, on the other hand, the teacher's way of working was to motivate and facilitate student learning, and to interest students in the daily lesson while making sure they mastered the necessary material for exams. She often used group and pair work, and students usually worked in groups with those beside, in front of, or behind them in the room. She was a fast speaker, gave instructions rapidly, and often had to repeat herself when students did not understand.

She actively sought new ideas for teaching, and at different times I observed her have students discuss a drawing on an overhead transparency, complete values clarification worksheets and use them to launch teacher-led class discussions, use information from class to apply to real problems in school and town, and do group projects involving interviews, photographs, and writing that were presented in class. She also adapted the Project Citizen (Kami Bangsa Indonesia)[2] model and had a class competition for the best presentation of a local problem and proposed solution. In contrast to many other classrooms I observed where teachers required quiet and order, hers was often productively chaotic, as the teacher bustled about and the students figured out what they were supposed to be doing. Ibu Dua often had prepared handwritten worksheets for class or homework, and she encouraged students to give their own views about many issues or curriculum topics, guiding them to the teaching point of the lesson. In one class, after a brief introduction to the topic, the teacher handed out a list of sentences for students to discuss, giving reasons why they agreed or disagreed. A full class discussion ensued.

The teacher made an effort to bring variety in classroom activities but also to be a less autocratic teacher—she said that the topic of democracy was meaningless without some evidence of it in the classroom and the school.

> One item on the agenda of *reformasi* is democratization. If we look at society now, everyone is confused about how to begin democratizing, so that now it is tending towards unlimited freedom. And school is society in miniature, so democracy should begin from the school environment. How to begin? It needs teachers to create democratic situations, and I see that the change in the 1998 curriculum is a change in that direction, but without being balanced by teacher behavior, the curriculum change is meaningless. We see that teachers are authoritarian in class, the teacher is like a god, like the ruler of the class. What would be wrong with empowering our students, with developing their potential? (interview, October 16, 2002)

She asked for student input about classroom management and agreed to student requests to change test dates and other matters. One worry that she had about using whole class discussion as a method was that she had observed that only the clever students spoke, while the rest remained silent. Another problem she identified was the school culture of devaluing teachers who were pro-student or too friendly with students.

Students of both teachers had to develop and practice habits of listening and responding appropriately to other students, of reading the textbook not simply for facts to repeat but for information to use in support of an argument or opinion. They had to think rather than memorize when discussing topics.

Teacher questioning techniques in both classrooms were varied. Like many teachers, both used rhetorical questions to introduce a teaching point. For example, "Is free fight liberalism[3] the same as a free and competitive economy or Pancasila economy?" (Padang notes, April 2003) was met with silence by the students, who recognized that the teacher was about to tell them the answer. Sometimes, however, the students did respond with a yes or no, and a teacher would follow up, often being satisfied with a formulaic answer from the textbook. "Is the archipelagic principle important in Indonesian society?" "Yes!" The teacher asked why as she wrote on the board: economically, socioculturally, politically, for defense and security, and for the unity of the nation. A student offered, "Economically," and the teacher called on another student to say why it was important economically. Getting no answer, she continued with her lecture, covering the points on the board.

More interestingly, however, were other types of questions that went beyond asking for recall of facts or provision of an example to illustrate a point. For instance, during student presentations, Ibu Dua would elicit details and ask students to evaluate information that was new to her and the other students. In both classrooms the teachers trained the students to listen to each other and ask questions directly to other students during presentations so that new ideas emerged that were not teacher directed.

CURRICULAR IMPLEMENTATION

The civic education curriculum in 2002 (the 1994 revised curriculum) was designed around a list of core values that support the Pancasila national ideology. One key problem with this was one of perception—the same values are taught at every level of schooling, although cognitive complexity is supposed to increase as students progress. In reality, by the senior secondary school level, students can recite the official definitions for terms such as democracy, and know key phrases and terms. They were generally not excited or motivated by this class compared with the other ten or eleven subjects they were taking. However, to move up a grade a student was required to pass civics, religion, and Indonesian language.

Ibu Dua thus tried to make the required topics engaging in a variety of ways, while following the set order of the curriculum. For example, for the topic of love for country she began, as many teachers did, with the concept of love. Students at this age were definitely engaged when naming the people or things one could love. Then she continued:

"Love of country has no meaning without sacrifice." The class erupts in laughter because someone in the back of the class has just said the exact same sentence. "Heroes and events are important." She puts up on the overhead projector a hand-drawn picture of a 1995 episode when Australians burned an

Indonesian flag in Australia. She asks the students to analyze it themselves and the classroom fills with murmurs of discussion. One student asks the teacher where the scene takes place, and she tells them to guess. One student says, "Siti Nurbaya Bridge," a new bridge in town, and another says "Semanggi," the cloverleaf bridge in Jakarta. The teacher does not say where it is, although the Sydney Harbor Bridge and Opera House are visible in the picture.

The teacher asks, "What do you think or feel about this picture?" Three students raise their hands and she picks on a boy first, making a joke about boys needing to progress more now that there is a female President. The boy says that perhaps flag burning is a sign of love for country by Indonesians who are fed up with the bad things being done in their country, although he adds that he does not agree with the method. A second student says, "If it is foreigners [burning our flag] we should be offended. They must be crushed." (Padang notes, September 2002)

In this passage, the notable features are the teacher's use of overhead projector technology, her open questioning, and her use of current events, although it must be noted that for students who were age sixteen in 2002, an event from 1995 was probably ancient history, hence the guessing about the location. The students clearly already had the message about loving their country and the need to sacrifice for it. The teacher allowed differing views of the meaning of the picture—she did not insist on one right answer, and in fact never did explain what the actual picture depicted. The students were active and offered opinions, but there was no serious questioning of the values ever evident during the class period. The discussion was managed by the teacher, and one student who was thinking critically about the situation was allowed to speak, but neither the teacher nor other students noted that he was proposing an alternate view—that Indonesians and not foreigners might burn an Indonesian flag for patriotic purposes. Rather, the teacher clearly wanted students to recognize how the values taught in the lesson were relevant to their lives and not merely slogans to be memorized.

Ibu Dua often introduced an activity and then directed students to use information in the textbook to do the activity. For the topic of vigilance, the teacher added group projects based on the Project Citizen model, asking students to identify problems that affected them personally and propose realistic solutions.

Now, you have the right to help change things. So we will be doing portfolio presentations. In your book there is information. We can look at ATHG [she uses an acronym that students know stands for threats, challenges, barriers, disturbances] and you can help find solutions to problems in school. So now *kewaspadaan* (vigilance) does not just mean to be careful, but also how to seek solutions. Look at page 122 for a list of attitudes that we need to be alert for nationally. Because we are more and more overwhelmed with problems of KKN [another acronym that students know stands for corruption, collusion, and nepotism], the economy, and socio-cultural imbalances. You read this at home already, didn't you? (no answer) Now let's get into groups one, two, three, four (the 39 students move into 4 groups). Groups one and four, and groups two and three join together to make two big groups. (Students move around again and push desks together until the two big groups are each around big, long tables). (Padang notes, March 2003)

This was an unusual and successful attempt to transform the theory and generalizations found in the teaching of values, specifically the value of vigilance in preserving and protecting the nation, into civic action. The teacher went beyond the curriculum to engage the students in looking at their environment and researching ways to improve it, rather than allowing them to memorize a set number of ways to be vigilant. The source of this teacher's inspiration for the lesson was her participation the previous semester as a judge in the Project Citizen project presentations for the junior secondary schools in the city. An unusual step she took was to invite other teachers to observe and to be on the panel of judges for her class presentations in an effort to share her work with colleagues.

The teacher got new ideas for teaching in an apparently ad hoc manner from seminars at the university, local teacher development sessions, and other sources. Because she was open to new ideas, Ibu Dua was willing to try student active activities in her classroom. She never lost sight of the final goal of semester exams but planned lessons with some active learning elements. She spent time talking to students in and out of class and urged them to be active in their homes and communities. This was her idea of good citizenship. Two examples from classes on the topic of *gotong royong* (mutual assistance) illustrate this. The teacher has said that the focus for the discussion would be the "people's economy" and asks how it works.

A student offers, "A cooperative spirit." (Three or four students are busy highlighting each other with highlighter pens.) Another adds, "A foster father system with big companies helping smaller ones." The teacher moves to the back of the room and asks two girls to comment. One says, "Big companies should stay owned by the government so they are run for the good of the people." A male student disagrees, "This is the business of government officials, to help. Some areas of the country have a lot of income from local resources and others do not. For example, Padang has cement."

The teacher tells the students they have the right to make their voices heard and influence public policy, e.g., concerning price hikes ("Mega's gift"[4])."You have the right to protest. Return to your own hearts and souls. If you have a heart you will help develop your own local place. Do you have courage to take action to affect policy?"

The students chorus, "Yes!" The teacher continues, "Ok, what would you look at? For example, state assets are being sold to Singapore, in the form of sand from Bangka Island." She continues, "Look at Section 33 of the amended version (2004 amendments to the 1945 Constitution)."

Another day, she covers the same topic in a different class.

"Let's focus on Demokrasi Ekonomi. Who can define it?" A male student offers, "economy based on the needs of the people." She asks, "Do you agree? Section 33 says that the economy is based on the 'familial principle' and the second clause is about public good, and Section 37 says. . . ." The discussion continues about the role of government in the economy. A student offers, "Control may be too strong a word—it could be used for corruption by the government."

The teacher says, "To prevent central control, we could have local invest-ment by the private sector-foreign or domestic. What is government involve-ment? Cooperatives, State-owned companies (BUMN). . . . The problem is not with the Constitution (UUD 45) but with implementation. People are work-ing for their own benefit."

A male student adds, "It is not the system but *oknum* [an official acting badly in an individual capacity] that is wrong. For example, it is prohibited to cut down the rainforest, but it is cleared anyway."

The teacher asks, "So if you don't trust private ventures or government—who do you trust? If your land contains '*mas segadang kudo*' [gold the size of a horse—i.e., riches] do you have rights or not? We can't be pessimistic-must start with ourselves. What is the solution?"

A female student sighs, "That is difficult. The roots of destruction are so deep."

The teacher responds energetically, "We can't be pessimistic, but must look ahead! So, for example, we need to figure out how West Sumatra can enjoy its own cement, and not be like Bangka that sells its sand to Malaysia." Various students are pessimistic about problems of corruption, collusion, and nepo-tism, but the teacher exhorts them to become involved in solving local prob-lems, "So we can't just say we are rich without working for it." (Padang notes, January 2003)

How are Pancasila democracy and Western ideas of democracy differenti-ated? When Ibu Dua taught this topic, she followed the curriculum so that students learned that Indonesian Pancasila democracy was based com-pletely on indigenous values drawn from the best of all the various indige-nous beliefs of the many Indonesian cultures. The purpose of the lesson and the conceptualization of the basis of Indonesian democracy was both to recognize all local cultures in the diverse nation that is Indonesia and to homogenize these many cultures into one national identity that every stu-dent must acquire to be a good Indonesian citizen. Additionally, the lesson aimed to differentiate Indonesian democracy from Western liberal democ-racy and from communism (both undesirable).

The teacher had prepared a list of statements for students to discuss in pairs and say whether they agreed or disagreed. One student said that he agreed with the statement that Pancasila democracy was a combination of Western and Indonesian democracy. He argued that, for example, voting was not part of the *musyawarah mufakat* (deliberation to reach consensus) pillar of Pancasila, yet it was part of Indonesian democracy. Other students agreed with him, pointing out that even the word democracy came from Greek, *musyawarah* from Arabic, and Pancasila from Sanskrit. The teacher was surprised but finally said that opinions are not right or wrong, so she could accept their arguments.

However, a week later when the teacher returned to class, she corrected herself, telling the class that the process of Pancasila democracy was different from liberal democracy and from democracy in communist countries. It was not a combination of Western and Indonesian ideas but came solely from the indigenous cultural values within Indonesia. She told me that she had talked to another teacher who said that she must correct the students' mistaken analysis. She also had read all she could find, and everything she read said that Pancasila democracy was indigenous to Indonesian cultures. Her husband, a civics lecturer at the university, also told her to "straighten out" the students' understanding so that they would not do badly on exams.

This incident reflected how complex the process of change can be for a teacher. Ibu Dua took a lesson that is usually memorized as fact and one where teachers at most might ask students for examples to illustrate the best indigenous values that have become part of national ideology. Instead, she asked students for their own opinions, and when they gave them to her with good reasoning, she accepted them.

However, she went home and "read everything [she] could find," but because she was reading sources intended to help teachers understand the lessons they should teach, and textbooks for university civics courses that were based on the same ideological framework as the school lessons, she found only the same answer as in her original lesson. Rather than questioning this, she asked for the ideas of two others, a teacher and a lecturer at the university. Both said she must change her teaching to match the lesson in the book or else the students would have trouble, although not because the student reasoning was erroneous. So she did, though with no strong supporting evidence that would refute the students' arguments.

Because most teaching is done through lectures, it was rare for a teacher to come to class and admit she had been wrong as Ibu Dua did. Nevertheless, student response was limited to some slight grumbling, as they were used to being told what they should learn for the exams. They had presented their views, but the teacher had the power to dictate the correct answer, and the students were very accustomed to learning what the correct answer was from the teacher and to presenting this answer when asked. Nobody questioned the teacher about whether it was acceptable for students to have a range of different opinions under Pancasila democracy.

One day, Ibu Satu had the first period class, when normally a student led a prayer. The date was October 1, when in 1965 a group of army generals were discovered murdered in what the government called an attempted communist coup; this eventually led to the downfall of President Sukarno. After the student-led prayer, Ibu Satu stood up at the front of the room and said that they should pray for the Pahlawan Revolusi (Heroes of the Revolution) because today was Kesaktian (Sacredness of) Pancasila Day. She is very solemn, as she led the prayer with, *"Doa mulai . . . selesai!"* (Let us pray. Begin . . . end!). Then she added that these days there were more and more problems with national security and misunderstandings among religions and groups in society. She continued in this vein. Later she told me that in the past the school had a big flag ceremony for this day, but under *reformasi* it had disappeared. No other teachers or students noted the day except for one class that had to go to the Governor's Office for the city flag ceremony. The teacher in this case chose to maintain the former regime's practices, while the school administration had let this particular patriotic ceremony lapse.

On another day in Ibu Dua's class the topic was human rights in Indonesia, and the students had worked in groups to list examples of how the rights listed in Pancasila and the 1945 Constitution were implemented in daily life. Following their group work, there was a whole class discussion. During the discussion the class had covered a number of rights, and had come to the topic of religion.

> Teacher: Next, Article 29 on freedom of religion.
> A student presents the main points and an example, then a female student asks about the Christianization movement. A male student replies that it is against Pancasila and the Constitution. The first student replies that people who have been Christianized have had their human rights violated. Is there any sanction for those who Christianize [i.e., convert] them?
> *Male student*: I don't know about legal sanctions, but a foreigner was deported.
> The teacher says that forcing religion on someone is a violation of Article 175 of KUHP (the criminal code) but one must have proof. The sentence is 5 years in jail for those who force a religion on a person who already has a religion, via economic or other methods. For those who do not have a definite religion (*belum punya agama yang jelas*), as in Samosir or Mentawai, it is allowed.[5]
> *Female student again*: But it doesn't appear like forcing, but more like persuading or making someone interested.
> *Male student*: Can all people freely embrace *kepercayaan* (traditional beliefs) because Kong Hu Cu is still a kepercayaan but it is the only one accepted in Indonesia?

Teacher: According to the Constitution only 5 religions are recognized, but normatively and morally Kong Hu Cu is recognized. Gus Dur even participated in the Imlek celebrations.

Male student: So can other *kepercayaan* be allowed?

The teacher again responds that they can only be accepted normatively. So one is not allowed to force any belief on others, except if another person listens to *dakwah* (religious proselytizing) and wants to join, that is OK.

Male student: Isn't *dakwah* the same as enticing or persuading?

Teacher: A person who proselytizes goes around giving talks to the public and nobody has to listen. Enticing is giving something to people so they listen.

Male student: What about the original Islamic missionaries, weren't they coaxing and enticing? Also, internally, there are those who make trouble about differences within one religion.

(bell) The teacher applauds, saying that the more debate, the better. (Padang notes, August 2002, Ibu Dua's class)

The whole class was attentive throughout this exchange. Nobody was doodling or doing homework for another class. All were listening to the discussion and appeared very interested even though two students and the teacher dominated it completely. The male student was trying to make a point that all forms of indigenous beliefs should be allowed, and therefore proselytization was not appropriate. The teacher was not asking other students for their opinions, but she clarified points and answered all the student questions herself. In other discussions, this teacher had directed students to both listen to and respond to each other and not go through the teacher. The teacher demonstrated tolerance through her encouragement of student questions that reflected divergent points of view, but she was very careful to differentiate for the students what was mandated by the Constitution and what was "normative" practice. She did not critique this constitutional limitation on religious belief, nor did she question whether people in Samosir or Mentawai had their own beliefs. This teacher was also the adviser to the school's extracurricular Islamic religion group, yet she was careful to include other religious perspectives when there was a non-Muslim student in the class (not every class had non-Muslim students).

USE OF TEXTBOOKS AND OTHER RESOURCES

Every student had a civics or government textbook. Teachers also had textbooks from other publishers as well as their university textbooks that they referred to when needed. Teachers' guides were not available for the textbooks. Each class also had a treasurer who collected money for photocopying and teachers had the class copy needed handouts or worksheets. At this secondary school the provision of textbooks was done through the faculty/

staff cooperative, which had an agreement with a publisher who paid a commission of 20 to 30 percent divided between the teachers and the cooperative. All students were required or encouraged to buy the textbooks, although they could get them from other bookshops for the same price. In addition, multiple copies of the government textbook were available in the school library. This book was out of date and was a very brief but dense outline of the material. However, as it was the official interpretation of the curriculum, students and teachers referred to it for guidance at exam time.

The two teachers differed in their approach to the textbooks. For Ibu Satu, the material in the textbook had to be mastered for the exam. So, as noted earlier, she organized her student activity to ensure mastery of the content in an engaging manner. The teacher required her students to bring in little outside material, although changes were occurring daily in the government form and function, as well as in legislative rulings. She did, however, give students some additional information during her lectures on new laws or changes in the government, and she corrected students who presented information from the textbook that was outdated.

In order for the teacher to monitor student preparation for semester exams, she required them to summarize each chapter in outline form and write it on a folding pocket-sized note card. The material in the textbook was thus transferred to the student cards and the teacher told the class she was helping them organize themselves to review for tests. Analytical and critical discussion was limited to a few comments and rather focused more on understanding historical and political facts and information, with the exception of a few times when the topics were controversial. Testing in Ibu Satu's class took the form of oral tests and classroom quiz games. In addition, midsemester and final exams were prepared at the district level, so all students in the city had the same exams. Most exams required students to provide facts and some application of facts to a situation or event in multiple choice and short answer format. Very little analysis or higher-level cognitive processing was required.

Ibu Dua also knew that the students had to take citywide exams and thus had to master the textbook content. However, because the civics curriculum was organized around values, she often used the textbook content as the framework for concepts that were to be applied to real life problems. For example, when teaching a lesson about democratization of the economy, the curriculum teaches that under Pancasila democracy, the economy is based on the "familial principle." The teacher assigned each student to interview someone who ran a business and to show how the business exemplified mutual assistance and the familial principle.

Because of the exam system, teachers had no choice but to cover all the curricular information in the order it was presented in the textbooks. And textbooks were all organized into neat categories, topics, and lists, making memorization easy. One common parent complaint I heard about teachers who introduced new and different activities into their teaching was that students did not do as well on exams, an important consideration for both families and for schools that were ranked based on their average final exam results. The two teachers I observed managed to use the curricular materials in ways that promoted differing types of student learning and student thinking and also produced good exam results.

Despite the school's location in the central area of the provincial capital and having many students whose parents were members of the provincial and city government, there were no visits to courts or city hall, nor were speakers invited from the provincial parliament or the community at large. Teacher Satu did not see local involvement as necessary for students to succeed in her government class. The emphasis was always on the national level, with international topics next, followed by local. Indonesian citizens produced in this school would be global and nationally competent, and the best of them would also have computer skills and English language proficiency to make them competitive economically.

THE SCHOOL ENVIRONMENT AND THE FORMATION OF AND EXPECTATIONS FOR GOOD CITIZENS

It is important that these two teachers worked in a school environment that allowed them to introduce different activities and teaching methods. The school prided itself on being a selective, academically strong school, and students were well aware that if they did not follow the school rules or perform well, they could be asked to move to another, less prestigious school. The principal was out of the school a great deal as the head of the city's association of principals, and he was ambitious to implement physical improvement of the school premises, an endeavor that required that he spend time fund-raising. He led the monthly teachers' meetings, speaking with a microphone and taking up all but a few minutes of the allotted hour speaking to the teachers. Each month the teachers brought up questions and issues during the brief question-and-answer period, often politely but firmly critical of school policies or the principal's ideas. According to Ibu Dua, the principal was overtly democratic but usually got his own way about things. For example, he held an election to choose two new assistant principals, but when the candidates he preferred were not chosen, he simply did not install the new people, postponing it for various reasons. He repeatedly told me that he promoted a democratic school.

The school supported the development of good citizens in a variety of ways, from the Monday morning flag ceremonies, to student-led prayers in

each class at the beginning and end of each day, to enforcement of attendance and uniform regulations. These are all common activities in Indonesian schools. At this school I was surprised to note that many teachers did
not attend the flag ceremony but stayed in the teachers' room rather than
modeling good citizenship behavior as was common at other schools I visited.

It was interesting to me that the school limited the number of extracurricular activities allowed at school because the principal thought students
should focus on academics. Yet when the school did compete in citywide
sports competitions, the teachers complained that the students were bad
sports, ready to get into fights with students from other schools, possibly
indicating a lack of experience at both winning and losing.

The student government leaders were also chosen through a schoolwide
election after a campaign. However, a panel of teachers interviewed the
candidates in order to ensure that they met the school's desired criteria.
Those that did not were not allowed to campaign. The school's democratic
and participatory activities kept the teachers busy managing those students
who displayed an excess of democratic zeal. Many of the more democratic
activities, such as protests and demonstrations, were toned down when
teachers became involved in monitoring.

The assistant principal for student affairs handled student disciplinary
matters. One day three boys who had had an altercation were disciplined.
The assistant principal came with them to the class I was observing. He
announced that the parents had been called in, punishment agreed on, and
if they fought again or had others fight for them, they would all be expelled
permanently. He gave a copy of a notice about this to one student, telling
her to photocopy it for all students to take home to their parents. As he left
classes with the three boys to continue on his rounds of the other classes,
he said, "Maybe Ibu Dua can talk to you about how to respect your friends."
The teacher announced to the class that this was an example of democracy
at school—the boys were not expelled, but a process of negotiation took
place (Padang notes, September 2002).

It was not only students who had to wear school uniforms. Teachers and
staff also did, and the city school district had recently begun to require
female teachers to wear Islamic dress (i.e., long skirts and long sleeves for
women) and "recommended" that they wear headscarves. This was an
attempt to promote local ethnic culture, which in this province is predominantly Minangkabau and Muslim. However, some female Muslim teachers
did not wear headscarves and reported to me that they had been called into
the principal's office and asked why they did not. Although they were not
told that they had to, it was understood that they were not following the
rules as expected, and they felt under some pressure to conform. There were
no non-Muslim teachers at the school.

Religion was present in the life of the school, with Muslim holidays and celebrations reflected in school life and extracurricular activities. There were only a few non-Muslim students in the school, and in each class that had one or more non-Muslim student the daily morning prayers that students recited in class were nondenominational prayers to the one God that all religions (even Hindu!) accept in Indonesia. Classes with all Muslim students had Islamic prayers, often in Arabic with an Indonesian translation. Teachers did not lead these[6] but simply prayed along with the class or waited quietly.

The published vision statement of the school was "To excel in achievement, pioneer in science and technology and in faith and beliefs, to be a model in behavior and culture, and to utilize available resources." In this era of reform, some teachers have been trying new ideas and methods in their teaching. Some had already been doing this prior to 1998 but reported that they found more acceptance in the post-1998 period. They operated under constraints of curriculum and exams that limited them in both time and scope of content. Ibu Dua mentioned that in the past she had tried to encourage debate and discussion in her classes and had been called in to the principal's office and warned not to be too radical, but that now things were a little more open. Other teachers reported that students were more willing to speak out and had more access than the teachers to information via the Internet, yet they still needed careful guidance to become good citizens.

The principal of the school said that his teachers also needed to improve:

Look, the students in classes are almost all *sudah pandai* (already smart), even though our facilities and resources are lacking. For teachers, only about twenty are *sudah pandai*, though we have over seventy teachers. So only one-third have reached [the desired level of quality for having democratic classrooms], and that is our complaint. (Interview, October 2002)

The principal was concerned with the quality of knowledge of his teaching staff, although Ibu Dua observed:

Actually, I see there is a change towards reform. But what interests me most is the strategy, the teacher behavior that we need to [change]; teacher behavior when teaching. I mean that teacher behavior has to be changed, the teaching strategy, because as we see one of the items on the reform agenda is democracy and democratization. (Interview, October 2002)

The principal wanted his teachers to be cleverer, in line with the first part of the vision statement, "to excel in achievement." The teacher wanted the school and teachers to educate students to be democratic members of society, in line with the second part of the vision statement, "to be a model in behavior and culture." These and other discussions are ongoing in the school and the nation as a new curriculum is being introduced and implemented throughout the country.

In the larger context beyond the school, this was a period of political campaigning in Padang, and there were many banners and news articles promoting "native" candidates for local government positions. This led to numerous discussions in the teachers' room about whether it was better to have a native teacher over someone from outside. And what was a native—how far away could you come from? Could you still be native if you were born and raised in Jakarta but were ethnic Minangkabau? What if you were born and raised in this city but your parents were Javanese or another ethnic group?

In the past such topics were banned from public discourse, particularly those falling under the acronym SARA, which stands for ethnic group, religion, race, and intergroup relations. During the New Order government of President Suharto, unity was important; loyalty to the nation and Pancasila over any ethnic, religious, or other group was demanded; and in school the national motto of "Unity in Diversity" emphasized the unity. Now with changing times, all people, including teachers, have begun to explore how to deal with diversity of opinion, culture, religion, ethnicity, geographic region, and social class. Some have been cautious and continued to avoid difficult discussions. Others have embraced the opportunity to allow students to think about such matters inside the classroom.

Students brought to their classrooms a wide range of experiences from outside school that formed the lenses through which they viewed the world. They were family members in families that may have been rich or poor, Minangkabau or Javanese or Chinese, Muslim or not. They were community members and may have worked in local markets after school or helped out with a family business or farm. But students were rarely called on to openly examine their experiences from outside the classroom although teachers often gave examples from their own lives as models of good behavior for students. Students may have been reluctant to be critical of the values being taught, even though they had experiences that taught them different lessons. They needed to pass the class in order to be promoted to the next grade.

A female student came privately to talk to a teacher I knew, upset because a relative was taking bribes in his government job. Yet one of the values she was being asked to espouse was truthfulness. She had strong family loyalty and, as a youth, was unable to confront her relative. She felt that although she could pass her civics exams with good grades, she was not putting the lessons into practice. Few students articulated this as specifically as she did. However, similar sentiments emerged in more general terms in classes I observed, making it clear that the good values and norms presented in school were not wholly embraced by students whose reality contradicted the lessons and left them with a critical awareness of local civic life. I observed lessons where this could be seen regarding questions of class and power, of religion and religious freedom, of moral values, gender issues, aspects of ethnic diversity, and individual rights.

Outside class every Indonesian is a critical thinker, having lived through a time when the press was tightly controlled and the government messages were often in direct contradiction to the realities of everyday life. At the same time, the emphasis in school on a single right way, right answer, and right religion has meant that students and adults have not had practice in considering alternatives and discussing alternative views and beliefs, nor in articulating how tolerance of diversity could work in school or in the community. They have memorized facts about diversity in Indonesia and the world, but until recently have not engaged academically with issues surrounding this diversity.

CONCLUSION

From the brief picture I have given here, it is evident that change at this school is a complex matter and that teacher decisions are as much about meeting administrative demands as they are about educating students. How did these teachers try to frame their practice around what they thought democracy should be?

Ibu Dua thought that democracy under *reformasi* meant that people should be free to, and moreover had the responsibility to, participate in society. They should speak up, debate, and pay attention to things that they could work to improve at both a local and national level. In school the teachers encouraged student participation, shared ideas with teaching colleagues, and sought new ideas for teaching to meet the challenges of continuing change.

Ibu Satu made it very clear to her students that a good citizen was well informed about the government and law of the nation, articulate in discussing them, and was organized, diligent, and composed in public discussions and when being tested or quizzed. She did not focus on local matters that were not in the curriculum and textbooks; instead, she worked to make the national system of government clear to her students, who would be voting for the first time in the first direct presidential election of the nation. As one of only a few teachers who did not wear the Muslim headscarf, she was also a visible presence in favor of individual freedom.

The teachers knew that they "should" use student-centered, active teaching methods and that students should become critical thinkers, able to understand issues and respond with imagination and agility to succeed in the world of global competition. They often reminded students that the nation would be at a great disadvantage when the regional trade agreement came into effect the next year, and that they must work diligently to be "modern and competitive" in the world. Civic education for Indonesia was complex from the start, with domestic diversity of nearly unimaginable magnitude. Increasing the focus on global citizenship only increases the felt complexity of the world the students are entering.

The schools play a role in ordering this complexity for the students. Teachers are guided by the curriculum, but the curriculum lags behind the changes in the country. In West Sumatra, the only experience some students had of the world outside their Minangkabau families and communities came from school and television.

The Ministry of National Education had always considered teachers to be important, and for years provided strict curriculum guidelines to make sure that they were educating students to be good Indonesian citizens of a speci-fied type. With *reformasi*, teachers could choose to what extent they wanted to change to meet the changing times, depending on their personal procliv-ities and their school environments. Both teachers in my study had relative autonomy in their classrooms and never had visits from the city school inspectors. However, tradition, curriculum, and exam systems, coupled with peer pressure to conform and maintain the status quo, were factors that controlled all teachers, who never forgot that they were civil servants first, and educators second. Thus their job security depended on receiving good performance reviews and not on student success, although arguably these ought to be related.

Furthermore, the teachers I observed, like their students, brought their personal identities into their school lives. For example, both were Muslim and saw religious, gender and legal matters from the perspective of Mus-lims. However, both were also Minangkabau women, in a matrilineal cul-ture where inheritance goes through the female line (unlike Islam, which gives women a lesser share than men), so this gave them a different per-spective from those of other ethnic groups. These teachers used their past experience and their own beliefs about teaching and about being a teacher in the government system to actively respond to the changing face of democracy in the country.

More changes are in store with the implementation of the 2004 curricu-lum being phased in over a three-year period. How this affects the larger population of teachers who must respond to a changing curriculum as well as a changing nation will be of interest to observers of Indonesian educa-tion. Decentralized support for central government curriculum changes provides opportunities but also challenges for teachers and teacher educa-tors nationwide, who need imagination and resources to respond to the needs of students as they become local, national, and global citizens.

NOTES

1. After I completed my fieldwork, a new 2004 draft curriculum returned to the title of Citizenship Education, and the competency standards for senior secondary school included:

1. The ability to seek, comprehend, communicate and use information about the nation and country; values and norms (religious, moral, etiquette, and legal); the upholding of human rights and its implications; political society; principles of democracy; and the relationship between the basis of the nation and the Constitution.
2. The ability to seek, comprehend, communicate, and use information about personal achievement; openness and the guarantee of justice; political systems; international relations; international legal systems and courts; Pancasila and the 1945 Constitution.
3. The ability to seek, comprehend, communicate and use information about government systems; the role of the press in democratic society; and the impact of globalization on the nation and people of Indonesia. (*Kurikulum dan Hasil Belajar*, 2002)

2. Project Citizen (Kami Bangsa Indonesia) is a civic education program developed by the U.S.-based Center for Civic Education and funded for adaptation for use in Indonesia by the U.S. State Department.

3. "Free fight liberalism" (in English) and *ekonomi Pancasila* are terms that the teacher and the students used on this day without defining them. Perhaps they have been defined in previous lessons or years. The curriculum teaches that Pancasila democracy, economics, and so forth, is always better than liberal (politics, democracy, economics) on the one side and communist ones on the other.

4. A reference to President Megawati.

5. The first pillar of Pancasila is "belief in one God" and Indonesian law specifies five religions as allowed in Indonesia: Protestant Christianity, Catholicism, Buddhism, Hinduism, and Islam. Traditional beliefs are also allowed, but this is a fuzzy and contested area at present, with, as the teacher says, normative acceptance of indigenous belief systems depending on the local situation. The ethnic groups living on the small islands of Samosir and Mentawai off the coast of Sumatra have their own traditional beliefs and are not Islamic, such as the ethnic Minangkabau of West Sumatra.

6. At the beginning of the school year, each class wrote or agreed on a prayer, and students took turns leading the prayer daily.

REFERENCES

Coleman, H. 1987. "Teaching Spectacles and Learning Festivals." *English Language Teaching Journal* 41, no. 2: 97–103.

Kurikulum dan Hasil Belajar, Rumpun Pelajaran Ilmu Sosial. 2002. Jakarta: Pusat Kurikulum, Balitbang.

Noer, Y. 2001. "*Sejarah Pendidikan Civic di Indonesia*." Unpublished manuscript, Padang.

3

Democratic Pentecost in El Salvador? Civic Education and Professional Practice in a Private High School

James G. Huff, Jr.

The challenges that El Salvador faces today are many. The consolidation of peace and democracy, the eradication of poverty and the enhancement of the country's economic competitiveness at the global level are among these. Education offers real answers to these challenges. Education is in fact fundamental to ongoing and sustainable development in El Salvador. Education, therefore, should contribute to national efforts to form new citizens who are more economically productive, more socially united, and more politically active and tolerant; citizens who are more respectful of human rights and more peaceful in their relationships with one another.

—Reforma Educativa en Marcha:
Linamientos del Plan Decenal, 1995–2005

Forming New Spirits (*Forjando Espíritus Nuevos*)
—School Motto, Colegio Evangélico School System

In August 2001, legislators in the Salvadoran National Assembly briefly considered legislation put forward by a member of the conservative National Conciliation Party (PCN) requiring all educational institutions in El Salvador to allocate ten minutes daily to a public reading of the Bible. Although short-lived, the proposed legislation demonstrated how preoccupations over the so-called moral condition of young people in El Salvador have framed much of the public discourse over the state of secondary edu-

cation since the conclusion of a twelve year civil war in 1992. Such preoccupations prompted Ministry of Education (MinEd) officials in the late
1990s, for example, to incorporate into various reform documents and government pamphlets clear language about the importance of teaching young
people values in the classroom (Lindo-Fuentes 1997; World Bank 1999).
The debate over the roles that high schools and their teachers should play
in the moral formation of Salvadoran youth, moreover, has corresponded
with real changes being made to the secondary education curriculum. In
fact, the implementation of comprehensive education reforms in 1997
established new curricular and pedagogical guidelines requiring high
school teachers to give more explicit attention to the instruction of so-called
social and civic values in the classroom.

Overlapping processes of religious change, privatization, and education
reform are shaping the contexts within which Salvadoran teachers are forming their pedagogies of citizenship education. The various national administrations in power during the postwar period have steadily advanced a so-
called modernization project of the public education system through far-
reaching education reforms. These reforms have not been unlike those
unfolding in other Latin American countries where governments are reor-
ganizing and reducing their financial commitments to public education,
while calling on a variety of social actors at the local level to increase their
participation in providing educational services (Collins and Lear 1995;
Gershberg 1999; Gill 2000; Munin 1998; Street 2001).

The transformations occurring in the education system, however, are not
exclusively the result of actions taken by government policymakers. The
proliferation of private schools during the last half-century has also caused
considerable change. The effects of these changes are especially pronounced
in the capital city of San Salvador, where the largest concentration of public
and private high schools is located. During the 2000 academic year private
high schools enrolled close to thirty-five thousand students, whereas public
high schools enrolled a total of twenty-four thousand students in San Salvador. By 2002, over three-fourths of the schools with secondary education
programs in metropolitan San Salvador were private.[1] To be sure, the recent
spate of education reforms has facilitated the growth of private high schools
by severely limiting the government's financial investments in secondary
education. Nevertheless, the de facto privatization of the secondary education system has intensified as different religious organizations have
expanded their institutional reach to include schools.

It is within this changing educational landscape that this chapter examines how pedagogical practices and instructional standards mandated by
education reforms are being appropriated by high school teachers. In the
following discussion, I critically examine aspects of the secondary civic edu-

cation program by detailing some of the educational practices developed by Daniel Ariaza, a social studies teacher. I became closely acquainted with Daniel during the course of carrying out fieldwork at a large private, Pentecostal high school located in San Salvador.[2] I explore how Daniel made use of key aspects of civic education policy, including the use of so-called participatory instructional methods and the allotment of instructional time to address students' "social problems" in class. By delineating the varied ideas and propositions that Daniel brought from other social and historical contexts to his educational work, I argue that civic educational policies, as well as the norms and practices they promote, do not make their way into schools in any predetermined or straightforward manner.

Policy, as Levinson and Sutton (2001) have noted, functions "as a legitimating charter for the techniques of administration and as an operating manual for everyday conduct; it is the symbolic expression of normative claims worked into a potentially viable blueprint" (2). Official educational policy in El Salvador has undoubtedly embodied certain assumptions about how civic education programs should be administered and how high schools—and, more specifically, those who teach in them—should conduct themselves in preparing students to be good citizens. Nevertheless, diverse social actors such as students, parents, school administrators, and teachers interact and bring their own interests to bear upon received policy. Teachers' routine engagement with civic education policies is especially complex. At times they reject received guidelines outright, while at other times they reconfigure such guidelines to form classroom practices that may not conform to official policy mandates. The norms and practices promoted by secondary education reforms—as well as the assumptions they make about the problems they seek to remedy—are but one of many reference points to which teachers like Daniel turned to in order to explain the need for their own civic education pedagogies.

Daniel's example clearly draws attention to the relative power of teachers to embrace, ignore, or reject outright state-mandated educational policy. However, this chapter is also attentive to the ways that education reform and the ongoing processes of privatization are circumscribing and problematizing teachers' contexts for collective social action. In a closing discussion, I briefly consider some of the difficult circumstances that teachers like Daniel are facing just as the private educational sector continues to expand with little regulation and oversight from MinEd and other state institutions. His experience, along with the experiences of a growing number of private school teachers, highlights some of the important contradictions embedded within the process of "democratization" occurring in El Salvador and elsewhere.

SECONDARY EDUCATION AND MORAL
FORMATION IN THE POSTWAR ERA

Education reform in El Salvador had its beginnings in the early 1990s shortly after the end of the country's protracted civil war. At the end of the war, the education system was in dire need of attention. The destructive effects of twelve years of civil conflict on education were considerable in both human and institutional terms. Large numbers of public school teachers and students had been the targets of state-sponsored suppression of labor and popular organizations during the war. Many were killed, tortured, and disappeared. School buildings were often the center of intense battles between national army soldiers and Farabundo Martí National Liberation Front (FMLN) combatants. Many schools located in rural areas were completely destroyed. Conservative estimates place the damage suffered by rural educational facilities at roughly $11 million in U.S. dollars (Segovia 1996). The war forced 671 schools to close down, leaving some eighty-two thousand students without a place to attend class (Moncada-Davidson 1995). Understandably, initial investments into the education system at the end of the war focused on reconstructing and remodeling schools in the rural zones most affected by the war. The Salvadoran government relied heavily on outside sources such as the World Bank and the Inter-American Development Bank for the funding of such projects.

Both the financial and technical assistance provided by these multilateral organizations have left a noticeable imprint on education policy in El Salvador. Notably, the various administrations in power since the end of the war have stressed that the national government should only play a subsidiary role in providing public services like education. As Collins and Lear (1995) have pointed out, such a strategy "restricts the national government to doing only what local communities presumably cannot" (128). Under the guise of institutional modernization and administrative decentralization, state agencies like MinEd have been reduced to performing supervisory and normative functions. MinEd's core functions now include the development of new curriculum and instructional methods and the creation of new professional standards for teachers. It is apparent, moreover, that such philosophies and practices have guided the government's efforts to transform the secondary education system.

Education reform in El Salvador had its formal beginnings in the joint efforts of a variety of national and international institutions. In 1993, Harvard University and the Central American University (UCA), along with several Salvadoran nongovernment organizations (NGOs), oversaw a diagnostic study of the country's system of education. The scope of the study was expansive and included all levels of education in the country. With financial assistance provided by the USAID, the study's participants collected information on different components of the education system, including educational access and quality, administrative systems, human resources, education legislation, and teacher training (Guzman 1999). Based on the recommendations made by the study, MinEd formally unveiled education reform in 1995. At its broadest level, education reform has consisted of three interrelated components. First, the government prioritized increasing basic education coverage among rural populations through the expansion of the locally managed EDUCO (Community Participation Education Project) schools program. The program, which was initiated by funds provided by the World Bank in 1991, has been moderately successful in improving primary education enrollments in rural areas (Moncada-Davidson 1995). And with the expansion of the program through the reform, the government has been able to increase educational coverage in rural areas while shifting much of the costs of maintaining rural educational services and facilities to the local level.

Second, education reform broadened the government's efforts to reorganize school management by decentralizing the financial, operational, and administrative functions of all public schools in El Salvador. Following the model established in the EDUCO program, the national government mandated in 1997 that all public schools form local school councils consisting of various parent, teacher, and staff representatives. MinEd identified decentralization as part of the government's efforts to modernize state institutions, the principal aim of which was to presumably improve the efficiency and effectiveness of educational administration at national and local levels (Guevera et al. 2000).

The third component of the reform, which MinEd refers to as improvements in educational quality, continues to be the principal recipient of funds distributed by multilateral institutions. The scope of MinEd's efforts to improve educational quality in the school system is broad. Plans outlined under this component of the reform include the development of new curricula and instructional methods, the creation of performance-based incentive programs for teachers and individual schools, the rehabilitation of school infrastructure, and the expansion of professional development programs for teachers. In actuality, MinEd has been highly selective in using funds that presumably target quality improvements. In 2000, for example, the World Bank disbursed a loan to fund one phase of the education reform. MinEd designated the largest percentage of the $83 million package for implementing additional curricular changes. Less than 3 percent of borrowed monies, however, were targeted for investment in professional development programs for teachers ("1 Mil Millones para Reforma Educativa," 2000).

While MinEd officials have largely ignored demands that education reform pay more attention to improving teachers' economic well-being, they have not been inactive in restructuring the kind of work teachers perform in the classroom. Most of the policies and practices introduced by the reforms to date have centered on curricular revisions and the introduction of new instructional guidelines. This has especially been the case at the secondary education level. The unveiling of the new high school curriculum in 1997 affected public and private high schools alike. The new curriculum streamlined existing academic and vocational programs and expanded instructional hours to include the so-called formative areas of education, which were the centerpiece of a new civic educational program for public and private high schools. The implementation of the new secondary education curriculum, therefore, was not simply an update to an "outdated" system of education but also formed an important part of the government's efforts to promote the teaching of "human, ethical and civic values" to the student population (Guzman 1999: 12).

Prior to 1997, high school curriculum in both public and private institutions was based on a highly diversified model established in 1968. In keeping with the government's promotion of domestic industrialization in the 1950s and 1960s, the content and organization of the 1968 curriculum was aimed at preparing a labor force for the country's small but growing industrial sector. Numerous vocational tracks in the curriculum provided students with the opportunity to develop job skills in a variety of fields, including commerce, agriculture, navigation, health, and tourism, among others. With the 1995 reforms, vocational subspecializations contained in the old curriculum were reduced substantially and new emphasis was placed upon developing a general academic curriculum and a more efficient vocational curriculum.

Education reforms not only revamped the content and structure of curriculum at the secondary level, however. Reforms also introduced new educational philosophies and instructional guidelines aimed at transforming the way that educators worked in the classroom. Curriculum specialists within MinEd were especially interested in using the reforms to officially endorse instructional approaches based in constructivist methods of teaching and learning. Constructivist theories of education made their way from Spain to El Salvador in the early 1990s as part of MinEd's efforts to develop educational curriculum that would be "in step with national reconstruction efforts" in the postwar era (Picardo Joao 2000: 173).

The changes introduced by MinEd curriculum specialists were broad. First, new instructional guidelines strongly discouraged the use of traditional forms of instruction whereby teachers dictated their notes aloud or wrote lessons on the board while students sat quietly in their desks copying assiduously. Instead, teachers were to make use of more interactive methods of instruction and learning. Participatory instructional methods would presumably encourage the development of specific social skills and civic values in students, including the capacity to work cooperatively with others and the ability to respect different points of view. New guidelines, therefore, required teachers to regularly facilitate *dinámicas* (interactive learning activities), *laboratorios* (laboratory), and *trabajo en grupo* (group work) in the classroom.

Second, the new secondary curriculum allocated instructional hours for the development of courses that would specifically address students' needs for moral and civic education. To this end, instructional time was divided into two different areas: one for the teaching of "basic subjects" like social studies, mathematics, and science and the other for "formative areas" consisting of adolescent psychology courses and seminars addressing "social issues" pertinent to youth (World Bank 1999: 40). A total of twelve hours out of forty available instructional hours were to be devoted weekly to instruction in the so-called formative areas of education.[3] Notably, content development for "formative" education courses, and, thus, the creation of a civic education program, was largely left to the local high school staff and faculty.[4]

Finally, the new secondary education curriculum stressed the importance teaching of social and civic values to Salvadoran youth. According to one MinEd educational consultant, teaching values associated with democracy and peace formed a key part of the larger effort to reconstruct Salvadoran society:

> Values formation is vital to the reform process and democratization in the reform is a model that stands opposed to the egocentrism, intolerance and authoritarianism of the past. In this way, the principal task of the educational system is to mend the social fabric damaged by the civil war by generating a socially democratic conscience based in rationality and civic ethics (Picardo Joao 2000: 247)

MinEd standardized particular instructional strategies and introduced a variety of activities to facilitate "values formation" in the high school classroom. School administrators were provided with didactic materials—including a *Methodological Guide for Formation in Human and Ethical Values*—that offered directions on how to teach values. In keeping with the emphasis upon more constructivist forms of teaching, the new curriculum also identified a "contextual" instructional approach as the pedagogical means by which civic values would be taught to high school students. Instructional guidelines required all teachers, regardless of their subject area, to address different "cross-cutting issues" (*ejes transversales*) in class, which included a variety of topics related to the environment, democracy, health, equity, and human rights.[5] For the 1998 and 1999 school years, MinEd developed calendars that identified particular values to be taught by educators on a weekly basis. In March, April, and May 1998, for example, high school teachers were to encourage classroom discussion around the themes of democratic participation, liberty, respect for authority, peace, and citizenship participation, among others (Picardo Joao 2000).

Teachers involved in my study generally welcomed the curricular updates that were prompted by the education reforms.[6] Most, however, held that what new guidelines called for—especially in terms of allotting instructional time in class to addressing the experiential predicaments students faced outside of school—was already present in their own teaching practices and classroom routines. During our interviews, for example, teachers frequently made distinctions between the "informative" and "formative" aspects of their work with the students. Teachers associated the former with instruction in their subject area and the latter with providing moral guidance or practical advice to students. Formally, providing students with moral guidance and practical advice was considered to be one of the primary functions of the class adviser or *orientador*.[7] Few teachers, however, adopted a strict approach in this regard. Teachers regularly took time in all of their classes to address a practical concern of the students or to stress the importance of a specific behavioral norm. One teacher at the private high school, whose observation was not unusual, noted, "In reality you are an orientadora for all of the students you teach."

Teachers clearly considered what they did with students in the classroom to be a transformative endeavor. To put it in the words of one teacher: "I tell the students that they are the clay that I am molding." Teachers, moreover, were well aware of the pedagogical mandates introduced by the secondary education reforms that made "formative instruction" a normative and standardized component of their work as educators. Nevertheless, the instructional practices that teachers adopted in class were not simply reproductions of pedagogical ideals embodied in the new curriculum (cf. Mercado 1994: 66). Rather, the norms and practices promoted by the secondary education reform were one of many reference points that teachers turned to guide educational practice. Teachers were very much active in appropriating official norms and practices and modifying them by bringing their own interests and concerns to bear on the work of forming students.

We now turn to consider how one high school teacher, who worked in one of El Salvador's largest private school systems, appropriated new curricular requirements for civic education into his own educational practice.

CIVIC EDUCATION AT COLEGIO CENTRAL

When I arrived in El Salvador in January 2000, Colegio Central offered classes from preschool to secondary education, employed approximately seventy full-time teachers, and began the school year with an enrollment of more than 2,500 students. The school was the flagship institution in a network of thirty-eight different Colegio Evangélico schools, which is affiliated with one of the largest Pentecostal denominations in El Salvador, the Assemblies of God.[8] Colegio Evangélico Central officially began in 1963 with a staff of seven individuals, consisting of six teachers and a school director.[9] In a period of roughly thirty years, the Colegio Evangélico school system grew to have one the largest private school enrollments in the country (Petersen 1996). By 1992, approximately 10 percent of all students enrolled in private schools in El Salvador attended a Colegio Evangélico school.[10] By 2001, the school system reported an enrollment of nearly twenty thousand students nationwide.

The high school at Colegio Central was the largest secondary school in the Colegio Evangélico school system. Secondary education was also the largest of the three programs at the school, with a total enrollment of 1,736 students, three-fourths of whom were enrolled in the morning session alone.[11] The school campus is situated in an urban development just north of downtown San Salvador. The area surrounding the school consists primarily of commercial buildings, including numerous auto repair shops, a bottling plant, and various street-level retail stores.

Daniel Ariaza was one of Colegio's newest teachers. He was not, however, new to the teaching profession. Daniel had been working part-time at a public high school located east of San Salvador since 1996, and he had held several full-time positions at different Christian private schools in the city since 1993. Daniel started working full time as a social studies teacher at Colegio High in 1999.

The hurried pace of the workday started early for Daniel and his colleagues. Colegio High offered both morning and afternoon sessions. The morning session began at 6:30 and concluded at 12:10 P.M., while the afternoon session commenced at 12:30 and ended at 6:20 in the evening. The first period bell signaled the beginning of a workday characterized by constant movement through the building's crowded spaces. Class periods were scheduled back to back. Students remained in their assigned rooms while teachers moved from room to room throughout the morning. The physical structure and organization of the building required teachers to climb and descend several flights of stairs as they made their way to each class. Two fifteen-minute breaks that began at 8:30 and 10:45 A.M. gave the teachers brief opportunities to literally catch their breath during the workday. Even though most teachers were required to watch over students in an assigned section of the building during each recess, these short breaks gave them an opportunity to sit down. The scheduling of class periods back-to-back left teachers little extra time to move from one room to the next. Most teachers began class several minutes after the official starting time because of these inefficiencies in the scheduling system.

Teachers at Colegio were knowledgeable about the curricular and pedagogical requirements mandated by secondary education reform. Many Colegio teachers had become familiar with the educational theories and instructional methods associated with the secondary education reforms as a result of participating in a series of courses offered at the end of the school year in 1999 by a private educational institution affiliated with the Colegio Evangélico school system. Teachers were also very conversant with official discourse that called for the abandonment of conventional, rote forms of instruction and the adoption new forms that were more participatory and constructivist in nature.

Daniel frequently brought it to my attention that his participatory and interactive teaching style was one of the main reasons why students particularly enjoyed his social studies classes. During May, for example, Daniel invited me to observe how he was making use of participatory forms of instruction in the classroom. All of his second-year students had been making preparations for an in-class competition that Daniel had described as the "Teacher–Student Challenge." The activity would form the capstone of a month-long unit entitled "Neoliberal Economic Policies in the Plans of the Government." At the beginning of the month, students in each of his classes had spent an entire period copying down a list of twenty-five items that Daniel had written on the blackboard. The twenty-five items included concepts and incomplete sentences related to different macroeconomic phenomena and the government's postwar economic policy. Some items on the list were very specific and required simple definition (i.e., "Relative poverty is . . ."), while others called for the explanation of wide-ranging phenomena or processes (i.e., "Stimulating the foreign trade of nontraditional products").

It was a typical example of the coursework that Daniel assigned in his classes—each student was required to provide answers for the twenty-five items in her or his notebook, which Daniel graded at the end of the unit. In the weeks prior to the competition, students worked in groups of four and five at least once a week to prepare their answers for the competition. The students also spent time recording lessons verbatim in their notebooks that Daniel either dictated or wrote on the blackboard. During the second week of May, for example, Daniel spent time in class dictating notes he had developed explaining neoliberalism.

At the end of the month, I accompanied Daniel to class to observe the Teacher–Student Challenge. Most students were enthusiastic about the event given the fact that it was a break from the routines of dictation and copying. Moreover, the students looked forward to the opportunity to compete with their teacher. The roughly fifty students were already energetic when we entered the room. Daniel needed close to ten minutes to quiet down the class. After explaining the rules of the game, Daniel called students forward one at a time to face him in answering a randomly selected question. Both Daniel and the student were given several minutes to respond to a different question. Responses were evaluated by a small panel of "judges," which consisted of two teaching coordinators. The entire class was rewarded a point when one of their classmates produced a reasonably coherent response. It became apparent that the activity also functioned as a subtle means of social control: students cheered classmates who produced correct responses and ridiculed those who fumbled through their answers. The class grew increasingly loud and excited as each new student walked to the front to face Daniel. Although Daniel occasionally pretended to struggle with a question in order to keep the competition close, the game ended predictably with Daniel winning by a considerable margin. Later Daniel reflected on the Teacher–Student Challenge:

> I spend almost twelve hours here. That's almost more than I spend at home. I feel that the students are like my family and I have to get along with them. . . . James, you know that if a teacher does not enjoy working with his students because he doesn't get along with them, because he despises them, then his life is stressful and angst ridden. Then he doesn't work well. I learned that since I spend most of my time with them I should live well [*vivir bien*] with them.

Working at Colegio required Daniel to manage a very large number of students—as much as seven different class periods in one day with as many as fifty students in each class—and saturated work schedule. For Daniel, encouraging students to participate in class through games and other activities was one way he could cope with such demanding working conditions. "Getting along" and "living well" with students were priorities that guided his professional practice and his appropriation of new instructional forms. Daniel added that the pedagogy introduced by MinEd only validated the efficacy of his approach:

> Then MinEd came along and implemented different seminars and in-service courses based on this, concerning interacting confidently and effectively with the students. All along, my approach had been similar to what MinEd was saying to do. I was already working this way with the students long before I had gone to one of those seminars to be trained. You know, hang out and have fun with them, and get down to their level. Never above them, but at the same level. When MinEd came to teach me this, I had already implemented it. What MinEd did was simply confirm [*abonar*] what I had already known.

Daniel and many of his Colegio High colleagues considered group activities, dinámicas, and student laboratories to be the ideal instructional methods for classroom work. Daniel's reflections, however, suggest that the newly introduced pedagogical guidelines were being mediated through his own interests and practical concerns as an educator at a private high school. To put it another way, the new knowledge Daniel encountered in the secondary education reform was but one of the elements he referred to in explaining the necessity and relevance of the activities he directed in class. His practical knowledge of the working conditions he managed from day to day, as well as his own assessments of students' needs and capacities, were also brought to bear on the instructional methods he developed. So, Daniel equated the new pedagogical forms with "hanging out" with students and "getting down on their level." Such interactional structures, more important, allowed Daniel to better manage classroom working conditions that were physically and mentally taxing. Daniel's comments also suggested that he carried ideas and propositions originating from a variety of "extra-scholastic experiences" with him to guide the instructional methods he adopted in the classroom (cf. Mercado 2002: 41). He insisted, for example, that he had been encouraging student participation in class long before MinEd officially made constructivist teaching methods the norm. When I asked him where he had learned such methods, he responded, "I began learning how to teach this way about eighteen years ago as a Sunday school teacher in church."

In a similar manner, Daniel drew on extrascholastic experiences related to his Pentecostal Christian identity to guide his formative and civic educational efforts with students both inside and outside the classroom. For example, he always started the first class he had with students each week with five minutes of what he called *orientación*. The routine usually included reading a short passage from the Bible, followed by brief commentary on the practical application of the passage to students' daily lives. The practice, as Daniel saw it, was the "oil that kept the engine running in class." He continued the metaphor in this way: "The oil is Christ, it is God, it is the Bible, the word of God. . . . I feel that if I don't put all of this into practice, then I am not carrying out what I should, or I am imparting something that is dry. It's like food without salt or flavor. So in order to give the teaching and the class some flavor, I involve the Bible."

Daniel worked hard to merge the so-called informative and formative areas of social studies education in the classroom. He associated informative work with instruction in his subject area, and formative work with that of providing moral guidance to students. On the one hand, Daniel suspected that most of his students were disinterested in social studies: "Students' lives are so full of necessities, of varied interests, and of problems, that the information they are presented with in social studies class is—how can I describe it?—it is just something secular to them." He remained optimistic, however, that he could stir their interests. Part of the challenge, as he described it, was to help students see the "spiritual significance" of the subject:

> But behind all of this information and behind the student is a huge spiritual need. Do you recall the verse I started the year with? The one from Proverbs 17:17, "A friend loves at all times and kinsfolk are born to share adversity." You've read it, right? This was the introduction I gave them. It really left a big impression on the students. They realized that this was no ordinary social studies class, but it was a moral education, a spiritual teaching. They said, "We needed this, we needed words of encouragement." And then they applauded and I thought, "How strange!" "But it is the Lord," I said, "I don't need the applause." They reacted this way because they felt that I had met some of their expectations—not all of them, because I cannot meet all of their needs—but, yes, I met certain spiritual expectations they had.

Daniel was somewhat exceptional among his colleagues in that he spent a great deal of time organizing activities for students outside class so that he could give them "practical examples" of the ideas he shared in class. During a weeklong break in August, for example, six third-year students accompanied Daniel on a three-day trip to a small coastal community where they assisted in a church-based program that provided medicine and free health consults to impoverished households. Daniel often told stories about the trips in his classes in order to help his students become aware of "social reality" in El Salvador. He added, "These students grew up here in the city, . . . They don't know what it's like to go hungry or to eat only once a day."

While Daniel's energetic and engaging teaching style won him popularity with the students, he felt that the content of his formative lessons often went against the grain. Daniel believed, for instance, that many students were only interested in discussing the government's culpability in creating social and economic problems in El Salvador. He added, "Sure, I don't agree with most of what the state does here in El Salvador, but I am trying to encourage the students to think about the good that government could do with their participation." Daniel wished to avoid, as he put it, "pointing the finger" because he did not want to "stir up hatred in the students." Rather, he hoped to inspire the students to see themselves as people who could change the future of the country. He explained:

> Look, I always tell my students that they are the future of El Salvador. That one day maybe they will be a representative in the legislative assembly or a mayor. And when they are in this position, they should work to improve the living conditions of people in need. I see myself as a voice for those who don't have the means to express themselves. I tell the students that they can be the ones to help the poor. They shouldn't try to make it to the top or try to obtain a

career to get rich; rather they should look to improve the conditions of those around them. Be an active citizen. Look out for the well-being of society.

For Daniel, such civic duties were clearly linked to his religious ideology. He concluded, "The idea is that they learn to help others. Christ wasn't against the government. He said, 'Render unto Cesar, what is Cesar's. But give to God, what is God's.' I am trying to encourage a Christ-centered approach (*cristo-centrismo*). Do you understand?"

COMMENT: THE SOCIAL CONSTRUCTION
OF FORMATIVE EDUCATION

Daniel and his Colegio colleagues were well aware of the pedagogical mandates introduced by secondary education reforms that made formative instruction a normative and standardized component of their teaching practices. These teachers clearly believed, moreover, that their work with students involved the teaching of certain behavioral norms, and in this sense, they saw themselves as helping their students to develop new orientations and "values" regarding their schooling, social relationships, and civic responsibilities. Nevertheless, Daniel's comments and his educative work complicate the assumption that any one isolated element is determinative of the teaching practices he adopted in class (Mercado 1994: 66). Rather, the preceding discussion suggests that there were "multiple reference points" in the orientation of his work (Mercado 1994: 66). An important task of analysis, therefore, is to make sense of the varied reference points guiding Daniel's instructional practices in the classroom.

The preceding account indicates, for example, that Daniel brought knowledge stemming from experiences lived outside the context of the classroom to the work of formative instruction. Daniel frequently shared stories of his past and present involvement in church-based activities where he and others provided food and medicine to the rural poor. He believed that these stories would inspire his students to become active citizens and take up the cause of the poor in El Salvador. He likewise drew on the experience of having used the bible for instruction in other contexts—namely, the local church—for guiding the formative educational practices he adopted in the classrooms. The choices that Daniel made with regard to addressing the formative areas of instruction were also shaped by his perceptions of the students he interacted with at Colegio High. In describing his lessons, Daniel recalled reflecting on the tendency of his students to "blame this one and blame that one without thinking about how to improve the situation." By combining social studies with his "spiritual teachings" in class, Daniel hoped to change students' minds and convince them of their civic duty to help the poor.

Knowing how to link "formative" and "informative" instruction in the classroom and knowing how to present students with situations that they might find significant are both examples of what Mercado (2002) refers to as *saberes docentes*, or "the knowledge that teachers have about instruction that they develop during the daily practice of teaching" (11). Daniel's comments suggest that the knowledge he held in relation to formative instruction was formed as a result of reflective activity, meaning that he was engaged in a process of weighing the new pedagogical requirements alongside other "social voices" while practicing instruction in the classroom (Mercado 2002). Daniel did not report adopting the pedagogical ideals identified in the reforms "as is," but indicated, instead, that he modified them according to his own concerns and interests and according to the practical knowledge he had gained from working in the classroom (cf. Anderson-Levitt and Alimasi 2001: 51).

In Daniel's case, it was the social voice of experiences lived outside the classroom along with the voice of the students that "dialogued" with requirements related to the formative areas of the curriculum (cf. Mercado 2002: 54). Hence, Daniel made the requirements to link "academic" and "formative" instruction entirely his own by drawing on personal experiences to provide content for and direction to the instructional practices he adopted in class. He then blended this knowledge with his own perceptions of what his particular students needed to learn with regard to the formative areas of the curriculum, hoping that the resulting instruction would resonate with the students. As Mercado (2002) notes, recognizing that teachers bring ideas and propositions from other social contexts to their work in the classroom provides a counterbalance to research claiming that teachers' work is largely controlled by the pedagogical materials they work with (89). This recognition of the "implacable agency" of teachers in the work that they do in the classroom, moreover, demonstrates the "power of teachers . . . to mediate national educational policies/reforms" at the local school level (Levinson 1998: 491). What emerges here is a picture of teaching as a socially constructed phenomenon wherein the intervention of state institutions (in the form of curricular reforms) is negotiated by the interests and actions of teachers involved in the daily workings of the classroom (Batallán 2002: 39). For Daniel and many of his colleagues at Colegio High, the classroom continues to be a space where they can maintain a relative degree of occupational autonomy and control over their classroom labor in the midst of changing and demanding working conditions.

Daniel's efforts to make the new secondary curriculum his own, however, draw attention to the contradictory nature of the kind of civic education that was occurring in his classrooms. Daniel was insistent that the emphasis upon participatory learning present in the new curriculum was already a part of his teaching practice. To be sure, the learning activities that occurred in class were often "participatory" in name only. Daniel, like many of his Colegio colleagues, continued to expect his students to memorize and reproduce select concepts and phenomena that had been outlined in previous lessons or identified in the curriculum received from MinEd. For example, Daniel made use of the Teacher–Student Challenge in order to motivate his students to commit more material to memory. Therefore, much of what counted as learning in class continued to be organized around the rote forms that the new instructional techniques were supposed to replace. It was not surprising then that classroom activities frequently took on a ritualistic quality: teachers and students "both became co-participants in a *simulacrum of learning* that never required them to actively engage the content or their own relationship to it" (Luykx 1999: 182, emphasis in original). Given the highly circumscribed nature of participation in Daniel's classroom, what kind of democratic norms or values were his students learning? Or, to put it another way, what is the nature of democratic citizenship that is on display in his classroom?

On the one hand, Daniel's classroom practice seemed to reinforce the neoliberal notions of "participation" being promoted by MinEd in the education reform. In the language of the education reforms, fostering participation at the local level was synonymous with encouraging teachers, parents, and students to take responsibility for the conditions of education at their school. Group activities in Daniel's class, moreover, were as much about the creative management of school work in an overcrowded classroom as they were about the formation of democratic citizens. In this way, Daniel's students were developing their abilities as workers "to identify problems and introduce improvements . . . [and] to work effectively in teams" (World Bank 1999: 30). As one of Daniel's colleague wryly observed such in-class activities were more apt to prepare students for work in a *maquila* than for critical political engagement.

Moreover, Daniel's belief that addressing student's spiritual needs was a fundamental part of their civic formation echoes the rhetoric of "values-formation" articulated by MinEd officials since the mid-1990s. Such rhetoric has clearly placed the blame for young Salvadorans' social problems on their own shoulders. What is notable about the values discourse is the way it has been invoked by MinEd officials to advocate, on the one hand, the view that Salvadoran youth are largely the victims of their own alleged pathological habits and philosophies, while at the same time aligning teachers' educative work in the classroom with the government's efforts to "empower" young people to "rediscover their internal capacities for self-help" (Brin Hyatt 2001: 221). In a similar manner, Daniel likened his formative work to convincing students that lasting social change in El Salvador would only begin with individuals who had undergone spiritual, moral, and philosophical transformation.

A fuller analysis of the content of Daniel's "formative" instruction suggests, however, a more complicated amalgam of citizenship education. Clearly, his notion of what counted as good citizenship was closely connected to his own religious beliefs as a Pentecostal Christian. Elsewhere, Burdick (1993) has noted the usual tendency to regard Pentecostalism as a "religion of the status quo" (226). He cautions, however, that the religious logic of Pentecostalism is "more politically ambiguous than this" and that it "can foster both passivity and activism" (226). Likewise, I am reluctant to interpret Daniel's interest in tempering his students' alleged tendency to "blame the government" for social problems in El Salvador as a by-product of a religious logic that endorsed the status quo. In fact, a strong case could be made for seeing Daniel's approach as an attempt to foster a critical social consciousness in his students. As a social studies teacher, Daniel was deeply concerned that Salvadoran youth were deeply apathetic about politics and civic engagement. By using the language of faith, Daniel hoped to convince the students of their Christian obligation to be engaged and active citizens. Political passivity was antithetical to Daniel's "cristo-centrismo."

Finally, and on a related note, Daniel's formative work also demonstrated a concern for the poor and for issues related to social justice. Daniel was deeply hopeful that his class field trips to impoverished, rural communities would encourage his students to develop a broader awareness of the kinds of material conditions that most Salvadoran citizens found themselves in. Daniel again borrowed from his religious beliefs to articulate the notion that "good citizens" were those who were concerned for the material welfare of others. In promoting such a notion of citizenship, Daniel hoped to persuade his students that their educational entitlements could one day be used to improve the living conditions of people in need.

CONCLUSION: CAUTIOUS
HOPE FOR DEMOCRACY

Colegio High is one of many private educational institutions in the metropolitan area that receives comparatively little oversight and regulation by state agencies like the Ministry of Education. And it is within this unregulated institutional setting where teachers like Daniel coped with working conditions that caused them considerable stress. Teachers working at the private high school encountered compensation structures that compelled them to work as many hours as possible in order to make a living. Spatial arrangements and work routines forced teachers to spend most of their time in the classroom and made fraternization with other faculty very difficult.

The centralized and hierarchical system of personnel relations gave teachers little opportunities to actively participate in determining the routines and conditions of their work. And, perhaps most important, members of the senior administrative staff—including those who were responsible for deciding which teachers would continue working at Colegio each year—were opposed to teachers' organizing any collective form of representation for themselves.

Elsewhere, I have interpreted (Huff 2004) the larger processes of educational change that are constraining more and more would-be teachers in El Salvador to accept employment in private educational institutions as evidence of what Morrow and Torres (2000: 39) aptly label as the "commodification" of educational activities. At a broad level, the increasing commodification of educational activities in El Salvador has facilitated the growth of a segmented labor market for would-be teachers.[12] This has involved the rapid growth of jobs in private institutions that offer low wages, contract teachers on an annual basis, and typically restrict participation in union activities. Such realities, I believe, offer an important and necessary caution to any examination of how teachers within these institutional contexts are exercising their agency in the classroom.

Daniel and his colleagues at Colegio, for example, were reminded daily that the occupational autonomy they exercised over their daily educative work was highly constrained. And despite their very real concerns about the working conditions they were forced to cope with at Colegio High, Daniel and other teachers were generally reluctant about taking deliberative action to openly confront these circumstances. Their avoidance of confrontation with school management was shaped by their belief that "hard experience proves that employers still hold the cards and use strikes to get rid of troublemaking workers" (Burdick 1993: 215). They were also painfully aware of the scarce opportunities available to them to work in public institutions where pay and job security would likely be considerably better. It is precisely these kinds of relational contexts, where teachers have little control over the conditions and terms of their employment, that are being facilitated by the commodification of educational activities in El Salvador.

These insights are especially important to consider in light of the history of struggle between the government and public school teachers in El Salvador. This study sees the shifting of responsibility for educational outcomes to the local level—through privatization and decentralization—by the Salvadoran government as part of a larger strategy to atomize and fragment teachers' contexts for action. Such processes threaten to redraw the lines of struggle so that teachers are increasingly competing with one another and with other local actors over the success of their school rather than turning their attention to state agencies like the Ministry of Education. Such a strategy is clearly part of the state's effort to exercise greater control over the actions of a bloc of social actors who have frequently contested the interests of the powerful and called for genuine and lasting democratization in El Salvador during the last fifty or so years.

So why consider the diverse schemes of motivation and action that teachers bring to their educative work in an age when the commodification of educational activities are making it increasingly difficult for teachers to actively and collectively defend their interests and needs as educators and workers? It is evident that educational policies in El Salvador envision certain kinds of subjectivities and, more important, attempt to regulate how educators do the work of forming these subjectivities in students. The preceding discussion, however, indicates that the curricular policies mandated by MinEd did not make their way into the classroom in any predictable or straightforward manner. The directives issued by MinEd concerning what should be taught and how it should be taught traveled across different institutional contexts and through a variety of social actors. Rather than assume that the educational practices endorsed by MinEd are adopted as is by Salvadoran high school teachers, I have explored how one teacher conceptualized and practiced so-called participatory, "constructivist" forms of instruction and formative education in the classroom. Close scrutiny of how Daniel made use of the new curricular and instructional guidelines introduced in secondary education reforms reminds us that teachers are always engaged in mediating and changing received policy. Such dynamics are particularly instructive for how conceptions of democratic citizenship are formulated at the local level, especially in a context where teachers have broad latitude to interpret the meaning of civic education.

In calling attention to Daniel's agency as a social subject, I do not wish to ignore the plain fact that many Salvadoran high school teachers find themselves working in situations where it is becoming increasingly difficult for them to provide for their basic social reproductive needs. Rather, I hope to highlight how the distinct beliefs and interests from which teachers' work emerged are indicative of the strong commitment shared by all teachers to a notion of occupational autonomy, especially as it relates to their educative work with students. The classroom continues to be a key space within which teachers like Daniel maintain a degree of autonomy and control over their professional lives. So, while I argue that education reform and the ongoing processes of privatization have highly circumscribed and problematized teachers' contexts for social action, the preceding discussion also offers the important reminder that Salvadoran teachers are clearly not powerless in the face of change. It is this basic recognition of teachers' shared sense of occupational autonomy, moreover, that compels researchers to pay more attention to the dynamic and sometimes contradictory ways that citizenship education and political socialization are unfolding within the four walls of the classroom.

NOTES

The larger project from which the data for this chapter are drawn was funded by a Dissertation Fieldwork Grant from the Wenner-Gren Foundation and a research grant from the Bryan S. Smith Foundation of Vanguard University. I would like to express my thanks to both institutions for their generous support.

1. By 2002, 168 of 232 total institutions with secondary education programs in the department of San Salvador were private. Of the 757 schools providing secondary education in El Salvador, 345 were private and 412 were public (MinEd 2002).

2. The data presented here form a small part of a much larger study (Huff 2004) that compares and contrasts the professional lives of a group of high school teachers working in a public and a private high school in San Salvador.

3. One instructional hour refers to a forty-minute class period. Of the twelve hours designated for formative areas of the curriculum, three hours were allocated for a psychology course, and the remaining nine hours were divided between six hours of "optional activities" and three hours for "seminars."

4. Two teachers at the public high school involved in my study, for example, voluntarily designed and cotaught a sex education course that met curricular requirements for "formative" education. The private high school, on the other hand, merged a number of preexisting courses and activities into the new curriculum. These included a weekly, one-hour Bible course, an orientation period, and a student chapel period.

5. I am using the translation of *ejes transversales* as provided by the author of the World Bank (1999) document. The phrase translates literally as "transverse axis" (a geometrical term).

6. The teachers I refer to here include the twenty-three women and men who participated in my dissertation research (Huff 2004). The group included twelve teachers from a private high school and eleven teachers from a public high school. The teachers, who were of different ages, professional tenures, and marital statuses, participated in lengthy and multiple, open-ended interviews and assisted me in recording their life and work histories.

7. The work of an orientador at both schools required teachers to manage similar administrative and advisory roles with an assigned section of students. Record keeping of student grades and attendance was also a primary responsibility of each class adviser.

8. See Huff (2004: 65–76) for a brief discussion of the history of the Assemblies of God in El Salvador and a fuller description of the formation of the Colegio Evangélico school system.

9. Colegio Evangélico Central is the school where I conducted most of my research. Hereafter, Colegio Evangélico will refer to the private school system founded by Juan and other church members. Colegio Central will refer to the system's first and, presently, largest school.

10. Total enrollment figures are based on data compiled from Colegio and Ministry of Education (MinEd 2002) statistics.

11. The total enrollment figure reported here includes students enrolled in both the morning and afternoon sessions at Colegio High. School records indicated an

enrollment of 1,234 students during the morning session and 502 students during the afternoon session. Class schedules were divided into multiple shifts (*turnos*), each of which constituted an entire school day. Colegio Central High had one morning and one afternoon session.

12. The reorganization of the instructional schedule and the addition of formative areas under the new secondary high school curriculum impacted private and public high schools in different ways. See Huff (2004: 165–204) for a comparative discussion of how the formative areas of education were being carried out in a private and a public high school in San Salvador.

REFERENCES

"1 Mil Millones para Reforma Educativa." 2000. *La Prensa Grafica*, November 29.

Anderson-Levitt, K. M., and N. Alimasi. 2001. "Are Pedagogical Ideals Embraced or Imposed? The Case of Reading Instruction in the Republic of Guinea." In *Policy as Practice: Toward a Comparative Sociocultural Analysis of Educational Policy*, ed. M. Sutton and B. A. U. Levinson. Westport, Conn.: Ablex.

Batallán, G. 2001. "Contradictory Logics in the Social Construction of Teaching in Argentina: An Ethnography of the Notebook of Professional Performance." In *Ethnography and Education Policy across the Americas*, ed. B. A. U. Levinson, S. L. Cade, A. Padawer, and A. P. Elvir. Westport, Conn.: Praeger.

Burdick, J. 1993. *Looking for God in Brazil: The Progressive Catholic Church in Urban Brazil's Religious Arena*. Berkeley: University of California Press.

Collins, J., and J. Lear. 1996. *Chile's Free-Market Miracle: A Second Look*. Oakland, Calif.: Food First.

Collins, J. L. 2002. *Threads: Gender, Labor, and Power in the Global Apparel Industry*. Chicago: University of Chicago Press.

Gershberg, A. I. 1999. "Decentralization, Citizen Participation, and the Role of the State: The Autonomous Schools Program in Nicaragua." *Latin American Perspectives* 26, no 4: 8–38.

Gill, L. 1999. *Teetering on the Rim: Global Restructuring, Daily Life, and the Armed Retreat of the Bolivian State*. New York: Columbia University Press.

Guevera, M. F., et al. 2000. *Los CDE: Una estrategia de administración escolar, local, participativa*. San Salvador: FEPADE.

Guzman, A. C. 1999. *Equidad de la educación en El Salvador*. San Salvador: FEPADE.

Huff, J. G. 2004. "Professional Practice in the Age of Neoliberalism: Teaching in Public and Private High Schools in Post-war El Salvador." Ph.D. diss., American University.

Hyatt, S. B. 2001. "From Citizen to Volunteer: Neoliberal Governance and the Erasure of Poverty." In *The New Poverty Studies: The Ethnography of Power, Politics, and Impoverished People in the United States*, ed. J. Goode and J. Maskovsky. New York: New York University Press.

Levinson, B. A., and D. Holland, D. 1996. "The Cultural Production of the Educated Person: An Introduction." In *The Cultural Production of the Educated Person: Critical Ethnographies of Schooling and Local Practice*, ed. B. A. Levinson, D. A. Foley, and D. C. Holland. Albany: State University of New York Press.

Levinson, B. A. U. 1998. "Review Essay: Mexican Educational Ethnography and the Work of the DIE: Crossing the Border and Finding the Historical Everyday." *Anthropology & Education Quarterly* 29, no. 4: 487–94.

Levinson, B. A. U., and M. Sutton. 2001. "Introduction: Policy as/in Practice—A Sociocultural Approach to the Study of Educational Policy. In *Policy as Practice: Toward a Comparative Sociocultural Analysis of Educational Policy*, ed. M. Sutton and B. A. U. Levinson. Westport, Conn.: Ablex.

Lindo-Fuentes, H. 1997. "Educating for Progress and Educating for Economic Growth: Liberal and Neoliberal Education Reforms in El Salvador." Paper presented at the Latin American Studies Association, Guadalajara, Mexico.

Luykx, A. 1999. *The Citizen Factory: Schooling and Cultural Production in Bolivia*. Albany: State University of New York Press.

Mercado, R. 1994. "*Saberes* and Social Voices in Teaching." In *Education as Cultural Construction*, ed. A. Alvarez and P. del Río. Madrid: Fundación Infancia y Aprendizaje.

———. 2001. *Los saberes docentes como construcción social: La enseñanza centrada en los niños*. Mexico City: Fondo de Cultura Económica.

MinEd. 1995. *Reforma educativa en marcha: Documento III, linamientos generales del plan decenal, 1995–2005*. San Salvador: Author.

———. 2002. *Estado actual de la educación*. www.mined.gob.sv/gestion_mined/pdf/Anuario_Estadistico_2002.pdf.

Moncada-Davidson, L. 1995. "La educación dentro del proceso de paz y la reconstrucción social y económica de El Salvador." *ECA* 557 (March): 215–31.

Morrow, R. A., and C. A. Torres. 2002. "The State, Globalization, and Educational Policy." In *Globalization and Education: Critical Perspectives*, ed. N. C. Burbules and C. A. Torres. New York: Routledge.

Munín, H. 1998. "'Freer' Forms of Organization and Financing and the Effects of Inequality in Latin American Educational Systems: Two Countries in Comparison." *Compare* 28, no. 3: 229–43.

Petersen, D. 1996. *Not by Might, nor by Power: A Pentecostal Theology of Social Concern in Latin America*. Oxford: Regnum.

Picardo Joao, O. 2000. "La reforma de la historia y la historia de la reforma: La reforma educativa en marcha de El Salvador." Unpublished document.

Rosen, L. 2001. "Myth Making and Moral Order in a Debate on Mathematics Education Policy." In *Policy as Practice: Toward a Comparative Sociocultural Analysis of Educational Policy*, ed. M. Sutton and B. A. U. Levinson. Westport, Conn.: Ablex.

Segovia, A. 1996. "Domestic Resource Mobilization." In *Economic Policy for Building Peace: The Lesson from El Salvador*, ed. J. K. Boyce. Boulder, Colo.: Rienner.

Street, S. 2001. "When Politics Become Pedagogy: Oppositional Discourse as Policy in Mexican Teachers' Struggle for Union Democracy." In *Policy as Practice: Toward a Comparative Sociocultural Analysis of Educational Policy*, ed. M. Sutton and B. A. U. Levinson. Westport, Conn.: Ablex.

World Bank. 1999. *Secondary Education in El Salvador: Education Reform in Progress*. www1.worldbank.org/education/secondary/documents/Winter.pdf.

4

Curricular Intervention and Greek-Cypriot Pupils' Constructions of Citizenship: Can "Europe" Include Immigrants?

Stavroula Philippou

Discussions over citizenship issues have been very frequent in Europe, as developing a sense of European identity and citizenship among young people became a key aim of the European Union (EU) educational policy over the last three decades (Brine 1995). The EU has been attentive to its "democratic deficit" and has created symbolic and legal markers of European citizenship such as common passports, a flag, an anthem, the euro, and, most recently, a constitution. In response to these political developments, academics have been discussing the impact of globalization and Europe on polity formation, democracy, the nation-state, citizenship, and education (see, e.g., Cederman 2001; Habermas 1994, 1996; Davies and Sobisch 1997; Osler, Rathenow, and Starkey 1995). Part of the prominence of the European terms *identity* and *citizenship* in political and academic discussions can be attributed to their contested meaning and complex educational implications.

In the study described in this chapter, these issues were explored using a social constructivist and critical approach to Europe in a curriculum development project that aimed to introduce a European dimension into history and geography by exploring different constructions of Europe across time, space, and culture. It was implemented among Greek-Cypriot ten-year-old pupils during the 2000–2001 school year. Cyprus, a country at the margins of Europe and characterized by an extreme nationalism that has long divided its society, must now respond to demands of revisiting its meanings of citizenship and democracy as a condition of its EU membership. No society can be judged fully democratic without sufficient provisions and protections for its minorities. Could the concept of "Europe" be used as a tool to challenge Greek-Cypriot pupils' xenophobic attitudes toward immigrants by reconceptualizing them as citizens of Cyprus and Europe?

IMMIGRANTS IN NATION-STATES IN THE EUROPEAN UNION: ARE THEY CITIZENS?

Discussing European citizenship is problematic because the notion of "citizenship" has historically been associated with the creation of nation-states and their efforts to define who "belonged" as "members of" their jurisdiction. Citizenship in nation-states had geographic, legal, political, cultural, and social aspects. As Habermas (1994) notes, the legal definition of citizenship consisted only of political membership, membership to a state. Since the 1990s, however, the concept has been expanded to cover the status of citizens defined in terms of civil rights. Citizenship has also been understood as a sociopsychological or affective state (e.g., national identity), as a set of legal rights and responsibilities, as guidelines of conduct, and as a means of participation (Heater 1990). In the case of the sociopsychological or affective state, national identity or citizenship is derived from self-identification with a particular national group and is used to denote identities associated with nation-states. Historically, however, the formation of nation-states has been based on an exclusive or ethnocultural model of community formation (Habermas 1996), a model that sought to draw a direct, causal link between culture and an ethnos (see Cederman 2001) and that, as social constructivists have argued, mobilized education—along with the media and other state mechanisms—to construct nation-states and to create shared national myths, heroes, symbols, ideals, and historical narratives (see, e.g., Anderson 1991; Hobsbawm 1994). Consequently, nation-states excluded or sought to assimilate minorities and recent immigrants who did not share the perceived national-cultural characteristics of "the nation." In this case, Danopoulos (2004) argues, democracy was threatened, since "democracy lacks quality unless it is able to produce a constitution that provides for fundamental liberties, minority rights, and a set of institutions and checks and balances that limit state power and ensure accountability" (42).

Similar arguments have been formulated to criticize the discourse with which the EU seeks to construct the notions of European citizenship and identity in education. A key EU document, the 1988 *Resolution of the Council and the Ministers of Education Meeting within the Council on the European Dimension in Education,* clearly linked education with a European identity for the first time. Notably, the first objective of this resolution was "to strengthen in young people a sense of *European identity* and make clear to them the value of *European civilization* and of the foundations on which the European peoples intend to base their development today . . . the principles of democracy, social justice and respect for human rights" (Council of the European Communities General Secretariat 1990: 19; emphasis added). Hansen (1998) argues that behind the 1988 Resolution and the 1993 Green Paper[1] lies the purpose to generate "a greater sense of identification with European culture, which . . . gets construed as something palpable, seemingly fixed, exemplary and simply 'out there' for people to discover and add on to their similarly construed national and regional cultural identities" (14). In the 1995 White Paper, this essentialist model of European identity again comes to the fore, where culture, heritage, and civilization are called on to justify the need for teaching the history of European civilization, "the legacy of a tradition which made Europe the first to bring about a technical and industrial revolution and thus change the world. . . . Being European is to have the advantage of a cultural background of unparalleled variety and depth" (Commission of the European Communities 1995, cited in Hansen 1998: 14).

Hansen (1998) thus concludes that the way "culture" is defined by EU educational discourse is nationalist and seeks to invoke an identity among Europeans on ethnocultural grounds. Thus, those nonwhite pupils who do not share the historical roots, the cultural tradition, and the Christian civilization of the European identity are excluded. This is especially evident in the role of language education in constructing a European cultural identity.[2] Other critics argue that the European dimension is restricted to the teaching of at least one European language and to an emphasis on mathematics, science, and technology—in other words, those subjects that are considered necessary for the highly skilled, flexible, and mobile worker that the global economy and the EU seek and that each member-state thinks it is responsible for preparing (Sultana 1995). Arguably, European citizenship (as defined in EU centers like Maastricht and Amsterdam) only includes economically active citizens and nationals of member-states, while it excludes immigrants (e.g., Turks and Muslims), third country nationals, refugees and asylum-seekers, non-Europeans and ethnic minority communities (Lewicka-Grisdale and McLaughlin; O'Leary 1996; Ritchie 1997; Hansen 1998). However, immigrants do define themselves as "Europeans" and do not always perceive themselves as "foreigners." For example a study by Adams and Tulasiewicz (1995) in France, Germany, and the UK revealed that the "new European" members of the Asian community in the London sample showed a very high degree of European consciousness and knowledge, something that the researchers associate with their frequent traveling around Europe to visit their extended families.

Discussions of the role of education in identity formation suggest that European citizenship needs to be understood as coexisting with other, multiple citizenships (e.g., Heater 1997). They also attempt to draw distinctions between various models of citizenship education such as "civics" and "citizenship" education. McLaughlin (1992) understands civics as the "minimal" definition of education for citizenship, a conception that restricts "education for citizenship" into the provision of information, "the development of virtues of local and immediate focus" (237), and the development of "unreflective socialisation into the political and social *status quo*"(238). He proposes the expansion of citizenship into a "maximal" version for education, which entails "the development of a broad critical understanding and a much more extensive range of dispositions and virtues. . . . It also requires the consideration of a more explicit egalitarian thrust" (238). Such virtues include citizens' responsibility "to actively question and extend their local and immediate horizons in the light of more general and universal considerations such as those of justice, and to work for the sort of social conditions that will lead to the empowerment of all citizens" (236–37). Lewicka-Grisdale and McLaughlin (2002) similarly argue that "any adequate form of education in 'European identity' must encourage and develop appropriate forms of critical reflection and assessment. . . . Education which is worthy of the name is as likely to problematise the notion of a 'European identity' as it is to encourage and promote it" (63). To achieve this "problematization" and to acknowledge multiplicity and complexity—which have been persistent, though unrecognized, characteristics of European states for many years (Coulby and Jones 1995)—a social constructivist standpoint was adopted for the curricular intervention that is described later in this chapter, after locating the study in its Cypriot political and educational context.

CITIZENSHIP, NATIONALISM, AND IMMIGRANTS IN CYPRUS: ISSUES AND DEBATES

Identity and the politics of recognition are the cornerstones of the Cyprus problem. Evidence of human presence in Cyprus dates back to 9000 B.C. The official historical narrative of the Greek-Cypriots commences with the arrival of the Greek Mycenaeans in 1400 B.C., while the Turkish-Cypriots identify with the beginning of Ottoman rule over Cyprus in 1571 A.D. Both versions of the past are saying that "historically Cyprus has been ours," and thereby illustrate the nationalism of each community (Papadakis 1995). When parts of mainland Greece first gained independence from the Ottoman Empire in 1829, the Greek-Cypriot community aspired to the unification (*Enosis*) of the island with Greece, a policy that after 1878 (when Cyprus was passed over from the Ottoman to the British Empire) also held strong anticolonial elements. Fearing Greek domination, during the 1950s, the Turkish-Cypriot community developed a policy of partitioning (*Taxim*) the island between the two communities. Cyprus gained independence from the British in 1960, with the signing of the Zurich-London agreements and the adoption of a constitution, which assigned Greece, Turkey, and Britain as guarantee powers of the island and which soon proved unable to balance the two communities' nationalisms. Thus, the postindependence period was characterized by "ethno-nationalism, inter- and intra-communal conflict, and eventually war" (Koyzis 1997: 31). The educational systems were left separate and were used as the cornerstone of both nationalist ideologies by Greece and Turkey to increase their influence, and thus widen the gap between the communities (Kizilyürek and Hadjipavlou-Trigeorgis 1997). A coup organized by the dictatorial government of Greece against the government of Cyprus led to a Turkish military intervention in 1974, which divided Cyprus into two parts separated by a demilitarized zone called "the Green Line" and still guarded by UN peacekeepers today. However, after an easing of travel restrictions by the Turkish-Cypriot authorities in April 2003, there has been unprecedented mobility between the two communities. The UN General Assembly has requested the withdrawal of foreign troops and the restoration of human rights in Cyprus and has coordinated a number of unsuccessful negotiation talks, of which the most recent, UN secretary-general Kofi Annan's plan, was rejected by 75 percent of the Greek-Cypriots in an April 2004 referendum.

The 1960 constitution defined citizenship clearly in terms of ethnic origin, language, culture and religion:

(1) the Greek Community comprises all citizens of the Republic who are of Greek origin and whose mother tongue is Greek or who share the Greek cultural traditions or who are members of the Greek-Orthodox Church;

(2) the Turkish Community comprises all citizens of the Republic who are of Turkish origin and whose mother tongue is Turkish or who share the Turkish cultural traditions or who are Moslems;

(3) citizens of the Republic who do not come within the provisions of paragraph (1) or (2) of this Article shall, within three months of the date of the coming into operation of this Constitution, opt to belong to either the Greek or the Turkish Community as individuals, but, if they belong to a religious group, shall so opt as a religious group and upon such option they shall be deemed to be members of such Community. (Appendix D: Part 1—General Provisions of Constitution, Article 2)

These provisions drew quite distinct categories of Cypriot citizens, "Cypriotness" being restricted to a state identity that was not as emotionally appealing as ethno-communal identities were. However, concepts of the Greek nation, nationalism, and Enosis began to be discredited (but not extinguished) among Greek-Cypriots after 1974 (Koutselini-Ioannidou 1997). This stemmed from the need to form political dialogue within the international community on the basis of Cyprus's independence and the violation of statehood in 1974. Greek-Cypriot society and education were turned into arenas of conflict between two ideologies or discourses of identity: *Hellenocentrism*, which emphasized the Greekness of Greek-Cypriots and has been supported primarily by the political right, and *Cypriocentrism*, which emphasized the Cypriot identity citizenship that all communities in Cyprus share and has been mainly supported by the political left (Spyrou 2001). Despite the rise of Cypriocentrism after 1974, "the curriculum continues to preserve its national humanistic character and supports the pervasiveness of a supremacist national ideology" (Koutselini-Ioannidou 1997: 407). More recently, due to increasing immigration in the 1990s, the Ministry of Education and Culture of the Republic of Cyprus for the first time used the rhetoric of multicultural education in a Memorandum at the beginning of the 2001–2002 school year to acknowledge that Cypriot society was "becoming multicultural." Yet this formal recognition of multiculturalism as a new (rather than old) phenomenon prevents reflection about the Cyprus problem from acknowledging ethnic violence and national anxiety that has historically marked difference in Cyprus (Gregoriou, in press).

The political situation has influenced constructions of Europe in education. Persianis (1998) has diagnosed a resistance to European cultural space, due to the traditional role of Greek-Cypriot education to inculcate the Greek national identity. Nonetheless, EU membership has been a broadly acceptable "ideal" to the public and political worlds in Cyprus (Office of the Chief-Cyprus-EU Negotiator 1999), and the Ministry of Education and Culture (1996: 13) has included the need to prepare children for the "European orientations" of Cyprus in its main aims for primary education. A closer investigation, however, of how the Ministry has construed the European dimension indicates that "Europe" has been identified with the EU; that the European dimension has been mainly associated with technological and economic development so that perceived EU standards in these fields are reached; and that it has been confined to the addition of EU languages or the participation in exchange programs (Philippou 2004). This approach leaves the traditional ethnocentrism of the curriculum untouched. It also leaves the potential of a European identity or citizenship as a way of shifting existing nationalistic tensions and exclusion of "Others" (communities, immigrants, minorities, etc.) unexploited.

These issues have also been identified in civic and citizenship education curricula. A study among principals and teachers in primary education in 1992 showed that perceptions about what constituted civic and social education were quite diverse (Persianis 1996). During primary education, teachers can use two textbooks titled *Becoming a Good Citizen* in the fifth and sixth grades (with ten- to twelve-year-old pupils).[3] Teachers can occasionally choose topics from these textbooks according to the time they have available. Given the large volume of the subject matter, time for civic education is very limited. A curricular analysis of these textbooks has shown that emphasis is given to theoretical knowledge of political institutions and the rights and responsibilities of citizens rather than to the actual practice of citizenship through pupils' democratic participation in decision making, organization, and management. It was also found that "the civic education curriculum has focused on issues underlying the roots of the national problem and consciously resists any alteration to the situation and opposes conflict resolution without prior restoration of human rights" (Koutselini and Papanastasiou 1997: 113). Consequently, the citizens portrayed in these textbooks have no active role beyond remembering the occupied areas and wishing to return there. It is also important to note that "old" minority groups protected by the constitution (Maronites, Armenians, and Latins) do not constitute a special topic in these textbooks (Koutselini and Papanastasiou 1997).

In the third year of secondary school (fourteen- to fifteen-year-olds), citizenship education is taught as a separate, obligatory subject in one trimester titled "Social and Political Education" for one teaching period (forty-five minutes) per week; it includes basic knowledge about institutions, the structure of the government, and citizens' rights and responsibilities. Even though citizenship education is seen by secondary education principals to be taught in all other subjects (mainly humanities) and extracurricular activities, Persianis (2003) has found that the emphasis is paid to developing good human beings, rather than citizens—the assumption being that a good person will also be a good citizen. Consequently, the emphasis is on the development of virtues that need to characterize humans, and the means by which this aim is pursued "are the traditional methods of providing knowledge, emphasizing the preparation of school events, referring to noble historical examples, making appeals, sermons and giving advice, as well as insisting on the implementation of school regulations" (133). These traditional strategies and approaches, Persianis points out, stem from cultural epistemological traditions. They have not been adjusted to the many social, political, and cultural changes in Cyprus, and therefore leave many students uninterested.

In the IEA civic education study, Cyprus scored above the international mean in civic knowledge, civic engagement (conventional citizenship and expected participation in political activities), and civic attitudes (trust in government-related institutions, positive attitudes toward immigrants and support for women's political rights) (Torney-Purta 2002a); however, together with Greece, Cyprus had the strongest national feelings and the greatest belief in the importance of military service (Torney-Purta 2002b). Very few studies focus on pupils' views of immigrants in Cyprus, and those that do involve young people, not children. A study conducted among European youth for the needs of the Eurobarometer (Konstantinou 2003) indicated that 79 percent of Cypriot young people state that there are "too many foreigners" in Cyprus, whereas the countries approaching accession had a mean of just 17 percent (for comparison, the second highest, Malta, reached just 34 percent). Accordingly, Cypriot youth were the least likely in Europe to agree that foreigners and locals have equal rights: only 25 percent agreed, while the mean in the thirteen accession countries is 51 percent. Finally, an even smaller percentage stated that they were "happy that foreigners live in my country." The thirteen countries' mean is 45 percent, while only eight in every hundred Cypriot young people feel happy about this.[4] Other studies among Greek-Cypriot children have identified primarily negative understandings and views toward a number of national outgroups, including migrant minorities such as the Pontioi (people of Greek descent from the Black Sea region) (Koutselini et al. 2002) and Gypsies, Bulgarians, and Russians (Philippou 2003). Finally, a recent study at a secondary school among 644 pupils revealed quite xenophobic attitudes toward recent immigrants, as well as toward peoples of different nationalities and religions in Cyprus. Specifically, 46.9 percent of the pupils thought that foreign workers cause social problems and 62 percent that they increase crime. In addition, 44.9 and 68.5 percent of the pupils agreed that the Greek nation and the Christian Orthodox religion are, respectively, the most superior nation and religion in the world (Kyriakidou 2005). This small-scale study provoked a heated political debate, and ministry officials cast doubt on these findings, arguing that they were not representative of the situation in Cyprus (Alexandrinou 2005).

These complex political and ethnocentric educational contexts, together with Cypriot pupils' extreme views and the current political will to include the concept of Europe in education, have led to the key question of this chapter: how could a European dimension be used to broaden pupils' constructions of citizenship in democratic ways to include immigrants in Cyprus? The findings of this study aim to provide a standpoint from which we may begin to address this question.

RESEARCH METHODOLOGY

The research design combined curriculum development, action research, quasi-experimental, and multiple case study strategies; it centered around a curricular intervention in which existing Cypriot curriculum materials in history and geography were revised to include a European dimension, with principles that aimed to address the ethnocentrism and traditional pedagogies encouraged by the official curriculum and textbooks. A total of forty worksheets were implemented during a four-month span in the 2000–2001 school year. The research sample consisted of 140 Greek-Cypriot ten-year-old pupils from six fifth-grade classes and their teachers. The intervention program was taught to three of those classes (experimental with sixty-three pupils, referred to as grades 5A, 5B, and 5C), whereas the other three (control with seventy-seven pupils, referred to as 5D, 5E, and 5F) followed the standard syllabi and textbooks for the two subjects.

Data among pupils was collected mainly with tests and interviews to compare any shifts or changes between pre- and postevaluation of pupils' historical and geographic understandings and their national and European identities. The same instruments were therefore used before the introduction of the intervention (December 2000) and after the completion of the program (June 2001). In this chapter, I present data produced in response to the test and interview items that investigated pupils' constructions of immigrants in Cyprus and Europe.

Two test items sought to cross-check pupils' attitudes to immigrants in Cyprus with attitudes to immigrants in Europe. The first item asked whether immigrants should be allowed to migrate to Europe, whereas the second asked, "Should permanent migration from other countries to Cyprus be allowed?" (choice of yes, not sure, or no, scored with 2, 1, and 0, respectively). This question also had an "open" part asking pupils to provide up to three reasons why they chose a particular answer.

Interviews were also conducted with six focus groups (one from each class) of four pupils (two boys and two girls). Two questions focused on immigrants. The first one included following "The Algerian Worker Story":

A large French company is hiring employees. Amongst those who applied for a job was an Algerian migrant to France. When it was his turn to be interviewed, the boss of the company saw his name in the catalogue, realized from that where the applicant was coming from and asked for his secretary: "Can you tell the next applicant that we only employ French people in this company?"

Pupils were then asked, "What is your opinion about his attitude? What do you think made him say this?" This story was used to see whether pupils' responses concerning immigrants would be any different toward an individual (a victim of racism and exclusion from French citizenry, as presented in the story) rather than a generic group of immigrants. Though the story could explore pupils' comments on the Muslim Algerian being rejected by a white Christian, they did not seem to have knowledge of the religions involved and their responses were restricted to nationality. The second interview question was "How do you feel about immigrants in Cyprus? Do you think they should be allowed entrance to Cyprus? Why (not)?" This question sought to further explore the similar test item, as well as whether pupils would differentiate their responses to immigrants when they were viewed within the Cypriot context as opposed to the European context. See the appendix at the end of this chapter for further details on how the data were analyzed in this study.

THE EUROPEAN DIMENSION PROGRAM

The intervention program will not be described in detail here,[5] but I will briefly refer to the principles implemented in its development that referred to migration and immigrants, in order to frame the findings, particularly those during postevaluation. The intervention program sought to address some of the problems of the standard national syllabi and single textbook used in history and geography. In these two subjects, Greek-Cypriot pupils study the Byzantine Empire and the geography of European countries. The syllabi and textbooks in question are characterized by ethnocentric as well as Eurocentric discourse, and they encourage traditional pedagogies (Philippou 2004). It was therefore important, while developing the European dimension curriculum materials, to address and to challenge both Eurocentric or ethnocentric narratives of citizenship and pupils' negative views toward immigrants. In history, the Byzantine Empire was explored alongside other empires in the rest of Europe and the world; its diversity and imperialism were examined, its "national heroes" (e.g., Akrites) were "normalized," and its culture and borders were construed in relation to others'. In geography, ground morphology, colonization, and ecological problems were examined to illustrate the construction of borders and the interdependency of Europe with the world, within Europe and the EU. The program construed Europe and the EU as multiple and diverse, promoted an awareness of their multicultural past and present societies, and questioned stereotypes, identities, and views that represented societies to be static, singular, or pure. In both subjects, the emphasis shifted from knowledge and information to the critical study of multiple sources and maps, the construction of concepts, and collaborative work. References to migration and immigrants occurred indirectly. For example, in history, the Byzantine Empire was represented as multicultural, multilingual, and multireligious (as opposed to Greek and Christian—the view of the standard textbook), with borders constantly in flux. In geography, "pure" European nation-states were replaced by morphological features of geography such as mountain ranges and rivers as concepts to organize content and show how borders are constructed and "ignored" by geography. European societies were represented as multicultural, particularly after World War II.

The concept of democracy was prominent in both the content and the pedagogy of the intervention program. In terms of content, democracy was discussed as a criterion that the European Union sets for candidate member states. Pupils engaged in discussions during which they had to distinguish between countries where democratic institutions and regulations were followed (and which were therefore eligible for candidateship) and countries where democracy was violated in various ways (and which therefore needed to improve democratic institutions). This discussion brought together the issue of immigrants and human rights, since democratic societies were understood as those respecting human rights, including those of recent immigrants and asylum seekers. Pedagogically, the program's principles attempted to challenge traditional pedagogies: the teaching materials (lesson plans for teachers and worksheets for students) encouraged diversity of opinion, independent thinking, greater democratic interaction between pupils and the teacher, and greater critical appraisal of information. These principles included a critical approach to knowledge, developing concepts (one of which was democracy) and organizing information, and learning actively through cooperation.

The pre-post design of the study aimed at exploring the potential impact of the curricular intervention on pupils' discourses of identity, citizenship, and immigrants as compared with their preevaluation responses, as well as to the responses of the pupils who continued to use the official/standard syllabi and textbooks. The findings are presented here through careful comparisons and content analyses of these discourses.

FINDINGS

An analysis of the quantitative data provided an overview of pupils' views of immigrants in Cyprus and Europe. Table 4.1 shows the means of their responses.[6]

During preevaluation, both experimental and control groups had similar views concerning migration of other peoples to Europe (mean = 1.06 and 1.08, respectively). The pupils of the experimental group demonstrated a statistically significant positive change in their attitudes toward migration of other peoples to Europe at the posttest (mean = 1.45). There was no significant change for the control group (mean = 1.14).

As far as attitudes toward people migrating and permanently residing in Cyprus, the control group was initially more positive (mean = 1.06) than the experimental group (mean = 0.88). Postevaluation showed that the

Table 4.1.   Pupils' Responses to Migration to Cyprus and Europe

	Experimental		Control	
Item	*Pre*	*Post*	*Pre*	*Post*
Immigrants should be allowed to migrate to Europe.	1.06	1.45**	1.08	1.14
Should permanent migration from other countries to Cyprus be allowed?	0.88	1.27**	1.06	0.95

experimental group became significantly more positive (mean = 1.27) about migration to Cyprus, while the control group, remained less inclined to agree with this statement (mean = 0.95).

Although the experimental group showed significant positive changes in their acceptance of migration to Cyprus and Europe by other immigrants, both groups were less positive about migration to Cyprus than migration to Europe during both pre- and postevaluation. Pupils were asked to provide up to three reasons to justify their view of immigrants coming to Cyprus. These answers offered some insights into how pupils constructed immigrants as citizens (or not) of Cyprus (see table 4.2).

Most pupils objected to immigration during preevaluation, citing reasons that represented immigrants as a "threat" against "small" (and consequently weak[7]) Cyprus: "because Cyprus is small." Pupils thought that immigrants would take Cypriots' jobs, outnumber Cypriots in the popula-

Table 4.2.   Reasons for Accepting or Rejecting Immigrants to Cyprus

	Experimental Group				Control Group			
	Pre		Post		Pre		Post	
Category of Justification	*N*	*%*	*N*	*%*	*N*	*%*	*N*	*%*
0. No answer	155	82.0	99	52.4	197	85.3	175	75.8
1. Unclear/misconception	2	1.1	0	0	0	0	2	0.9
2. Self-understood/unjustified	0	0	2	1.1	1	0.4	2	0.9
3. Each-one-to-their-own	4	2.1	0	0	2	0.9	6	2.6
4. Disadvantages for Cyprus	0	0	16	8.5	11	4.8	18	7.8
5. Ambiguous/conditional	0	0	7	3.7	5	2.2	5	2.2
6. Benefits for the immigrants	0	0	12	6.3	4	1.7	1	0.4
7. Positive impact on Cyprus	7	3.7	18	9.5	4	1.7	5	2.2
8. Personal reasons	0	0	8	4.2	4	1.7	5	2.2
9. Humanistic reasons	0	0	17	9.0	2	0.9	12	5.2
10. Human rights justification	0	0	10	5.3	1	0.4	2	0.9
Total	189	100	189	100	231	100	231	100

tion, extinguish "our customs," cause trouble and crime, cause environmental pollution, require buildings for accommodations, and spy. Immigrants were largely constructed in racist and xenophobic terms. Other answers revealed that pupils understand the world to be divided into mutually exclusive nation-states, countries, and their nationals, while changing or multiple citizenships were not conceived of as a possibility. Some typical justifications for opposing immigration included "Every country must have its own people" and "We don't want them to come to our country. They should go to their own country."

Very few positive reasons were provided, and they involved "helping us with our [political] problem once they see what an [beautiful] island we are," "to see our hospitality," increasing the population of Cyprus, and having an opportunity to meet new people. These reasons were "ethnocentric" because they adduced benefits for Cyprus from immigrants. Rarely was there reference to "humanistic" reasons, involving immigrants' personhood, and these answers were flavored by pity: "they might be poor" or "need help."

Interestingly, these ten-year-old pupils associated immigrants with the political problem of Cyprus in two contradictory ways: Some statements were strongly negative, providing reasons such as "because Cypriots are few and in the other half of Cyprus they are Turks, then Cyprus will be filled with foreigners." Other pupils considered migration an advantage and a lesser danger than the Turks: "because we would have more people in Cyprus and that way Denktash[8] will leave." The first group constructed immigrants as non-Cypriots, foreigners who would "add" to the "otherness" of the Turks and reinforce the "enemy." The second group expected immigrants to become Greek-Cypriots, to be assimilated, thus rendering Cyprus stronger against the "enemy."

During postevaluation, a greater number of pupils attempted to answer this item—particularly from the experimental group—which perhaps indicates a greater understanding of the two items and/or stronger views about them. Pupils who responded also gave a greater number of reasons to justify their responses. The xenophobic rhetoric against immigrants in Cyprus was repeated in the posttests with statements like "Cyprus must have Cypriot inhabitants not foreign peoples." Such statements "excluded" immigrants from Cypriot citizenship. Table 4.2 shows that these constructions were accompanied by an increase in the "humanistic" and "human rights" categories by both the experimental and control group; this shift was again greater for the experimental group. These arguments indicated some understanding of the causes of migration and that these causes also apply in Cyprus—for example: "to find a better way of life"; "some countries may be poor and so people are forced to migrate"; "to help their family"; "to have food"; "so that they can live"; "because they might be maltreated where they live now." The "human rights" rhetoric was mobilized particularly by the experimental group with statements like "we must respect other people because they are all equal"; "thus they will go to another country freely"; "because every human being may come and leave freely whenever they want"; more clearly, "because we must respect human rights."

Some of the reasons provided revealed an openness to encountering and interacting with immigrants. For example "to get to know them," "because people will meet others, they will make new friendships," "so that they cooperate with other countries and take ideas," or "because Cyprus must have many nationalities." Religion was referenced to justify more positive views: "because God said we are all brothers and that is why we must all be together."

These answers indicated shifts in some pupils' views of immigrants, though some of the rhetoric that excluded immigrants was repeated during postevaluation. The disruption of this rhetoric in the experimental group became clearer during the interviews, discussed next.

"The Algerian Worker Story"

The interview data provided deeper insights into pupils' thinking around immigrants in relation to Europe. After this story, students were asked their opinion of the boss's words, "We only employ French people in this company." Pupils from both the experimental and control groups were critical of this comment during preinterviews, arguing that a single worker could be no real threat to the company as "he would only be working there, he wouldn't take the company from him [the boss]!" and mentioned reasons like poverty and unemployment as reasons why the boss should hire the worker. For example, from grade 5B, an experimental group:

Aris: It's a shame . . . if they are poor, they must work. . . .

Sofia: He [the boss] doesn't trust him [the worker]. . . . He should have tried him. How could he know? There are many who are bad. We know that some are thieves, but how could he know? He [the worker] trusted them to come to France and live permanently with all his pleasure, but they [French] rejected him.

Aris: Maybe he would have better behavior than the others. . . .

Leo: What, he would hire only French. Can't someone from another country work there?

Aris: For example, if Americans came. . . .

Researcher: The boss said he didn't want anyone else, only French. . . .

Leo: Maybe there weren't many jobs in their country. Say Africans were poor and they wanted to earn money. . . .

Aris: Say if he came . . . if an American came, he would take him.

Researcher: Why do you think?

Aris: Because them [the Americans] all the world knows them that they have civilization, whereas with the Africans, how could he [the boss] know that he [the worker] would be able to do it [the job]?

This group seemed to empathize with the disappointment of the rejected worker, since it meant the collapse of his dream to live in France. The group even tried to differentiate among Algerians, saying that this worker might have "better behavior" than the rest. They later indicated how they considered Algerians "uncivilized," at least in comparison with Americans. Pupils would also reformulate the situation by putting the boss or a Greek in the position of the worker:

Pambo: It's . . . it's bad what he said because it's got nothing to do with where the employees are from, say us, for example—we have Greeks and English in a job. . . .
The rest: Aha [nodding in agreement].
Researcher: Aha, yes Tony?
Andony: And English. . . .
Maria: I believe that it was bad what he said to the other employee because this man might not have been able to find another job to work and he found a position there . . . just like he [the boss] wouldn't have liked it himself to get thrown out if he went to another country to work. (grade 5A, experimental group)

Christos: That was a bad thing he did because others come, too, to work in other countries; it can't be just the French. For example, us in Cyprus, my father is from Nicosia and now works in Larnaca, and he works where our house is in [a local town]. . . .
Elena: I say it is necessary . . . a French person, for example, can't throw out a Greek one from working. The Greek person needs the job to work and earn money, take care of his wife, his children. He needs money. (grade 5D, control group)

Only one control group (grade 5F) approved of the boss's comment, suggesting that the migrant could cheat or even destroy the French company and that the (French) customers wouldn't have liked to see an Algerian working there; they thus recognized and agreed with how immigrants might not be welcome within French society.

Becoming a Citizen

During postevaluation, some of the preinterview rhetoric reappeared; the experimental group variably and evidently drew from the intervention program's involvement of stereotypes, borders, and migration to respond. One experimental group, grade 5A, was certain that the Algerian worker would become a French citizen by naturalization because he would live all his life in France:

> *Pambo:* Ehm, he made a mistake that one, because he didn't know if that Algerian was good or bad. . . .
>
> *Rea:* Miss, that is a stereotype again because he [the boss] might have had a bad opinion about the Algerians, but it could be that only a few people who did bad things or something that was harmful to that persons who only wanted the French.
>
> *Andony:* He made a mistake because the Algerian migrant went to live all his life, he may. . . .
>
> *Pambo:* . . . He became French now, that he went to France to live all his life there, he became French; he must have become French. . . .
>
> *Researcher:* So he could get the job?
>
> *Pambo:* Yes, he could.
>
> *Maria:* It was a mistake what the manager of the company did, because he didn't give the Algerian a chance to work and see his work, because the Algerian could be working better than the French, and it was a mistake of his, that he didn't give him a chance. . . .

This group thought that the immigrant could become French because of living there, indicating an understanding of citizenship as changing in different contexts. There was also reference to stereotypes as an obstacle to the boss's judgment, since they led him to overgeneralizations. It was interesting to see that the group also thought that the boss should make a decision on meritocratic grounds and should hire the immigrant if he was better for the job. This rationale also came up with another experimental group, grade 5B:

> *Gea:* Very wrong again, because . . . what, that he is Algerian; they are humans too. Say he went to ask for a job. He may have the same qualifications as the others who want to get the job. He may be better than them, so why shouldn't he get the job? . . . He is just from a different country. . . .
>
> *Sofia:* They should let him because it's borders that separate countries, and they say that, that one is French, this one is Algerian, German, borders. If borders weren't there, we wouldn't judge people like that. . . . But if they didn't exist, we would have fights about what [area] is ours, what is somebody else's. . . .
>
> *Leo:* It's a wrong view because if in Algeria, eh . . . they opened a factory and asked for employees and a Frenchman went there say and asked for a job, would he like it if they told him, "We only get Algerians"?
>
> *Aris:* They are humans too, they are not . . . so we are all humans, and we are brothers. We must love each other.

What is particularly interesting for this group is that they invoked the existence of borders to challenge the boss's reaction. They thus problematized the concept of "borders," arguing that merely being from another country should not be a reason for rejecting someone; in Gea's words "he is just from another country." Borders were also "blamed" for judging people "like that" by Sofia. Grade 5C also thought the boss should make a decision based on the individual applicant rather than his nationality. There was also reference to the colonial link between France and Algeria to explain why the boss might have been afraid that the Algerian could cause problems as a reaction to past colonial oppression:

> *Pavlos:* It's not good what he said to his secretary to call the next [candidate], because say it may be . . . he wasn't . . . if he had anything bad with Algerians, say if he had a problem with them, he should have interviewed him to see his character first, and then tell him . . . only French. . . .
>
> *Akis:* I think . . . Algeria was a colony to France if I remember well, and he must have known it . . . the boss and he didn't allow it because he [the migrant] would hate him and destroy his company. . . .

The control groups referred to a mixture of reasons. They argued that since there is freedom of work within Europe, then anyone should be allowed to work anywhere. Other reasons for disagreeing with the boss was the unemployment and poverty of the migrant; given these problems, they considered it inhuman not to give the immigrant a job. There was also reference to meritocratic reasons suggesting that the migrant could more be able than others to perform the job. What prevailed, however, was again the construction of immigrants as a threat; the next example from grade 5D shows how the Cypriot context was invoked to respond in a negative way:

> *Angie:* Like us now that immigrants come to Cyprus, and they don't let them. I think it's good what the boss did, because they [immigrants] might do something to his factory; something bad may happen.

What about Cyprus?

Pupils' constructions of immigrants became more extreme when Cyprus was involved. During preevaluation, grade 5F was very negative to the prospect of immigrants in Cyprus; they explained that they didn't feel well because "Cypriots want a job and because they've got immigrants in the job, ours [Cypriots] can't get a job and so we are gonna be beggars in our own country!" Indeed, most of the replies were somewhat different in comparison with those given for the Algerian worker. Pupils were more reluctant to view immigrants positively, and the rhetoric of "threat" to their identity and the identity of Cyprus, of economic and ecologic danger, of criminality, and so forth, came to the fore more saliently, as it did in the questionnaires. Some pupils even paralleled immigrants to the Turks and other "strangers": "We shouldn't allow them because they might get us, as our parents say, when we go out at night, the foreigners [strangers] might catch us!"

However, some groups did try to differentiate within the category of "immigrants," arguing, for example, that "To some that are good with us and they love us and we trust them, we should allow them [to migrate to Cyprus]." When Cypriots could benefit from immigrants financially or by learning new customs, then immigrants should be allowed, other pupils argued. And others invoked immigrants' personhood or humanity: "[they] are humans too." Others were willing to consider migration to Cyprus, but only from "friendly" countries. For example, from grade 5E, a control group:

> *Soula:* I think that for good . . . no, we could get a law so that only those that we want could come.
> *Researcher:* Meaning who?
> *Soula:* Not Turks, because Turks are from Turkey and Cyprus might hate them, maybe they will make another war in these places.
> *Oli:* Countries that we are sure will not cause us a problem.
> *Soula:* Like Yugoslavia or Bulgaria.

During postevaluation, the experimental group were overtly positive to immigration to Cyprus and referred to the financial benefits for Cyprus, but also to how immigrants had a "human right" and should be allowed to enter Cyprus just as Cypriots should be allowed to migrate to other countries. Grade 5B even said, "We should appreciate that they chose our country to migrate, because it means that they like Cyprus, that they consider it a rich country, and so they want to migrate to Cyprus."

The control group seemed to hold more reservations, since for them, migration was associated with illegality and crime. For example, grade 5D said:

> *Andros:* No, we shouldn't allow them to come because on the television, it shows many immigrants in the planes and the buses and . . . sometimes that immigrants get and they hold prisoners in the buses, and . . . some migrant went and got into a bus with a gun, and it sped on and it collided with many cars, and the police got him and it got into the bus, the police, and they got him.
> *Elena:* I say we shouldn't host foreigners, because like it showed last night on the [Cypriot TV Channel] evening news that some immigrants attacked the policemen, and the policemen had to catch them and take them to prison. . . .
> *Christos:* No more should come, because black people may come, too, and threaten us with . . . and kill us.

Grade 5F accepted hiring "foreigners," but only in jobs that Cypriots didn't want:

> *Joe:* If Cypriots want to go to that job, they should hire the Cypriots; if they [Cypriots] don't [want to], they should hire the foreigners
> *Vera:* For the Cypriots, they will have more. . . . They know how to do many more things.
> *Fotini:* If some customer comes and sees a foreigner, he might not trust the employee to tell him what he wants.
> *Kyri:* They [customers] will be more sure with Cypriots than with the foreigners.
> *Joe:* And they will know their language, to understand each other better, and as Fay said we will trust them [Cypriots] more than the foreigners.

For this control group, out of necessity, and because some jobs are disliked by Cypriots, "foreigners" could be employed in Cyprus; Cypriots, however, were more desirable as employees, because they can do more things, they are more trustworthy, and they can communicate better with customers.

DISCUSSION

This study indicates the xenophobic constructions pupils held of immigrants to Europe and particularly to Cyprus, as well as the reasons they provided for constructing them as Cypriot/European citizens or not. The findings validate research showing that Greek-Cypriot pupils do not identify much with Europe or European identity (Philippou 2005a; Pachoulides 2003) because they did not feel as threatened by immigration when the discussion focused on Europe rather than Cyprus. Because the Cyprus problem remains unresolved, a uniquely stable educational culture has been created in which an enhanced national consciousness tends to dominate policymaking, curricula, and textbooks (Koutselini 1997). Hellenocentrism prevails in the schools, and, indeed, signs of this Hellenocentric discourse appeared in justifications opposing immigration such as "Then Cyprus will not be Greek." Such views not only assume that Cyprus is monocultural and exclude Turkish-Cypriots, Maronites, Armenians, and other ethnic groups in Cyprus but also suggest that migration and recent immigrants threaten their national (Greek) identity. Discussions, debate, and conflict over the content of "European," "national," "ethnic," and "communal" identities in Cyprus have been lively not only because of the political problem but also due to Cyprus's recent entrance to the EU. Such debates perhaps cause great uncertainties, ambiguities, and confusion over national identity and citizenship and, given the Cyprus problem, encourage narratives of exclusion against "Others" (including immigrants). It was revealing that pupils would often associate immigrants with Turks.

The study supports social constructivist arguments that education can play a critical role in developing democratic societies that support and respect the human rights of minority groups. Soysal (1994) has argued that broad, transnational definitions of human rights have eroded the power of various European states to exclude noncitizens from social benefits and civil rights. If the countries of Europe have begun to "include" immigrants whom they excluded from citizenship in the past, this change must inform curricular documents, syllabi, textbooks, teacher education and teaching practice, although such a change might prove more difficult in countries such as Cyprus that have a long history of conflict and division. Indeed, this is the challenge for researchers and educators. The postnational citizenship developed in Europe to accommodate human rights could be used to broaden Greek-Cypriot pupils' constructions of Cypriot citizenship. This change was found to "disrupt" the experimental group's views against immigrants whom they had initially represented in terms of threat and danger. Exposure to ideas about human rights encouraged some pupils to acknowledge immigrants' humanity. The study of borders, colonization, and migration that occurred during the program was also appropriated by pupils to challenge the exclusion of immigrants from Cyprus. Finally, immigrants' role in the economic development of Cyprus was acknowledged and was again an argument, though utilitarian, that pupils employed.

The findings have limitations, to be sure: this was not a representative sample of pupils. The pupils who participated were those whose teachers agreed to participate as experimental or control classes in the research project. In addition, the reported shifts by no means suggest that all participating pupils progressed in the ways that they viewed immigrants. However, these findings do provide some insights into how pupils in Cyprus think and talk about immigrants, and they offer some conceptual tools for future research and curriculum development. Indeed, my argument in this chapter is not that the program was equally effective with all pupils but that, in a conflict-ridden and divided society, it succeeded to *some* extent and among *some* pupils in shifting ethnocentric and Eurocentric narratives of "exclusive" citizenship. It also succeeded to some extent in broadening their understandings of migration in democratic ways by using a constructivist approach to the concept of "Europe" and borders, as well as the discourse of human rights, as curricular tools.

APPENDIX: DATA ANALYSIS

Quantitative data were analyzed with SPSS (Statistical Package for the Social Sciences), version 10.0. Nonparametric (Wilcoxon), and parametric (paired-samples)

Table 4.3. Hierarchical Topic Guide of Pupil Responses to "Should Permanent Migration from Other Countries to Cyprus Be Allowed?"

Value	Label of Codes	Description of Codes
0	No answer	
1	Unclear answer	The answer does not give a clear meaning; the reader cannot be sure of what the answer is trying to say or indicates misconception
2	No justification	Reasons repeat the question/no justification
3	Each-one-to their-own reasons	Reasons indicating that each people should stay in their country
4	Disadvantages/harm for Cyprus	Reasons indicating that migration to Cyprus has a negative impact on the country
5	Ambiguous and conditional reasons	Reasons showing indecisiveness
6	Benefits for the immigrants	Reasons indicating belief that immigrants will benefit from coming to Cyprus
7	Positive impact on Cyprus	Reasons indicating belief that Cyprus will benefit by incoming migration
8	Personal reasons	Reasons revealing that pupils face the prospect from a personal, positive point of view, according to how they could benefit personally
9	Humanistic reasons	Reasons indicating a humanistic point of view (i.e., acknowledging immigrants' humanhood and feeling sorry for them)
10	Human rights reasons	Reasons using terms of human rights and freedom

tests were conducted to compare pupils' responses to pre- and posttest. Qualitative data consisted of data collected with an open-ended test item and interviews. Interviews were fully transcribed in the language conducted, Greek, and transferred into the qualitative analysis package Atlas.ti, chosen for its ability to handle Greek fonts. For the test item, the coding framework described in table 4.3 was used.

The numbering of the codes shown in the table aims to indicate that they were "evaluative" in the sense that they were hierarchized from the most simple, wrong, or naive answers to the most complex ones. The coding of each question was transferred to SPSS; frequencies and Wilcoxon tests were used to identify changes from pre- to posttest in the number and level of reasons pupils would use to respond.

NOTES

1. A Green Paper released by the European Commission is a discussion document intended to stimulate debate and launch a process of consultation, at the

European level, on a particular topic. Usually it presents a range of ideas and is meant to invite interested individuals or organizations to contribute views and information. It may be followed by a White Paper, an official set of proposals that is used as a vehicle for their development into law.

2. EU's language policy is seemingly inclusive, in that it promotes the teaching of "minority," "regional," and "least widely used" languages spoken in the member states. However, it only includes those languages that are considered traditionally indigenous to the EU; it excludes the languages of immigrants or artificially created languages despite their long use by large groups—for example, Turkish, Arabic, Kurdish, and Persian communities in the EU. "Rather than breaking with the legacy of discriminatory principles of language selection that permeated the formation of European nation-state and its education systems, [the EU] is actually in some important respect working in compliance with these same principles" (Hansen 1998: 19).

3. A single-textbook policy applies in all subjects and grades in Cyprus. Half of the textbooks used in Greek-Cypriot schools are imported from Greece. Several textbooks and materials are produced by the Curriculum Development Service of the Ministry of Education of Cyprus to replace or supplement those from Greece; the two civic education textbooks are published in Cyprus.

4. Of course, these data are highly quantitative and do not reflect in-depth understandings and views of immigrants and foreigners. One limitation of such surveys, for example, is that the wording itself may "produce" responses. Such "objections" are particularly intense by fields such as discursive psychology, which argues that "social categorisation is a situated and flexible discursive practice, and that category labels as linguistic devices have the power to construct the very nature of a group, and are thus inherently evaluative and ideological" (Augoustinos and Quinn 2003: 29). They thus argue that people's evaluations and attitudes toward asylum seekers differed when research instruments used different social category labels such as "illegal immigrants" as opposed to "asylum seekers" and "refugees." Participants in the "illegal immigrant" condition of their study produced the most negative attitudinal judgments in comparison with the other two conditions. However, overall, there was a significant tendency by all participants, regardless of category condition, to ascribe more negative than positive traits to each of these three categories (Augoustinos and Quinn 2003).

5. A detailed description of the intervention program, the cross-curricular, content, and pedagogical principles used to develop it, as well as a critical content analysis of the geography and history fifth-grade standard syllabus and textbooks used in Cyprus, are conducted elsewhere (Philippou 2004, 2005b).

6. Whenever there is a statistically significant change in the means of the answers between pre- and posttest (as shown by paired samples t-tests), this is marked with asterisks on the posttest column. A single asterisk indicates significance below 0.05, and a double asterisk indicates significance below 0.01.

7. Children's understanding of Cyprus as a small, weak country, "only an island," also came up in their responses toward national out-groups and Europe, which were perceived as more powerful and therefore dangerous for Cyprus. Negative views of Bulgarian, Russian, Gypsy, and Arab immigrants (groups that have

been forming minority groups in Cyprus since the 1970s) occurred in items investigating children's views of the national out-groups in question. I have begun to explore these views elsewhere (Philippou 2003).

8. Rauf Denktash, a leader of the Turkish-Cypriot community from the 1960s until 2004, has been considered by Greek-Cypriots as one of the main obstacles to the solution of the Cyprus problem.

REFERENCES

Adams, A., and W. Tulasiewicz. 1995. *The Crisis in Teacher Education: A European Concern?* London: Falmer.

Alexandrinou, G. 2005. "Vouleftes amfisvitoun tin poiotita erotimatologiou Erevnas: I xenophovia den einai ratsismos" ("Parliament Members Question the Quality of a Research Questionnaire: Xenophobia Is Not Racism"). *Politis* (*Citizen* newspaper), March 16, p. 40.

Anderson, B. 1991. *Imagined Communities.* London: Verso.

Augoustinos, M., and C. Quinn. 2003. "Social Categorization and Attitudinal Evaluations: Illegal Immigrants, Refugees or Asylum Seekers?" *New Review of Social Psychology* 2, no. 1: 29–37.

Brine, J. 1995. "Educational and Vocational Policy and Construction of the European Union." *International Studies in Sociology of Education* 5: 145–63.

Cederman, L. E. 2001. "Nationalism and Bounded Integration: What It Would Take to Construct a European Demos." *European Journal of International Relations* 7, no. 2: 139–74.

Coulby, D., and C. Jones. 1995. *Postmodernity and European Education Systems.* London: Trentham Books.

Council of the European Communities General Secretariat. 1990. *European Educational Policy Statements: Supplement to the Third Edition (December 1989).* Luxembourg: Office for Official Publications of the European Communities.

Danopoulos, C. P. 2004. "Religion, Civil Society, and Democracy in Orthodox Greece." *Journal of Southern Europe and the Balkans* 6, no. 1: 41–55.

Davies, S., and A. Sobisch, eds. 1997. *Developing European Citizens.* Sheffield: Sheffield Hallam University.

Green, A. 1997. *Education, Globalisation and the Nation-State.* Basingstoke: Macmillan.

Gregoriou, Z. In press. "Reckoning with the Divide in Cyprus: The Performativity of Borders." *Hagar, Studies in Culture, Polity and Identities* 7, no. 1: 1–26.

Habermas, J. 1994. "Citizenship and National Identity." In *The Condition of Citizenship,* ed. B. van Steenbergen. London: Sage.

———. 1996. "The European Nation State: Its Achievements and Its Limitations: on the Past and Future of Sovereignty and Citizenship." *Ration Juris* 9: 2.

Hansen, P. 1998. "Schooling a European Identity: Ethno-cultural Exclusion and Nationalist Resonance within the EU Policy of 'The European Dimension in Education.'" *European Journal of Intercultural Studies* 9, no. 1: 5–23.

Heater, D. 1990. *Citizenship: The Civic Ideal in World History, Politics and Education.* London: Longman

———. 1997. "The Reality of Multiple Citizenship." In *Developing European Citizens*, ed. J. Davies and A. Sobisch. Sheffield: Sheffield Hallam University.

Hobsbawm, E. J. 1994. *Nations and Nationalism since 1780: Program, Myth, Reality.* 3rd ed. Cambridge: Cambridge University Press.

Kizilyürek, N., and M. Hadjipavlou-Trigeorgis. 1997. "An Analysis of the Cyprus Conflict: Its Structure and Causes." In *Cyprus and the European Union: New Chances for Solving an Old Conflict?* ed. H. J. Axt and H. Brey. Munich: Südosteuropa-Gesellschaft.

Konstantinou, K. 2003. "Apeleftheromenoi alla kai xenophovoi oi Kyprioi neoi symfona me erevna tis Evropaikis Enosis" ("Progressive but Xenophobic Are Cypriot Young People, According to a Survey by the European Union"). *Politis* (*Citizen* newspaper), November 4, p. 22.

Koutselini, M., L. Neophytou, G. Taliadoros, and G. Mylonas. 2002. "Protimiseis kai etoimotita synyparxis me xenous pou zoun simera stin Kypro kai me xenous genika: mia erevna ton antilipseon ton Kyprion mathiton tis St? taxis tou dimotikou ("Preferences and Coexistence Readiness with Foreigners Who Live in Cyprus Today and with Foreigners in General: A Study of the Perceptions of Cypriot Students in the Sixth Grade of the Primary School"). In *Praktika tou 7ou Pagkypriou Synedriou tis Paidagogikis Etaireias Kyprou: I ekpaideytiki erevna stin epochi tis pgakosmiopoiisis, Tomos A?* (*Proceedings of the Seventh Pancyprian Conference of the Cyprus Pedagogical Association: Educational Research in the Globalization Era, vol. 1*), ed. A. Gagatsis, L. Kyriakides, N. Tsaggaridou, H. Phtiaka, and M. Koutsoulis. Nicosia: University of Cyprus.

Koutselini, M., and C. Papanastasiou. 1997. "Civic Education in Cyprus—Issues in Focus: A Curriculum Research Study." *Children's Social and Economics Education* 2, no. 3: 113–29.

Koutselini-Ioannidou, M. 1997. "Curriculum as Political Text: The Case of Cyprus." *History of Education* 26, no. 4: 395–407.

Koyzis, A. A. 1997. "The Politics of Secondary School Reform in Cyprus 1976–1993." *History of Education Society Bulletin* 59: 30–36.

Kyriakidou, C. 2005. "Me ratsistikes taseis pente stous deka mathites" ("With Racist Tendencies Five in Ten Pupils"). *Phileleftheros* (*The Liberal* newspaper), March 3, p. 1.

Lewicka-Grisdale, K., and. T. H. McLaughlin. 2002. "Education for European Identity and European Citizenship." In *Education in Europe: Policies and Politics*, ed. J. Ibanez-Martin and G. Jover. Dordrecht: Kluwer Academic Publishers.

McLaughlin, T. H. 1992. "Citizenship Diversity and Education: A Philosophical Perspective." *Journal of Moral Education* 21, no. 3: 235–50.

Ministry of Education and Culture. 1996. *Analytika Programmata Dimotikis Ekpaideysis* (*Primary Education Curricula*). Nicosia: Ministry of Education and Culture, Curriculum Development Unit.

Office of the Chief Cyprus-European Union Negotiator. 1999. *Cyprus-EU Accession Negotiations.* www.cyprus-eu.org.cy/eng/ome.htm.

O'Leary, S. 1996. *European Union Citizenship: Options for Reform.* London: Institute for Public Policy Research.

Osler, A., H.-F. Rathenow, and H. Starkey, eds. 1995. *Teaching for Citizenship in Europe.* London: Trentham Books.

Pachoulides, K. 2003. "Poreia oikodomisis tis ethnikis taytotitas: i periptosi tis Kyprou" ("Ontogenesis of National Identity: The Case of Cyprus"). Paper presented at the Greek Psychological Association Annual Conference, Aegean University, May 21–24, 2003 (Greece, Rhodes).

Papadakis, Y. 1995. "Nationalist Imaginings of War in Cyprus." In *War, a Cruel Necessity? The Bases of Institutionalized Violence*, ed. R. Hinde and H. Watson. London: Tauris Academic Studies.

Persianis, P. 1996. "I koinoniki agogi sto dimotiko sxoleio: ta porismata mias pagkyprias erevnas kai i filosofiki ermineia tous" ("Social Studies in the Primary School: the Results of a Pancyprian Study and Their Philosophical Interpretation"). In *I ekpaideysi tis Kyprou mprosta stin proklisi tis Evropis* (*The Education of Cyprus in Front of the Challenge of Europe*), ed. P. Persianis. Nicosia: Author.

———. 1998. "Cultural Resistance to the Structuring of the European Space in Greece and Cyprus." In *Education and the Structuring of the European Space: North-South, Centre Periphery, Identity-Otherness*, ed. A. M. Kazamias in collaboration with M. G. Spillane. Athens: Seirios.

———. 2003. *Mporoun simera ta sxoleia tis Kyprou na ekpaideysoun polites* (*Can the Schools of Cyprus Educate Citizens Today?*). Nicosia: Author.

Philippou, S. 2003. "Eksikonizontas ton ethniko eayto Ellinokyprion paidion: dipolikotita kai taytotita" ("Depicting the National Self of Greek-Cypriot Children: Bipolarity and Identity"). Paper presented at the Greek Psychological Association Annual Conference, Aegean University, May 21–24, 2003 (Greece, Rhodes).

———. 2004. "The European Dimension in Education and Pupils' Identity: A Study of the Impact of a Primary School Curricular Intervention in Cyprus." Ph.D. diss., University of Cambridge.

———. 2005a. "Constructing National and European Identities: The Case of Greek-Cypriot Children." *Educational Studies* 31, no. 3: 293–315.

———. 2005b. "The 'Problem' of a European Dimension in Education: A Principled Reconstruction of the Greek Cypriot Curriculum." *European Educational Research Journal* 4, no. 4, 343–68.

Republic of Cyprus. 2001. *Constitution of the Republic of Cyprus 1960: Appendix D: Part 1—General Provisions, Article 2*. www.cyprus.gov.cy./cyphome/govhome.nsf/Main?OpenFrameSet.

Ritchie, J. 1997. "Europe and the European Dimension in a Multicultural Context." *European Journal of Intercultural Studies* 8, no. 3: 291–301.

Soysal, Y. N. 1994. *Limits of Citizenship: Migrants and Postnational Membership in Europe*. Chicago: University of Chicago Press.

Spyrou, S. 2001. "Those on the Other Side: Ethnic Identity and Imagination in Greek-Cypriot Children's Lives." In *Children and Anthropology: Perspectives for the Twenty-first Century*, ed. H. Schwartzman. Westport, Conn.: Bergin & Garvey.

Sultana, R. G. 1995. "A Uniting Europe, a Dividing Education? Supranationalism, Euro-centrism and the Curriculum." *International Studies in Sociology of Education* 5, no. 2: 115–44.

Torney-Purta, J. 2002a. Patterns in the Civic Knowledge, Engagement, and Attitudes of European Adolescents: The IEA Civic Education Study." *European Journal of Education* 37, no. 2: 129–41.

———. 2002b. "What Adolescents Know about Citizenship and Democracy." *Educational Leadership*, 45–50.

II

NOT JUST FOR KIDS: ADULTS (RE)LEARNING DEMOCRATIC CITIZENSHIP IN CHANGING SOCIETIES

Political transitions from authoritarianism present two problems for the preparation of citizens. First, it is not sufficient to limit citizenship education to children in schools. Adults must learn about the new institutions of the state and how to function in a changed society. Yet without universal, compulsory schooling for adults, adult education in particular can take a variety of forms, from individual reflection on lived experience to formal study offered by nongovernmental organizations (NGOs) within civil society. Furthermore, the civic education teachers in schools are themselves a key category of adults who did not have the experience of democratic citizenship education in the classroom. Because they lack experience with more democratic forms of pedagogy and are stuck in institutional hierarchies that often retain authoritarian tendencies, teachers often know democracy more as an abstract idea than as lived experience.

The second common challenge stems from economic changes. Authoritarian societies, especially those without enormous wealth in natural resources, tend not to be prosperous. The challenging economic circumstances in which people in post-authoritarian transitions live are further complicated by the need to adjust to the new and unfamiliar mechanisms of free markets. Economic pressures can reduce participation in civil society and put additional demands on earners, further limiting their possibilities for political participation.

Brazilian literacy scholar Mariana Souto-Manning returns to her native state of Pernambuco to study the contribution of "culture circles," the legacy of the great Brazilian educator Paolo Freire, to the construction of contemporary democracy in Brazil. Souto-Manning has spent a good deal of time participating in these culture circles for adults. Her familiarity with the scene allows her to develop an analysis of their possibilities for educating adults as democratic citizens. She also develops a powerful theoretical-methodological tool for conducting the analysis. Calling it "critical narrative analysis," Souto-Manning highlights the importance of grounding concepts for social action in people's stories to and about themselves. Intriguingly, her research methodology mirrors the educational process under study; both critical narrative analysis and Freirean pedagogy are highly reflective and dialogical, driven by the stories and concrete referents that build up narrators' understandings of the world. At the heart of the chapter, Souto-Manning presents a couple of extended analyses of interactive sequences that take place in the culture circles. By following up on the consequences of some of these key educational interactions, she shows how the democratic process of the culture circles themselves, where participants are given voice and encouraged to think critically, inform the expression of democratic citizenship in the wider world.

Audra Skukauskaitė demonstrates that the economic logic of markets that drove a reform of the school funding formula for Lithuania has produced results quite different from the democratic principles it claims to seek. She doesn't make suppositions about the sincerity of the stated goals by asking whether the outcomes reflect a successful but deliberately misrepresented set of aims, or whether the stated aims were the real goals, but failed as a result of ideological misunderstandings. Instead, she shows that even in this democratizing context, policy remains a top-down affair, too often excluding teachers from the construction of policy or the implementation of goals that would be difficult to carry out without them. While teachers do not directly implement the distribution of funds to schools, an analysis of their discourse reveals a lack of familiarity with the purposes and workings of so central a reform. Those with direct knowledge and experience of the transformations that have resulted from school-funding reform still lack the opportunity to bring their expertise to bear within democratic structures of education policymaking. Teachers feel keenly that they have been devalued by the changes that have taken place since Lithuania's secession from the Soviet Union, and paradoxically, they feel less powerful than they did in a nondemocratic system. The implementation of a voucher-style educational funding system, in their view, not only has allied school administrators with students' families against teachers in any conflict but also has contributed to lower-quality education for everyone. They are not effectively informed about key policy initiatives, nor do they feel a role in their implementation. Instead, they express a combination of powerlessness and apathy, hemmed in by reduced economic security, and in essence disempowered in what should be empowering, democratizing times. While early reform documents inscribe a vision of active citizenship for teachers, the actual consequences of its funding reform directly subvert that very goal. By analyzing and contrasting the discourse of teachers, educational policy documents, and media discussions of education reform, Skukauskaite lays bare the unintended consequences of ideologically conceived reforms.

In chapter 7, U.S. researcher Dolores Foley and national program manager Mpho Putu investigate the workings and outcomes of a model citizen-leadership program in South Africa. The Citizen Leadership for Democratic Governance program, run by the Institute for Democracy in South Africa (IDASA), is designed to equip citizens with the skills to get involved and to handle the difficult tasks of governance in their South African communities. With South Africa's emergence from apartheid, the need to equip citizens to respond more effectively to the challenges of creating and sustaining democracy became clear. Initially, IDASA offered civic education programs throughout South Africa, but in recent years it has concentrated efforts on developing citizen leaders. The intensive program concentrates on a small group of citizens. The larger goal in developing citizens' leadership capacity is to strengthen civil society throughout South Africa. We learn about the impact of the program through the voices of the participants. Their narratives provide insight about the importance of citizen-education efforts in the consolidation of democracy.

5

Education for Democracy: The Text and Context of Freirean Culture Circles in Brazil

Mariana Souto-Manning

No educational experience takes place in a vacuum, only in a real context—historical, economic, political, and not necessarily identical to any other context.

(Freire 1985: 12)

Forty years ago, Brazil's democracy came to an end, and Paulo Freire's "circles of culture" were outlawed. In 1964, the military forcefully took over the government, overthrowing Brazilian president João Goulart, accusing him of supporting communism. The Brazilian presidency was then occupied by General Castello Branco, who established a dictatorship and promulgated a new constitution.

The coup d'état came as Freire's circles of culture were yielding quick and remarkable results in the promotion of literacy and active democratic citizenship (Yamasaki and Santos 1999). Peasants were questioning their positions in society and engaging in social action to change their conditions. These circles were so successful, in fact, that they were perceived as an imminent threat by the new military government. Within two weeks of the coup, Freire's circles of culture were closed down by government decree. Twenty years later, however, they again became a reality when a democratic government was reestablished in Brazil. This chapter reviews both the history of Freirean circles of culture in Brazil over the last forty years and their role in education for democratic citizenship today. It also explores the component parts of Freire's approach, illustrating them with observational fieldwork. These observations revealed a technique of analysis that I call critical narrative analysis (CNA). I apply CNA, a form of praxis for change, to make a methodological contribution that transcends the limitations of discourse analysis and narrative analysis, overcoming the false dichotomy that divides macroinstitutional power discourses from microconversational approaches.

CONTEXT AND HISTORICITY: CIRCLES OF CULTURE AS A POLITICAL THREAT

Historically, illiteracy has been a reality for Brazilians. In 1890, 67.2 percent of Brazilians were illiterate (Haddad and Freitas 1991). In 1920, even though a republic had been established in 1889, 60.1 percent were still illiterate, reflecting the lack of democratic access to education. Brazil's first large-scale adult literacy campaign happened in 1947 (Yamasaki and Santos 1999), after the end of the Vargas dictatorship (roughly 1930–1954). During the 1950s, there was no specific method to teach adult literacy. According to Yamasaki and Santos (1999), "the illiterate adult was made responsible for his/her condition, being considered incapable of taking on responsibilities; society was not given . . . any historical responsibility for this social exclusion" (7). Psychologically, the illiterate adult was classified as having serious learning problems, and treated as a child. This contributed to the marginalization of these adults as well as to prejudice, limiting the social and political effectiveness of the illiterate adult in the world in which he/she lived.

With the prominence of peasant movements in the 1950s, which inspired political and intellectual support of emancipatory movements, including the redistribution of lands throughout Brazil (Santos 1999), these adults started being recognized as "victims of an exclusionary historical-social process" (Yamasaki and Santos 1999: 8). Haddad and Freitas (1991) have blamed the extremely high Brazilian illiteracy rate—46.7 percent at the end of the 1950s—on the lack of a specific pedagogical approach to teach adult literacy that both involved the situated contexts of the learners and engaged them in purposeful or meaningful learning. In this context, such a possibility arose.

During the 1950s, Freire developed a new vision for the pedagogical process of an adult literacy program that involved learning not only how to read the word but how to read the world. Freire's method invited students to learn and value their own culture while questioning the existing system. Peasants analyzed their own situations as they started to mobilize against the system that subjected them to very poor living conditions and very few opportunities for change. They wanted opportunities and possibilities for people like themselves to be in power; as Freire himself put it, to be part of a "true democracy," supporting a democratic citizenship (Instituto Paulo Freire, n.d.-a). This aim is implicit in much of Freire's work and is made explicit by the interpretations of Shor (1990), Macedo and Costa Freire (1998), and Gadotti (1994).

From 1960 to 1963, Freire was involved with the Popular Culture Movement (Movimento de Cultural Popular, or MCP) in his native Recife, the capital of the northeastern state of Pernambuco. Today, Recife is a fast-growing urban area with a very wide salary gap between the haves and have-nots. This gap is perhaps most clearly symbolized by juxtaposition of luxurious buildings—ones that could have been transplanted from Beverly Hills—standing side-by-side with cardboard houses that have no plumbing. Its population is officially about 1.5 million inhabitants but is closer to three million if the surrounding suburbs are included. Recife is the fourth-largest city in Brazil (Koreisha 2004).

Gerhard (1993) reported that Freire's literacy method, the circles of culture, were first implemented and developed in an MCP culture circle that Freire coordinated in one of the suburbs of Recife. Paulo Freire was invited by the mayor of Recife at the time, Miguel Arraes, to construct and implement a literacy program under the umbrella of the MCP. Taking a critical perspective, this program was intended to transform the socioeconomic situation of the northeast (de Castro 1969).

Having achieved success in Recife, Freire was invited by the governor of Rio Grande do Norte, another northeastern state, to head a pilot project in the city of Angicos. Angicos happened to be the governor's hometown; he wanted to do something significant for his town, especially considering elections would occur in the following year, 1964. Freire agreed to work in Angicos, but he made it clear to the governor that he was not going to campaign in the classroom to convince voters to vote for the incumbent. He then recruited the help of university students to conduct these circles of culture and promote liberation and democracy through education.

Although there are inconsistencies between several accounts of this period (Brown 1975; Elias 1994; Pelandré 2002), it is clear that Freire's new program worked extremely well. The exact amount of time the process took is uncertain.

The success of the Angicos project was such that Freire was invited by his friend, Paulo de Tarso, newly appointed minister of education in the populist government of President João Goulart (1961–4), to become the director of the Brazilian National Literacy Program. . . . In that capacity Freire drew plans for 20,000 circles of culture to involve two million people by 1964, extending the pattern of literacy work throughout the country. (de Figueiredo-Cowen and Gastaldo1995: 65)

In 1964, a year after the implementation of the circles of culture in Angicos, the military, assisted, organized, and funded by the United States government (Azevedo et al. 2004; Coben 1998), forcefully ousted the elected Brazilian government. A military dictatorship, initially supported by the Kennedy administration and subsequently by the Johnson administration, was established.

In 1964, Freire's program was extinguished within fourteen days of the coup d'état. Freire was arrested and put in prison for seventy days in Recife (Gadotti 1994). He was then exiled to Bolivia, where he went without his wife Elza and their five children. The following year, Freire went to Chile, where he rejoined his family and resumed his critical literacy programs. From Chile to the United States and Europe and on to various countries in Africa, he continued to develop his work, which he detailed in *Pedagogy in Process: Letters to Guinea-Bissau* (1978).

Following a two-year transition, democracy was finally reestablished in Brazil in 1986. In that same year, Miguel Arraes, who had been exiled for his revolutionary ideas and for sponsoring circles of culture, was elected the governor of Pernambuco in an emotionally charged campaign (Araújo 1991). He represented the return to a time before the dictatorship. Anti-American feelings were widespread. Arraes was elected and reestablished circles of culture in Pernambuco, making them the model for adult literacy programs in the state.

Today, Luis Inácio Lula da Silva, a former factory worker with a fifth grade education and a native of my home state of Pernambuco, is the president of Brazil. He is the first member of the Worker's Party (of which Freire was a founding member) to be elected president. Part of his governing platform includes a program called Zero Illiteracy (Analfabetismo Zero). Something simple to say yet difficult to achieve, this program has taken the first step and funded circles of culture in many locations, including those I studied in Bezerros, a rural community in Pernambuco. Freire's aspiration wasn't to aid people in functioning better within a given system. Instead, he wanted them to become aware of injustices and to act and change them (Finger and Asún 2001). According to Senge et al. (2000):

Freire['s] . . . success in the national adult literacy campaign in Brazil in the 1960s influenced literacy campaigns around the world. . . . Freire believed that literacy was one means to democracy, and felt that being able to "read the word" was intimately tied to being able to "read the world"—that is, to analyze the political and social conditions that circumscribe people's lives, in order to envision how these conditions should be changed. (208)

CULTURE CIRCLES

Culture circles exist to enable people to promote change in oppressive situations. In the circles, literacy is proposed as a tool for social change (Freire 1998). The program discussed here was supported by both the government of the state of Pernambuco and many nongovernmental organizations (NGOs). Before the culture circles were implemented, rural workers would complain that they would work the whole day in the field, and could not cope with going to school to learn things that were not important in the field. School was regarded as a luxury or as something that gave people something to do until they could find a job. The underlying thought was that if one already had a job, one did not need to go to school, because one attends school in order to find a job. In 1996, upon the implementation of these circles by the state government with the support of some NGOs, 34 percent of the population of the state was illiterate. Even worse, 59 percent of the population in Pernambuco's rural areas was illiterate (Secretaria de Educação e Esportes 1997).

In culture circles I observed, fifteen to twenty-five participants met five days per week; each session lasted between two and three hours. The program employed an emergent curriculum, in which learners identified their own problems and issues and looked for the answers to their problems. The circles I observed were located in the rural town of Bezerros. Established in the eighteenth century, Bezerros has a large concentration of artists. The artistic and cultural production by locals is incredibly rich and diverse. The many nonprint texts (Fairclough 2003) represented in the culture inspired the city government to think about a way to use the culture of the place in combination with education to construct a meaningful and enjoyable program. Considered to be a form of civic education by the government, this interdisciplinary program has the objective of educating its illiterate youth and adults. The program presents thematic relationships unifying their history and place. Through generative themes, emerging from participants' own lives, issues, and locations in society, historical-social processes and injustices are explored and problematized dialogically. With these premises in mind, the program adopted many of Freire's ideas of circles of culture and liberatory education (Freire 2002), combining basics (e.g., comprehension, interpretation, explanation, implications) with thematic situations, such as nature and culture, the relationship between culture and economy, and social activism.

Circles of culture are grounded in four components: problem posing, critical dialogue, problem solving, and action. The aim is conscientization, or critical meta-awareness, of each participant's condition. For example, in one of the sessions I observed, Maria was concerned she was failing. Contrary to the popular belief that every hard worker will succeed, she was selling sandwiches but losing money. The episode related here took place in one of the circles in which I was a participant-observer. (All names are pseudonyms, and the facilitator is noted by "F.")

Maria: I don't know what to do anymore. Everybody says that if you work hard--
Lurdes: --you
           will earn money.
Cida: Yes.
Maria: But--I am working hard . . . every day . . . all day selling sandwiches.
Luiz: Good.
Maria: But I never have money.
           ((many participants look at her puzzled))
Marlene: Why?
Maria: I don't know.
Zé: So, I guess it's not enough to work hard.
Lurdes: What else, then?
Zito: How much is a sandwich?
Maria: One real. [Real is the Brazilian currency.]
Tonho: How many sandwiches do you sell?
Maria: About thirty each day.
Cida: ((hahaha)) you earn thirty Reais per day and you are complaining, woman?
Dete: It takes me ten bags of corn to earn thirty Reais [plural for Real].
Michele (F): Folks, let's let her explain her situation.
Desa: We need to listen.
Maria: But then I have to buy bread, hot dogs, ketchup, mustard, potato sticks, peas,
           corn, mayonnaise, tomatoes, onions, tomato sauce . . . and then I see, I don't have
           money to pay for the [hot dog] cart rental.
Michele (F): Do you calculate what you spend?
Maria: No. I just thought that one Real was a little less than what other people were
           selling for, so I would sell more.
Desa: But you are not making money
Maria: No. . . . And I am working hard.
Zito: So, what do you buy for each day?
Maria: I buy every week . . . 20 packs of bread, 200 hot dogs, one box of canned peas, one
           box of canned corn, one big jug of ketchup, another one of mustard, mayonnaise.
           Tomato sauce is three. And the potatoes.
Bia: And where do you keep all of that?
Maria: In the refrigerator.

Zé: So you pay for that too. . . .
         ((Maria nods))
Dete: And where do you cook it?
Maria: At home, so I don't have to spend money.
Lurdes: But you use more gas, don't you?
Maria: Yes.
Nita: So you spend money there too.
Cida: Oh . . .

From here, after problematizing the common saying that if you work hard enough you will succeed, the group goes on with the dialogue, and then engages in problem solving.

Tonho: So, you need to know what you spend with everything before you decide on a price.
Nita: Or you will work hard, every day.
Luiz: And not make any money--
Maria: --Like me.
Zito: So, now you can calculate what you
Bia: Then, if you take the money that it takes you to buy the food, napkins and bags, rent the cart, pay for energy and gas--
Zé: --And put everything together
Maria: Then I can sell the sandwiches and make money.
Cida: Nobody tells you about this.
Nita: Just that if you work hard enough
Michele (F): I think there is a course at SENAC [a government-supported school for technical skills to aid commerce]
Dete: Maybe we can ask the person who teaches the courses to come visit us and talk about how to make money.
Michele (F): This extra money is called profit.
Desa: Let's invite them to visit many circles--
Maria: --So that other people won't lose money too.
Tonho: You know, this is education too, [you] know--
Bia: --This is what we need, so we can have an opportunity and try to have a better life.
         ((many participants nod and show agreement))

After Maria posed her problem (working hard and not earning money), the group discussed it, and came up with the means to find solutions for her problem. The group concluded that in addition to hard work, calculating expenses and earnings were necessities required to make a profit and succeed. This affirms the importance of the four components that ground this program—problem posing, dialogue, problem solving (through critical reflection), and action—as conveyed by Darder (2002):

> It is virtually impossible to speak of a revolutionary practice of *problem-posing*
> education outside the dialogical process, since dialogue is truly the cornerstone
> of the pedagogy. Central to Freire's concept of education is an understanding
> of *dialogue* as the pedagogical practice of [*problem solving through*] *critical reflec-*
> *tion* and *action.* . . . [P]roblem-posing serves to [promote] . . . the emergence of
> critical consciousness in the learning process. (102, emphasis added)

While the interaction above emerged naturally, there were challenges,
especially in Freire's first meetings. As Bee (1980) reported, "Freire and his
team needed to convince the people . . . that no matter how denuded of
dignity . . . they were in fact makers of culture, of history, and subjects in
life, not merely objects of manipulation" (40). Participants had difficulty
talking about their own problems initially and problematizing what for
them was, many times, the only reality they knew.

Freire addressed these problems through the use of generative themes—
themes that emerged from the daily lives of circle participants used to initiate critical dialogue. Freire used pictures to evoke themes, which allowed
the students to discuss situations relevant to them without exposing themselves or making themselves vulnerable. These pictures captured the generative themes expressed by students. They allowed students to start engaging
in critical dialogue and problem solving, as the pictures posed problems
that were part of their very own collective realities.

Generative themes are codifications of situations arising from participants' lives, with varying levels of complexity, charged with political significance and likely to generate considerable discussion and analysis. They
derive from a study of the history, circumstances, and discourse of the circle's participants. In culture circles, generative themes can be codified into
generative words—syllabic words that can be broken down into syllabic
parts and used to "generate" other words. Words emanate from the vocabulary and reality of the participants. These codifications, which can take the
form of paintings, photos, or words, represent participant's every day lives.
One such codification may be represented by Pernambuco artist Bren-
nand's painting of a worker toiling in the sugar cane fields. Codifications
are dialogue-initiating abstractions, leading to analysis of concrete realities.
Such words, paintings, and/or photos serve as a bridge between realities
and their theoretical context, and between facilitators and participants.
Generative themes are the very first step in culture circles. Then, the participants problematize, or decode, the generative theme/word. This is when
dialogue happens, unveiling previous meanings of reality.

In culture circles, participants engage in dialogic exchanges about their
own situations. The group serves to provide theoretical context for reflection, and transforming interpretations of reality into more critical knowledge leading to social action. Participants engage in critical analysis of their

own narratives and/or institutional narratives, thereby appropriating language (Chouliaraki and Fairclough 1999). More than literacy as it is traditionally conceived, the method used allows participants to engage in the problematization of their positions in society and practice of a process that leads to conscientization (Freire 1970), to critical meta-awareness.

Circles of culture aim to promote *conscientização* (Freire 1970, 1990). "In concrete terms, his methods of 'conscientization' with adults in literacy programmes was basically constituted by a process of coding/decoding linguistic and social meanings, organized through a number of steps" (Apple, Gandin, and Hypolito 2001: 131). Although there are a number of steps, there is no simple formula for the implementation of circles of culture. According to Apple and colleagues (2001), the first step is to generate themes from the community in which students live. These words are "socially and culturally relevant to those communities" (132). After the generation of words, they are employed in dialogues in the circles. "[S]pecific steps are taken to achieve the process of reading . . . consist[ing] of a process of decoding written words . . . from a coded existential situation. This connection to the real existential situation is . . . crucial, . . . enabling students . . . to use . . . knowledge to reconstruct their lives" (132). Circles of culture intend to eliminate the dichotomy between theory and practice often present in the traditional schooling environment as the practice depends on the theory and the theory depends on the practice in the implementation and maintenance of circles of culture.

Critical meta-awareness is attained through an ongoing process of conscientization. While consciousness-raising involves the transmission of particular knowledge, which Freire (1970) called "banking education" whereby passive learners receive ready-made knowledge just as banks accept deposits, conscientization problematizes the status quo, breaking through prevalent discourses and practices in order to reach a deeper level of awareness. This new level of consciousness includes awareness of their own positions as objects rather than subjects in society.

Once situations are problematized and conditions are identified, they progress on to dialogue. From dialogue, participants bridge their location as objects to that of subjects, as they negotiate and plan action geared at change in both personal and social realms. Critical meta-awareness is, therefore, a deeper level of awareness and interpretation of situations and problems than mere knowledge transfer. Critical meta-awareness—the state achieved by conscientization—rejects passivity, and entails dialogue leading to a shift from object to subject positioning. The process is initiated by collective praxis (cyclic process of action, reflection, and action), not by a single individual effort. Through becoming "conscientized," participants question both traditional discourses as well as socially and culturally constructed concepts, such as the concept of working hard and not earning money, as explored in the episode presented earlier. Figure 5.1 represents the components and phases employed in culture circles following the generation of themes and/or words (as explained earlier).

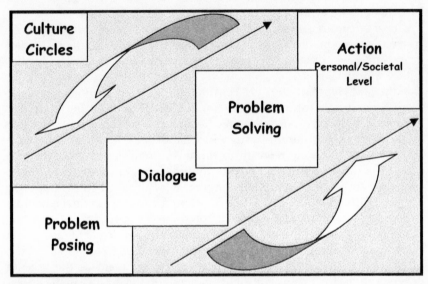

Figure 5.1.   Culture circles.

The sequence represented by figure 5.1 plays out in culture circles and leads to collective agency according to the conversational narrative that is analyzed later in the chapter. It includes "four components necessary for personal and group empowerment: belief in self-efficacy, validation through collective experience, knowledge and skills for critical thinking and action, and reflective action" (McNicoll 2003: 46). Internalizing this process is a way to foster the development of individual agency and action, and for these circle participants to start reenvisioning, reinventing their lives within the system, or enacting change on the structure. After all, personal and social change are dialectically related, and as such they are interactive and inseparable (Breton 1995; Getzel 2003).

ANALYZING THE DISCOURSE IN ACTION: CRITICAL NARRATIVE ANALYSIS OF CLASSROOM DISCOURSE

Envisioning Critical Narrative Analysis

In this section, I apply a technique that arises from the culture circles themselves: critical narrative analysis. This methodology connects practices and contexts and words and worlds. It also transcends the artificial dichotomies of micro-macro in discourse analysis and of personal and institutional discourses. It uses a mostly macroanalytic perspective (critical discourse analysis, or CDA) to inform a predominantly microanalytic perspective (analysis of personal/conversational narratives), and vice versa. In the combination of these two analytic approaches to data analyses, inspired by and compatible with the very framework employed in the culture circles themselves, I explore the "link between macro-level power inequities and micro-level interactional positioning" (Rymes 2003: 122).

As in Freire's culture circles this methodology, which is aligned with critical or emancipatory pedagogical approaches to education, aims at promoting critical meta-awareness. Critical meta-awareness allows common people to engage in social action to solve problems and address issues that they identify in their own narratives. This meta-awareness (achieved through conscientization) allows people to establish a relationship of appropriation in which they use language as a resource, as opposed to being colonized by language (Chouliaraki and Fairclough 1999; Fairclough 2004). By appropriating language, participants considered and problematized multiple perspectives and discussed their social-historical construction, as opposed to taking one view as the sole truth. To engage in the process of problem posing, dialogue, problem solving, and action, participants needed to use language as a tool for deconstructing previous beliefs and understandings, analyzing authentic issues together, and collectively charting a plan for action.

Wedding CDA with narrative analysis brings CDA closer to dealing with real-world issues and promoting changes in society. CDA views most institutional discourses as colonizing; however, it assumes that institutional discourse has the power to transform social relations. Narrative analysis and CDA can productively inform each other, but narrative analysis without CDA can remain at an uncritical level.

A discourse is made powerful when it is recycled in stories everyday people tell. If we only look at macrolevel power discourse without looking at narrative construction at the level of conversation, we cannot be certain if it really is power discourse. While there is a call for a joint and balanced focus on social issues as well as linguistic (textual) analysis in discourse studies, much is needed to unveil the complex ways in which language and the social world are intertwined.

Here I employ a new discourse analytic approach, a hybrid of narrative and critical discourse analyses, which I call critical narrative analysis. CNA deals with institutional and societal differences in power as they relate to language, how people make sense of their experiences in society through language, and power and language within the context of society. It critically analyzes conversational narratives, a form of discourse that is more concrete because it is closer to a person's experiences and it is temporally organized. CNA analyzes conversational narratives and deconstructs the different discourses present in a particular narrative. In demystifying social constructions of reality, just as the culture circle participants do, this methodology addresses real world issues and seeks to develop critical meta-awareness (Freire 1970) with the intent of changing the way interactions work, thereby allowing such socially constructed discourses and practices to be challenged and changed.

"[W]hen the listener perceives and understands the meaning (the language meaning) of speech, he simultaneously takes an active responsive attitude towards it" (Bakhtin 1986: 68). The critical meta-awareness of how institutional discourses are recycled in conversational narratives allows narrators to understand the social construction of the reality in which they live. It also invites them to comprehend that there are indeed multiple understandings of a certain issue (Chouliaraki and Fairclough 1999).

It is through conversational narratives that narrators and conarrators begin to question their realities and problem solve, because "[s]torytelling is a site for problem solving. . . . [M]any problem solving narratives happen and delineate roles, relationships, values, and worldviews" (Ochs, Smith, and Taylor 1996: 95). Finally, once narrators identify the social construction of their own situations in the context of institutional discourse that they have recycled within their own narratives, they challenge their position in society and engage in social action. This is the sequence present in culture circles (Freire 1959). Participants in the culture circles engage in CNA of their own tellings.

When someone is telling a story, it is harder for one to dialogue with the narrator and to disagree because it isn't an explicit position. Narrative tellings have a deeper meaning than what is conveyed explicitly by what is said. What is left unsaid can say as much as what is said. As a result, it is harder to challenge ideology disguised in narrative formats. Disseminating political views though narratives, through storytelling, thus gives the false impression of the absence of political views and ideological concepts. The political materials and views can slip past the critical eye because they are framed within a narrative in the story world (Chafe 1980), due not to intellectual levels but to prevailing language socialization practices. These political narratives have been shown to carry great power as they are often recycled in personal stories. Some of the ideas or positions conveyed employing the narrative genre would generate conflict if they were framed in the interactional world (Chafe 1980). As a result, these political issues framed as everyday stories don't get broken down into parts; they can bypass rationality and are accepted on the level of emotion. Storied worlds are harder to break out and analyze; they are impenetrable in terms of critical questioning as long as the moral stances align themselves (Ochs and Capps 2001).

Stories (as a genre) can serve as a means of colonization, creating and justifying object locations in society while solidifying the subject positioning of those in power. This happens when there is no critical questioning of the stories' components or parts; no problematization of discourses. Taking advantage of stories as a colonizing device, politicians such as the president of the United States (Bush) and the president of Brazil (Lula) have been using everyday narratives embedded in their speeches via television or even completely separate in the form of advertisements.

For example, in early 2004, a minimum wage increase was approved in Brazil. This would have been cause for celebration, except that the president had promised an even bigger increase during his campaign. To avoid protests, the government put out TV ads. These ads used everyday narratives to explain to people that the government could not give a bigger raise because there were other items the budget needed to cover. Instead of giving this message in a detached and abstract way, and thereby making it open to questioning and vulnerable to protests, the government's ad was framed within a conversational narrative. In it, a couple is talking. The husband is telling the wife that it is taking longer and will be more expensive to build their house than he had initially thought because he is putting a lot of effort into building a strong foundation, but when it is ready, it will be very strong, long lasting, and better than they had expected in the beginning. Then, the husband tells the wife that this is exactly what the federal government is doing, building a strong foundation for their house (the country), and this is why they could not raise the minimum wage further.

During the time in which this ad was running, I asked Elena, a thirty-three-year-old domestic worker who was not a culture circle participant, whether she was happy with the small raise in minimum wage. She responded that she was not, but the government was "building a strong foundation for the country and that later it will be much better because of this strong foundation." The government discourse was thus being recycled in everyday conversations throughout the populace. I suggest that had the government used the interactional world as opposed to the story world (Chafe 1980) to justify the small raise in the minimum wage, many more people would have questioned what other items the budget had to cover and if indeed these were as important as the minimum wage—the means by which many Brazilians meet basic needs such as food and shelter. This type of civic education, based heavily on the "banking model of education" (Freire 1970), shapes how people think about government action. Democratic citizenship, on the other hand, requires the critical meta-awareness to make informed choices, to appropriate the discourse in use as opposed to being colonized by it, believing in it as if it were the sole truth, as Elena did, absent of problematization. Narrative in this case involved the dissemination of the institutional discourse, allowing language to serve as a colonizing device (Chouliaraki and Fairclough 1999). In instances such as this, people like Elena are obligated to be receivers of discourse. The TV ad was not exposing Elena to multiple understandings of the issue, and as a result denied her tools to move toward critical meta-awareness. In such a case, language was employed as a tool for attempting ideological colonization of viewers like Elena.

Here we can see that institutional discourse (which is typically analyzed by critical discourse analysts) and stories (which are typically analyzed by narrative analysts) merge to become a hybrid genre: critical narrative analysis. This new methodology allows me to assess culture circles through the tellings of participants. It is also used by the very participants whose conversational narratives I analyze, because it aims to promote critical meta-awareness, allowing common people to engage in social action to solve problems and address issues they identify in their own narratives. This meta-awareness (conscientization) in turn allows people to use discourse as a tool to change their social locations and situations, promoting democracy, while challenging the deterministic claim that "[w]e are stuck in the vicious circles of mutually reinforcing cultural and economic subordination" (Fraser 1997: 33).

Analyzing a Culture Circle in Action

On a Monday evening in June 2003, as darkness began to settle and the heat gave some signs of weakening, women and men, from late teens to early seventies, started entering the room in which they routinely met for their culture circle. Some of them came right from work, as noted from their clothes and hands, which were dusted with soil and signaled their agricultural employment. Some of them talked about the work on the tomato farms in the region, since many of them were engaged in this kind of work. Others looked tired, as if ready to go to bed. It was almost seven o'clock. The facilitator was there, but could hardly be identified from among the participants, as she sat and talked with some of them. There wasn't an official start routine. Conversations about everyday themes and issues that started small developed to a point in which they involved everyone, as the people engaged in dialogue and problem solving, two of the crucial parts of culture circles.

From the beginning, work was clearly the topic of the night. Whether in the tomato fields or in someone's kitchen, they all kept difficult work schedules; many led double lives, working inside and out of their homes. As they started talking about their work, money and salary issues emerged naturally as the focal point, a theme to which they could all relate. Josi expressed her frustration: "It doesn't matter how much I work, I am always owing something to someone; I am always late with my bills. I live with fear. Fear that one day I will get home and not have enough money to pay the rent, or to give food to my children." Participants, men and women, nodded. Another woman, Sandra, asked Josi, "But don't you make a minimum [wage] salary?" Josi answered positively. "What does that mean?" asked Sônia, the facilitator. Sandra immediately answered, "That means she should have enough to live." They continued in the following dialogue:

Josi: I work hard, but the salary is not enough. I don't know what I am doing
           wrong--
Tonho: --Wrong?
Josi: Yes, because I work, earn a minimum [wage] salary, but it's never enough to
           pay the bills and put food on the table.
Sandra: But the minimum [wage] salary is enough. Isn't it? ((looks around seeking
           approval))
Miriam: I don't have enough money for all my bills either. Do you have--
Sandra: --What?
           Enough money?
Josefa: Yes--
Sandra: --No. I am not the owner of my own house. I pay rent every month. I
           can't buy everything that my family needs. Some days all we eat is [manioc]
           flour. A handful of flour to fill the belly. We don't have meat on the table.
           ((Many nod, showing agreement and empathy))

The group started talking about the minimum wage salary and how most of them could identify with Josi's situation. They all made minimum wage salaries, which, according to governmental definition, should allow for a decent living, but they arrived at the conclusion that it didn't, at least in their experiences. They worked hard, but the minimum wage established by federal law was what most of them earned. Some earned even less. After arriving at the understanding that the minimum wage salary wasn't allowing most of them to lead a decent life—to have food on the table and to pay utility bills and housing expenses—they started problematizing the definition of a minimum wage salary.

Tonho: So who decided how much is enough?
Marina: I don't know. It wasn't me.
           ((laughter))
Sandra: Who was it?
           ((side talk as they try to figure out who sets the minimum wage salary))
Sônia (F): The government is who approves the minimum [wage] salary--
Josi: --That's not
           fair. They don't earn a minimum salary. I just saw Lula [the Brazilian

president] in a big car on a store's television. I can't buy a car like that. I
can't even pay to go to work by bus. I go walking.

Miriam: Me too.

Sandra: Who earns a minimum [wage] salary?
            ((most raise their hands))

Sandra: Who earns less than a minimum [wage] salary?
            ((four women raise their hands))

Tonho: Do you work the entire day?

Laurinda: I work--

Neto: --the entire week?
                   ((women who earn less than the minimum wage nod))

Laurinda: Who earns more than the minimum [wage] salary?
            ((five of the eight men in the room raise their hands))

Sônia: What do you perceive?

Luís: That we earn more than they [do].

Sandra: Men earn more money--

Neto: --but it's not enough to live.

The women and men in the culture circle realized that there was economic injustice, but also gender discrimination in terms of salaries. The
gender issue erupted through the problematizing of salaries as a theme of
discussion. Even though the minimum wage salary was clearly not enough
to lead a decent life in the experience of this culture circle's participants, the
women had a clear disadvantage as they made less money than the men—
even if they worked at the same place and performed the same kind of job,
as was the case with two circle participants, Neto and Miriam.

After much discussion, dialogue, and reflection on the issue of economic
and gender-based discrimination and injustice, these people decided to calculate what would be a decent, livable, minimum wage. After adding rent,
utility, and transportation to and from work, clothing, and food (not
restricted to manioc flour and water) for a family of three, one adult and
two children, they arrived at 650 reais, which amounted to around three
times the minimum wage salary at the time (or approximately U.S.$230
per month). They concluded that session by developing two plans for
action—one on the personal and one on the societal level. On the personal
level, they were going to further their studies so as to be better qualified to
take on better-paying jobs. Both men and women also decided to ask their
employers why the women were making less money than men for the same
job. Bridging the personal and the institutional realms, they were determined to attempt to dialogue with their employers about the importance
of equal pay across genders for the same kind of work. Finally, on the institutional level, they decided to write a letter to their governmental representative that read, "Three salaries is what allows [us] to live. [We] have to
study very much." The letter ends by calling for action on the institutional

level. The participants' nonuniform lettering and limited literacy did not stop them from taking action, from attempting to promote change.

In the circle described here, the participants, women and men, engaged in problematizing salaries, something that they believed they could do nothing to change. Through problematizing and dialoguing about some of the issues involved, such as gender disparity in earnings, they dialogued and designed a plan of action. Participants, therefore, were becoming aware of tools they could use (problem posing, dialogue, and problem solving) to question the status quo and to start believing in and even negotiating for change.

As subjects who guided their own learning, participants brought authentic issues to the circles and engaged in meaningful learning experiences, applicable to their everyday lives—and thereby gained ownership of their learning. The culture circles that I observed discussed salary, working conditions, job skills and ethics, parenting, children, education, elections and politics as they related to the participants' lives. Through the exploration of relevant issues and themes, the participants engaged in inquiry, questioning, and charting courses of action. As they problematized themes and issues, old knowledge and assumptions collided with new knowledge. Participants could then construct their own knowledge in a critical manner. This happened as they shared their experiences, their perspectives, and listened to other perspectives as alternatives, from a multiplicity of angles, as explanations. The facilitator, Sônia, took advantage of certain moments to further the participants' queries and inquiries; she provided information, but did not necessarily dictate what went on in the circles, nor did she take the stance of teacher as the holder of knowledge.

Implications of Critical Narrative Analysis

Critical or liberatory education encourages learners to problematize the world in which they live and engage in social action and change, instead of uncritically accepting it and adapting to its conditions. All participating parties (participants, facilitators, and community) are collectively responsible for the content and curriculum of a liberatory education program. Through a dialogic curricular structure, participants seek political, economic, and personal empowerment.

As exemplified earlier by the second narrative episode about sandwiches, participants in the culture circles constantly engaged in the analysis of their own narratives. They considered multiple perspectives (both personal and institutional) and became researchers of their own situations. Given that texts interact with contexts, an issue conveyed through a particular institutional discourse may have many "understandings" (Chouliaraki and Fairclough 1999: 67), as different people see the same issue differently.

Participants, through a dialogic process, must choose one explanation, take a stand, when analyzing their own stories with regard to the impact of institutional discourses intertextually woven in their own narratives. After dialogue, together, participants in the earlier example planned two courses of action, one on the personal realm and another in the societal sphere. The societal plan was to make the politicians in office aware of the disparity and of the need to approve a minimum wage that equaled a living wage. In the personal realm, they realized that by further developing schooling skills such as literacy and problem solving they would be better prepared to take a higher-paying job, therefore addressing the situated issue. This exemplifies a first step toward engaging in the concrete critical research that CNA seeks to accomplish.

Being able to create distance from a story in order to see how it was constructed is a metalinguistic skill that requires insight into the power of language to mislead and/or deceive (Parmentier 1994). "Such meta-awareness is an important life-skill . . . listen[ing] critically and consider[ing] life's challenges from multiple perspectives. . . . Through reframing . . . narrative portrayals . . . [comes] aware[ness] of how the perceptions of others challenge or support their own views" (Rymes 2001: 168).

IMPLEMENTING CULTURE CIRCLES: FREIREAN METHODS

As Freire (Instituto Paulo Freire, n.d.-b) wrote, "It is as impossible to negate the political nature of the educational process as [it is] to negate the educational character of the political act" (translation by author). Overall, the circles of culture are based on two basic tenets, the political nature of education (Freire 1985) and the centrality of dialogue in the process of educating. These tenets manifest themselves within the context in which the learners live, as their problems are analyzed critically and politically, and dialogue is used as a way to overcome and find solutions to those problems. Dialogue became such a central concept for Freire that in the 1980s, he began writing books in dialogue format, as his method itself proposed (Instituto Paulo Freire, n.d.-a).

As detailed earlier, there are four steps in the circles of culture. These are not prescriptive and need to be re-created as new instances occur and circles of culture are implemented in different contexts. They are (1) thematic investigation (investigation of the social and linguistic context of the learner); (2) thematization (selection of generative themes and words); (3) problematization (the antithesis of problem solving; seeks to do away with our innocent and simplistic views of the world or any specific situation, allowing us to treat all previous conceptualizations as questionable and leading us to look critically at, and transform, the situation in place); and (4) action.

COMPARING FREIREAN CULTURE CIRCLES AND TRADITIONAL CLASSROOMS

In establishing a democratic culture circle, Shor (1990) asserted "that the initial challenge of the critical educator is to deconstruct authoritarian modes of discourse in traditional classrooms" (Steiner et al. 2000: 121). In circles of culture, students' experiences are invited, valued, and central to the construction of meaning. According to Freire (1987), "a progressive position requires democratic practice where authority never becomes authoritarianism, and where authority is never so reduced that it disappears in a climate of irresponsibility and license" (212). There is no simple definition of circles of culture, nor a formula for implementing them. One of the "most empowering [aspects of circles of culture] was the way . . . Freire expanded the notion of literacy to include reading the world and writing the world as cultural agents and subjects rather than as objects of history . . . establishing a culture circle as a pedagogical space" (Steiner et al. 2000: 122).

In the circles, I perceived the seating arrangement to break hierarchies set in traditional banking education classrooms in which the teacher is the holder of knowledge, standing in front of the classroom, while students face the teacher from whom they are to receive and learn. According to Kincheloe and colleagues (1998), the physical seating arrangement in circles is essential to employ dialogue and problem-posing education (Freire and Macedo 1996). In the sessions I observed, participants all sat in circles facing one another.

Discourses, knowledge, curriculum, and learning must be redefined for circles of culture to be implemented successfully. The facilitator, who is trained within a curricular structure that mirrors that of culture circles, does not know where the circle is headed, in accordance with the very premise of critical pedagogy. He or she helps the group become conscious of its potential and power to act on and to transform situations. Circles are "space[s] in which all views can be voiced freely and safely. Only when all views are heard can we claim that the heterogeneous nature of our culture is most widely represented in the circle" (Steiner et al. 2000:123). According to Marsiglia (2003):

> The group becomes a laboratory for democracy where all opinions count. . . .
> In becoming a transformative force, the group initially decides on small action steps, develops plans, and implements them. Once the course of action is

implemented, the group reflects on its accomplishments and shortcomings, relates the outcome to the larger societal phenomena they are concerned about, and starts planning the next action step. Group members are more capable of challenging and rejecting messages from the larger society that says that nothing can be changed. (84)

Participants in culture circles start to articulate solutions to their personal challenges through dialogue and problem solving. As some of the participants narrated, a number of them were starting to reconstruct themselves, exploring the implementation of discursively constructed solutions in their lives and engaging in change enacted on the personal level. This personal action can contribute to democratic social change over time. Being part of culture circles allowed the participants access to education, after failing to succeed in formal schooling environments, to take a more agentive role, to have tools with which they might be able to promote change. In culture circles, the participants "experience interpersonal processes with others who share their predicament of exclusion that can provide a most powerful potential for personal, interpersonal, and social change" (Shapiro 2003:19). Together, they began negotiating a new set of collective morals, which can serve to illuminate the start of personal change processes. In the circles, the participants had a chance to lay a foundation for better understanding of the process of questioning the status quo, their own locations in society, to get a glimpse and imagine the potential for action and change on a broader scope. Such was the case of the example described earlier, in which the participants in the culture circle questioned the minimum wage salary and re-imagined themselves, coming up with actions on the personal and societal levels, hints of a better future.

POSSIBLE IMPLICATIONS: CRITICAL NARRATIVE ANALYSIS AS PRAXIS FOR CHANGE

The prospects of circles of culture in the United States are exciting, but we must remember what Freire himself said when talking to Donaldo Macedo: "I don't want to be imported or exported. It is impossible to export pedagogical practices without reinventing them. Please tell your fellow American educators not to import me. Ask them to re-create and rewrite my ideas" (Freire 1998: xi). Many times, when educators speak of Freire and literacy, they reduce the complex concept of literacy to a set of pre-scripted skills linked to learning how to read and write.

Literacy education is an act of knowing, . . . of creating, and not the act of mechanically memorizing letters and syllables. . . . [It] must originate from research about the vocabulary universe of the learners, . . . to understand culture as a human creation, an extension of the world by men and women through their work, helps to overcome the politically tragic experience of immobility caused by fatalism. . . . Literacy education must be characterized by dialogue as a path to knowledge. . . . [It] must be premised on remembering what it means for . . . adults, used to the weight of work instruments, to manipulate pencils . . . be premised on remembering the insecurity of illiterate adults, who will become upset if they feel they are being treated like children. There is no more effective way to respect them than to accept their experiential knowledge for the purpose of going beyond it. (Freire 1996: 128–29)

To fully implement Freire's ideas, it may be helpful to remember that he defined literacy in terms of culture (Freire 1970). Students "look at themselves as persons living and producing in a given society" (Macedo and Costa Freire 1998: xi). As a result, "[w]hen men and women realize that they themselves are the makers of culture, they have accomplished . . . the first step toward feeling the importance, the necessity, and the possibility of owning reading and writing. They become literate, politically speaking" (xi) and walk toward a true democracy (Shor 1990; Gadotti 1994; Macedo and Costa Freire 1998).

Critical narrative analysis is an essential part of what goes on in three of the phases of culture circles—problem posing, dialogue, and problem solving. Problem posing can only take place when a person or a group sees the situation as problematic as opposed to accepting it as is. Often, people are not aware of the problems that need to be posed as they construct their own narratives.

There is a process through which narrative tellings are shaped and how they come into existence. Personal events and institutional discourses blend together in narrative tellings. Without being aware of the distinct ingredients of this mix, narrators perceive the wedding of these two to be personal beliefs shaped according to their own ideas. Adopting institutional discourse as one's own set of beliefs and espousing them in one's narratives is one easy way to accepting one's position in society. Culture circles invite students to engage in problem posing, a process that seeks to investigate which parts of the narrative tellings are portraying institutional discourses, which parts are constructed to fit normative morals, and which parts are geared at understanding what happened (personal events). In circles, participants dialogue and seek to recognize the infiltration of institutional discourse, and challenge its absolute voice. They come to view institutional discourse as one understanding of an issue, an understanding that might actually be curtailing their agency and trapping them in a cycle of low socioeconomic status (SES) and poor working conditions. As for the participants in this study, when they dropped out of school, they believed such things as "women stayed home and helped their mothers" to be the truth. Ultimately, many of them recognized the traditional patriarchal discourse that framed many issues.

Culture circles encourage the problematization of its participants' situations. Communities cannot preserve their unique social identities and worldviews if they are not aware of them. Promoting social justice, therefore, often starts at the cultural awareness level or with conscientization efforts (Freire 1995; Marsiglia 2003). Fostering the appropriation of discourse, the understanding of discourses as framed in a particular way, circles seek to counter the all too common colonization—the maintenance of oppressive structures, such as the ones that keep low SES women in rural areas from being formally schooled. The process seeks to promote dialogue aimed at deconstructing narrative tellings.

Replacing perceived personal beliefs with internal conversation (individually) or dialogue (collectively) allows participants to deconstruct narrative tellings into their basic components, thus identifying the institutional discourses infiltrating their narratives and questioning some previously conceived universal truths, or facts. This process explicitly outlined in circles models the process of internal conversation. Seeking to teach adults how to read, circles also provide participants with tools to engage in critical narrative analysis of their own situations, therefore giving them tools to enact agency at an individual level. Circles foster not only the teaching of reading and writing, but higher order skills, such as problem solving. This process goes from deconstruction to constructivism. From this perspective, language is not representational; it is potentially colonizing. Even the structural, grammatical regularities of language are infinitely manipulated so that their ability to represent is reduced to mere play at best or, ideological confusion at worst. The role of circles and the process it fosters, then, is to uncover this ideological component, so that people will not be taken in by it. The constructivist, building his or her own resistant analysis, rises from the deconstructed ashes generated by the process of problem posing and dialogue.

In the circles, the process of analyzing narratives in the lifeworld (Habermas 1987)—the everyday stories people tell—and deconstructing the different discourses present in these narratives allows participants to deal with real world issues and develop critical meta-awareness (Freire 1970), demystifying the social construction of reality, making social interaction a place for norms to be challenged and changed, and bringing the individually situated deliberations and the person into focus within the context of CNA. In terms of praxis, beyond incorporating a focus on narrative in our own investigative and communicative practices, culture circles have immediate lifeworld implications, built within the lifeworld of its participants and based on an understanding of their unique agency, both individual and collective. This is consistent with an empowering agenda centered in theory and research that is always tied to praxis—an engaged praxis that accounts for the deliberative capacity of all individuals.

One way of envisioning this sort of praxis is the culture circles—in which individuals engage simultaneously with the word and the world. This approach emphasizes that my research is about people who can be encouraged to read and write, making sense of their own world, instead of living in the world that someone else is making sense of on their behalf. Participation in these circles is also internalized, and allows participants to engage in critical meta-awareness, to become individually "conscientized."

The collective nature of the culture circles allows its participants to find the strength needed for self-empowerment as well as to "attain actualised, unique personhood [and] personal responsibility" (Lee 1994: 24). As we've seen through the analysis of the conversational narratives above and supported by additional interview data, the problem-solving component of culture circles led to an increased confidence in the participants' own abilities to embody an agentic stance, feel better about themselves, project more hope into the future, and become more empowered. Problem solving, after all, led to both personal and social change. Through participation in the community of circles, women and men who had been alienated from their culture were encouraged to recognize, scrutinize, and take action regarding their location in society and their oppression (Gutierrez and Lewis 1998). This happened through the steady and recurring action-reflection-action chain of group behaviors, praxis (Freire 1970) involving dialogue and action (Freire 1995). Praxis encompasses the action of participants who recognize issues, describe or label them, and explore ordinary solutions.

Participants link personal problems and political issues (Gutierrez and Lewis 1998). As a group, they start to envision their capacity for change, projecting future endeavors and seeking to promote social justice (Marsiglia and Zorita 1996). Freire's focus was on "textuality, on the text and text analogues for understanding the world; his emphasis upon subjectivity, experience and culture; and, to some extent, his understanding of oppression and the exercise of power" (Peters 1999: 117). Freire intended that people themselves actively engage in listening to and considering other understandings, other perspectives, respecting diversity, questioning the status quo in hopes of change; in hopes of forming a truly democratic citizenship. This is what they are doing today.

REFERENCES

Apple, M., L. Gandin, and A. Hypolito. 2001. "Paulo Freire, 1921–97." In *Fifty Modern Thinkers on Education: From Piaget to the Present Day*, ed. J. Palmer. London: Routledge.

Araújo, V. C. 1991. *Democratização, educação e cidadania: caminho do Governo Arraes*. São Paulo: Cortez.

Azevedo, C., T. Domeneci, M. Amaral, S. Tendler, N. Viana, J. Arbex Jr., et al. 2004. "O golpe de 64." *Caros Amigos Especial* 19.

Bakhtin, M. 1986. *Speech Genres and Other Late Essays*. Austin: University of Texas Press.

Breton, M. 1995. "The Potential for Social Action in Groups." *Social Work in Groups* 18, no. 2/3: 5–13.

Brown, C. 1975. *Literacy in 30 Hours*. London: Readers and Writers Co-op.

Chafe, W. 1980. *The Pear Stories: Cognitive, Cultural, and Linguistic Aspects of Narrative Production*. Norwood, N.J.: Ablex.

Chouliaraki, L., and N. Fairclough. 1999. *Discourse in Late Modernity*. Edinburgh: Edinburgh University Press.

Coben, D. 1998. *Radical Heroes: Gramsci, Freire, and the Politics of Adult Education*. New York: Garland.

Darder, A. 2002. *Reinventing Paulo Freire: A Pedagogy of Love*. Boulder: Westview.

de Castro, J. 1969. *Death in the North-East*. New York: Vintage.

de Figueiredo-Cowen, M., and D. Gastaldo. 1995. *Paulo Freire at the Institute*. London: Institute of Education, University of London.

Elias, J. 1994. *Paulo Freire: Pedagogue of Revolution*. Malibar, Fla.: Krieger.

Fairclough, N. 2003. *Analysing Discourse: Textual Analysis for Social Research*. London: Routledge.

Finger, M., and J. M. Asún. 2001. *Adult Education and the Crossroads*. New York: Palgrave.

Fraser, N. 1997. *Justice Interruptus: Critical Reflections on the "Postsocialist" Condition*. New York: Routledge.

Freire, P. 1959. "Educação e atualidade brasileira." Ph.D. diss., Universidade de Recife, Recife, Brazil.

———. 1970. *Pedagogy of the Oppressed*. New York: Continuum.

———. 1978. *Pedagogy in Process: The Letters to Guinea-Bissau*. New York: Seabury.

———. 1985. *The Politics of Education*. Westport, Conn.: Bergin & Garvin.

———. 1987. "Letter to North-American Teachers." Trans. C. Hunter. In *Freire for the Classroom: A Source Book for Liberatory Teaching*, ed. I. Shor. Portsmouth, N.H.: Heinemann.

———. 1990. *Education for Critical Consciousness*. South Hadley, Mass.: Bergin & Garvey.

———. 1996. *Letters to Cristina*. Trans. D. Macedo. New York & London: Routledge

———. 1998. *Teachers as Cultural Workers: Letters to Those Who Dare Teach*. Oxford: Westview.

———. 2002. *Educação como prática da liberdade*. São Paulo: Paz e Terra.

Freire, P., and D. Macedo. 1996. "A Dialogue: Culture, Language, and Race." In *Breaking Free: The Transformative Power of Critical Pedagogy*, ed. P. Leistyna, A. Woodrum, and S. Sherblom. Cambridge, Mass.: Harvard Educational Review.

Gadotti, M. 1994. *Reading Paulo Freire: His Life and Work*. Albany, N.Y.: SUNY.

Getzel, G. S. 2003. "Group Work and Social Justice: Rhetoric or Action?" In *Social Work with Groups: Social Justice through Personal, Community, and Societal Change*, ed. Association for the Advancement of Social Work with Groups. Binghamton, N.Y.: Haworth.

Gutierrez, L., and E. Lewis. 1998. "A Feminist Perspective on Organizing with Women of Color." In *Community Organizing in a Diverse Society*, 3rd ed., ed. F. Rivera and J. Erlich. Boston: Allyn & Bacon.

Habermas, J. 1987. *The Theory of Communicative Action. Vol. 2, Lifeworld and System: A Critique of Functionalist Reason*. London: Heinemann.

Haddad, S., and M. Freitas. 1991. *Diagnóstico dos estudos e pesquisas*. Brasília: Ministério de Educação e Cultura.

Instituto Paulo Freire, producer; M. Gadotti and A. Antunes, directors. n.d.-a. *Paulo Freire: Coleção grandes educadores*. Motion picture. Available from ATTA Mídia e Educação, Rua Ministro Sinesio Rocha, 209, São Paulo, São Paulo, Brazil.

———. n.d.-b. *Paulo Freire em ação: Alguns retratos*. São Paulo: Cortez Editora & Xerox do Brasil.

Kincheloe, J., S. Steinberg, N. Rodriguez, and R. Chennault. 1998. *White Reign: Deploying Whiteness in America*. New York: St. Martin's.

Koreisha, S. 2004. *Recife*. http://darkwing.uoregon.edu/~sergiok/brasil/recife.html.

Lee, J. A. B. 1994. *The Empowerment Approach to Social Work Practice*. New York: Columbia University Press.

Macedo, D., and A. M. Costa Freire. 1998. "Foreword." In P. Freire, *Teachers as Cultural Workers: Letters to Those Who Dare Teach*. Oxford: Westview.

Marsiglia, F. F. 2003. "Culturally Grounded Approaches to Social Justice through Social Work with Groups." In *Social Work with Groups: Social Justice through Personal, Community, and Societal Change*, ed. Association for the Advancement of Social Work with Groups. Binghamton, N.Y.: Haworth.

Marsiglia, F. F., and P. Zorita. 1996. "Narratives as a Means to Support Latino/a Students in Higher Education." *Reflections* 2, no. 1: 54–62.

McNicoll, P. 2003. "Current Innovations in Social Work with Groups to Address Issues of Social Justice." In *Social Work with Groups: Social Justice through Personal, Community, and Societal Change*, ed. Association for the Advancement of Social Work with Groups. Binghamton, N.Y.: Haworth.

Ochs, E., and L. Capps. 2001. *Living Narrative: Creating Lives in Everyday Storytelling*. Cambridge, Mass.: Harvard University Press.

Ochs, E., R. Smith, and C. Taylor. 1996. "Detective Stories at Dinnertime: Problem Solving through Co-narration." In *Disorderly Discourse: Narrative, Conflict, and Inequality*, ed. C. Briggs. New York: Oxford University Press.

Parmentier, R. 1994. *Signs in Society: Studies in Semiotic Anthropology*. Bloomington: Indiana University Press.

Pelandré, N. 2002. *Ensinar e aprender com Paulo Freire: 40 horas 40 anos depois*. São Paulo: Cortez/Biblioteca Freireana.

Peters, M. 1999. "Freire and Postmodernism." In *Paulo Freire, Politics and Pedagogy: Reflections from Aotearoa–New Zealand*, ed. P. Roberts. Palmerston North, N.Z.: Dunmore.

Rymes, B. 2001. *Conversational Borderlands: Language and Identity in an Alternative Urban High School*. New York: Teachers' College Press.

———. 2003. "Relating the Word to World: Indexicality during Literacy Events." In

Linguistic Anthropology of Education, ed. S. Wortham and B. Rymes. Westport, Conn.: Praeger.

Santos, R. 1999. *Camponeses e democratização no segundo debate agrarista.* www.aces sa.com/gramsci/?page=visualizar&id=100.

Secretaria de Educação e Esportes, Governo do Estado de Pernambuco, producer. 1997. *Círculos de educação e cultura.* Motion picture. Available from TV VIVA, Rua de São Bento, 344, Olinda, Pernambuco, Brazil.

Senge, P. M., N. Cambron-McCabe, T. Lucas, B. Smith, J. Dutton, and A. Kleiner. 2000. *Schools That Learn: A Fifth Discipline Fieldbook for Educators, Parents, and Everyone Who Cares about Education.* New York: Doubleday.

Shapiro, B. Z. 2003. "Social Justice and Social Work with Groups: Fragile—Handle with Care." In *Social Work with Groups: Social Justice through Personal, Community, and Societal Change,* ed. Association for the Advancement of Social Work with Groups. Binghamton, N.Y.: Haworth.

Shor, I. 1990. "Liberation Education: An Interview with Ira Shor." *Language Arts* 67, no. 4: 342–53.

Steiner, S., H. Krank, P. McLaren, and R. Bahruth. 2000. *Freirean Pedagogy, Praxis, and Possibilities: Projects for the New Millennium.* New York: Falmer.

Yamasaki, A., and E. Santos. 1999. "A educação de jovens e adultos no Brasil: Histórico e desafios." In *Cadernos de EJA 2: Educação de jovens e adultos, uma perspective freireana,* ed. A. Yamasaki, E. Santos, L. do Nascimento, and S. Feitosa. São Paulo: IPF—Instituto Paulo Freire.

6

Examining Peripheries of Substantive Democracy in Lithuania from the Point of View of Teachers: Intended and Unintended Outcomes of the Financial Reform in Education

Audra Skukauskaitė

> When independence started, there was no explanation that democracy is not anarchy. And what we have now, we shouldn't call it democracy; it is not a democratic, but an anarchic state. Everyone does as they wish. And it's not surprising that it becomes apparent in school especially strongly.
>
> Now, if you have conscience, if you are a decent citizen, you prepare [for your classes], you do your best, you give your best to all that hard work, but you can also do nothing, joke around, and you will exist just as successfully and will receive the same salary. Both [teachers] will be paid the same— pennies, as a joke. Only one will walk around worrying, will keep planning, thinking of how to make [lessons] better, more interesting. The parents will say—we have a great teacher, the kids will praise the teacher, but you won't be satisfied with this praise for long.

I begin this chapter with an excerpt from an interview with Aldona, an English-as-a-foreign- language (EFL) teacher, who has taught foreign languages (English and Russian) for twenty-five years. Here Aldona expresses her view on the status of Lithuanian democracy and its linkage with schools. To her, the Lithuanian state appears to be more "anarchic" than "democratic" because "everyone does as they wish" and because, apart from one's "conscience," there are no accountability systems. Such accountability measures, as Aldona suggests, need to provide support for good teachers ("decent citizens") as well as ascertain that teachers get paid for the effort and the results of their work, not merely for putting in the hours ("do nothing, joke around").

Moreover, Aldona's choice of words for teachers' work—"juodas darbas" (black/dirty work)—indicates the low status of teaching, insufficient compensation, and devaluing of teachers, who in former times (both Soviet and pre-Soviet) were seen as "rays of light" or "torches of wisdom" (Bartkus 1991; Žilienė 2001). The phrase "juodas darbas" in Lithuanian is typically associated with the work that requires little, if any, education and little creativity, and is marked by low pay and inflexible long hours, similar to work in factories. The salary that teachers are paid Aldona calls a "joke" (salary anyways is a joke—"alga vistiek ant juoko"), reinforcing her view of teachers as doing the "dirty" work—work that is not valued and is laughed at in society. By using the words "tuo gi sotus ilgai nebusi" (you won't be satisfied/satiated with that for too long), Aldona notes that the praise teachers, who put much effort into their work, get from students and parents is not sufficient to sustain them. Her choice of "sotus" here has a double meaning: (1) the praise is not sufficient to help teachers feel valued, and (2) praise does not put food on the table, and thus is not to be seen as a substitute or even complement to salaries.

When taken together, Aldona's choices of words (her *discursive choices*; see Ivanič 1994) about the nature, value, and remuneration of teachers' work and the relationship of these phenomena to the democratic processes of Lithuania's development, point to one of the key conditions of sustainable democratization—that of socioeconomic well-being (Kaldor and Vejvoda 1999). Even though scholars in comparative education argue that economic development alone does not indicate the level of democratization in a state (McGinn 1999), the economic basis, nevertheless, is usually taken into account when examining democracy, whether in particular countries or in cross-country comparisons.

All nine Lithuanian EFL teachers participating in this study[1] on the intended and unintended consequences of Lithuanian educational reforms referred to a range of economic issues that influence their work and participation in educational and societal changes. Among the issues discussed were low salaries, the need for teachers to hold additional jobs to make ends meet, devaluing of teachers, especially as compared with the status of "rich parents," and problems with educational funding. To understand what the socioeconomic basis of teacher's work includes, how it is situated in the larger sociopolitical developments of Lithuania, and how it supports and constrains teachers' participation in educating democratic citizens, in this chapter I analyze Aldona's and other teachers' views and experiences around the reform of funding of schools of general education (Government of the Republic of Lithuania 2000). At first, I present the larger context of Lithuanian democratization processes, followed by analyses of the goals of education and the roles for teachers indicated in the Lithuanian *Concept of Education*. In the latter part of this chapter, I consider the intended outcomes of the Financial Reform of Education and then contrast reform intentions with the views expressed by teachers in ethnographic open-ended interview-conversations. I end the chapter with a discussion of the consequences of the financial and related reforms for teachers, noting how these consequences are embedded in the larger sociocultural and economic factors of the Lithuanian state.

DEMOCRATIZATION IN LITHUANIA: FORMAL AND SUBSTANTIVE DEMOCRACY

In 1990, Lithuania declared its independence from the Soviet Union and a goal to "return to Europe" as a democratic state. Despite Soviet military attempts to regain control and an economic blockade imposed by Russia, Lithuanian independence was soon recognized by the world. The unity and euphoria of the independence movement years (1989–1991) slowly dissipated as the nation was faced with enormous tasks of rebuilding its political, economic, and social systems (Donskis 2002; Girnius 1999; Peck and Mays 2000). Despite the difficulties of the transitional period (Peck 1998; Peck and Mays 2000; Polyzoi, Fullan, and Anchan 2003; Radó 2001), in the last sixteen years, Lithuania has been advancing fast toward its goals of democracy and economic improvement, as indicated by its acceptance into NATO and the European Union (EU) and its consistently improving gross domestic product (GDP) ratings. When formal criteria of democracy are taken into account, Lithuania rates highly in virtually all democracy indexes (Berglund et al. 2001; Haerpfer 2002; Kaldor and Vejvoda 1999; Karatnycky, Motyl, and Schnetzer 2003). According to Freedom House evaluation (Karatnycky et al. 2003; Piasecka 2003), based on democratization and rule-of-law scores (1.88 and 2.63, respectively, on a seven-point scale, with 1 representing the highest and 7 the lowest level of democratic development), Lithuania is considered a "consolidated democracy," along with Poland, Slovenia, Hungary, Slovakia, Estonia, Latvia, and the Czech Republic—eight of the twenty-seven East Central Europe and Eurasia countries represented in the report. Democratization scores are based on scores for electoral process, civil society, independent media, and governance, while rule-of-law scores are based on constitutional, legislative, and judicial framework and corruption assessments. These scores are consistent with more detailed criteria for democracy, outlined by Robert Dahl (1982) and represented in Kaldor and Vejvoda's (1999: 4–5) volume: (1) inclusive citizenship, (2) rule of law, (3) separation of powers, (4) elected power holders, (5) free and fair elections, (6) freedom of expression and alternative sources of information, (7) associational autonomy, and (8) civilian control over the security forces.

Going one step beyond the discussion of the formal democratization criteria, Kaldor and Vejvoda (1999) point out that "democracy, however, is not reducible to institutions, rules and procedures; that is, to its formal aspects. It is a way of life of the individual citizen in the societies born out of modern democratic revolutions" (7). The authors, in examining democracies in Central and Eastern European countries, make an insightful and analytically useful distinction between *formal* and *substantive* democracy. Key to their conceptualization of substantive democracy is an individual citizen's sense of security, ability, and willingness to participate in political decision making and other aspects of democratic life. The authors claim that though it is hard to measure the depths of impact and take-up of democracy by individual people, a focus on substantive democracy, often unexamined by formal surveys, can reveal some features of what democracy looks and sounds like in the lives of people living in those democracies.

In reviewing Lithuania's struggles with developing an active civil society and professional associations, a number of researchers have noted that part of the explanation for the lack of active civic life can be attributed to the economic difficulties (Anderson et al. 2001; Mitter 2001; Peck and Mays 2000; Piasecka 2003) and the demand for people to "concentrate their energies on finding second and third jobs, leaving neither time nor energy for civic activity" (Girnius 1999: 64). This observation is consistent with the results of the ethnographic-interview study presented in this chapter. As will be noted below, all nine teachers participating in the study revealed that in addition to their jobs in the public schools, they had additional tutoring and private teaching jobs—jobs they had to have to make ends meet.

Since the economic aspects of teaching and education became foregrounded in interviews with nine English teachers, in this chapter I use the financial reform of education as an anchor for making visible links between conditions for teaching and substantive democracy. In analyzing teacher discourse and juxtaposing it with the language of education reform documents, I seek to make visible a range of civic, economic, historic and sociocultural factors that play out in the lives, work, experiences, and language of Lithuanian EFL teachers. By examining teacher discourse about educational reforms in general and the reform of educational funding in particular, I unravel ties between educational funding, democratization, and conditions of teachers' work that shape their ability and willingness to participate in democratic processes of the state. The focus on teachers is purposeful because, as implicated in many of the educational reform documents in Lithuania, teachers influence young people's understanding of democracy as well as their ability and willingness to become active citizens of the Lithuanian nation-state and the larger European community. EFL teachers are chosen for this study because, as a number of teachers claimed, knowledge of the English language opens doors to the broader world and expands people's minds to other ways of thinking and living, thus fostering an openness to the "other" (Donskis 2002) needed in pluralistic, increasingly multicultural societies.

In the next section, I discuss the role assigned to education in reshaping Lithuanian society and advancing democracy. By examining the language of the *Concept of Education*, a key document that shapes educational reforms, I make visible how the active role ascribed to teachers both provides and limits teacher opportunities to act as agents of change. This discussion serves two goals: it provides an overview of the overarching goals of Lithuania's educational reforms, and it suggests a possible explanatory framework for understanding why teachers feel devalued and are unable and/or unwilling to participate proactively in educational and societal change processes.

EDUCATION FOR DEMOCRACY: THE *CONCEPT OF EDUCATION* AND THE ROLE OF TEACHERS

Lithuania's secession from the Soviet Union in 1990 and intent to "return to Europe" created a need for reenvisioning Lithuanian education goals as fitting a democratic nation. *The General Concept of Education in Lithuania* was drafted in 1988–1989 by an underground group of educators and other members of the intelligentsia (Kagarlitsky 1990, in Kohli 1992), who were united by a common goal of creating an "ethnic school" autonomous from the Soviet educational system. The *Concept*, which shaped the Law of Education of 1991 but which was itself officially announced only in 1992, stated:

> The historic shift in national development demands a change in the mental climate of the society: a basic comprehension of democratic values, a new political and economic literacy, the maturation of a moral culture. These social changes are possible only if Lithuanian education is radically reformed and given new objectives. Education is a fundamental factor in the development of society, the basis for all social reforms. On the other hand, education can

successfully achieve its goals only when its development surpasses the development of society in general. For this reason, it is essential that education
become a State-supported priority. (Lukšienė et al. 1992: 8)

By designating education as state priority, the government of Lithuania
envisioned education as a venue for advancing democratic principles and
ideals. The main principles of Lithuanian education as stated in the *Concept*
included humanism, democracy, a commitment to Lithuanian culture and
the preservation of its identity and historic continuity, and renewal (Lukšienė et al. 1992: 11). The principles of democracy were defined as "learning of and ability to base one's life on democratic values; the creation and
application of democratic relations in education; the universal access to
education; and the recognition that morality is fundamental to democracy"
(Lukšienė et al. 1992: 11).

The *Concept* also envisioned teachers as active participants in the processes of redesigning Lithuanian education and re-creating the democratic
society:

> The goals of the renewal of Lithuanian education and society will be success-
> fully achieved only with the training of teachers who are able to develop as
> much as possible the inborn physical, mental, and spiritual powers of the stu-
> dent and create conditions for the free expression of individuality and
> improvement of personality. Therefore, it is most important that future teach-
> ers be creative individuals, nurturers of human beings, and not only conveyers
> of objective information. They must be able to base fostering and pedagogical
> interaction on dialogue, tolerance, respect, fairness, insistence on high stan-
> dards, and creativity. Teachers with their value systems and professional com-
> petence determine the nature of institutions, the goals of training, and the
> methods of achieving objectives. Teachers at educational institutions of all lev-
> els and stages must be culturally, morally, civicly, intellectually, pedagogically,
> and scientifically competent. (Lukšienė et al. 1992: 36–37)

Along with the Law of Education, the *Concept* envisioned teachers as willing and able to carry out the goals of the reforms. This paragraph from the
section on teacher training not only identified the role of teachers but also
defined what kinds of teachers Lithuania needed, and what teachers "must"
be able to do—for the learners, learning environment, educational institutions, and the Lithuanian society. It defined what kind of a human being
and, by implication, a citizen, a teacher must be, and emphasized (as in the
last two sentences of the excerpt) that the ways of enacting reform goals
depended on teachers.

The *Concept of Education*, the Law of Education, and other reform documents constructed by policy makers and visionaries of Lithuanian democ-

racy, assumed not only that teachers would be well-informed of the reform goals but also that they would take it upon themselves to carry out those goals and visions. However, as Phillipou, Reed-Danahay, and Whitman discuss in their chapters in this volume, particular assumptions and definitions of democracy, citizen, nation, or educational goals on the part of policymakers do not translate into singular definitions and understandings of everyday people, including teachers, students, and community members, among others. I also argue that teachers do not share the same visions of educational reforms, not only because they do not know the big picture of the reform ideals and goals, but also because the conditions and demands of their everyday lives and teaching are not conducive to active involvement in educational and societal change processes.

Furthermore, as recent research on policy impact indicates, reforms and documents are not simple documents or top-down mandates to be enacted by teachers and schools. Instead, policies are *complex social practices*, written, read, heard, interpreted, resisted, or appropriated by varied actors in varied ways, across social and institutional settings over time (Chrispeels 1997; Dixon et al. 2000; Levinson and Sutton 2001; Stein 2004).

Even though the *Concept of Education* envisioned teachers as active change agents, by marking teacher role as merely enacting educational goals, that same document delimited teacher agency to be creative, respectful, and fair within the framework of the goals defined by the concept. By failing to take into account teachers' views, capacities,[2] and willingness to participate in reform formulation, policymakers limited that same agency with which they were entrusting teachers. These reform documents became "contested cultural resources" (Levinson and Sutton 2001)—differently (re)defined, understood, and experienced by different actors—teachers, administrators, parents, students, and writers of the documents.

In the next section, I examine the reform of general school funding to illustrate what differences occur when knowledge and understanding of reform goals and implementation processes differ. First, I describe the intended outcomes of the reform, as described in the documents, also noting how the reform is situated in the sociohistorical context of Lithuania's development. I then examine teacher understandings and views about this reform, highlighting the unintended consequences of the new funding system. The reform of funding is chosen as the focus for the analysis for two reasons: (1) it directly addresses one of the main issues raised by teachers in interview-conversations—the financial/economic aspects of teachers' work; and (2) this reform, announced in 2000, uncovers the past and the present challenges of educational and societal change and outlines directions for the future.

THE REFORM OF FUNDING OF SCHOOLS OF GENERAL EDUCATION: INTENDED AND UNINTENDED CONSEQUENCES OF THE "STUDENT BASKET"

The Model of Financing Lithuanian Education: Official Intended Outcomes

The Guiding Principles for Reform of Funding of Schools of General Education, a policy approved by the Lithuanian government in October 2000, presents sociohistoric, political, and economic contexts of the Lithuanian educational system. It does so by listing eight "main flaws of the current funding arrangement" (Government of the Republic of Lithuania 2000). By naming the present "flaws," it also indicates developments in the state that have shaped the current situation of education. Among the problems with the system of educational funding that existed for the decade since regaining independence are issues of varied spending in different municipalities, inefficient school network,[3] and the lack of incentives for schools to use allocated funds efficiently. One of the key "flaws of the current funding arrangement" (listed as number 5 in the document), directly addressed by the reform, includes principles of money distribution for each academic year:

> When distributing funds for the teaching plans for a certain academic year among the schools of general education the money is allocated per number of class sets not per number of students. This leads to funding of a large number of vacancies in classes. Schools are not interested in new enrollment because if they accept new students into the existing sets of classes they usually do not get additional funding for education of those students. Municipalities try to limit formation of new sets of classes because even if only a few students add, funding must be allocated as per full class set. (Government of the Republic of Lithuania 2000: 1)

At least three problems with educational funding prior to 2000 are embedded in this one "flaw": funding based on numbers of class sets, not numbers of actual students; vacancies in these class sets and, implicitly, inefficient use of funding; and lack of incentives for schools and municipalities to increase enrollment. The latter issue implies the lack of agency to implement changes or take independent action on the part of schools or municipalities. Together, these three aspects of one flaw also indicate that the design of the reform and its implementation is a top-down process, marked by discursive choices such as "distributing funds," "money is allocated," "schools are not interested," and "do not get additional funding." The only active role is written into the third sentence for municipalities who "try to limit formation of new class sets." However, this active municipality role is seen as negative, one of resisting, instead of taking charge and enacting changes. Though not intended in the document, this interpretation becomes visible when examining how policy is seen as "social practice" and how it affords opportunities for action by various members of the system—one of the aspects that potentially can characterize substantive democracy (Kaldor and Vejvoda 1999).

To rectify flaws of funding such as the one quoted above, the *Guiding principles* list eight objectives (see table 6.1, "Objectives" column) for implementing the changes in funding. Though not explicitly stated, these objectives inscribe a range of democratic principles and thus particular definitions of democracy (Davies 2002; Reed-Danahay, this volume). For

Table 6.1.   Objectives for the Funding Reform

Objectives	Focus
1. Through more efficient use of education funds, to improve the quality of education services and to provide the public with access to such education services that would meet the abilities and needs of the public	Efficient use of funding; quality of education; public access for all; education as service for public
2. To optimise [*sic*] the network of schools of general education and to ensure equal opportunities to rural and urban students regarding their access to quality education	School network; use of funding; equal opportunities; access for all
3. To create conditions for the network of non-governmental schools of general education to develop	School network; choice; equal opportunities
4. To reduce the number of children who do not attend school	Children's right to education; education for all
5. To strengthen the financial independence of schools	Financial independence
6. To create a transparent education funding arrangement	Transparent (and equitable) funding
7. To provide students and their parents with a choice of an institution of education and to ensure the conditions for exercising this choice	Children and parent choice; school network; access to education
8. To increase the responsibility of education managers of all levels for making sure—when shaping the education policy—that implementation of all decisions is supported with realistic financial resources	Responsibility of managers; accountability in shaping policy; efficient and equitable funding

example, equitable funding (objectives 1, 3, 5, 7, and 8), public access to education (objectives 1, 2, 3, 4, and 7), choice and equal opportunities (1, 3, 5, and 7) and accountability of managers and policymakers (5, 6, and 8) can be seen as democratic issues that the financing reform seeks to address. These issues are consistent with both formal and substantive criteria of democratic states, as explicated by researchers cited in the previous section.

In achieving these objectives of the funding reform, the "student basket" (moksleivio krepšelis) is introduced as a new unit of funding at the core of this reform. The *student basket* is defined as "the amount of basic funding for education of a conventional student (a student in normal health attending the eighth grade in an urban school)." The amount of money allotted for each school no longer depends on the number of classes but on the number of students attending that school. This funding innovation directly addresses flaw 5 and becomes an incentive for schools to work at increasing and retaining the number of students attending the school, thus potentially reducing the numbers of children out of school (table 6.1, objective 4). In addition to taking into account the real number of students attending a particular school, the reform includes provisions for monetary adjustments depending on the number of special needs children in the school as well as the type of school, among other factors. This provision directly addresses objectives 1 and 2 (see table 6.1) of serving the needs of the public and can be seen as linked to the 1998 reform on special education and integration of special needs children in regular classes.

The funds from the student basket are designated for direct educating of students and not for capital improvements of schools, salaries of technical staff, or costs of maintaining the "teaching environment" (e.g., heating, building maintenance, student transportation). Among the direct costs to be covered by student baskets are teacher salaries, textbooks, "teacher in-service training, teaching aids, management, school library and pedagogical psychological assistance" (Government of the Republic of Lithuania 2000: 3). As will become visible in the section on the unintended outcomes of this reform, these varied allocations and uses for the "student basket" are, for the most part, unknown by the teachers.

The official expected results of the Reform of Funding of Schools of General Education and the objectives they address are represented in table 6.2. These intended outcomes of the reform seek to ensure transparency of funding, equitable distribution of funds, including timely payment of teacher salaries, and support of the five required days of teacher in-service training, among other direct costs of the "teaching process." However, the intended outcomes do not directly translate into educational practice. The next section presents analyses of teacher discourse about educational reforms to make visible how educational policies become sociocultural

Table 6.2.   Expected Results of the Funding Reform

Article	Expected Results	Objectives Addressed
21	The means for education will be used more efficiently when allocation is based on the same principles.	Transparency (6)
22	Competition of schools will result in better quality of education services.	Quality of services (1, 2)
23	The number of children not attending the school shall decrease, because the schools will be interested in keeping the existing and attracting new students.	Children in schools (4); institution accountability (7, 8)
24	The school community will know how much funding they can expect per year, which enables better planning and organisation [sic] of services.	Transparency (6); accountability (7, 8); quality of services (1, 2)
25	Conditions for operation of nongovernmental schools will be created.	School choice (3)
26	The school network will suit better the needs of students and parents, as well as ensure implementation of the national education standards.	Network (2); quality of services (1, 2)

practices, interpreted and appropriated differently by different actors of the educational system (Levinson and Sutton 2001).

Funding Reform: Teacher Interpretation of the Student Basket as a Unit of Funding

Juxtaposing the language of the funding reform documents with teacher inscriptions of educational changes revealed that only the outcome of "competition of schools" (outcome 22 in table 6.2) and a related outcome of school interest in attracting increased numbers of students (outcome 23) are mentioned by teachers. The positive model of competition inscribed in the intended outcomes of the document analyzed in the previous section was designed to ensure "better quality of education services." However, this official intention turns into a negative unintended outcome when described by teachers. For example, according to Renata, a midcareer teacher, this increased competition for money has resulted in decreased quality of education, especially in schools such as gymnasia—secondary schools designed to provide differentiated education to learners of various abilities and focus on the academically inclined students (Organization for Economic Co-operation and Development [OECD] 2000). Renata commented that gymnasia had to eliminate entrance examinations and accept every student who knocked on the door, equalizing opportunities for all students. However, since equal is not necessarily equitable, such increased interest in the numbers of students, according to Renata, became a factor that limited opportunities for students with different academic abilities and resulted in an unintended outcome of decreasing the quality of education (contrast to objectives 1 and 2 of table 6.1). Renata (and five of the other teachers) claimed that they have seen how such competition for student numbers, when combined with governmental prohibitions to refuse students based on their abilities, has decreased the quality of education and has done a disservice to all, especially the academically inclined and gifted students.

Furthermore, when teachers talked about the "student basket," they saw this reform as one that has not been carefully thought through and thus resulted in "fighting" among and within schools. Though the official documents stated that a portion of the money of the student basket (31.5 litas in 2001)[4] is to be designated for acquisition and renewal of textbooks, only two of the nine teachers knew that this provision had been made in the student basket. All teachers mentioned the lack of funding for textbooks, but either they did not know the provisions of the reform, or, as one teacher indicated, the amount of funding for textbooks per student was not sufficient for covering all textbook costs. Renata mentioned that for example, one Lithuanian-English/English-Lithuanian dictionary cost 99 litas, and thus the 31.5 litas allotted per student for all textbooks was not sufficient to cover the needs of foreign language teachers or their students. Parents often pitched in and/or teachers had to wait for years to receive funding to order new classroom sets and supplementary materials.

Not knowing what the "student basket" entailed, some teachers mentioned fellow teachers and their subjects (e.g., math, Lithuanian language and literature) as the culprits getting all the money, blamed administrators, the ministry, or simply resorted to accepting the perceived fact that there was no money for textbooks. Renata and Aldona (quoted at the beginning of this chapter) were the only two of the nine teachers who indicated that they knew the amount allotted for textbooks. Renata, who had familiarized herself with the student basket reform by finding the documents on the Ministry's website and reading about them in an educational newspaper, described how she approached the school administrators to negotiate that a certain amount of the funds be allotted to the English classes. Together with the administrator and teachers of other subjects, in her secondary school Renata created a more transparent system of textbook money distribution: who got the money, when, and how much was decided on a rotating basis per subject, the frequency of changing textbook editions and student need, among other factors that came into play on a yearly basis. Renata's actions are indicative of the potential for civic action and individual agency even within certain financial and institutional constraints. It is also an example of a checks and balances system built into the different levels and structures of democratic institutions.

However, unlike Renata, seven of the nine teachers did not know about the intentions of the funding reform, the designated purposes of the student basket or methods of basket calculation. Ilona, a young teacher who had been teaching English for four years and tutoring to supplement her small teacher salary, noted that the "baskets came" but the teachers did not know much about those baskets, and, as far as she was concerned, "the baskets have nothing to do with me." An excerpt from her transcript[5] is presented in table 6.3 to indicate how the words Ilona chooses disclose her perspective and reasoning about the student baskets as a unit of the financial reform of education. Both the original Lithuanian transcript and the English translation are represented here for analytic purposes, for English alone would not be sufficient to uncover the nuances of meaning inscribed in Ilona's original Lithuanian discursive choices (Ivanič 1994).

In lines 1–3 of this excerpt, Ilona notes one of the changes associated with the student basket, a change that is indeed indicated as an intended outcome of the funding reform—schools interested in attracting larger numbers of students. However, in naming the student basket, instead of the official word *krepšelis*, Ilona chooses a less commonly used word, *krepšiu-*

Table 6.3. "Student Baskets Have Nothing to Do with Me"

Line	Lithuanian Transcript	English Translation
1	o dabar kai atė-	and now when it came
2	atėjo krepšiukai	the baskets came
3	kai reikia daug mokinių prisirinkti	[schools] must collect lots of students
4	nors mes pavyzdžiui kaip mokytojai	but for example we as teachers
5	aš nežinau	i* don't know
6	aš to krepšiuko	for me that basket
7	man tai visiškai tas pats	for me it's all the same
8	ar jis yra	it exists
9	ar jo nėra	or it doesn't exist
10	mokykla gal gauna daugiau tų kažkokių lėšų	the school maybe receives some kind of funding
11	ten tiem projektam paskirsto	distributes it for some projects
12	aš manau	i think
13	gal kažkokiem remontam ten	maybe for some renovations
14	nežinau	i don't know
15	aš kaip ten	i so to say
16	aš į tokius dalykus nesigilinu	i don't examine all those things
17	nes su manim nesusiję tai	because it has nothing to do with me

*The pronoun *I* is purposely lowercased in this context, as part of the theoretical approach to transcribing (see endnote 5). Only words that are markedly emphasized are capitalized in the transcript.

kai. Even though in Lithuanian both words technically mean the same thing, Ilona's discursive choice of *krepšiukai* stated in plural instead of the official singular form ("mokinio krepšelis") is one instance that signals Ilona's potential unfamiliarity with the reform.

Moreover, in lines 1–2, Ilona uses *atėjo* (came), an active past tense form of the verb *to go* (eiti), treating the "baskets" as animate objects, which influence what others must and can do (schools must find more students (line 3) and distribute money for "some projects" (line 11). She contrasts the agency and actions of the "baskets" with the teachers' lack of knowledge about the baskets (lines 4 and 5), accentuating that it doesn't matter to her whether these baskets exist or not (lines 7–9). The passive, unknowing role of the teacher is further contrasted with the actions afforded by the reform to the school. Similar to active, animate "baskets," the school as a whole, as an institution is personalized, animated, and is the one actor that has some ability to "distribute" money. The word *distribute* in line 11 is an active verb, but its potential for action is delimited by the verb *receive* of line 10. By juxtaposing *receive* and *distribute*, Ilona reveals her understanding that though schools as institutions have more knowledge and ability to act than do teachers who don't know about the baskets, even schools are constrained by what they "receive" from the baskets that "come" without anyone at school having any say about it. Thus, the school and the teachers remain powerless recipients of top-down reforms. *Power*, a term often used ambiguously or contested by many (Bloome et al. 2005), is used here to mean an ability and knowledge to act in relationship with others to influence one's own and others' work, life, and environment. It also alludes to notions of civic participation as used by political scientists and comparative education scholars (Anchan 2003; Anderson et al. 2001; Haerpfer 2002; Kaldor and Vejvoda 1999; Karatnycky et al. 2003).

Ilona's powerlessness, implicated by her repeated statements of not knowing ("I don't know" and her statement that the existence of the basket is of no consequence to her ("it's all the same to me if it exists or not," lines 7–9) is confirmed in the last line of this excerpt. She claims that whatever schools do with the basket, she neither knows nor pays attention nor attempts to "examine those things" (line 16) because "it has nothing to do with me" (line 17). How this powerlessness and lack of knowledge is consequential for her participation in school decision making (and, by extension, civic life in the state), becomes apparent when examining her words about what the baskets do and then contrasting her stance with that of Renata, whose understanding of the baskets and consequential actions were described earlier.

Not only does Ilona use a word (*krepšiukai* instead of *krepšelis*) that is not an official word for the funding reform, but by explaining about what schools can do with the money (lines 10–14), she confirms her lack of knowledge of the reform intentions, positioning herself as a passive recipient. In lines 10–14, Ilona indicates two uses for student basket—projects and school renovation. When the text of the reform document is examined, it becomes clear that even though projects and other extracurricular activities may in fact be funded from the student basket, such use is never explicitly mentioned in the reform documents. The second use Ilona mentions, that of money from the basket being allotted for school renovation, is in direct contradiction with basket purposes outlined in the official documents. Article 13 of the Resolution No. 1520 (Government of the Republic of Lithuania 2001) states that renovation and other "school environment" needs are to be determined by the founder and allocated from municipal budgets, not student basket. Not knowing the intentions of the reform, how much money is in the basket for what purposes, or how the amount of money is determined, Ilona can do nothing to affect any change in her own or other teachers' lives. Her sense of powerlessness and her feeling that the reform has nothing to do with her is in contrast with Renata's ability to implement changes in her school. Renata could act because she sought out opportunities to learn about the reform, whereas Ilona remained powerless because she did not know and thus was attributing the power to the inanimate "baskets" and the policy that instituted them.

How such powerlessness is shaped by and shapes larger educational and societal change processes, is explored in the next section by analyzing Gintarė's and Vilmantė's views about the introduction and implementation of the reform of funding of general education. Gintarė, a teacher of twenty-five years and Vilmantė, who has taught English for eighteen years, tie the student basket reform to the devaluing of teachers occurring in schools and society.

Unintended Outcomes of the Reform: Teacher Powerlessness and Devaluation

In discussing the student basket reform, Gintarė makes an insightful observation about differential values ascribed to students and teachers by the reform: students as "gold" and teachers as "servants." Like other interviewees, Gintarė notes that in the past thirteen years of independence, the young people have become freer and have more opportunities both in school and in the larger society within Lithuania and beyond—a positive outcome of the societal and educational changes. However, she couples that observation with a concern that ties to the reform of educational funding. She claims that in schools she often hears that "a student and parents are in first place because a student is worth gold—the basket." Teachers' status is contrasted with this "gold" student status; a teacher, according to Gintarė, has become a mere "servant, but such a servant at times, that she

becomes totally crucified and unable to have any opinion of her own."
Gintarė attributes such elevated status of students and parents to the money
("gold") associated with the student basket and by implication, the funding
reform of education.

Because the basket money is tied to the student and travels from school
to school as the student moves, Gintarė notes that such a financial arrangement overprivileges students and their parents, while at the same time
devaluing teachers and their work. Even though 80 percent of educational
funding goes to teacher salaries (OECD 2000), the money is not directly
tied to teachers. Even if the *Concept of Education* intends to portray teachers
as crucial actors of the educational system, teachers do not see themselves
in positions where they can affect change or even attract students to their
schools. Because the money of student baskets is tied to the students, teachers see themselves as replaceable commodities, useful as long as they can
"serve" students and their parents (note Gintarė's inscription of "servant"
as well as the official use of the word *services* in tables 6.1 and 6.2).

Moreover, six other teachers noted that this elevated student status has
posed a risk to teachers' sense of safety in schools. Teachers recounted
numerous events when students and their parents threatened them because
of the low grades they gave to students or because students wanted to have
high grades for the assignments they didn't do or did with minimal effort.
They attributed this increased number of undeserved threats and verbal
abuse to the increased student and parent sense of power and decreased
value of the work of teachers. Gintarė and other teachers argued that
because the money came to schools from student and parent choice to
attend that school, administrators were afraid of disagreeing with parents,
and in conflict situations sided with the parents. As noted by Vida, a teacher
of thirty-two years, such financial arrangements have resulted not only in
the devaluing of teachers, but also in teacher fear for their own safety and
security in schools.

An excerpt (table 6.4) from the first interview with Vilmantė, a teacher of
the middle generation, reiterates Gintarė's, Vida's, and other teachers'
observations of the increased rights of students and devaluation of teachers.
In her discursive choices referencing the "student basket," Vilmantė not
only inscribes some of the unintended consequences of the reform but also
offers a plea to policymakers for a more careful process of policy design.
Again the transcript is presented in message units (see endnote 5), but
because of the length of the transcript, message unit breaks are represented
by a slash.[6] Though such transcribing makes reading difficult, it is necessary
to make claims about meanings, purposefully and carefully chosen to be
conveyed through Vilmantė's discursive choices.

In the first section of this transcript (lines 1–9), Vilmantė indicates that
in the last two years (the interview took place in 2003), there has been a

Table 6.4.   Reform Consequences: Positioning Students as "Gold" and Devaluing Teachers

Line	Lithuanian Transcript	English Translation
1	Vilmantė: dar mokiniui/ teisės yra kur kas	Vilmantė: now student/ rights are much
2	di-/ didesnės/ moki-/ ii/ atsirado teisės prieš	more gr-/greater/ stu-/ ii/ it happened two
3	du metus/ kadangi mokin-/ iiii/ moksleivio/	years ago/ because pupi-/ iii / student/ this/
4	ta/ ko-/ kaip tenais/ kerte-/ ne kor-/ korte-/	ca-/ how/ what's that/ bar-/ no ca-/ car-/
5	moksleivio kortelės/ tokios atsirado /	student cards/ appeared/ i* mean/ baskets/
6	reiškia/ krepšeliai/ va/ moksleivių krepšeliai	that's it/ student baskets were
7	atsirado/ ir reiškia jau už tuos krepšelius	implemented/ and for those baskets now
8	kovoja/ ir taip toliau/ ir mokinys / jau yra	there is fighting/ and so on/ and the
9	pastatytas jau/ gan geroj vietoj/	student/ is already positioned/ in a very
		good place/
10	bet mokytojas/ yra/ iiii/ visokiais / būdais	But the teacher/ is/ iiiii/ in all kinds of
11	žeminamas/ už tuos krepšelius/ už tą/ čia/	ways humiliated/ for that/ here/ anyway/
12	mm/ čia vis dėl to/ vistiek/ turi/ turi /	there/ some mechanism/ must/ must/ start
13	suveikti kažkokia mašina/ kad būtų/ uh/ uh/	working/ so that it would be/ uh/ uh/ more
14	atsargiau tai daroma/ ir ta reforma/	carefully done/ and that reform
15	A: uhu/	A: uhu
16	V: jai turi būti pasiruošta/ dabar va/ dirbs	V: and they must get ready for it/ a task
17	darbo grupė/ eksperimentuos/ išeis /	force will work/ will experiment/ it will
18	neišeis/ uh/ čia/ turi būti labai atsargiai	turn out well/ it won't turnout well/ it
19	daroma/ nes čia yra žmonės/ čia yra/ mmm/	must be done very carefully/ because
20	ne/ ne triušiai/ kažkokie bandymo/ o/ o / čia	these are people/ these are/ hmm/ not/ not
	yra žmonės/	some guinea pigs/ but/ but these are
		people/
21	ir pavyzdžiui kiek/ kiek/ žmonių / vien per	and for example how many/ how many/
22	praeitus metus/ aš nesakau/ aš savo	people/ only during last year/ i can't say/ i
23	mokykloj/ sakė padaugėjo/ pedagogu	[speak] only for my school/ they said/ in
24	kolektyvuose/ hmmm/ šitų/ biuletenių	educator communities/ hmmm/ the
25	skaičius/ žmonės neperneša krūvio/	number of illnesses/ has increased/ people
		can't handle the load

*The pronoun *I* is purposely lowercased in this context, as part of the theoretical approach to transcribing. Only words that are markedly emphasized are capitalized in the transcript.

marked increase in the rights of students. She attributes this change to the implementation of student baskets (line 6). However, though Vilmantė does name the core aspect of the funding reform—the student basket—she does not directly indicate that those baskets have anything to do with funding. The way she struggles to name (lines 3–5) and finally identifies the change (lines 5–6) reveals her unfamiliarity with and/or uncertainty about what the change and its objectives are. After identifying the time frame (line 3) and historically positioning the change, Vilmantė attempts to explain the reasons and inscribe causality (the use of word *because—kadangi*) between the increased rights of students and the implementation of student baskets.

Her speech is choppy as she struggles to name the change and offers a range of beginnings for the reform name (cards/*kortelė*, bars/*kertelė*—as in "raising the bar"), all of which she aborts until the "basket" is identified in line 5. Once the change she attributes to increased student rights is identified, the speech gains more fluency and Vilmantė proceeds to name two outcomes of this educational change: "fighting for those baskets" (lines 6–7) and student positioning in a "good place" (lines 8–9).

In lines 10–11, she contrasts student positioning in a "good place" with the humiliation experienced by teachers. Vilmantė does not explicate this contrast but offers a suggestion that policymakers need to be more careful and establish some mechanisms for introducing and implementing new changes (lines 12–14). After the researcher responds, or backchannels (Tannen 1989), with the "uhu" (line 15), expressing her interest and engagement, Vilmantė proceeds with a suggestion that people must get ready for reform implementation (line 16) and that task forces should be established to carefully consider reform outcomes (lines 17–18). In lines 18–20, Vilmantė provides the reason for her call for careful consideration of reform processes and outcomes: reforms are "experimenting" with lives of people, not guinea pigs, and thus carry important consequences and implications. This consequential nature of educational change is highlighted in lines 21–25. She initially starts by naming that consequences were felt in the larger Lithuanian population of teachers (line 21–22), but then backtracks and specifies that she is speaking only about her observations at her school (line 23). However, in lines 24, by choosing the words *educator communities*, Vilmantė infers a population of teachers affected by the reform as broader than her school. She names increased numbers of teacher illnesses as a direct outcome of the overloads associated with implementation of the student basket (and other educational changes, which can be intertextually tied to the financing reform).

Such intended and unintended consequences of educational reforms have been in part summarized in an article in the independent educational weekly *Dialogas*. Elena Tervidytė (2004), chief editor of the paper, in an article on the limitations of individualism in schools includes a section on the "Dark Side of the Basket." Her pointed description of some of the issues resonates with the discourses of teachers participating in this study. Tervidytė claims that one of the positive outcomes brought about by the introduction of student baskets included timely payments of teacher salaries. She attributes this change to direct allocation of basket money for educational needs, thus preventing municipalities from using state money for fixing roads, organizing special events, or other city needs. Introduction of student baskets also encouraged municipalities to take an active part in the politics of optimizing school networks (i.e., contributing to improvements in the density of schools, closures of small schools, reorganization of other schools). However, as Tervidytė states, "no rod has only one end." The "dark side" of the basket resulted in competition, a broad issue to be sure, and she elects to highlight only a couple of aspects of competition—the advantageous position of students and teacher unwillingness to share their expertise:

> Students quickly reacted to the competition created between schools ("Aha, teachers need us . . ."), and gained psychological advantage: teachers cannot choose students, but students can choose teachers. In small towns, groups of students started running from school to school. A teacher pushes harder—I am changing the school; if I don't like it in that school, I will go back. Everyone takes me in because I walk around with a basket of 1500 litai.
>
> In addition, competition among schools practically eliminated any possibility for sharing expertise. . . . If teachers hid their experiences only from teachers from other schools, it might still be bearable, but they also don't share with colleagues at the same school. (3, translation mine)

Though like the nine teachers in my study Tervidytė notes some of the negative unintended consequences of the financing reform, she also outlines some positive changes that have occurred. Her role as the chief editor and her description of both the positive and the negative outcomes indicates her knowledge of the reforms. Unlike Tervidytė, teachers, as represented by Ilona's or Vilmantė's struggles in naming the reform, largely were not familiar with reform documents or reform intentions. Even if the documents are publicly available on the ministry's website, the economic conditions of teachers' lives, combined with their views of their devalued role in society, shape teacher ability and willingness to participate in reform efforts. For example, seven of the teachers in the study had no personal computers, only one had access to the Internet at home, and all had extremely limited or no access to overcrowded (by students) Internet-powered computers at schools. Moreover, eight of the nine teachers held additional jobs (including tutoring and adult EFL courses) because they said their teacher salaries were not sufficient to cover even their basic needs (e.g., apartment utility costs, food, or telephone).

COMPLEXITIES OF EDUCATIONAL CHANGE

As illustrated throughout this chapter, teacher understandings and participation in reforms cannot be analyzed apart from the sociocultural, political, and economic contexts of teachers' lives. In the IEA report on civic education in Lithuania, Zaleskienė (1999) notes that "civic education," and, I would add, all educational changes, "[remain] disadvantaged" by certain obstacles.

Habits of work, thought and behavior developed during the Soviet period remain. Informed understanding of democracy is rare among the public. Citizens have little faith in the Constitution or laws since their implementation is sometimes hampered by administrative bureaucracy, corruption and the inefficiency of institutions of justice. Growing unemployment, declining productivity and an acute decrease in buying power constitute serious economic problems. Even though education is a priority in national policy, state financing of education is insufficient. The activities of those in charge of carrying out educational reform are poorly coordinated, and the functions of different levels of administration (ministry, district and municipality) are not divided clearly enough. It will take competent, responsible and nationally-minded citizens willing to take initiative to realize the transformation into a healthy civil society. (421)

As indicated by Renata's actions of taking up the opportunities to seek out and learn about the student basket and then helping institute changes in her school, potential for civic participation exists in the Lithuanian educational system and the larger society. However, as this chapter demonstrates, actions like Renata's are rare because teachers do not know the visions or mechanisms of the reforms and are unable (or unwilling) to participate due to multiple factors and demands.

Analyses of document language and teacher discourse around the funding reform of education uncovered a range of complex factors embedded in implementing democratic educational changes. Some of the challenges teachers faced in their daily lives and work included the need to hold multiple jobs; a lack of a sense of safety in school; a lack of information about the reforms; limited opportunities, resources, and time to seek out that information; and a feeling of powerlessness. This chapter has uncovered some of the ways in which the democratic mechanisms, envisioned by the *Concept* and the Reform of Funding of General Education, resulted in unintended consequences, partially because the processes of constructing and implementing such reforms were top-down, with limited opportunities for input and action on the parts of the teachers and schools. As argued by Levinson and Sutton (2001) and others who have conceptualized policies as complex sociocultural practices, and as highlighted by Vilmantė (table 6.4), in order for reforms to reach their intended outcomes, policy implementation needs to be considered through the eyes and experiences of people who are affected and can potentially affect those changes (Hargreaves et al. 2001; Lieberman 1995).

The potential for such changes can be seen both in Renata's actions discussed earlier and in a chapter by Landis and Mirseitova (forthcoming), who document how a grassroots movement and sustainable dialogues among educators at all levels in Kazakhstan resulted in a widespread educational reform. They note that in the beginning stages of involving any new

member in the Reading and Writing for Critical Thinking movement, leaders helped the new members understand the underlying philosophy and
goals of the movement. Landis and Mirseitova's chapter and chapters in this
volume, as well as research on policy as social practice and teacher participation in reforms, indicate that actors at all levels of the educational system
need to know the visions, goals, and mechanisms of the reforms in order
to participate in the intended changes effectively. The opportunities for
civic action as well as the challenges of the democratic educational and
societal systems need to be seen as embedded in the larger social, political,
economic, and historical contexts of the nation as well as in the global and
supranational changes. The economic, social, historic, and political and
local-global interrelationships of all kinds, as illustrated throughout this
volume, make a difference in what counts as democracy, citizenship, learning, or educational change to different actors, under a variety of circumstances and with a variety of intended and unintended outcomes and
consequences. In examining these consequences and outcomes, the perspectives of those directly impacted by the policies and changes need to be
examined to understand policy appropriation and to inform further policymaking and implementation at all levels of educational and societal systems.

NOTES

1. The study presented here draws on a program of research that examines
intended and unintended consequences of educational reforms in Lithuania, as
inscribed in qualitative interviews by three generations of teachers (nine teachers,
three per generational group). Teacher discourse is juxtaposed with discourse of two
different types of newspapers and the official reform documents. In juxtaposing
teacher, media, and document language, a larger research program, still in progress,
explores factors that support and constrain educational changes and that shape
teacher opportunities for developing, taking up, or rejecting particular professional,
personal, and civic identities and actions. By interviewing three generations of
teachers whose careers span Soviet, post-Soviet, and independent eras, I examine
how opportunities for learning, actions, and professional and personal development afforded teachers at particular times in society's development shape teacher
capacity for agency and their work with children of a different generation.

2. Though it is beyond the scope of this chapter to review the changes in teacher
training, professional development opportunities, and teacher education reform, it
is important to note that the reform of teacher education, was finally signed by the
outgoing minister of education only in 2005—fifteen years after independence.
Though drafted in the late 1990s, the reform was long contested by universities and
teacher training institutions, which had held the autonomy on teacher training
since Soviet times. Two of the three young teachers participating in this study noted
that their recent teacher training was out of touch with the reality of public schools,

the goals of education reforms, and were guided more by professors' obsolete academic knowledge than by the need to prepare teachers for schools of the twenty-first-century democratic Lithuania and Europe.

3. *School network* refers to the density of schools in the country. During the Soviet times, each village had its own school and city schools were within walking distance for most of the students. All schools housed grades K–12 and were divided into two parts, primary and secondary, though both parts were in the same building. In attempting to restructure the educational system after independence, the Ministry of Education attempted to "optimize school network" by closing down small, financially inefficient schools and bussing children to larger schools. The primary-secondary division was also restructured and a three-tier system of schools appeared: primary (1–4), basic (5–8), and secondary (9–12), the latter of which was further separated into regular secondary schools and gymnasia (with different accreditation and admission criteria). Basic schools, which previously had housed grades 1–12, did not have the right to provide education in grades 9–12, and students had to change schools after grade 8. In many cases, grades 1–4 were also moved into former kindergarten buildings, which became partially empty due to a low birthrate and decreasing enrollment. This restructuring was not well liked

among teachers, students, or parents because it created competition among schools and because children had to move from school to school during the twelve years of schooling (ten grades are compulsory).

4. Currently, 1 litas is about U.S.$2.5. Until 2002, the litas was pegged to a dollar, and the rate was 4:1. Ninety percent of student basket money goes to teacher salaries, substitute teaching, and social security funds. "The average monthly salary of a teacher in 2003 was 1,168 litas while the average wage for the fixed pedagogical norm was 806 litas (18 contact hours per week)" (www.smm.lt/en/edu_reform-.htm, "Resolution on the New Payment System for Teachers").

5. Ilona's and other transcripts analyzed in this chapter were constructed in message unit format. The message units (one unit per line) in Ilona's transcript can be seen as building blocks, like LEGOs, which gradually build a representation of Ilona's perspective about student baskets. Message units, or minimal bursts of speech on the part of the speaker (Green and Wallat 1979 1981), are determined by prosodic, paralinguistic, linguistic, kinesic, and /or proxemic contextualization cues (Gumperz 1982, 1992) that people in interaction use to signal meanings to each other. Representing interview conversations in message units keeps the researcher accountable to the coconstructed discourse. Moreover, unlike block quotes that represent only the main focus of the content, message unit-level transcripts make possible to see not only *what* content is being coconstructed but also *how* the content gets talked into being through the interview interaction (Bloome et al. 2005; Holstein and Gubrium 2003). Message unit-level transcribing, like any transcribing, is a theoretically grounded approach (Green, Dixon, and Franquiz 1997; Ochs 1979). This form of transcribing, presented and analyzed throughout this chapter, is based on anthropologically informed conceptualizations of language and culture (Agar 1994; Bloome et al. 2005; Bloome and Clark 2006). According to Agar (1994), "Language carries with it patterns of seeing, knowing, talking, and acting" (71). Message unit transcripts allow the researcher to investigate those patterns as they are coconstructed in the conversation and are shaped by larger sociocultural contexts.

6. Faulty starts as well as uttered and aborted words are included to make visible the flow of speech. Self-corrections and faulty starts are represented by the hyphen at the end of the unfinished word (e.g., *gr-* or *di-* in Lithuanian, where Vilmantė starts saying "great-" but aborts her first start and after a slight pause utters "greater" [*didesnės*], or *stu-* for student, aborted and soon restarted as "pupil"). The "iii" in the transcript represents Vilmantė's audible beginnings to utter a word that remains unarticulated. These indecipherable but audible sounds are important because they serve as placeholders and indicate that Vilmantė is consciously searching for words (is thinking) that would best describe her meaning.

REFERENCES

Agar, M. 1994. *Language Shock: Understanding the Culture of Conversation*. New York: Quill.

Anchan, J. P. 2003. "Foreword." In *Change Forces in Post-Communist Eastern Europe: Education in Transition*, ed. E. Polyzoi, M. Fullan, and J. P. Anchan. London: Routledge Falmer.

Anderson, R. D., S. M. Fish, S. E. Hanson, and P. G. Roeder. 2001. *Postcommunism and the Theory of Democracy*. Princeton, N.J.: Princeton University Press.

Bartkus, V. 1991. *Mokytojo odiseja: Puslapiai iš dienoraščio apie krašto švietimą ir istorinius įvykius*. Vilnius: Saules Delta.

Berglund, S., F. H. Aarebrot, H. Vogt, and G. Karasimeonov, G. 2001. *Challenges to Democracy: Eastern Europe Ten Years after the Collapse of Communism*. Cheltenham, U.K.: Elgar.

Bloome, D., S. P. Carter, B. M. Christian, S. Otto, and N. Shuart-Faris. 2005. *Discourse Analysis and the Study of Classroom Language and Literacy Events: A Microethnographic Perspective*. Mahwah, N.J.: Erlbaum.

Bloome, D., and C. Clark. 2006. "Discourse-in-Use." In *Handbook of Complementary Methods in Education Research*, ed. J. L. Green, G. Camilli, and P. B. Elmore. Mahwah, N.J.: Erlbaum for AERA.

Chrispeels, J. H. 1997. "Educational Policy Implementation in a Shifting Political Climate: The California Experience." *American Educational Research Journal* 34, no. 3: 453–81.

Dahl, R. 1982. *Dilemmas of Pluralist Democracy*. New Haven, Conn.: Yale University Press.

Davies, L. 2002. "Possibilities and Limits for Democratization in Education." *Comparative Education* 38, no. 3: 251–66.

Dixon, C. N., J. L. Green, B. Yeager, D. Baker, and M. Franquiz. 2000. "'I Used to Know That': What Happens When Reform Gets through the Classroom Door." *Bilingual Education Research Journal* 24, nos. 1 and 2: 113–26.

Donskis, L. 2002. *Identity and Freedom: Mapping Nationalism and Social Criticism in Twentieth-Century Lithuania*. London: Routledge.

Girnius, K. K. 1999. "Democracy in Lithuania." In *Democratization in Central and Eastern Europe*, ed. M. Kaldor and I. Vejvoda. London: Pinter.

Government of the Republic of Lithuania. 2000. *Guiding Principles for Reform of Funding of Schools of General Education*. www.smm.lt/en/edu_reform.htm.

———. 2001. *Resolution Regarding Approval of the Provisions for the Financial Reform in General Education*. No 1520. www.smm.lt/en/edu_reform.htm.

Green, J. L., C. N. Dixon, and M. Franquiz. 1997. "The Myth of an Objective Transcript: Transcribing as a Situated Act." *TESOL Quarterly* 31, no. 1: 172–76.

Green, J. L., and C. Wallat. 1979. "What Is an Instructional Context? An Exploratory Analysis of Conversational Shifts across Time." In *Language, Children and Society: The Effect of Social Factors on Children Learning to Communicate*, ed. O. Garnica and M. King. London: Pergamon.

———. 1981. "Mapping Instructional Conversations—A Sociolinguistic Ethnography." In *Ethnography and Language in Educational Settings*, ed. J. Green and C. Wallat. Norwood, N.J.: Ablex.

Gumperz, J. J. 1982. *Discourse Strategies*. Cambridge: Cambridge University Press.

———. 1992. "Contextualization and Understanding." In *Rethinking Context: Language as an Interactive Phenomenon*, ed. A. Duranti and C. Goodwin. Cambridge: Cambridge University Press.

Haerpfer, C. W. 2002. *Democracy and Enlargement in Post-Communist Europe: The Democratization of the General Public in Fifteen Central and Eastern European Countries 1991–1998*. London: Routledge.

Hargreaves, A., L. Earl, S. Moore, and S. Manning. 2001. *Learning to Change: Teaching beyond Subjects and Standards*. San Francisco: Jossey-Bass.

Holstein, J. A., and J. F. Gubrium. 2003. "Active Interviewing." In *Postmodern Interviewing*, ed. J. F. Gubrium and J. A. Holstein. Thousand Oaks, Calif.: Sage.

Ivanič, R. 1994. "I Is for Interpersonal: Discoursal Construction of Writer Identities and the Teaching of Writing." *Linguistics and Education* 6, no. 1: 3–15.

Kaldor, M., and I. Vejvoda. 1999. "Democratization in Central and East European Countries: An Overview." In *Democratization in Central and Eastern Europe*, ed. M. Kaldor and I. Vejvoda. London: Pinter.

Karatnycky, A., A. Motyl, and A. Schnetzer, eds. 2003. *Nations in Transit 2003: Democratization in East Central Europe and Eurasia*. New York: Freedom House and Rowman & Littlefield.

Kohli, W. 1992. "Reflections of a Critical Theorist in the Soviet Union: Paradoxes and Possibilities in Uncertain Times." *International Journal of Qualitative Studies in Education* 5, no. 1: 29–38.

Landis, D., and S. Mirseitova. Forthcoming. "Confirming Beliefs about Citizenship by Striving for Education Reform in Kazakhstan." In *Winning Hearts and Minds*, ed. E. D. Stevick and B. A. U. Levinson. Stamford, Conn.: Information Age.

Levinson, B. A. U., and M. Sutton. 2001. "Introduction: Policy as/in Practice—A Sociocultural Approach to the Study of Educational Policy." In *Policy as Practice: Toward a Comparative Sociocultural Analysis of Educational Policy*, ed. M. Sutton and B. A. U. Levinson. Westport, Conn.: Ablex.

Lieberman, A., ed. 1995. *The Work of Restructuring Schools*. New York: Teachers College Press.

Lukšienė, M., M. Barkauskaite, G. Dienys, et al., eds. 1992. *General Concept of Education in Lithuania*. Vilnius: Lietuvos Respublikos Kulturos ir Švietimo Ministerijos Leidybos Centras.

McGinn, N. F. 1999. "Education, Democratization, and Globalization: A Challenge for Comparative Education." In *Comparative Perspectives on the Role of Education in Democratization: Part I. Transitional States and States in Transition*, ed. N. F. McGinn and E. H. Epstein. Frankfurt am Main: Lang.

Mitter, W. 2001. "Education for Democratic Citizenship in Central and Eastern Europe in the Mirror of Globalization and Transformation." In *Democratizing Education and Educating Democratic Citizens: International and Historical Perspectives*, ed. L. Limage. New York: Routledge Falmer.

Ochs, E. 1979. "Transcription as Theory." In *Developmental Pragmatics*, ed. E. Ochs and B. B. Schiefflin. New York: Academic.

Organization for Economic Co-operation and Development. 2000. *Reviews of National Policies for Education—Lithuania: Examinators' Report*. www.smm.lt/en/ stofedu/docs/edu_reform/OECD_report.pdf.

Peck, B. T., ed. 1998. *Teaching and Learning in Lithuania: A Challenge for Teachers and School Directors*. Huntington, N.Y.: Nova Science.

Peck, B. T., and A. Mays. 2000. *Challenge and Change in Education: The Experience of the Baltic States in the 1990s*. Huntington, N.Y.: Nova Science.

Piasecka, A. 2003. "Country Reports: Lithuania." In *Nations in Transit 2003*, ed. A. Karatnycky, A. Motyl, and A. Schnetzer. New York: Freedom House and Rowman & Littlefield.

Polyzoi, E., M. Fullan, and J. P. Anchan, eds. 2003. *Change Forces in Post-Communist Eastern Europe: Education in Transition*. London: Routledge Falmer.

Radó, P. 2001. *Švietimas pereinamuoju laikotarpiu: Švietimo politikos kūrimo kryptys vidurio Europos ir Baltijos šalyse*. Trans. I. Jomantiene. Vilnius: Garnelis.

Stein, S. J. 2004. *The Culture of Education Policy*. New York: Teachers College Press.

Tannen, D. 1989. *Talking Voices: Repetition, Dialogue, and Imagery in Conversational Discourse*. Cambridge: Cambridge University Press.

Tervidytė, E. 2004. "Individualizmo spazmai rakina mokyklas." *Dialogas*, March 12, pp. 1, 3.

Zaleskienė, I. 1999. "National Identity and Education for Democracy in Lithuania." In *Civic Education across Countries: Twenty-four National Case Studies from the IEA Civic Education Project*, ed. J. Torney-Purta, J. Schwille, and J.-A. Amadeo. Amsterdam: International Association for the Evaluation of Educational Achievement.

Žilienė, D. O. 2001. *Eglė-amžinas žaliavimas: Apybraižos, analitiniai straipsniai, esė*. Vilnius: Lietuvos Valdorfo Pedagogikos Centras.

7

Developing Citizen Leaders for Democratic Governance in South Africa

Dolores Foley and Mpho Putu

A vibrant civil society is necessary for democracy to flourish. While citizens in mature democracies have many opportunities to absorb and practice democratic principles and norms over the course of their lives, how is civil society created and maintained in countries emerging from long periods of authoritarian rule? Civic education is one clear answer.

Civic education programs are broadly divided between school-based programs and adult civic education. In countries trying to make the transition into a strong democratic structure, it is essential to apply multiple approaches to create the required knowledge base on all levels. This chapter will describe one way that the Institute for Democracy in South Africa (IDASA) seeks to promote active citizenship.

IDASA is an independent not-for-profit organization that has been working to promote a sustainable democracy in South Africa since its founding in 1986. Their original focus was to promote dialogue between groups, to help define legitimate political groups for the elections scheduled for 1994, and to assist in the negotiations for the release of political prisoners. Between 1990 and 1994, the period of transition from apartheid to a democratically elected government, they ran programs to bring together conflicting groups to work together toward building inclusive democratic processes, as well as mass citizen education efforts in voter education and citizens' rights and responsibilities. IDASA has offices and programs that work throughout different sectors and regions in South Africa and the continent. Although IDASA has expanded substantially over the years, the guiding principle has not changed:

> One of IDASA's main tenets of consolidating democracy involves the education of citizens and encouragement of their participation in democratic practices. . . . Rather than a specific set of norms and procedures, democracy is better understood as a principle that informs the development of political institutions, norms and procedures. (www.IDASA.org.za)

IDASA's efforts to promote citizen participation are primarily conducted through the Community and Citizen Empowerment Program. This chapter describes an innovative citizen leadership program more recently developed by IDASA: the Citizen Leadership for Democratic Governance Program. This program focuses on building democracy through developing the capacities of small groups of citizens in selected areas in South Africa. It nurtures citizen-leaders through a multifaceted effort to develop and to utilize their skills in community projects and to link them with mentors, government officials, and other community leaders. The assumption is that an in-depth, experientially structured program is required to create citizen-leaders who can translate democratic knowledge, values and skills into effective and responsible leadership in their communities.

We will begin by sharing the stories of several participants in IDASA. With their cases as a foundation, we will then discuss the history, context, and framework of the leadership program at IDASA. We will then discuss the general impact of IDASA using quotes from a wide range of participants. We will use the stories and narratives from the participants to convey the dynamics of how the program develops the capacities of the participants to be active citizens. The authors worked on gathering the stories from participants and staff in 2004–2005. Mpho Putu is the manager of the Citizen Leadership Unit. Dolores Foley spent three months at IDASA during a sabbatical to research different approaches to promoting civic engagement, deliberation, and action on public issues. She became interested in studying IDASA's approaches through workshops sponsored by the Kettering Foundation that bring participants together from around the world to share their experiences in promoting democratization. Through this research she became convinced that Citizen Leadership is one of the most innovative and successful programs in promoting the development of citizen leaders she has observed.

PARTICIPANT STORIES

Many stories describe how the participants have gone on to have major impact in their communities. The following stories have been obtained through interviews with participants and staff, written reports, and evaluations.

Mary Choma says that she gained confidence and skills through the IDASA training program. She says she "got clarity about human rights, citizenship and the benefits of networking." Mary participated in a training program that brought together participants from towns and communities outside Pretoria, the capital of South Africa. She has been involved in a number of initiatives, but one in particular stands out as a model to the other participants. Mary is an entrepreneur and has tried to make a living by washing cars and selling various products. After being exploited in one project they had started, she and other women saw an opportunity to sell produce outside a mall. South Africa has many markets where individuals come to sell products, and they are known as *informal traders*. They may be along roads or outside malls where there are established vendors. Street vendors are ordinary people, previously and historically disadvantaged community members who may not have the lowest education levels, but who have developed means of surviving by selling fruit and vegetables and other necessary items to earn a living. Due to high levels of unemployment, over the years most of these people have developed some entrepreneurial skills and they are found in many parts of the country. They are mostly operating on the street corners, at bus stops, at taxi stands, and outside train stations—basically where many people are circulating. In Mary's case, she is operating in the urban setting, in the townships, places that were previously reserved for black Africans. Sometimes there are conflicts over space and other matters, and the informal traders often feel they are the most vulnerable and are sometimes exploited. She helped organize other informal traders and the civic association, Denneboom Informal Traders, was created.

The intent was to stay independent and help others make a living. But they constantly faced problems. To address their concerns they had to organize meetings. These meetings, even up to today, are organized in their workplace, which is on the street corners where they sell their products. Their meetings are not as formal as one would think. They are firstly organized and called to meetings by word of mouth; basically no written notices are sent out. There are no proper chairs or sitting arrangements, and the meetings are run in an open field, next to their stock, or products. Issues discussed vary from safety, selling space, problems with the police, municipality, and many more. Members are given an opportunity to raise their concerns, problems, and challenges. Decisions are made democratically through consensus. At times disagreements arise, but the most important element is that people are given an opportunity to participate in discussions.

The association faced many problems, and Mary went to the mayor of the town and others in the community, but to no avail. Mary was frustrated that she couldn't get the mayor or other officials to hear about the problems of informal traders. She was frustrated and was told no one would listen to her. Mary said that there was a time when she thought the government knew all the problems that citizens faced, but through the IDASA program she learned that it is the "responsibility of citizens to communicate their needs and those of their community." So after she was turned down by so many she decided she was going to meet with President Mbeki. She was determined to meet with him. She said that the president needed to know how ordinary people were suffering. She said she was not going to leave until she talked to him. Her persistence paid off. She succeeded: not only did he meet with her, but he also invited her to lunch. "Suddenly doors that were closed were now open," Mary said. He had told her that he could not fix things overnight, but things did improve. It is clear that the story has not only inspired Mary but also inspired others in reminding them that they can have an impact. Many of the other participants repeat the story as symbolic of how community members can make a difference.

Mary has gone on to work with a number of other projects. She appears to have boundless energy and wants to help other women become leaders. She has been involved in a project with domestic workers, and with school children, and she continues to be involved with organizing and training for the informal traders. She said the most important thing she learned through the course was "the realization that citizens should not expect the government to do everything. I am convinced that democracy means taking responsibility and working with the government." She credits IDASA with learning important skills to organize while at the same time recognizing her own limitations and need for more management skills.

Another participant is Nomthi, who went on to work on a number of initiatives. She established a study circle focused on developing personal leadership skills and a manual titled *The Leader in You*, which she and others have used to train other citizens. She credits the citizen leadership program with giving her the skills and capacities to organize citizens. The study circles she organized focused on developing leadership skills with topics such as "Democracy and Leadership," citizen leaders interfacing with government, representing, and motivating people. She and her team integrated this work with another project and they became involved in a local water delivery initiative. She also worked with her team on a water delivery initiative in a community that was constantly running out of water. After presenting the results of their surveys and research, they were promised that they would have running water by the summer of 2005. Nomthi believes that "the course gave me the skills so I could be effective. It's wonderful to work with others and see people taking charge of their own lives." She says the course taught her the "golden rule of organizing," which is to get others to see what they can do for themselves. Nomthi has gone on to establish the

Vukani Community Development Organization. She says Vukani faces many challenges. They lack financial resources, the residents in the area have had little education, and they are often unwilling to challenge local government. She says she is working to help the citizens understand the basic issues of democracy and their rights and responsibilities. Despite the challenges, Nomthi is optimistic and says she gets a lot of support from IDASA and others she has met through the program.

Virginia Mashigo credits the program with giving her the skills and the capacity to expand and improve the Luvuyo Orphanage, which now is able to cater for 220 children (a few years ago they could only serve 80 children). Virginia says one of the training modules has had great impact. Other participants also credit "power mapping" as being critically important in getting them to understand where power lies and how to tap into it. Virginia says she learned how to empower herself and develop leadership skills in other women in her community. Virginia worked with women to provide them with marketable skills, and now she has trained over 250 women in detergent manufacturing, bead making, or flower arranging, and she has motivated them to become leaders in their communities.

Themba Sibeko, one of the founding members of the Congress of South African Students, helped make the country "ungovernable." With a liberated South Africa, he vowed to use his skills to make a difference once he was released from prison. He says, "We must be involved in the government. This government must be accountable to the people." His organization has helped people obtain identity documents, and he runs awareness campaigns that help people understand the laws of the country. He's setting up a business referral and information network.

In December 2004, a group of ten IDASA alumni initiated a "Walk for Democracy." They wanted to mark ten years of democracy by taking a 1,400-kilometer journey to Cape Town. They arrived in Cape Town at the end of January, stopping in towns along the way to meet with students, public officials, and communities. The group formed the Open-up with Democracy Institute to advocate self-empowerment in a democratic country. "We believe that, as South Africans, we cannot sit and wait for government policies to become magic wands and solve the diverse problems we are faced with in our daily lives," explains democracy ambassador Ntebogeng "Tebogo" Kau. The walk "is to signify that democracy is just an idea; it only comes to life when we do it." They hope to build the capacity of citizens through study circles and other efforts to address issues together as partners with a common stake in the community.

These are only a few of the many inspiring stories of the participants of the leadership program that highlight the impact of IDASA. In the following sections we will discuss the history, context, and framework of the leadership program.

BACKGROUND

In 2004, South Africa celebrated ten years of democracy. Momentous changes have occurred since the end of apartheid and the democratic elections of 1994. The feelings of optimism about the promise of democracy and a new system are prevalent throughout the country, but there are also deep concerns and problems. An unemployment rate of 40 percent, HIV/AIDS, a high infant mortality rate, low life expectancy, and high levels of criminal activity continue to plague the country. The system of apartheid left deep scars and a legacy of deep divisions between the wealthy and the poor, educated and educated, skilled and unskilled. Radical reforms have been undertaken in nearly every sector but it will take years to repair the damages wrought. For more than forty years, the country's majority black population suffered under a system of racial separation that fostered white supremacy and denied blacks the right to vote, access to free basic education, and freedom of movement. Under apartheid, South Africa maintained disparate education systems organized along racial lines, with vastly inferior institutions for black students. South Africa is still a country of great contrasts. One travels down modern highways to shopping malls that could be in any developed country. Yet one also passes people living in abject poverty and disease. Fifty percent of South Africa's forty-seven million people live below the poverty line. Blacks make up 75 percent of the population, yet wealthy areas are still mostly white enclaves. The policy statement of the Congress of South African Trade Unions (COSATU) highlights the lack of socioeconomic progress since the end of apartheid:

> In contrast to this political progress, in socio-economic terms the legacy of apartheid remains entrenched and, with the massive loss of jobs in the past decade, even appears to be worsening. Wealth is still concentrated in a white minority. The nature of capital remains largely the same—concentrated in the mining-finance complex, which continue to dominate the commanding heights of the South African economy. Serious inequalities persist, with signs of worsening particularly among the formerly oppressed. The number of people living in poverty is staggering. Almost half of the population lives in poverty, including many of the employed—the "working poor." Unemployment and underemployment are on the rise as more jobs are shed and people rely on survivalist activities to make ends meet. The complex nature of the transition emerged in deeply contradictory government policies. (COSATU policy statement, July 2001)

While the conditions of poverty, unemployment, disease, and crime are daunting, the optimism one hears from citizens about the prospects of democracy and reform are inspiring. South Africa has experienced: a complete overhaul of government services; the creation of a democratic constitution grounded in human rights; and the development of a free press including newspapers, radio stations, and television stations. It is also promising that legislation in just about every domain, from policing and education to local government, will place particular emphasis on the importance of public participation. In fact, it is a constitutional requirement, without which no policy or legislation-making process can advance. Despite this, citizen participation in governance is considered weak in South Africa, from public meetings to voter participation. In 1996, three million fewer people voted than in 1994. In both local government elections, in 1995–1996 and 2000, less than half the electorate participated in elections. As Naidoo (2001) argues, although fewer and fewer people participated in public life compared with the levels of energy in the apartheid era, participation in the public sphere is an "essential to do thing."

Because democracy was believed to herald such broad improvements across society, its failure to meet those expectations has created a significant obstacle to wider participation. People are still trying to make sense of democracy and the links between democracy and economic development. Many promises were made at the end of apartheid about what democracy would bring. Even today, several people still question these relationships. Democracy is not only equated with personal freedom but also economic freedom and justice. Although the country is in its eleventh year of democracy, many still lack basic services. Yet people are patient, optimistic, and hopeful. Many are trying to make ends meet, believing and trusting that things will get better and that it is better now than in the past.

Several reasons are cited for the lack of citizen involvement. Although there was an extensive range of civic associations in black townships during the struggle for democracy, many now point to a crisis of civil society in post apartheid South Africa. South Africa's civil society was the most vibrant during the mass democratic movement in the country. There was a dynamic, broad-based movement of people's organizations ranging from religious organizations, youth and students, professional organizations, trade unions, civic associations, to professional bodies, among others. It was focused on making the townships ungovernable and was characterized by civil disobedience, noncompliance, nonpayment of rent, and violence. It reduced the state to the exercise of repressive violence and ultimately delegitimized the government. These features were necessary in the struggle to end apartheid but not conducive to building a culture of civic obligation, responsibility, and democratic behavior. These associations were critical as agents of the liberation struggle, but it was easier to organize boycotts of council rents than to persuade residents to become responsible citizens (Waldmeir 1994).

South Africa does have a history of civil organizations that many emerging democracies do not. The struggle against apartheid and the resulting growth of organizations were essential to the emergence of civil society as it appears today. However, the dynamics of the struggle necessitated resistance, secrecy, and violence, which often resulted in organizations with inadequate governance structures, a lack of accountability, and a reluctance to cooperate and share information. The dynamics of secrecy, conflict, and violence in these organizations also created difficult challenges for the transition and development of organizations in the postapartheid era. Many civic organizations that once focused on protest and civil disobedience had difficulty finding a role in relation to the new South Africa (Gyimah-Boadi 1996). Also, many of the leaders of the civic organizations left their communities to assume posts in the public and private sectors. The loss of leadership, mission, and international funding in the NGO sector after 1994 further weakened South Africa's civil society. Much of the international funding that supported the NGOs during the struggles, and the phases of voter education and elections, diminished once there was a democratically elected government.

Few would dispute Diamond's statement on the importance of civil society in Africa in promoting democracy: "Civil society has become the cutting edge of the effort to build a viable democratic order" (in Diamond, Linaz, and Lipset 1988: 26). However, as Gerwel (2001) has concluded, the role played by civil society has diminished significantly since democratic change and the lack of capacity in civil society organizations could threaten the success of democratic consolidation. While there is a vocal embrace of democracy, there is also confusion when it comes to people's responsibility and experience with the institutions of direct democracy. Southhall (2003) argues that the "unrealized hopes of participatory democracy have led to growing cynicism and political demobilization, which pose long term dangers to the rooting of democracy in South Africa" (22).

IDASA, along with other NGOs, feared the leadership gap in civil society had the potential to rapidly weaken civil society participation in democratic processes and further perpetuate the divide between elected officials and grassroots communities.

THE RESPONSE

In response to this need, IDASA developed a program geared toward promoting citizen participation through the empowerment and development of community leadership. For more than five years, IDASA has been involved in leadership development programs for civil society organizations. The course aims to strengthen the leadership of local-level civil society organizations, because the local government system requires the active participation of citizens. Through this course, IDASA aims to equip a group of citizen leaders who are able to make positive changes in their communities.

The mission of the program in Citizen Leadership for Democratic Governance is to help strengthen democratic practices by developing local leadership capacity. Courses are designed to build the capacity of citizens to make an impact by equipping a group of citizens with necessary skills. Participants learn community-organizing skills and strategies for both interacting with government and increasing their organizations' impact. They also develop their leadership strengths and the skills needed to develop civic responsibility and leadership in others. Since training modules alone will not do this, the program is designed to be intensive and concentrates on involving a relatively small number of participants over an extended training period. In addition to providing comprehensive training, the program links the participants with mentors and councilors to work on community projects.

The initiative also links the alumni through the Swedish model of study circles and other programs in order that they may continue to work on issues of concern and network with others. Participants are encouraged to initiate study circles in their communities at the conclusion of the training. Several participants have begun multiple study circles in their communities. They found that many others were also willing to participate on issues critical to their community. As Bron (2001) argues, the experience of study circles has shown that citizens learn democracy by allowing participants to make decisions about the content of what they learn. One of the distinctive features of the program is its effort to provide continuing linkages and support to the participants. Participants stay involved through an alumni program where they can share their experiences and learn from each other. Many participants also continue to work with other participants on the community projects that they started as part of the course.

THE FRAMEWORK

Many leadership courses focus on management principles, organizational development and personal development. In contrast, this course, while covering these issues, focuses on developing the political awareness and skills for people from organizations involved in the tough, creative work of community organizing and strengthening democratic principles in their communities. In contrast to earlier mass-based public education strategies, this program represents an intensive investment in a relatively small number of individuals. IDASA believes that the lack of capacity in civil society organizations necessitates an in-depth leadership program and that this will have far greater impact in the long term. The stated goals of the program are as follows:

Goal 1: To strengthen civil society by creating new leadership and strengthening existing leadership within civil society

Goal 2: To strengthen civil society by capacitating leadership trainees to proactively organize the community effectively around important community issues

Goal 3: To strengthen the participative practices of local government by ensuring that civil society actors are well equipped to play a part in a wide range of cooperative governance initiatives at the municipal level

PROGRAM STRUCTURE AND CONTENT

The course entails twenty training days, distributed between four five-day workshops, which take place over a period of four months. Thirty participants are selected for each course. The participants are young and middle-level leaders in the twenty-five to forty age group. They are volunteers and nonprofessionals based in civil society organizations (ward committees, resident associations, civic associations, squatter committees, HIV/AIDS groups, youth groups, women's groups, religious organizations, environmental groups, etc.).

IDASA uses participatory training methodologies, and the course makes extensive use of group work and other experiential learning techniques. The course is residential, and all participants are required to stay at the same venue during training to facilitate the completion of group homework assignments. Between each training block, participants are also expected to complete an assignment. Those who attend the full course and complete all required assignments are awarded a certificate of attendance. Workshops are also held for mentors and for municipal elected councilors. These workshops are intended to help government leaders work more effectively with citizens and to promote understanding and networking opportunities between citizens and government officials.

The work of community organizing is placed within a conceptual framework emphasizing citizens as cocreators of democracy, not simply as voters or protesters. The emphasis on developing the skills critical to active citizenship can be seen in a listing of some of the modules:

• Problem framing
• Deliberation
• Policy analysis
• Interfacing with government

- Community consultation
- Communication skills
- Negotiation and persuasion
- Conflict management
- Consensus building
- Getting and sharing power
- Alliance building
- Facilitating collaboration
- Lobbying and advocacy
- Campaign planning/implementation
- Mobilizing resources

The course is designed to be intense, with participants working at nights outside of programmed activities. The participants develop strong networks that help them with their projects and other community work. Between each training block, participants work in learning communities on projects.

PARTICIPANTS OF THE LEADERSHIP PROGRAM

Many people in the cities have been urbanized and adopted different ways of living than those in the rural areas where traditional culture is still dominant. Cities like Pretoria, the capital of South Africa, are cosmopolitan; people of different backgrounds, both rich and poor, live and share the urban space. People in the cities have been shaped and influenced mostly by the years of struggle for democracy, and the development of democracy has challenged many, young and old, to look at choices and options differently. Differences in the style and level of sophistication are evident in the different areas where the trainings are given. Some of the trainings are given in remote rural areas, while others are in or near urban centers. Of course, whether the setting is rural or urban, many people still grapple with the same issues and challenges in terms of understanding democracy and its principles.

In South Africa, citizens are confronted by the sheer scale and depth of poverty they are trying to address. The need for development and for change is huge, but the resources, opportunities, and ideas at their disposal are extremely limited and not always as useful as one might hope. Great numbers of marginalized people seem to be stuck in a hole, unable to dig themselves out; unable to see what is on offer; unable to see what they can do for themselves, what is possible, or what is their right; unable even to ask.

When this citizen leadership project was developed in 2000, the aim was to develop an active citizen who not only would be engaged with government and would develop both their own communities and their own version of democracy, but also would fill the leadership gap. This gap or vacuum in community leadership was pronounced after the loss of highly capacitated community leaders, who were recruited by the national, provincial, and local governments. There was also the fact that those who took over as leaders were not politically developed to meet the challenges of the newly developed South African democracy. IDASA took on the challenge to help bridge the leadership gap, and to develop a sense of ownership and pride in community members. In its attempt to do so, IDASA partnered with community-based organizations and municipalities to help identify suitable emerging young leaders who could be developed into future leaders.

The twenty days of training, divided into four five-day blocks, was presented to thirty-five participants (twenty-five females and ten males) selected for the training, coming from various community-based organizations or a particular municipality. Participants selected had various levels of experience in community development. Some of the participants had never attended a workshop before the IDASA training. Among the challenges they faced in their organizations was the fact that they were struggling with leadership issues that could assist them in building strong organizations. Many participants were not exposed to this type of information and education except for work-related activities. They found the course demanding and challenging, due to their lack of exposure to, and knowledge of, concepts such as politics, power, and lobbying. Some participants thought the course was irrelevant to them; they did not see how the course could be applicable in their own work environment.

Interestingly, women are at the forefront of most community-based organizations. They are actively organizing and mobilizing against social crimes. Most of them work and have extensive knowledge about issues communities face. Issues of particular concern to them include sexuality, alcohol abuse, HIV and AIDS, family violence and victim support, and local economic development. They acknowledged that they needed simple and workable methods of dealing with all these issues. Even though they struggled with the concepts, through assignments and presentations their confidence level grew; those who appeared shy took up the challenge and appeared to grow a great deal. This was evident during the joint sessions with councilors and later with their mentors. The kinds of questions raised showed that there had been a lot of growth, and participants were able to reflect on what they have learned. Also, during the project report, facilitators observed tremendous growth and development in most participants. In general, most participants benefited from this training. They felt that they gained experience and skills that equipped them to be more outspoken, confident, and proactive in their organizations.

Overall, participants felt that sharing knowledge, ideas, and experiences among the participants was a valuable opportunity for growth. Participants felt more confident to work across ideological and cultural differences, and in public settings characterized by a diversity of views and interests. As one participant described, she was more tolerant and valued others' ideas and experiences: "We came from different backgrounds, and we learned how to understand different views and approaches to dealing with the community."

Interestingly, a couple of participants mentioned that they initially thought it was unnecessary to focus on community organizing. After the course, however, all respondents realized its importance and their gaps in knowledge. As one respondent explained, "At first you look at community organizing, and you think, 'That is something I know.' But when they get into it, they deal with things we are not aware of but deal with daily." Having made trainees aware that more interaction with communities as a community-based organization was important, most participants found the course highly relevant and useful for their work in their respective organizations. Indeed, most participants acknowledged the importance of community organizing and the need to consult with the community. As participants highlighted:

- "One always needs to include all stakeholders and the community in decision making and projects because the end product will be in the hands of the community."
- "I have learned and understood in detail how to organize and public speaking."
- "Most importantly I learned the correct approaches when organizing the community (i.e., that the community organizer must follow the right channels, gathering enough information required for whatever activity)."

Many participants shared that they learned more about democracy and the duties of citizens in public participation, including the need for citizens to be active and involved in issues affecting their communities. They realized that "[they] didn't know everything about democracy—thinking it was only about politicians—but actually includes all of us." Another trainee "realized that as a leader you have to participate."

Participants shared information with the community by attending and participating in local meetings. They were also able to inform community members about their role in local government issues and their responsibilities as citizens, and were able to encourage increased community participation in, for example, Integrated Development Plan (IDP) processes.

For the majority of participants the topic that stood out most was leadership. Some felt that it was helpful to deal with the topic of leadership at the beginning of the course before moving on to issues such as IDPs and governance, as it helped them understand their role and responsibilities as a leader. As one participant shared, "If you don't understand yourself or what type of leader you are, you start approaching people and you end up with problems, you make mistakes you should not have made. So when things are brought into perspective, you understand and you know what you can offer."

In particular, the topic of power was very popular among participants. Participants found the topic of power very informative and learned that power results from hard work and can be beneficial to the community, but that constraints need to be put in place so that power is not abused. Some participants found this part of the course humbling, as they realized how at times they themselves might abuse power: "I think power was the most important topic because at one stage, as a leader, you think you have all the power in the world, but you don't understand where the boundaries are—where you should go and where you should stop." Another said, "As a leader you need to know what your powers are and what the powers of the people you are leading are. You need to know how to respect their power and yours as well, and you need to balance that."

Human rights and democracy were also highlighted as an important topic since "[they considered] it very important to inform the community of their rights and of the constitution because most people think that such matters only belong in Parliament." Other participants mentioned the importance of understanding the duty and role of citizens as one of the most valuable topics in the course.

Participants mentioned that they did not only benefit from the course professionally, but also personally. They felt that they had grown as individuals because of what they had learned, and felt that as a result they were more effective in their work and within their communities. Most participants said that they developed presentation and public speaking skills. One participant describes herself as very shy before but now enjoys public speaking. Another felt unable to speak to his colleagues freely because he lacked confidence but now felt empowered to discuss and share ideas, "through making presentations."

Participants also reported increased confidence in organizing community events, advocacy and lobbying skills, and speaking to senior government officials, illustrated by the following quotes:

- "The training helped me to organize stakeholders and going out to talk to the community. It gave me the confidence to speak to government officials and empowered me to be strong."
- "The course assisted me with presentations and to have confidence so

that people will have confidence in me and think, 'This person knows their story.' Now the community takes me seriously."

One trainee applied the skills to start her own business. She ascribed the success of her business to the skills she learned from the IDASA training, including "how to advocate, and because of the 'spider web' training, we are able to find out who is interested and approach them waiting for any response, whether positive or negative, it is OK."

All mentors except for one believed that the trainees were using their new skills and believed that as a result their organization and their community had benefited. For example, having recently written a proposal for collaborating with other organizations without any assistance, a mentee was able to initiate projects on his own. Another mentioned that his mentee felt knowledgeable enough to start his own organization after the training. Even though this would mean that the organization might lose capacitated staff, most mentors encouraged such enthusiasm. Only one mentor felt his mentee worked only on his strengths and not weaknesses, and chose only the easy tasks.

Leadership trainees believed that their style of leadership changed. As one respondent explained, "I used to be confrontational, but after the course I improved in my leadership quality. I now deal with things in a professional way: I get the facts straight, follow procedures, and don't shout." Another changed from being "an autocrat—I used to tell people what to do and impose things on them. Now I discuss things because I realize that I have to include everyone in decision making." A number mentioned gaining a better understanding of the importance of participatory leadership, "learning that I need participation. It is not a one-man show. I learned about cooperation and now I am able to use those skills."

LINKAGES WITH GOVERNMENT OFFICIALS

Another element of the program is to foster linkages between the community leaders and locally elected councilors. The intent is to help government leaders work more effectively with citizens and to promote understanding and networking opportunities between citizens and government officials. Some leadership participants described as tense the initial meeting with councilors as part of the course. Similarly, a few of the councilors interviewed found it difficult to meet with community leaders at first since both parties had different views and biased perceptions of the other. For example, one councilor thought trainees would be "radical or nasty to us" and that "[the leadership trainees would] believe what the media is saying about corruption and to expect us all to be this way." But any tensions that existed were resolved during the meeting. Trainees seemed to develop an "understanding that being a councilor is hard," and "they gained respect for us." As one respondent described:

> At the start it was difficult because we were working from a different viewpoint. The community leaders believed that councilors are hiding issues, and on our side it was said that people form organizations but when we call them for meetings they don't attend. In the end we realized that information does not always reach them. After engaging with each other, we came to a better understanding.

A number of councilors were also apprehensive before the meeting because they were concerned that they would not be able to answer questions put to them. However, they were able to get back to the participants on questions they could not answer at the time. Another councilor expressed his surprise at the level of interest of community leaders in learning more about government and realized that "[we] got a wake-up call to do our homework to be able to answer their questions."

Despite these initial apprehensions, the interviewed councilors found meeting with community leaders (part of the IDASA training) a very valuable exercise. They were able to discuss mutual problems with community leaders, resulting in a better understanding between the two parties and in some cases a working relationship. Interviewed councilors spoke of the importance of building and maintaining relationships with community leaders. "We learned the importance of continuity, maintaining relationships with people, which helps to get them involved on the ground." Another councilor said it was an opportunity for community leaders and councilors to discuss issues related to council, and in fact found they had a lot in common. Yet another mentioned that community leaders were able to learn more about how the municipality works, and as a result had more realistic expectations in terms of service delivery.

Leadership trainees also believed that the meeting provided the opportunity to initiate dialogue and to clear up misunderstandings on the part of both parties. Some participants even suggested setting more time aside for the meeting with councilors. Participants felt that it had provided a good basis for developing sound relationships with the representatives, as a number of participants reported a better working relationship with their councilors and establishing relationships where none existed before. One of the participants said the manner in which he interacts with the councilor has changed from merely accepting his answers, to questioning, to holding him accountable. The following quotes illustrate this change:

- "I didn't have knowledge of ward committees, I didn't know who to consult but now I am able to identify channels for complaints and communication. I am now able to interact with [councilors] and understand them. I used to think that they are only taking money, now I realize that they need us, too."

- "I am on good terms with my senior councilors because of this course. I have even been nominated to a ward council because of this course."

COMMUNITY PROJECTS

Key to the training is the requirement that participants develop community projects with other participants. Participants had to identify an issue of concern. Out of these issues identified, participants were then divided into groups according to the areas they come from, mostly in their own local municipalities. They then had to develop projects to work on for the two months. This included the work to research an issue, design an appropriate intervention, and to build public awareness on the issue. Some participants initially objected that they couldn't work on an issue that interests them but rather had to work on an issue the group had chosen and about which they knew little or lacked interest. This changed over time with participants becoming so excited about issues that some created new organizations to tackle the issue. The results have been impressive, with participants taking action on issues ranging from crime against women, to alcohol abuse, domestic violence, disabled access, and so forth.

The facilitators of the course report how impressed they are with what participants are able to achieve. Meleney Tembo, one of the trainers, said she is motivated by the development she sees in the participants: "They are empowered to do things they weren't before." They challenged one another to think differently—to see opportunities not just obstacles, to become involved in transforming their communities. She reported that it is inspiring to see how these participants go back to their communities and are able to capture people's imagination; they brought citizens together and encouraged them to take risks. She believes that the vision, energy, and commitment of these community leaders will continue to foster positive changes in their communities.

IMPACT: ACTIVE CITIZENSHIP DEVELOPED

The responses have been overwhelmingly positive from the participants, mentors, and councilors—and the trainers. The benefits of the program are best illustrated through the voices of the participants:

- "Learning advocacy helped me. Now I know how to approach and to talk to government officials if we need them to help us. We make sure

that our foundation is strong and then they want to help us. The training played a big role."

- "I have learned how to be a good organizer—to listen and give feed-
  back and most importantly to implement what I have planned."
- "I see myself as a cocreator working in partnership with government."
- "The course made me realize that I am a very important player in the
  nation."
- "I see myself as a citizen leader that can do more for my community
  and who can now teach others to become good leaders."
- "I have learned that politics does not actually refer to the politicians.
  It simply teaches me that as a leader I have to engage myself in public
  by knowing my community and things happening around it."

ANALYSIS

Ridden and Turner (2001) distinguish between a vision of active citizenship
aimed at developing solidarity and social obligation and not on transforming social and political structures and a conception of active citizenship.
They propose that the most effective initiatives are ones that "emphasize
universal access to resources within nation-states, grass roots participation
in public debates about identity, values and social and political change"
(46). This "thicker" version of citizenship is essential in a vibrant democracy (Putnam 1993). Programs like the citizen leadership program play an
important role in providing the critical thinking, skills, political literacy,
and access to resources that are essential for citizens to be able to participate
fully. The stories from and about the participants demonstrate the value of
the program in creating active citizens.

Earlier programs that focused on democratic education for citizens built
essential awareness of the democratic process in South Africa. They focused
on citizens and reached many citizens, but they did not build citizen leaders. This initiative is creating grass roots leaders who will lead other citizens
in building and sustaining their democracy. As a result of the skill development and interactive nature, the program deepens participants' understandings of how government functions and what role citizens can play in
sustaining governance initiatives. The capacities of emerging leaders can't
be developed only with short training modules. The program in Citizen
Leadership for Democratic Governance has developed an intensive and
integrated program that goes beyond most leadership development
courses. It emphasizes a multiagent approach. Citizen leaders must be well-
informed and learn how to work strategically with government, other organizations, and their communities. The approach is highly participative,
emphasizing interaction with other participants, mentors, councilors, and

communities. Participants leave the program enthusiastic about their abilities to create change. When the course ends, participants are encouraged to continue their involvement through an alumni association and through study circles. Many of the alumni join study circles to continue their learning and to join with others on acting what they have learned. Individuals report their personal transformation, and on their efforts to transform their communities. This program is clearly helping to build social capital one community at a time. As Putnam (1993) concludes in *Making Democracy Work*, "Building Social Capital will not be easy but it is the key to making democracy work" (185). It is our opinion that this program is an effective model for developing active citizens. The challenge in building and sustaining democracy is enormous in South Africa, where democratic ideals and practices are being developed within an environment of extraordinarily high rates of unemployment and crime, and a history of institutional racism and repression. South Africa's success in consolidating democracy may well depend on the development of active citizens and programs such as Citizen Leadership for Democratic Governance.

REFERENCES

Bron, A. 2001. "Learning for Democracy and Citizenship." In *Civil Society, Citzienship and Learning*, ed. A. Bron and M. Schermann. Münster: Lit Verlag.

Community Agency for Social Enquiry. 2004. *Civil Society in South Africa: Opportunities and Challenges in the Transition Process*. Braamfontein, South Africa: Author.

Cooperative for Research and Education (CORE) and the Institute for Democracy in South Africa. 2001. "Two Commas and a Full Stop." *Civicus Index on Civil Society, South Africa Country Report*. Cape Town: Authors.

Diamond, L., J. Linaz, and S. Lipset, eds. 1998. *Democracy in Developing Nations: 2. Africa*. Boulder, Colo.: Rienner.

Gerwel, J. 2001. "The State of Civil Society in South Africa." *In Conversation*. Cape Town: IDASA and Civil Society Initiative.

Gyimah-Boadi, E. 1996. "Civil Society in Africa." *Journal of Democracy* 7, no. 2: 118–31.

Institute for Democracy in South Africa. 2004. *Taking the Lead*. Pretoria: Author.

Naidoo, K. 2001. *Rethinking Governance: The Case of South Africa*. Development Outreach, World Bank Institute, www1.worldbank.org/devoutreach/winter01/.

Putnam, R. 1993. *Making Democracy Work: Civic Traditions in Modern Italy*. Princeton, N.J.: Princeton University Press.

Ridden, J., and B. S. Turner. 2001. "Balancing Universalism and Diversity: Cultural Citizenship, Civil Society, and the Problem of Transformation through Adult Education." *Bochum Studies in International Adult Education* 2: 29–59.

Southhall, R. 2003. "Democracy in Africa: Moving beyond a Difficult Legacy."

Democracy and Governance Research Programme, Occasional Paper 2. Cape Town: HSRC.

Waldmeir, P. 1994. "Is Democracy Achievable in Russia and/or South Africa?" In *South Africa: Twelve Perspectives on the Transition,* ed. H. Kitchen and C. Kitchen. Westport, Conn.: Praeger.

III

STATES FORMING CITIZENS: POLICY AND CULTURAL CONTESTATION

The forms that democratic citizenship education takes emerge from complex webs of power and influence. Policymakers, curriculum specialists, textbook authors, and teachers all employ their own tools and leverage to influence the education that children in their societies receive. These attempts at influence take place against the backdrop of popular culture, which provides yet another set of influences and perspectives. Students in schools draw on these diverse sources and their competing interpretations of societal change to form their own understandings. Very often, curriculum documents and textbooks are themselves the products of political struggles in which different understandings of such sensitive topics as globalization, immigration, and pluralism play out. These political struggles are hardly new or unusual, but they often reflect trends that can be traced back for decades.

American anthropologist Deborah Reed-Danahay draws on her recent fieldwork in France to explore the various educational sites for creating a sense of pan-European citizenship. She looks not only to schools and textbooks—traditional vehicles for creating national citizenship—but to a variety of other means of shaping the new European citizenship, including websites, shopping malls, and a new genre of film. Reed-Danahay suggests that these new means are being employed mainly by political and cultural elites to "invent tradition"—that is, to envision a timeless, unified Europe—but she is skeptical that they will take hold across a broad swath of the French public. For one thing, historically French schools have been particularly successful in creating a nationalist "common sense" (or *doxa*, as Bourdieu calls it). Such nationalist understandings may now serve as a source of resistance to new calls for supranational citizenship. Moreover, as Reed-Danahay shows, the stakes and meanings of European citizenship differ considerably by social class and by citizenship status in the traditional political sense. In the examples she provides, neither long-standing regional farm families nor recent urban immigrants from Africa feel particularly drawn to the promise of European citizenship. In order to meaningfully take hold, then, concepts of European citizenship will need to be cast even more inclusively. This is not just a pedagogical problem. As Reed-Danahay suggests, it is also a political-economic challenge of the highest order.

The U.S. anthropologist Bradley Levinson presents a critical analysis of an ambitious reform of Mexico's secondary-level program for civic education, which began in the late 1990s. The chapter begins with a brief historical review of the Mexican secondary school (*secundaria*) and then moves on to consider the institutional dynamics through which the new program, called *Formacion Cívica y Etica* (FCE), came into being. Levinson highlights the influence of what he identifies as three prevailing societal discourses—the need to recover "lost values," the need for a "critical citizen," and the need for greater "accountability." These discourses influence the thinking of the major actors charged with designing a curriculum and making a plan for implementation. Levinson also highlights the novel ways that this program took shape within the national education ministry. He then presents a thematic analysis of the new published curriculum and study program, which puts heavy emphasis on the development of democratic citizenship skills and habits. At the heart of the program is an emphasis on a "dialogical" and "communicative" pedagogy, which the authors of the FCE program hope will come to permeate the entire school culture. Finally, Levinson draws on interviews with a variety of educational actors to highlight some of the challenges that have been identified for the program's successful implementation. Many of these actors express skepticism about whether the reform can meaningfully take hold. They note that the FCE espouses a progressive democratic ideology and pedagogy but that it lacks a supportive democratic political culture, an appropriate structure of school governance, or adequate training for in-service teachers. Even as Levinson outlines the challenges to successful implementation of the FCE, he also notes that the broader "culture," including the family, the church, and the communications media, must play its part in shaping democratic dispositions beyond the school.

American researcher Doyle Stevick uses a case study of the adoption of a Holocaust remembrance day and the strident resistance it sparked to illuminate some of the obstacles to the civic integration of Estonians and Estonia's large Russian-speaking minority. The emphasis given to the Holocaust is controversial among ethnic Estonians because it singles out the Nazis' racially driven genocide from other devastating crimes, like that of the Soviet occupation of the Baltic states. Many Estonians note that more deaths can be attributed to the Soviets than the Nazis, and they feel that the Soviet Union targeted the Estonian nation for destruction, with devastating consequences. Consequently, they are unwilling to acknowledge any qualitative of quantitative distinction between what they suffered and the Holocaust. While foreigners recognize the types of suffering and mass murder inflicted by the Nazis, their emphasis on the Holocaust is often understood to disparage the victims of Soviet crimes as somehow less important than Nazi victims. Although Germany has officially apologized for Nazi atrocities, Russia never has taken responsibility for Soviet crimes, and Russian-Baltic relations remain strained. Some Russian nationalists have expressed openly their desire to reconquer—or to destroy—the Baltic states. Estonia's small size and feeling of vulnerability made NATO membership seem critical to its future survival, while the United States held out commemoration of the Holocaust as a virtual prerequisite for membership. Cornered into paying lip service to a policy its citizens loathed, the Estonian government formally adopted a Holocaust day that inevitably drew attention to Estonia's suffering at the hands of the Soviets; attention to Soviet crimes, however, complicates the country's need to develop an inclusive civic identity that can include both Estonians and Russian residents of Estonia.

Japanese educational researcher Yoko Motani illuminates how educational policies and practices are influenced by broader sociopolitical changes of wider society through a case study of a progressive educational movement that emerged during the mid-1990s in Japan, global citizenship education. Drawing on various published reports and documents as well as interview data with global citizenship educators, Motani surveys the recent development of global citizenship education and considers its implications for democratic citizenship education in Japan. Motani's analysis reveals that the educational reform ideas actually come from neoliberal/neoconservative business leaders and politicians, whose main interest was to create more cost-effective education by applying free market principles. Their desire to produce more competitive workers and entrepreneurs contrasts with progressive educators' call for independent thinking and better decision-making abilities that can be used to overcome school problems, but their proposals converged nevertheless. Although Japanese society is maturing—evidenced by the growth of civil society—the impact of global citizenship education is limited because more traditional civic education remains marginal.

Finally, Joan DeJaeghere explores how Australia has responded to global changes with a posture of increased openness, as it looks both inward and outward. Australia has achieved positive reform of its citizenship policies. Moving away from its old "White Australia" policy, it increasingly granted rights to Aboriginal citizens just as it welcomed greater immigration from non-European countries. The simultaneous openness to immigrant and Indigenous communities had important implications for citizenship, implications reflected in a turn toward multicultural, intercultural, and Indigenous education. These changes in citizenship, which are occurring in a changing global context, naturally portend reexaminations of citizenship education as well. What meanings does globalization hold for Australian educational policy elites? Is globalization construed as an opportunity, a challenge, or a threat? How do these elites want Australia's future citizens to think about their role in the world and the growing diversity within Australia? Using methodologies rooted in hermeneutic thought to disentangle interwoven threads in the curricula, and applying a conceptual scheme drawn from theories of critical citizenship, DeJaeghere notes the sometimes divergent, sometimes comingled presence of minimal and critical approaches to the three primary areas of emphasis that run throughout Australian citizenship education: the comparative dimension, intercultural dynamics, and global systems. The expansive conceptions of civic education at work in Australia, which include multicultural and environmental education, also institutionalized Indigenous education, which explores how rights and responsibilities of citizenship have been extended to Aboriginal groups in Australia and elsewhere. Previously called Aboriginal education, Indigenous education links closely to constructions of global education both through its attention to cultural diversity and intercultural contact, but also by creating a link between the broader connections of Australian cultures within the world to diverse cultures within Australia.

8

Citizenship Education in the "New Europe": Who Belongs?

Deborah Reed-Danahay

This chapter is about the ways in which the supranational identity of the European citizen is being shaped in contemporary cultural settings in Europe. It is based on multisited ethnographic research in France, as well as a variety of other sources—including online documents published by the European Commission, municipal celebrations of Europe Day, and two feature films that portray images of European citizenship. As we observe the ways in which Europeans are "imagining" a new community of Europe (Anderson 1991) and "inventing" new traditions (Hobsbawm 1992) of European identity practices, it is important not to lose sight of who is benefiting from this and who is being excluded. My focus here is primarily on the role played by social class in the process of Europeanization. Social class is a factor in the exclusion of both impoverished new immigrants to Europe and those "natives" who are in the urban and rural working class. As Balibar (2004) cautions, the "new" Europe is being built around notions of exclusion and inclusion, and this issue must be confronted and explored so that more equitable notions of belonging in Europe may be created.

Children and adults learn about the meanings of citizenship in many ways, and formal education in schools is just one of these. Education for citizenship is a broad process that occurs both inside and outside of formal classroom settings. I argue that we should "de-center"[1] the school in our analyses of civic education if we are to best understand the broader cultural and social meanings and practices that shape how messages about citizenship are transmitted and received in classrooms. Thus, although I will reference some of my own ethnographic work in French classrooms concerning European citizenship,[2] this will not be the major focus of my remarks and analysis. I do not mean to imply that we should not do intensive fieldwork in schools; rather, that work must be placed within the wider social and cultural contexts of schooling, to interrogate other sites of cultural production and meaning that may conflict with or enhance the messages conveyed by and in schools.

Pierre Bourdieu argued that, in modern nation-states, commonsense views of the world are largely constructed and inculcated through educational institutions. In his book *Pascalian Meditations*, Bourdieu (2000) wrote that the aim of these institutions is "to construct the nation as a population endowed with the same categories and therefore the same commonsense" (98). It is in this way, he argued, that what we call "national character" is created—although he cautioned against concepts that would essentialize national character as something primordial or "in the blood." For Bourdieu, national identity was socially constructed through schooling processes. Bourdieu suggested that this is why we feel out of place when visiting a foreign country, even when we have proficient language skills: we do not share the same commonsense understandings of the world. He referred to this commonsense understanding as *doxa*. Schools deliberately attempt to construct shared "commonsense" understandings of the world through both formal and informal citizenship training. Both in and out of schools, the European Union (EU) is currently trying to find ways to instill such "commonsense" understandings associated with a sense of belonging in Europe. So far, these efforts are not entirely successful.

In taking Bourdieu's very brief remarks on this subject a bit further, I suggest, following some of his earlier work on education and social class, that a child's primary experiences outside school (in the family, in the "social milieu") will affect how receptive he or she is to the messages of the school. This is part of Bourdieu and Passeron's (1990; see also Bourdieu 1996) arguments about habitus and cultural capital. We should, therefore, broaden our scope to look at wider cultural models and cultural dialogues regarding citizenship, and at other modes of socialization regarding citizenship that may complement, negate, or compete with those at school.

EUROPE AND CITIZENSHIP

The "new" Europe is a prime location for exploring issues of citizenship today. The EU is trying to instill a sense of belonging and identity connected to Europe as a social unit and to get its inhabitants to see themselves as European citizens. This project is not, however, intended to supplant national identities; rather, it is intended to supplement them with an additional frame of reference. Several programs targeting youth, in particular, have been established by the European Commission (a branch of the EU) in order to promote a European identity and to educate the public about the meanings of European citizenship. In this context, the countries of Western Europe are attempting to reconfigure their long-standing citizenship education programs aimed at national identities in light of EU integration and expansion, whereas many former Soviet bloc countries are inventing or rediscovering democratic citizenship education programs. (See Stevick and Skukauskaite, this volume, for their contributions regarding Estonia and Lithuania, respectively.)

The European Union now has twenty-five member states and is poised to expand further. It has its origins in the immediate period after World War II and marks it anniversary, Europe Day, with the 1950 "Schuman Declaration" that established cooperative agreements on trade and the economy among the first six members—Belgium, Germany, France, Italy, Luxembourg, and the Netherlands. There are currently five major European Institutions, including the European Parliament (a representative body elected directly by all citizens of member countries) and the Council of the European Union (the main decision-making body that has one member from each member state). The primary institution is the European Commission, which conducts and oversees the main work of the EU and is based in Brussels. This is a board that shall never be larger than twenty-seven men and women from the member states, aided by more than twenty-five thousand civil servants. The European Commission drafts laws and then, once passed, sets up committees to oversee their implementation. Among the committees, called Directorate-Generals, is one focusing on Education and Culture. Each committee has programs and agencies within it that interact with national governments and their own agencies.

The issue of European citizenship is complicated by differences among its member states concerning what is the basis for citizenship and what such citizenship entails. The French, British, and German models are frequently contrasted in this context.[3] The tensions and problems associated with this process of expansion have been recently illustrated with the recent failure to ratify a new EU constitution in late May 2005. Each member country was to hold a general vote among its entire electorate and, after the startling news of France's refusal to vote in favor of the constitution and then that of the Netherlands, many subsequent elections were halted, and a "crisis" for Europe was bemoaned by its supporters. Europe is also experiencing a new influx of immigrants (both documented and undocumented) from its former colonies and from the former Soviet bloc, and anxieties about these immigrants have complicated the discourse about EU expansion and free movement across borders for its citizens. Many right-wing political parties in Europe oppose expansion of the EU because of racist and xenophobic fears about these immigrants—fears that they will take away jobs, use up scarce resources in health and social services, or more generally dilute national identities by introducing cultural difference and diversity. While most of the criticism comes from the right, some leftist opponents to globalization also oppose the EU due to its neoliberal economic policies that they fear are undermining social welfare policies, as well as their concerns about the economic impact of some of its policies on local jobs.

This notion of a European citizen is thus both "under construction" and highly contested. And it was only quite recently that the architects of the EU realized that formal education should be a part of this process of the Europeanization. The European Economic Community (EEC) was first established in 1957 with the Treaty of Rome, which did not mention citizenship or education at all. It was not until 1992 and the Maastricht Treaty, establishing the European Union, that citizenship played a major role in the creation (or "invention") of this evolving social formation. The Maastricht Treaty explicitly states that anyone who is a citizen of a member state is a citizen of the EU. This citizenship affords certain rights, such as the right to move freely within and between member state borders and to receive protection from any member's consulate or embassy when traveling outside the EU. It also confers the right to vote in European elections. After the Maastricht Treaty was ratified, the leaders of the EU realized that it needed to promote a European identity through education among youth in order to realize its other goals.

The European Commission's Directorate-General for Education and Culture created the Socrates program, which initiates and manages several educational initiatives from the level of primary schooling to higher education and adult education. Its initial phase lasted from 1995 to 1999, and it has been renewed for a second phase (2000–2006). Socrates is administered through national agencies in the member countries. The stated aims of Socrates are "to strengthen the European dimension of education at all levels; to improve knowledge of European languages; to promote cooperation and mobility throughout education; to encourage innovation in education; and to promote equal opportunities in all sectors of education" (European Commission 2002: 3). Promoting the notion of "active citizenship" in Europe is also part of its charge. An example of the Socrates programs is Children's Identity and Citizenship in Europe (CiCe), through which universities train educators and teachers who will work with children and youth on issues of new European identities. Another is the Comenius program at the elementary school level, which encourages cooperation, exchanges, and collaboration between schools in different member states. While older European nation-states, such as France, created national identities through universal and mandatory schooling and prescribed curricula, the EU must find other ways to create a supranational European identity through the different state school systems, which may be resistant to change. The Socrates program funds educational initiatives that foster a sense of European identity in schools, but such initiatives are not mandatory in any particular member state, and the programs operate through a system of calls for proposals and grants to schools and universities.

The European Commission has recently taken a more aggressive role in attempts to promote belonging in Europe, with a new proposed program called "Citizens for Europe," based on the rationale that "mutual understanding, solidarity and the feeling of belonging to Europe are indeed the building blocks for the involvement of citizens" (Commission of the European Communities 2005: 2). This proposal was submitted to the European Parliament in spring 2005, and the initiative would last from 2007 to 2013. In its proposal, the European Commission explicitly states that, despite its growth,

> the European Union is, however, currently facing a paradox: despite the successes and achievements of the European Union since its creation, European citizens seem to have developed a distance towards the European institutions and to have difficulties identifying themselves within the process of European integration. The low level of participation in the last elections of the European Parliament is a recent illustration. The European Council has recognized on several occasions the need to bring the European Union and its institutions closer to the citizens of the Member States and it has encouraged the Union's institutions to promote citizens' participation in public life and in decision-making. (Commission of the European Communities 2005: 2)

The Commission has recognized that the process of building this sense of European identity and citizenship is difficult and faces many obstacles. The main goal of Citizens for Europe would be to enhance what is being called "active citizenship," which refers to civic participation. It seeks better cooperation among citizens of the EU and more active participation by finding ways to make Europe "more tangible" for its citizens.

WHO BENEFITS? WHO BELONGS?

There are, indeed, gaps and tensions between the ideals of the social engineering associated with attempts to form a European identity (which include numerous educational initiatives) and the degree to which inhabitants of Europe's member states identify with this supranational entity. The goals of forming a European identity include not only those jural rights associated with EU citizenship but also a sense of "belonging," in a less tangible sense, to a unit broader than the nation-state. There is also a gap between awareness of the changes associated with the EU at the supranational level and everyday experience.

The European Union website (http://europa.eu.int) is an attempt to create a virtual "community" in many languages, with a wealth of information on this social, political, and economic unit. Those who access the website will get a sense of their counterparts in different national settings. Although it is still not clear how successful the EU will be in forming a sense of belonging to the "supranation," the website works in similar ways to the newspapers and novels that Anderson (1991) suggests helped create the "imagined community" of the early nation-states. Some of this information is for technocrats working within the EU administration, but much of it is distributed on the website for educational purposes for the "consumers" of the new Europe. One such site is called "Europe in 12 Lessons" (http://europa.eu/int/abc/12lessons/index_en.htm), and it includes a chapter on "A Citizen's Europe." Here, in various languages, a reader can access materials on the advantages of European citizenship. The text begins with a statement recognizing that many people see the EU as a technocracy, but then goes on to explain that it is more than that. One reads that "a sense of being European and being together cannot be manufactured. It can only arise from a shared cultural awareness—which is why Europe now needs to focus its attention not just on economics but also on culture." A bit further on, there is the statement "The idea of a 'citizens' Europe' is very new. Making it a reality will mean, among other things, rallying support for symbols that represent shared European identity." Listed after this are such things as the passport, the European anthem, the flag, and the euro. These are all newly invented "traditions" that Europe is hoping will create emotional and symbolic ties to the EU.

This text and its message convey several basic assumptions that underlie the construction of Europe. One assumption is that a common European identity, most often stated as based in "Christian Europe," is a historical fact, and so there is no need to manufacture this but, rather, to bring something already in existence into greater consciousness among the public. The second assumption is that another aspect of Europe, that of a democratic, citizen's Europe, is a more recent idea, associated with new, shared rights and responsibilities. This aspect of European identity must be enhanced, therefore, through the use of symbols. An important question to ask about this website is, Who reads it? Few Europeans, other than policymakers, bureaucrats, researchers, and educators are even aware of, let alone read, the voluminous websites of the EU.

The website is not, of course, the only venue or outlet for promoting the European agenda. One example of the types of print materials being produced for children (both by the EU and by other groups that support its aims) is a French-language homework assignment booklet prepared for elementary school children. This was published by Generation Europe Foundation, not part of the EU, which is based in Brussels. In this booklet, as with much of the educational material I have seen on Europe for children, there is a mix-and-match approach to European countries: each member state is paired with one flag, one language, one spot on the map of Europe, and so on. Any fundamental cultural or political differences either within or between countries are minimized. On one page of this booklet, the topic is "We Are All Citizens of Europe" and the booklet tells children that to be a national citizen means having certain rights: "freedom (to vote, to study, to travel if we wish . . .)," "to be respected (by the police, the law, government . . .)," and "to have the same rights in a hospital, mass transit, schools, and social security." When you are eighteen, it continues, "you will be a citizen of Europe, and then you can vote for the European Parliament, travel freely in the member nations of Europe with a European passport, study, travel, and live in any European country just like its other inhabitants, appeal to the European Court of Justice if necessary, and create European associations (e.g., for the protection of nature, animals, children, food quality, art)" (Fondation Génération Europe, n.d.: 32). The booklet is part of an informal curriculum for European identity. Rather than being presented as a textbook on civic education, the content is part of the packaging of a typical element in each French schoolchild's backpack (the assignment notebook). While this mode of communication to children about the potential benefits of European citizenship gives them the factual information, the "tangible" understanding of the implications or advantages of this remains remote to many Europeans, whatever their age.

What has been the outcome so far of EU programs and materials aimed at children and youth? Various surveys have been conducted by both the EU and in particular nations to interrogate attitudes toward Europe and European citizenship, and to find out who is positively responding to the messages and who is not. One study, which surveyed middle and high school students in several EU countries, concluded that there was a wide range of orientations toward European, national, and regional identity. The author found, for example, that "in France, the adolescents who are attached to Europe and knowledgeable about it are those who have had many experiences, who think about going to university, and maybe living in another European country, who are from families of high socioeconomic levels" (Tutiaux-Guillon 2000: 42; my translation). In Bourdieu's terms, these youth already have the social capital that permits them to enjoy the benefits of European citizenship. The implication of this is that those who lack such symbolic capital are less apt to see themselves getting actively involved as European citizens. Social class is thus a strong indicator of interest in being "European," and it is among the more educated and urban that this identity is taking hold.

In my own ethnographic research in rural France on EU identity and elementary schooling, I found little active interest in assuming a European sense of belonging among the farm families with whom I conduct research. These farm families, by and large, associate the European Union with restrictive agricultural policies that have changed their practices and given them less autonomy. While some of their children have completed internships abroad (primarily in the U.K.), they have not accepted a "European" identity or sense of citizenship. In contrast, a professor who lives in the nearby city of Clermont-Ferrand proudly announced to me that her daughter was a "European," living and working in the U.K. Social class differences, perhaps also recalling the dichotomy of locals and cosmopolitans (Hannerz 1990; Merton 1957), are being expressed in these newer forms of social and economic mobility. This also recalls Robert Whitman's discussion (this volume) of education on an American Indian reservation, in which the creation of "global citizens" as promoted at school risks threatening the social ties that create a sense of local civic culture.

I think part of this split between the more educated and affluent and the more working-class people I know in France can be effectively explained in terms of the cultural capital model used by Bourdieu and Passeron (1964) to explain different tastes in music among college students. Just when the working-class students had learned to like classical music, they write, the bourgeois students had turned to jazz. Being "European" entails a certain form of cultural and symbolic capital among the upper-middle class in France. If the Auvergnat farmers among whom I have done long-term research for over twenty years start to see an economic or social advantage to being "European" and can acquire the cultural capital to make use of it, I have no doubt that they will eventually promote this among their children.[4] These are people who eventually came to teach their children French at home, rather than Auvergnat (a dialect of the southern *langue d'oc*), when it became evident that this was necessary for the limited educational success they aspired to for their children. I could cite many more examples of their receptiveness to selective changes when these were seen as advantageous (see Reed-Danahay 1996). A more serious issue, however, is that of a divide in Europe between those considered to have rights to claiming European identity and those who do not—that is, between those who already have rights to a national citizenship identity and those who do not. While Auvergnat farm families are unquestionably French citizens in the broadest sense of the term and associated with what is frequently referred to as *"la France profonde,"* many newer immigrants in Europe, considered "other," are the most vulnerable in the creation of this European identity.

There are, therefore, two sides to the growth of a European identity and the privileges associated with it. Those who are of the middle classes and elite sectors of the member nations profit from an unfettered mobility from country to country, new educational and economic opportunities, and forms of social and cultural capital that enable them to take advantage of the "new Europe." At the same time, however, those who are excluded from this, primarily those immigrants who lack any citizenship in the EU or its member states, labor on the margins to support new forms of economic growth and experience profound forms of social and physical suffering.

TWO FILMS/TWO IMAGES OF THE "NEW EUROPE"

Two recent feature films first released in Europe in 2002, *L'Auberge Espagnole* by Cédric Klapisch and *Dirty Pretty Things* by Stephen Frears, display opposite images of European citizenship. The first is an optimistic movie about possibilities and inclusion; the second, a cautionary story of exclusion. *L'Auberge Espagnole* presents a lighthearted view of the youth of Europe and the new freedoms they will enjoy as citizens of Europe. This film, made in France but as part of a European collaboration with Spain, is about the new mobile and multilingual European bourgeoisie. It concerns a group of students in the European-funded educational program for higher education called Erasmus, which is part of the larger Socrates program of the European Commission. This is a successful program, which has grown significantly since it began in the late 1990s. Erasmus encourages transnational mobility for students and teachers, who spend three to twelve months studying in one of the thirty countries participating in the program. Spain and France are the two most popular destinations and also send the most students abroad. The Erasmus program fosters these exchanges in education primarily to create a mobile workforce with transferable university credentials in a new, neoliberal Europe. Equally important, however, is the wider goal of instilling a sense of "belonging" to the supranational unit of Europe.

The protagonist of *L'Auberge Espanole* is a likeable young Frenchman named Xavier. We see him apply for the Erasmus program in France at the beginning of the film and, leaving his girlfriend behind, taking off for a year of study in Barcelona. Barcelona represents a site of the New Europe—a city with strong regionalist sensibilities where Catalan is spoken along with Spanish. The EU encourages regional languages and diversity in many of its programs, and so the regionalism of Barcelona and its Catalan speakers is not inconsistent with the growth of the EU.[5] Homogeneity or uniformity of culture, central historically to the development of such nation-states as France, is not part of the EU program of citizenship. The film displays this confluence of regionalism and supranationalism that, as I have written about in a previous essay (Reed-Danahay 2003), eclipses the nation-state.

The household Xavier and his fellow students create is a multicultural "salad bowl" of different nationalities. An *auberge* is a place of warmth and shelter, literally meaning "inn," and *l'auberge de jeunesse* is also the French term for "youth hostel." The English translation of this film in American distribution, however, is *The Spanish Apartment,* while the more common title in other English-speaking nations is *Europudding.* These students are transients in their Barcelona setting, but their mobility is one of privilege, the same type associated with tourism. Their place in Europe is secure in that they are the middle-class, educated elite who will help shape the new EU. The apartment residents in the movie playfully display stereotypical national personality characteristics. There are seven students in the apartment from seven different countries, including the somewhat uptight German student, the gregarious and naive English girl with a loutish brother who comes to visit, and a free-spirited lesbian from Belgium, among others. The movie focuses on their adjustments to living in Spain and to living with each other and dealing with their cultural and linguistic differences. The students' national identities are portrayed as personality quirks rather than fundamental differences that create unbridgeable gaps between them. No visible class differences are apparent.

The movie is also a coming of age story for Xavier, who has recently graduated from college and is experiencing a transitional postgraduate year of study abroad. He has an affair with a married Frenchwoman who is also living in Barcelona, having accompanied her businessman husband, and who teaches him a few tricks of romance and seduction. Through his experiences in Barcelona, Xavier learns how to be "European" and not just French. He struggles with his French girlfriend left at home, who is anxious about his departure and absence. She represents the France he left behind—like her, attractive and beautiful, but also too constraining in a way. Xavier's attraction to a married woman who is also like him, separated from her native France and living in Barcelona on a temporary basis, symbolizes their shared experience of rootlessness. Over the course of the film, Xavier is, little by little, "liberated" through his European experience. When he returns to France to assume a boring office job in finance arranged by his father (the main reason for his training in Barcelona), he rejects it, having somehow found a more authentic "self" through his travels and experiences abroad. His true love of writing prevails, and he is thus prompted to record this story, so that the film is presented as a dramatization of Xavier's Bildungsroman.

Whereas *L'Auberge Espanole* portrays the upper-middle-class experience of Europe, one of personal growth and shared experiences with those in the same situation from other nations, *Dirty Pretty Things* is about the shared experiences of the underclass of Europe. It tells a darker story—that of a group of (mostly) illegal immigrants who work at a hotel in London, a sort of "non-place," in Augé's (1995) terms. According to Augé, non-places are artifacts of supermodernity. They are transitory locations, where people pass through with other strangers also passing through, such as supermarkets and airports, where a sense of belonging is not possible or even imaginable.

While the Spanish apartment had a cozy connotation, even though it was also a temporary home for its inhabitants, the non-place of the hotel in *Dirty Pretty Things* holds a very different meaning for its workers. For them, it is a place of underground, unspeakable horrors and the exploitation of vulnerable people in this New Europe. This film provides a bleak view of noncitizens who are desperately trying to avoid immigration officers and earn a living while suffering the whims of employers who commit both symbolic and real violence upon them. For the most part, these are people from Turkey, the former Soviet bloc, and the former colonies of the British Empire.

The protagonist of this movie, Okwe, is, like Xavier, presented as a likeable person, although he is about a decade older than Xavier. He is a Nigerian exile living illegally in the U.K. and working two jobs—one as a night clerk at the hotel and the other, his day job, as a taxi driver. He stays awake by chewing a powerful herb that he acquires at a street market in the city. He was a medical doctor at home but had to flee due to political pressures, leaving his orphaned daughter behind. Okwe struggles to evade the immigration officials and to hold down his two jobs. He befriends a maid at the hotel, a young Turkish woman named Senay who is an asylum seeker and not officially permitted to work. Senay lets Okwe keep his things at her apartment and to catch a few hours of sleep between his shifts and before she returns from her night shift at the hotel. Okwe also has other friends among a variety of immigrants in the community, who offer an underground system of mutual aid to each other—including his Chinese friend who works at a hospital morgue and helps him get access to medications for others in need.

Along the way, Okwe discovers that the manager of the hotel, a Spaniard, is trafficking in human organs. The illegal immigrants who work at the hotel help bring contacts to him of people so desperate for forged identity documents that they are willing to sell body parts. This trafficking in body parts makes the symbolism of the "body politic" quite lucid in the movie.[6] Here we see the underbelly of the problems facing Europe today—an influx of undocumented immigrants who are all but invisible to the general public. In fact there is a line in the movie, toward the end, when a middleman in the organ trade says to Okwe and some of his friends, "How come I've never seen you before?" and Okwe responds, "Because we are the people you never see."

Okwe and Senay eventually outsmart the system in which they are exploited and escape from England. Their goal is not to become European or British citizens, however, but to leave for a better life—she to join a cousin in America, and he to rejoin his daughter in Nigeria. This film illustrates what Balibar (2004) labels the "new apartheid" in Europe, whereby those with full citizenship in a member nation can travel freely and enjoy the rights and privileges of European citizenship, while many new immigrants from the margins are excluded from this system. Whereas mobility and the right to work and travel throughout Europe are the cornerstones of European citizenship, the immigrants in *Dirty Pretty Things* are, unlike the students in *L'Auberge Espanole*, prohibited from free movement. Some are forced to sell their own organs (or, literally, lose part of themselves) in order to obtain the paperwork that would permit them to travel. In one scene of the film, in which Okwe helps a very sick African man who has sold his kidney, a female member of the family proclaims, "He is English now," to which Okwe responds, "He swapped his insides for a passport."

By juxtaposing these two films, we can see that they both address cultural anxieties in a neoliberal Europe of shifting identities, economic globalization, and geographic mobility. Whereas Okwe will flee the diaspora of London and return to his native Nigeria, both rejecting and rejected by Britain, Xavier will return to a France that is, for him, increasingly "European," and he will bring with him a newfound sense of his own entitlement in this new social order. For one man, Europe is a place of inclusion and opportunity; for the other, one of exclusion. "Not to worry," seems to be the message of *L'Auberge Espagnole* to those parents and students who wonder how various Europeans, not long ago at war with each other, can set a common course and "get along" with each other. Immigrants and "others" (those portrayed in *Dirty Pretty Things*) are banished from this idyllic setting, in which the children of the elite come together in a shared understanding.

Both of these films were major feature films released to broad viewing across their own countries as well as globally. Each is now available widely on DVD in various languages. These films received good reviews in their own countries and were made by popular filmmakers who previously had successful films. It is significant that *Dirty Pretty Things* was made in England, rather than France. Britain has been much more open to accepting its multicultural population (especially in terms of educational programs targeted at them) than has France, whose Republican model of citizenship historically has occluded cultural or linguistic differences. France is very much a nation of immigrants, but has only recently recognized this aspect of its national identity. In 1999, 7.4 percent of the population was composed of immigrants, and many immigrants in France have become incorporated into the citizenry from nations such as Portugal and Italy, as well as from Eastern Europe and North Africa.[7]

One final observation about these films is that they share a French actress, Audrey Tautou—who plays Senay in *Dirty Pretty Things* and Xavier's girlfriend in *L'Auberge Espanole*. This underscores, in a way, the transnational privileges of the elite. As an actress, Tautou has the privilege of, and desire for, free travel and mobility not enjoyed by either of her characters (Senay because she is denied this; the French girlfriend, because she is not sufficiently cosmopolitan). Moreover, that a French actress should portray a Turkish asylum seeker is also symbolic of the postcolonial legacies facing Europe today.

ETHNOGRAPHIC PERSPECTIVES FROM FRANCE: EUROPE DAY AND OTHER OBSERVATIONS

While films, such as the two discussed here, deploy various emotional and symbolic meanings to attract viewers and at the same time imagine contemporary settings of Europe, other contexts for the promotion of ideas about Europe are more consciously developed by the European Union itself as well as by political actors at the local level. One of these is Europe Day, a tradition that was established at the 1985 Milan Summit of EU leaders. Celebrated on May 9, it marks the date in 1950 when then–French foreign minister Robert Schuman declared the creation of the European Coal and Steel Commission, ancestor to the EU. The striking thing about Europe Day is that it was marked by its absence from the classrooms that I study in a rural region of central France, despite the existence there of some projects funded by the EU, which I have discussed elsewhere (Reed-Danahay 2003). It is not part of the formal curriculum in French elementary schools, and would have to be introduced by a teacher specifically. At the local level, some group or groups must take the initiative to organize events surrounding this day.

I was in France for two Europe Days, 2001 and 2002. In Clermont-Ferrand, the closest city to my fieldwork sites, Europe Days (in the plural) 2001 were celebrated by a series of events lasting from a Wednesday through to a Saturday, beginning on May 9. The theme that year was "To Live Europe and to Make Europe Live Locally" (*Vivre et Faire Vivre l'Europe Localement*). There were some conferences and debates scheduled at various venues in the city, and a Finnish chorus was invited to perform for two nights. In an indoor shopping mall, Centre Jaude, various information tables were set up around the halls outside of the shops by groups that were interested in promoting Europe or tying their own association into a European theme.

Like the EU itself, Europe Day is politicized in France, where there are mixed feelings about Europe among both the left and the right. Most of its support comes from political centrists who align themselves with neoliberalism, although they, in turn, differ on what Europe should look like and about what sorts of social and economic programs it should promote. While Clermont-Ferrand is itself a left-voting city, due to the presence of a strong worker population at the Michelin tire plant, the region is mostly center-right in voting patterns. Valéry Giscard d'Estaing, the former president of France, hails from this region and currently represents it in the European Parliament, and he is a strong supporter of Europe. At the 2001 event, there was a table about the euro, still to be adopted at that time, with informational packets for children and chocolate covered euros wrapped in gold foil. There was a table about economic development in the region funded by the European Union, a table organized by a teacher group that supports Europe and European education, and a table staffed by amateur ham radio operators. There were speeches by local politicians and officials and a *vin d'honneur* (or toast) in front of the French equivalent of a chain cafeteria in the mall. From what I gathered by newspaper coverage elsewhere, this event in Clermont-Ferrand was a fairly modest performance of European identity compared with that in some cities, whose mayors staged parades and more ostentatious displays of support for Europe. Most of the shoppers in the mall were oblivious to the meaning of the event, and went about their shopping and other errands without stopping at the tables, while my informants in the countryside claimed to have never heard of Europe Day when I mentioned having attended the events.

There is obviously a chasm between those who are and are not actively participating in this construction of Europe. For my dairy farming informants, Europe represents harsh economic controls that they perceive to be destroying their livelihood, and they are unsure of what it represents otherwise. Nevertheless, they receive satellite television programs from across Europe, and their children participate in a popular youth culture that crosses European boundaries. With or without their consent or conscious knowledge, "Europe" is seeping into their consciousness and their identity.

Still, European citizenship education is only slowly being overtly incorporated into French elementary classrooms. France is a nation that has used its centralized educational system in order to promote concepts of French citizenship. Primary schools were, historically, the major vehicle for promoting this national identity. Citizenship education was historically part of what was called "moral education"—a concept dear to the heart of the sociologist Emile Durkheim, who wrote a book with that title and influenced turn-of-the-century educational reforms. Today, it is in French middle schools that civic education and citizenship are most promoted, and it is there that concepts of European citizenship are being introduced, primarily in the context of discussions of rights and duties (Osler and Starkey 2001; Tutiaux-Guillon 2000). Since my own observations have been in elementary schools, I cannot comment on the implementation of these curricula. However, in my observations in two rural French elementary schools in central France, I noticed that despite the absence of a formal civics curriculum in primary schools, one can still see evidence of what is called the "European dimension" at work in these schools. Even though France does not introduce Europe formally until the middle school level, elementary school students are exposed to it through geography lessons.

In comparing older and newer textbooks stored in these classrooms, I observed that there is a shift in the geographic mapping of France and Europe. This is seen in geography texts (geography is part of the elementary school curriculum) in particular. France is increasingly shown on a map of Europe, whereas earlier texts (before the 1990s) did not place it in this context and provided disembodied maps of France standing alone in space. Another sign is in the common pedagogical approach in early primary schooling in France, which has been to go from the local to the global. In the French school curriculum, the idea is to show the child how he or she is part of a local community, a region, and a nation. Teachers start with the local community and then expand out in subsequent years of schooling. Europe has begun to appear as yet another level or layer of identity in this approach. Therefore, even though France lacks an "official" curriculum at the elementary level aimed at teaching Europe, the overall content of schooling is encouraging this through these types of approach to geography.

Europe Day is just one among many means for educating the general public about European identity and citizenship. I have studied several of these as I try to survey the terrain of the spread of these notions. There are numerous publications and brochures (including comic books) aimed at children as well as their parents. There are educational websites on Europe, such as the European schoolnet, aimed at both teachers and students. There are centers throughout France that inform people of the economic programs funded by the EU. A large European site at the commercial center La Defense in Paris, called Sources d'Europe, includes a library for scholarly research, a bookstore and gift shop, and a room with dozens of free brochures (including posters) on various aspects of the EU for the public to take. This infocenter also includes a European "classroom" (literally called a "route of discovery") where school groups may receive a lesson in European citizenship, which I have observed. This lesson takes a similar approach to that in the homework assignment book described above, or to the notions of national identity displayed in *L'Auberge Espanole*. The children are encouraged to notice cultural differences among European nations but then also to see somehow that they are all part of one big European Union that supplements their cultures, languages, cuisine, etc. To an anthropologist, these displays of cultural difference are quite superficial and stereotypical. Yet, as a political anthropologist, I am aware that nations employ such stereotypes regularly in order to instill in-group and out-group feelings among their citizens. If it is assumed that the differences among them are superficial and based on minor variations of such things as what people eat, then an in-group feeling can be constructed among Europeans.

CONCLUSIONS: NOTIONS OF CULTURAL CITIZENSHIP IN THE NEW EUROPE

Any school curriculum aimed at developing a sense of European citizenship is going to be limited in its efficacy as long as the wider tensions about Europe as an idea, and social divisions within Europe, persist. My own previous research in classrooms, discussed elsewhere, shows the uneven impact of a European curriculum at the local level in rural France (Reed-Danahay 2003). In several rural schools that had received grants from the EU for programs fostering exchanges between schools in different member states, for example, there were problems of communication and a lack of the full resources needed to implement these programs. In one program, computers were acquired to foster e-mail communication between a French and an Italian school, but teachers were not adequately trained in the use of the computers, and language barriers prohibited the children from writing to each other directly. In some cases, applying for an EU grant was a vehicle for getting more resources to a school, and not necessarily for the primary purpose of creating a European identity among the children.

Renato Rosaldo's concept of cultural citizenship, though based in the context of Latino identities in the United States, is useful in thinking about citizenship in a multicultural European Union. Philippou (this volume) also proposes, in greater detail than space permits me to do here, that a variety of understandings of citizenship must be taken into account. Rosaldo (1994) writes that "the central question raised by the concept of cultural citizenship is whether or not one can be different and be a full citizen too" (252). Cultural citizenship "stresses local, informal notions of membership, entitlement and influence" and takes into account what Rosaldo terms "vernacular notions of citizenship"—that is, the claiming of distinctive and special rights, representation, and cultural autonomy that is different from official or unitary models of citizenship. For example, Rosaldo suggests that among Latinos the notion of *respeto* is linked to concepts of cultural citizenship. It may be, therefore, that Europeans can best articulate a European citizenship that is based on more vernacular forms of citizenship that are not seen to conflict with the EU supranational identity.

The implications of these theories of doxa and cultural citizenship are that European citizenship will best be welcomed with a more grassroots approach rather than one that is exclusively top-down. The current attempt, despite a rhetoric which often denies this, is one that seeks to impose European identities and a sense of belonging on those who are not receptive to or familiar with it. It is also exclusionary of newcomers in its emphasis on stereotypical notions of European national identities, where there is no place for other religious and cultural backgrounds. Where does one fit a Turkish Muslim woman in the various models of Europe that are being promoted?

Citizenship education in France and Europe is occurring in a multitude of ways and through a variety of pedagogical means—through the mass media, on the Internet, through the invention of new ritual and symbolic forms, through programs targeting schools but not made mandatory, and through explicit and official school curricula. We are witnessing a slow and often subtle change in commonsense understandings of identity among people in Europe that may eventually lead to a shared set of beliefs and practices associated with European citizenship. What that will be, however, is still to be determined. The looming question is whether European identity will be part of the symbolic capital of the elite (a supranational or transnational class of a mobile, educated workforce) or whether it will be able to promote a sense of "active" citizenship among all inhabitants of European soil. An educational program aimed at active European citizenship will only go so far without wider supports for it in the attitudes of, and resources available to, inhabitants of European member states. To de-center schools in our understandings of citizenship education is to understand the wider contexts in which children, their teachers, and their parents are exposed to cultural models that can inform what goes on in the classroom. One could argue that various commonsense understandings of the world inculcated through national educational systems, which previously sought to instill strong national identities, are now at work in creating resistance to the newer doxa associated with European citizenship.

NOTES

This chapter is a revised and expanded version of a paper delivered at the 2003 American Anthropological Association Meetings, called "French Citizenship and European Citizenship: Education for a 'New Europe' in Contemporary France" and presented at a session organized by Bradley Levinson. I am grateful for the research and travel support I have received for my work on education in the European Union from a research grant from the Fulbright Commission in 2001 and a Visiting Scholar position at the Institut National de Recherche Pédagogique (INRP) in Paris in 2002. I would like to thank Doyle Stevick and Bradley Levinson for their helpful comments and suggestions.

1. I also argued for the need to "de-center" the school in my analysis of rural French primary schooling (Reed-Danahay 1996).

2. See Reed-Danahay (2003) for an analysis of these programs.

3. Cf. Brubaker (1992); Eder and Giesen (2002); Osler and Starkey (2001). See also Schnapper (1998).

4. I have previously written about the contextual and fluid nature of Auvergnat identity elsewhere (Reed-Danahay 1996).

5. With the Euromosaic study of 1992, the EU surveyed regional language with the intent to protect minority languages and cultures. The report was published in 1996 (see European Commission 1996). There is also a website on the project, notably in Catalan, English, and French (www.uoc.edu/euromosaic/).

6. Scheper-Hughes (2004) has focused more extensively on the organ trafficking theme of this movie in an article based on her research on this topic.

7. Noiriel (1996 [1988]) and Grillo (1995) provide good introductions to the issues of education and immigration in France.

REFERENCES

Anderson, B. 1991. *Imagined Communities: Reflections on the Origin and Spread of Nationalism.* Rev. ed. London: Verso. (Originally published in 1983.)

Antony, D., and M. Bourgeois. 1999. *Citoyenneté et république.* Franche-Comté: CRDP de Franche-Comté and CDDP du Doubs.

Audigier, F. 1999. *L'education à la citoyenneté.* Paris: Institut National de Recherche Pédagogique.

Augé, M. 1995. *Non-Places: Introduction to an Anthropology of Supermodernity.* Trans. J. Howe. New York: Verso. (Originally published in 1992.)

Balibar, É. 2004. *We, the People of Europe? Reflections on Transnational Citizenship.* Trans. James Swenson. Princeton, N.J.: Princeton University Press. (Originally published in 2001.)

Bourdieu, P. 1996. *The State Nobility: Elite Schools in the Field of Power.* Trans. Laurette C. Clough. Stanford, Calif.: Stanford University Press. (Originally published in 1989.)

———. 2000. *Pascalian Meditations.* Trans. Richard Nice. Stanford, Calif.: Stanford University Press. (Originally published in 1997.)

Bourdieu, P., and J.-C. Passeron. 1964. *Les héritiers: les étudiants et la culture.* Paris: Editions de Minuit.

———. 1990. *Reproduction in Education, Society and Culture.* Trans. Richard C. Nice. London: Sage. (Originally published in 1970.)

Brubaker, W. R. 1992. *Citizenship and Nationhood in France and Germany.* Cambridge, Mass.: Harvard University Press.

Commission of the European Communities. 2005. *Proposal for a Decision of the European Parliament and the Council Establishing for the Period 2007–2013 the Programme "Citizens for Europe" to Promote Active European Citizenship.* http://europa.eu.int/comm./dgs/education_culture/activecitizenship/new_pro gramme_en.htm. Brussels.

Eder, K., and B. Giesen, eds. 2001. *European Citizenship between National Legacies and Postnational Projects.* Oxford: Oxford University Press.

EUROPA. n.d. "What Is Europe Day?" http://europa.eu.int/abc/symbols/9-may/euday_en.htm.

European Commission. 2002. *Socrates: European Community Action Programme in the Field of Education (2000–06)*. Luxembourg: Office for the Official Publications of the European Communities.

———. 2006. *Euromosaic: The Production and Reproduction of Minority Language Groups in the European Union*. Luxembourg: Office for the Official Publications of the European Communities.

Fondation Génération Europe. n.d. *Notre Europe*. Brussels: Author.

Frears, S., et al. 2004. *Dirty Pretty Things*. DVD, Miramax Home Entertainment. (Original, U.K.: BBC Films, 2002.)

Grillo, R. 1985. *Ideologies and Institutions in Urban France: The Representation of Immigrants*. Cambridge: Cambridge University Press.

Hannerz, U. 1990. "Cosmopolitans and Locals in World Culture." *Theory, Culture, and Society* 7: 237–51.

Hobsbawm, E. 1992. "Mass-Producing Traditions: Europe 1870–1914." In *The Invention of Tradition*, ed. E. Hobsbawm and T. Ranger. Cambridge: Cambridge University Press. (Originally published in 1983.)

Klapisch, C., et al. 2003. *L'auberge espagnole*. DVD, Twentieth Century Fox Home Entertainment. (Original, France: Studio Canal, 2002.)

Merton, R. K. 1957. *Social Theory and Social Structure*. Glencoe: Free Press.

Noiriel, G. 1996. *The French Melting Pot: Immigration, Citizenship, and National Identity*. Trans. Geoffrey de LaForcade. Minneapolis: University of Minnesota Press. (Original published in 1988.)

Osler, A., and H. Starkey. 2001. "Citizenship Education and National Identities in France and England: Inclusive or Exclusive?" *Oxford Review of Education* 27, no. 2: 287–305.

Reed-Danahay, D. 1996. *Education and Identity in Rural France: The Politics of Schooling*. Cambridge Studies in Social and Cultural Anthropology. Cambridge: Cambridge University Press.

———. 2003. "Europeanization and French Primary Education: Local Implications of Supranational Policies." In *Local Meanings, Global Schooling: Anthropology and World Culture Theory*, ed. K. Anderson-Levitt. New York: Palgrave Macmillan.

Rosaldo, R. 1997. "Cultural Citizenship, Inequality, and Multiculturalism." In *Latino Cultural Citizenship: Claiming Identity, Space, and Rights*, ed. W. V. Flores and R. Benmayor. Boston: Beacon.

Scheper-Hughes, N. 2004. "Parts Unknown: Undercover Ethnography of the Organ-Trafficking Underworld." *Ethnography* 5, no. 1: 29–73.

Schnapper, D. 1998. *Community of Citizens: On the Modern Idea of Nationality*. Trans. Sévérine Rosée. New Brunswick, N.J.: Transaction Books.

Tutiaux-Guillon, N. ed. 2000. *L'Europe entre projet politique et objet scolaire au collège et au lycée*. Paris: Institut National de Recherche Pédagogique.

9

The Politics of the Holocaust in Estonia: Historical Memory and Social Divisions in Estonian Education

E. Doyle Stevick

In her April 24, 2002, remarks at the Stockholm Security Conference, Heather Conley, the U.S. Deputy Assistant Secretary of State for European and Eurasian affairs, praised the three Baltic states—Estonia, Latvia, and Lithuania—for the progress they had made to qualify for entry into NATO. She continued:

> However, all the NATO aspirants need to do more to better prepare themselves for membership so that they are ready and able to contribute to European security in tangible ways. For the Baltic States, this means hard work—not just words but concrete action. (Embassy 2002)

The description of what was needed—hard work, concrete action, and tangible contributions to European security—creates an expectation that some military changes will be prescribed: better facilities, training, or hardware, for example, or perhaps even some specific contribution the Baltic states could make in Afghanistan or against Al Qaeda, the Taliban, or terror generally. The very first example she cited, however, of the concrete action and

hard work necessary to contribute to security in tangible ways, was (following directly from the previous quote)

> on complex domestic issues like dealing with the history of the Holocaust.

However improbable this criterion may have seemed to those assembled,
the message for aspirants to NATO was clear. Just a half year after the surprise attacks on the United States, the American government was willing to
wield the promise of NATO membership as a carrot to influence domestic
policies about history, historical commemoration, and education. Estonia
obliged. Even before the next school year began, on August 6, 2002, the
"Estonian government . . . named January 27—the anniversary of the liberation of the Auschwitz-Birkenau Nazi concentration camp—as official
Holocaust Day" (*City Paper's Baltics Worldwide* 2002).

While January 27 is the commemoration date for twelve other European
countries, the date has no direct connection to Estonia, Estonia's Jews, or
the Estonians who participated in Holocaust atrocities (Zuroff 2005). The
date that the announcement was made, however, is an important anniversary for Estonians: August 6, 1940, marked the day that "the Supreme
Council of the Soviet Union met the 'request of the Estonian people' and
incorporated Estonia into the Soviet Union" (Laur et al. 2002: 266). The
juxtaposition of these two anniversaries—and the symbolic role they play
in the competing narratives and meanings of World War II—tap into some
of the deep divisions that linger both between the junior and senior members of NATO and the European Union (EU) and between Estonia's ethnic
Estonians and ethnic Russian minority. These differences, which impinge
powerfully on concepts of national and civic identity, have profound implications for the future of democracy both within Estonia and in the EU.

To explicate these differences and the complexity of issues surrounding
the adoption of Holocaust Day in Estonia, this chapter will first discuss the
origins of this research and the involvement of foreign partners in Estonia.
It will then explore the reactions to Holocaust Day in Estonia, ranging from
the highest levels of government and media forums to the full range of education policy, from the Ministry of Education to classroom teachers. The
chapter will focus particularly on the teachers and policymakers who participated in my multisited ethnographic study of the policy and practice of
citizenship education in Estonia. It will then provide some historical context about the Soviet and Nazi occupations of Estonia that helps make sense
of both Estonian reactions to Holocaust Day and the divisions in Estonian
society and beyond.

ADDRESSING THE HOLOCAUST: DEMOCRATIC CITIZENSHIP EDUCATION AND RACIST EXTREMISM

Though my research in Estonia concerned civic education generally and, in particular, its international dimensions, my initial questions dealt more with the democratic transition, the role of the Soviet legacy in it and the effectiveness of international cooperation in transforming that legacy: Were teachers' interpretations of the radical political and economic changes influenced by their indoctrination into Marxism/Leninism? Were international partners knowledgeable enough about the local languages, cultures, and issues to respond to local needs and to engage effectively with Estonians, or were they more concerned with advancing particular doctrines? I had no inkling when I began that the Holocaust would emerge as a major issue inextricably linked to my research. In fact, however, it both united my concerns with democratic citizenship education and racist extremism, and served as a window into many of the divisions that permeated Estonian society, from global geopolitics to ethnic relations.

My research focus on democratic citizenship education had grown out of encounters with racist extremism in the United States. A former student, Benjamin "August" Smith, and a former neighbor, Richard Baumhammers—both inspired by Hitler's racist ideology—independently launched racially motivated shooting sprees ten months apart, killing seven and wounding nine more between them. These men were well-educated products of elite American schools and good universities. Their actions made me question the ability of schooling to promote tolerance and to undermine antisocial ideologies. When I discovered that the United States had never attempted a nationwide program to overcome racism through schooling, I began to wonder what such an attempt to change attitudes and dispositions through schooling might look like. Believing that the same set of attitudes and dispositions is necessary both for developing tolerance and for sustaining a democratic society—the core mission of civic education—I set out to investigate how Estonia was trying to generate a democratic orientation through schooling in the wake of the country's liberation from the Soviet Union.

When I first visited Estonia, I was startled to see occasional swastikas among the graffiti on the sides of apartment buildings in the capital city, Tallinn. Fully aware of the horrors carried out by those who continue to be swayed by Nazi doctrine, I was reminded of media representations of East German skinheads perpetrating attacks on Turks. Though painting swastikas—the starkest symbol of vicious and virulent anti-Semitism—was clearly an act of hostility, it took some time for me to understand that this act of hostility in this context was primarily directed not at Jews but at Russians. History is never far from the surface in Estonia, a place where most adults can recall life in the Soviet Union and many of the elderly have firsthand experience with war, Nazi and Soviet occupations, and deportations—all of which are related in complex ways with the issue of the Holocaust.

By invoking Estonia's treatment of the Holocaust, the international community laid bare fault lines that run through Estonian society and beyond. For Western Europe, the United States, Israel, and also Russia, the Nazis constitute the transcendent evil of world history. Yet for Europeans who endured a half century or longer of Soviet domination, personal experience and national narratives are often incompatible with this conception. For them, the Soviets generally constituted an equal or even greater evil. As a corollary, service with the Nazis may not represent for them complicity in advancing Hitler's aims but at worst a reasonable choice between two evils, and sometimes even heroic resistance to Soviet occupation. These views are not marginal among ethnic Estonians, the people about whom I will be primarily speaking here.

The fault lines evoked by discussion of the Holocaust extend beyond Estonians' resistance to pressure from their allies, the governments of the United States, Western Europe, and Israel. The issue of the Holocaust also hit at the core divisions between Estonians and the Russian-speaking residents of Estonia. Estonians' civic identity is closely linked with their cultural identity and language. To be able to incorporate Russians and other Russian-speaking minorities effectively, Estonia must develop a more inclusive civic identity that transcends ethnicity. For that end to be attainable, Estonians will have to accept that the future can be much different than the past, because Estonia's independence was gained largely by fighting off Soviet forces—mostly Russian—and was later lost to the Soviets—again mostly Russian. Indeed, Budryte (2005) notes the argument that "historical memory about the past wrongs committed by the former occupying powers is likely to be one of the sources of resistance to accepting the recommendations of outsiders to extend rights to the minorities associated with the former occupying powers" (7). Discussion of the Holocaust invariably draws increased attention to Estonia's troubled history. To the extent that Estonia's political existence and independence are bound up closely with Estonians' opposition to the Soviets and hence to Russians, focus on those key historical periods of gained and lost independence inevitably places Russians and Estonians on opposite sides.

The politics of commemoration, which are inherently divisive in Estonia, pose a direct challenge to the development of a common civic identity for today's Russian residents and Estonian citizens of Estonia. Several Estonians who work in the Ministry of Education or nongovernmental organizations that are involved in civic education have also been outspoken on the

issue or directly involved with international efforts concerning the Holocaust. History teachers, often the teachers responsible for teaching civic
education, play a key role because the historical narratives that they accept
and convey have implications for relations between groups in Estonia. The
ability to work across such fault lines—to work across not only such different understandings but also sometimes distrust, opposition, and hostility—
will be critical to the future of democracy both in multicultural states like
Estonia and in the dramatically larger and more complex European Union.
A central component of this task is making some sense of these widely
divergent understandings.

These are important issues because tolerance, a precondition for a more
inclusive democratic civic identity, remains elusive. According to a recent
study, 53 percent of ethnic Estonians were classified as tolerant, while 47
percent were classified as exclusionary (Pettai 2002; cf. Poleshchuk 2005:
74). The exclusionary group breaks down to 28 percent who are less tolerant and 19 percent who are considered to be radical nationalists. (Among
non-Estonians who are residents of Estonia, the numbers are 21 percent
and 14 percent, respectively.) Furthermore, the cases of Estonia, Latvia, and
Lithuania suggest that "inclusive citizenship laws and minority-friendly
policies do not guarantee that tolerant multi-cultural communities will be
created" (Budryte 2005: 9).

Previous experience suggests that foreign involvement in the issue of the
Holocaust could have a positive effect. A study of ethnic policies in the Baltic states and Romania concludes that "the promise of EU membership and
'concerted international efforts' (the coordinated action of several international organizations) helped to subdue domestic opposition to policy
changes that involved minority rights" (Budryte 2005: 2). In fact, however,
the dynamics of this case are much more in line with the findings of Lynn
Tesser. "Tesser argued that the elites in post-Communist countries chose to
adopt European norms emphasizing minority rights for strategic reasons,
such as trying to escape from Russia's sphere of influence. This is why ethnic tolerance has been a 'geopolitical matter' that lacks genuine domestic
support" (Budryte 2005: 3). These circumstances point to twin ironies: first,
that in order to gain security from Russia and to escape its influence, Estonia accepted policies that are intended to make it more accommodating of
its own Russian minority; second, that the adoption of Holocaust Day, one
of whose goals is to promote tolerance within Estonia, exacerbates the historical tensions between Estonia's majority and minority populations.

FOREIGN INVOLVEMENT
IN HOLOCAUST ISSUES

The international community's efforts regarding the Holocaust have been
manifold. Through the Support for Eastern European Democracies (SEED)

initiative, the U.S. Embassy in Tallinn invested close to $2.5 million in a wide variety of issues in Estonia between 1994 and 2004. Five of these early projects explicitly dealt with the Holocaust. First, the Embassy funded a research project called the President's Roundtable whose mission was to investigate the oppression of Estonian citizens between 1939 and 1991. The commission's task involved the investigation of both the Nazi and the Soviet occupations of Estonia. The embassy then sponsored a trilingual virtual exhibit on the Holocaust.[1] The embassy also supported the publication of several books, including a book about Jewish history for high schools, *Tell Ye Your Children*. Another volume, *Who Are the Jews and What Is the Holocaust?* was sponsored soon after. A third book's translation was funded by the embassy, bringing into Estonian the account of Holocaust survivor Benjamin Anolik, a Pole who had made it through camps in Estonia.[2]

The difficulty with producing such materials is that they may never be used. Civics teachers in particular have been provided with an enormous stock of resources, funded largely by groups across Europe and the United States, but they are allotted so little time in a curriculum whose required topics easily fill the classes that there is scant opportunity to use them, nonetheless look at them. In the six classrooms that I attended regularly to observe civic education classes, and in the ten I visited once or infrequently across Estonia, I never spotted a single copy of the embassy-supported materials. In the period following September 11, 2001, the embassy broadened its education activities related to the Holocaust beyond the production of materials and began pushing for more extensive treatment in schools.

Most visible in the international effort to promote the commemoration and study of the Holocaust were the Simon Wiesenthal Center's (SWC) Efraim Zuroff, who leads investigations into Nazi war crimes and tracks war criminals, and the U.S. Ambassador during this period, Joseph Michael DeThomas. Although they emphasized different priorities, from cooperating with international investigations and tracking down Nazi war crimes suspects to erecting monuments to victims of the Holocaust in Estonia, and although they represent different groups, both see as a central issue the instruction and commemoration of the Holocaust in schools. Simon Wiesenthal, who passed away in 2005 at the age of ninety-six, dedicated his life to tracking down Nazi war criminals and gave his name to the center, which bills itself as an "international Jewish human rights organization" whose mission has expanded beyond Nazi-hunting to include "Holocaust and tolerance education; Middle East Affairs; and extremist groups, neo-Nazism, and hate on the Internet" (Simon Wiesenthal Center, n.d.).

The ambassador, who built on the remarks by Conley and comments about the lingering traces of fascism in Eastern Europe that he quoted from Senator Joseph Biden, proposed in a newspaper column three "modest steps": prosecuting those who had committed crimes, recognizing that the Holocaust was part of Estonia's history, and teaching children about it. He was not specific about the forms that historical acknowledgment and education should take, noting simply that "I have been told Estonian school textbooks treat the Holocaust in about one-and-a-half pages. If this is true for most of Estonia, I would suggest that history texts on this subject already in other states in this region be translated into Estonian for use here" (DeThomas 2002). He further suggested that Estonia participate in the Task Force for International Cooperation on Holocaust Education, Remembrance, and Research. Founded by the Swedes in 1998—although Sweden has received an F for "Total Failure" from the Simon Wiesenthal Center for its efforts and cooperation in the prosecution of war criminals—the task force had twenty members by September 2005, including Latvia and Lithuania, but not Estonia.

The Simon Wiesenthal Center also encouraged the implementation of a Holocaust Day in Estonia. When asked for his own vision for addressing the Holocaust in Estonian schools, Zuroff was not prescriptive but replied that it "can be based on the vast experience in teaching the Holocaust already acquired in Israel and the US. The best place to start is in junior high or high school. Estonian pupils should certainly know more about the history of Estonian Jewry and how Jewish history affected world history" (*Online Intervjuud* 2002). If the measures themselves seem modest, the response was unequivocally opposed. These measures were, in fact, highly contentious for Estonians.

THE ESTONIAN RESPONSE

The public was not at all receptive to Holocaust Day. One former Estonian prime minister, who was carrying and reading a recent book about the gulags when we spoke, insisted to me in an interview that Holocaust Day would never have been adopted under his administration.[3] "I would not support it. During my government, I would not allow it. Mostly it feels that it is coming from outside so it is not helping. . . . The communist terror took more lives than the Holocaust. It must be combined with crimes against humanity" (interview transcript, June 2003).

Although this sentiment was widely shared, the depth of the resistance to foreign activity in Estonia concerning the Holocaust and the fault lines dividing outsiders from those in Estonia became evident in a shocking turn in January 2003—the week of the first official Holocaust Day in Estonian schools—when the SWC sought to publish an advertisement for its "Operation Last Chance," an effort to encourage people to come forward with information about Nazi war criminals so they could be brought to justice before they died. As Radio Free Europe reported, "Chairwoman of the Estonian Jewish community Cilja Laud, Chairman of the Association of Former Prisoners of Ghettos and Concentration Camps Vladimir Perelman, and Rabbi Shmuel Kot sent a letter to the Media House advertising agency asking it not to publish the advertisements of the Simon Wiesenthal Center" ("Baltic States Report," 2003a). Estonia's own Jewish community split with the SWC, apparently rejecting the approach it took, and may have feared that its approach promoted antagonism within Estonia. Zuroff declared the refusal "shocking" and "unheard-of" ("Baltic States Report," 2003a).

The text of the ad was likely similar to the one published in Lithuania, which had a large Jewish community: "'Jews of Lithuania did not disappear! They were mercilessly massacred in Vilnius, Kaunas, Siauliai and over 100 other places of mass murder,' read the text of the large black-and-white ad, featuring a photograph of Nazis beating Jews to death" (*City Paper's Baltics Worldwide* 2002). The Simon Wiesenthal Center acknowledged that the text included this line "During the Holocaust, Estonians murdered Jews in Estonia as well as in other countries" (*City Paper's Baltics Worldwide* 2003). The translation into Estonian introduced a key ambiguity. In the Estonian language, which does not use articles, *Estonians* can mean either "some" or "the" Estonians. Prominent Estonians went on record condemning the ad. Peeter Torop, the head of the prestigious Semiotics Department at Estonia's leading institution of higher education, Tartu University, "said that although the text of the advertisement does not call for violence, it instigates ethnic hatred and 'accuses Estonians as a nation of murdering Jews'" (*City Paper's Baltics Worldwide* 2003). The article mishap intersected with complex notions of collective suffering and responsibility.

An attempt was made to revise the ad. According to the Baltic News Service, the revisions meant that the ad "no longer says Estonians as a nation collaborated with Nazis but that some Nazi henchmen did" ("Baltic States Report," 2003b). Even so, the major newspapers still refused to publish the ad, claiming that printing the ad "would violate the law and good journalistic practice" ("Baltic States Report," 2003b).

THE ESTONIAN RESPONSE: THE MINISTRY OF EDUCATION AND SCHOOL DIRECTORS

The Holocaust Day policy was adopted, yet this recently restored democratic government was not carrying out the will of its people: public opinion steadfastly resented what they saw as foreign meddling and opposed the move, leading a frustrated Zuroff to claim that "93 percent of the [Estonian] public oppose the establishment of a memorial day for the victims of the Holocaust"[4] (Simon Wiesenthal Center 2004).

Public opposition to foreign initiatives concerning the Holocaust put the government, and particularly the Ministry of Education, into a difficult position at a time when Estonia's memberships in both NATO and the European Union were pending. Officials sought ways to satisfy the demands on them for memberships in these organizations without alienating Estonian voters. The Ministry finessed the challenge effectively. As we will see, different messages went out to different audiences: foreign officials might hear one version in English, while the schools received a different one in Estonian. No effort was made to win public support for the policy, and it seems doubtful that there was ever any intention to see Holocaust Day through to full implementation or to ensure that it was carried out.

Even the timing of the announcement is significant. The unpopular policy was announced at the beginning of the month during which many Estonians vacation or begin extended stays in countryside homes. Announcing unpopular policies at such convenient times is an old tactic. But the date of the announcement also has symbolic value for Estonians. Announcing the policy on August 6, a day that evoked their half century of foreign domination, contextualized the unpopular policy in a larger historical frame; in this way, government officials could communicate implicitly with the national majority, almost as if in code, without tipping off the broader international audience.

The government's resistance to such a memorial day is also evident in its choice of January 27, the anniversary of the liberation of Auschwitz, to commemorate the Holocaust. January 27 had no relationship either to the fate of Estonia's Jews—because none of them were sent to Auschwitz—or to the crimes perpetrated by ethnic Estonians during the war (Zuroff 2005).

> Estonian officials rejected a suggestion by the Simon Wiesenthal Center that they choose either 20 January, the date of the infamous Wannsee Conference in 1942, at which the implementation of the Final Solution was discussed and Estonia was declared *Judenrein* (free of Jews), or 7 August, the date on which the 36th Estonian Security Battalion murdered Jews in Nowogrudok, Belarus. (Zuroff 2005)

Such a decision distanced Estonia from the crimes it was to be commemorating, either by denying responsibility (August 7, which, it should be noted, would not be a school day) or by not associating Estonia with the fate of Estonia's Jewish population (January 20).

If the rejection of alternative dates was a relatively clear symbolic statement, the possible meanings evoked by the August 6 announcement's historical subtext can only be understood in the context of a complex web of interrelated ideas or themes that recur in Estonia's political discourse. These are not universal sentiments but prominent strands that are heard on a reg-

ular basis from the op-ed pages to the teachers' rooms. They include continued fear of Russian aggression, resentment of foreign interference in
domestic affairs, and frustration with the Russian-speaking minorities "who
have been here for fifty years and still not learned Estonian." The resentment of foreign meddling is augmented by a sense that Estonia is not
understood or respected by outsiders, while its suffering and losses are held
to be less important than those endured by others. This lack of understanding also contributes to a sense of freedom, the feeling that Estonia can pay
lip service to foreign pressure while continuing to do what it sees fit. Such
lip service is appropriate in part because Estonians also believe that they
understand more clearly the true nature of oppression and of world events
as a result of their experience under occupation. That the predominant historical narrative of the Estonian nation as a victim is being challenged—and
by accusations that are perceived to imply collective guilt in certain atrocities of the Holocaust—only reinforces these notions.

The timing of the Holocaust Day policy announcement contextualizes
both the policy itself and the international politics surrounding it within
the historical experiences of the Estonian nation. This historical context
thus makes the policy resonate with the common ideas and themes of Estonian discourse that were discussed above. On the one hand, the anniversary
of Estonia's involuntary incorporation into the Soviet Union plays into
Estonia's antipathy to foreign meddling of all kinds in its domestic affairs;
this specific example—the Holocaust Day policy—emerges as a typical
example of such meddling. The notions that Estonia's losses are unrecognized and that foreigners do not understand Estonia combine with the
announcement's timing to produce a counterargument about the significance of the Holocaust; implicitly, they suggest that Nazi crimes were not
any more deserving of attention than those inflicted on Estonians by the
Soviet Union. Finally, calling to mind the Soviet Union's long-term dominance evokes both the continuing fear of Russia and the fact that Estonia
was able to persevere through the occupation with its language and culture
generally intact. Conjuring up the perceived dangers posed by Russia makes
the announcement's timing seem to be a justification of the policy itself:
the need to obtain security against Russia justifies Estonia's acquiescence in
this minor policy matter, which it need not execute any more faithfully
than it did Soviet doctrine. Estonia's perseverance through the half-century
occupation also suggests that this matter is one that can be waited out, with
Estonia paying lip service now and simply doing as it sees fit once this issue
has passed.

Among those reacting negatively were the principals of two of Estonia's
most elite high schools. These school directors have something like celeb-
rity status in Estonia; they are public intellectuals, appearing frequently in
the media, and are known to most Estonians (Baltic News Service, August

26, 2002). Under the headline "School-directors Condemn Holocaust Day," the two directors announced that they would do nothing to mark the newly declared Holocaust Day, one asserting that it was inappropriate to put someone else's horrors above Estonia's own. This declaration came just days before the school year was to begin and three weeks after the announcement of the establishment of Holocaust Day.

If their departure signified a rebellion against official policy, little was made of it. On the contrary, the policy and its presentation seemed designed to pay lip service to the event while rejecting its premise that the Holocaust deserves consideration above and beyond Estonia's own troubles. One Internet commentator captured concisely a common interpretation by writing, "Holocaust day is the entry-ticket for NATO" (mauri [*sic*] 2003). This seems to have been the view of the Ministry of Education.

In its original announcement, the ministry framed the day in terms of foreign policy: "According to a Ministry of Education statement, its observance would foster understanding of genocide and would underline 'as an important foreign policy factor, solidarity with the European and transatlantic community'" (*City Paper's Baltics Worldwide* 2002). This explanation clearly did not make the case for establishing a Holocaust Day based on the intrinsic value of the subject. The extent to which the ministry actively wished to draw attention to the day is evident on its website, where this announcement was expunged from its extensive archive of press releases.[5]

Before the first day was officially carried out, the Minister of Education sent a clear message that victims of the Holocaust should not be singled out: "Education Minister Mailis Rand in a circular sent to the schools in the fall noted that not only the Nazi crimes against Jews but also all other victims persecuted for ethnic, racial, religious, and political reasons should be remembered. The ministry gave the schools a free hand in deciding how and in which classes the subject should be handled" ("Baltic States Report," 2003a).

This message explicitly rejected the notion that something distinguished the Holocaust from other atrocities and thus merited special attention in Estonian schools. As if to reinforce the point, the Ministry of Education's many press releases conspicuously pass over any acknowledgment of Holocaust Day.[6] Only three references to Holocaust Day can be found on the entire site. Although the country prides itself on how well connected it and its schools are to the Internet, the ministry provides no guidance, information, or links to teachers about how they might carry out even the diluted recognition of the day discussed in the school flyer.

Attitudes had not shifted by the time late January arrived. A curriculum specialist was interested in this question and conducted some informal research about it. In an interview, the specialist explained:

When we at the Curriculum Development Center were having some lectures in Tartu University . . . and one of the homeworks for 30 different school directors and headmasters was to examine the way the Holocaust Day was spent the first time in Estonia in 2003. We asked them to get the information from another school: to ask how it was spent and what people were thinking about the Holocaust Day. People were very bitter, most of the people in their responses, they were very direct and very honest, saying that this is not the day that is celebrated in Estonian school, and not in a nice way. But public opinion and the opinion of teachers and head directors was that this came from outside . . . and from these 30 answers that we got, we had zero responses that this was an important day that we need to have in our school system.

Indeed, many teachers also had no qualms about publicly expressing their dissatisfaction with the day and its conception. The newspaper of one large city cited many of the arguments teachers used to justify their approaches to Holocaust Day:

"I think that holocaust day is nothing but an activity for activity's sake, nothing more," adding that it brought the theme to the students on just one day.

The Soviet occupation interests students more, because they have more connections with this, more relatives were deported.

You shouldn't traumatize a child with description of this, how a baby was thrown into the air as target practice, the idea of history is not to shock youth. Rather on this day we should emphasize the danger of all types of violence.

This is foolish, I'm not going to make the students march or do something else on Holocaust day; with this I would perhaps destroy the history period.

The uprising on Juri's Night[7] took more Estonian lives, that could be commemorated by the government. Let every nation commemorate its own day of mourning. (Nielson 2003)

Even the country's main representative for an international network concerned with the Holocaust did not hold the view that the Holocaust itself was a qualitatively different event that should be discussed independently of other human rights violations. The official gave a presentation about the Holocaust and Estonia to this network. In keeping with the dominant sentiment within Estonia, she discussed the suffering not just of the Jews and not just the suffering inflicted by the Nazis.

They stopped me and said, "What are you speaking about?" And I said that I am speaking about the human rights violations that occurred in Estonia, as said by our President, Lennart Meri, and the commission that investigates human rights violations in Estonia, that we should speak about all of them side-by-side, and not single one out. And they yelled at me. It was horrible. It was a horrible experience.

This attempt to link the atrocities committed against the Jews and against the Estonians and to gain recognition for the suffering of Estonians under both the Nazis and Soviets may make the selection of this official for the leading position in a Holocaust network questionable. In fact, it would be hard to find a selection who was more sympathetic to the cause. Indeed, this official had been very much in favor of Holocaust programs:

The Swedish Institute just came to Estonia—they wanted to create a relationship and start a Holocaust program, a tolerance program and I know from Latvian colleagues that they were very successful in Latvia and I really just supported their idea because, as it worked in Latvia, it is important for us, too, because all the questions of violence in the classrooms and at school and tolerance and its all very much related, and we know what it means to be tolerant, but how to teach it, just methods or models or something we have to learn. (interview transcript, November 2004)

This case illustrates the challenge facing foreign groups who seek out partners in countries whose languages and cultures they do not understand: they often offer enticing opportunities—frequently including international travel that they would be unable to afford independently—while having no effective mechanism to consider the ideological or philosophical inclinations of those whom they select. Their results are inconsistent at best and can go badly astray. While such enticing opportunities may provide an incentive for partners in less privileged countries to downplay their philosophical differences, the prospect of greater economic security creates an even greater incentive. Economic pressures on those at the mercy of the market in transition economies are, by circumstance, often more willing to participate in projects with which they do not agree. While such foreign-funded projects—such as those dedicated to raising awareness of the Holocaust—can be quite valuable in the hands of effective advocates, a recent study of racist extremism in Central and Eastern Europe provides a hint about what can go wrong. The author of the chapter on racist extremism in Estonia, emphasizing that the "teaching of the Holocaust in Estonian schools . . . needs serious elaboration and change," went on to cite as his illustration the fact that, "one of the local textbooks on history states that some Jews were killed as an act of revenge for Bolshevik abuses" (Poleshchuk 2005: 74). The author of this claim and of this textbook had been selected to lead the teacher-training sessions on the Holocaust in Estonia.

The importance of the Holocaust to foreigners is well understood. In 2006, the Foreign Ministry of Estonia put out a press release in English:

"During the Second World War, the Nazi regime systematically eliminated on the occupied Estonian territory both Estonian Jews, and those that had been brought here from elsewhere," the statement read. "There is no justification for the participation of anyone in these shameful and morally condemnable acts. Even if they have not directly shed the blood of anyone, they are nevertheless morally responsible. Knowing the past teaches tolerance and helps to achieve that the crimes of the last century will never be repeated," the statement said. (Estonian Ministry 2006)

It continued, "The Ministry of Education and Science called on all Estonian schools to explain to students the tragic events of the last century" (Estonian Ministry 2006). This precise line appeared in Estonian in the third paragraph of a brief article in one of Estonia's two leading papers. The other paper had no mention of this encouragement. The reference to "the tragic events of the last century" is open-ended; while a foreign reader would likely take this as an allusion to the Holocaust, Estonians might think first of the Soviet occupation.

If the Education Ministry did make such a bland and ambiguous announcement, it was subtle. No mention of the announcement was to be found in the ministry's own press release archive. In fact, all records of announcements related to Holocaust Day were scrubbed from the electronic archive of press releases.

I asked a curriculum specialist whether he had heard about any educational events or announcements connected to Holocaust Day in 2006. "Basically, Holocaust Day does not exist in Estonia," he replied.

HISTORY AND MEMORY: ESTONIA UNDER NAZI AND SOVIET OCCUPATIONS

To understand why Holocaust initiatives have faltered so badly in Estonia, we need to consider both the meanings of history for Estonians in light of current domestic politics and the missteps made by foreign actors.

In its February 2006 report on Estonia, in a subsection concerning anti-Semitism, the European Commission against Racism and Intolerance states, disapprovingly, that "many Estonians view the Nazi occupation in a more positive light than the Soviet occupation" (European Commission 2006). The report never seems to stop to ask why that might be.

The apparent assumption that Estonians would draw the opposite conclusion if only they were better informed about the Holocaust seems to be at the root of many of the initiatives coming from outside Estonia. This assumption may well be incorrect. To understand why, we must consider the complicated history of a small country trapped between two great powers and two destructive ideologies.

Estonia first gained independence at the end of World War I. Estonian forces fended off German units and then the Soviet army. (An earlier attempt to achieve autonomy from the Russian empire in 1905 had been suppressed.) Independence was achieved through military force that, generally speaking, pitted Estonian nationals against Russians. Soon after the war, the Soviet Union pledged in a peace treaty to respect Estonia's independence but two decades later broke that pledge. The Soviet occupation, though interrupted by the Nazis, would continue for a half century. As an Estonian civic education teacher with whom I worked liked to say, "For us, the Second World War ended when the Russian troops finally left in 1994." Mart Laar (2004), a historian who was twice prime minister of Estonia as head of the nationalist Fatherland Party, elaborated in the *Wall Street Journal* that for Estonia, "Aug. 31 1994 . . . is now marked as the end of World War II . . . with celebrations each year."

Hostility between Russia and the Baltic states did not end with the removal of Russian troops. Hundreds of thousands of Russians had been moved into Estonia during the Soviet period and remained after independence, a fact that provided Russia with a pretext to stay involved in Baltic affairs. Even today some of Russia's militant nationalists make menacing statements about retaking the Baltic states. (Vladimir Zhirinovsky, deputy state chairman of Russia's lower house of parliament, the Duma, has spoken of annihilating Latvia, for example, as recently as 2004.)[8] Estonian independence is thus inextricably linked to conflict with Russians and with strong Russian opposition. It is not only a consistent thread of Estonian history, but also an ever-present obstacle to social integration of the large Russian and Russian-speaking minorities who live in Estonia. Indeed, Estonia, with a population of 1.4 million, is home to fewer than one million ethnic Estonians; a large proportion of the ethnic minorities have no citizenship status whatsoever.[9] The Russian-speaking peoples, whose numbers before the war were still quite small, are themselves constant reminders to the Estonians of the half-century Soviet occupation.

The long history of conflict and enmity with Russia explains in part the common sentiment among ethnic Estonians that holds the Soviet occupation in an even worse light than the Nazi occupation. Other factors include the lack of access to historical truth and the uneven distribution of casualties among different ethnic groups.

Two decades after Estonia first achieved independence, the Nazis and Soviets signed the secret protocols of the 1939 Molotov-Ribbentrop pact that divided Eastern Europe between these military powers; the Baltic states were quickly occupied by the Soviet Union and were involuntarily incorporated into the Soviet state. During the first year of the Soviet occupation, the Soviets killed or deported approximately sixty thousand of Estonia's population of one million (Estonia was about 90 percent ethnic Estonian at the time). These casualties were extensive enough to affect a great proportion of Estonia's families and communities.

There is disagreement over how well-known the provisions of the secret pact were to Estonians. A leading civics expert within the Ministry of Education explained in an interview to me that

> it isn't true, what [historian and former Prime Minister] Mart Laar is saying, [that everyone knew about] . . . the case of the secret protocols of Molotov-Ribbentrop pact. My mother was an historian and these things were not discussed at home. . . . We didn't know about that, but probably they tried to save the younger generation because the situation was like it was. . . . Some people had literature at home, but not everybody was informed about the history. (interview transcript, August 2004)

If, indeed, most people were unaware of this secret agreement, then the Nazis' complicity in handing over the Baltic states to the Soviet Union was unknown to them. Tactically, this move worked effectively for the Nazis because when German armies arrived in Estonia to drive out the Soviet forces, they were often perceived as liberators. Even liberation may have been secondary to simply putting a stop to the horrors inflicted in that single year. Many Estonian men who were eager to defend Estonia enlisted with the Germans.

Although the Nazis occupied the Baltic states for three years before the Soviets retook control, memories of suffering under the Nazis do often pale next to the recollections of what was inflicted by the Soviets, who remained for a half century. The difference cannot be attributed to a lack of Nazi atrocities:

> Some 125,000 people were executed in the concentration camps of Estonia during the years of German occupation. The bulk of these were Soviet prisoners of war and Jews from Western Europe. There were about 4,000-5,000 Estonians among those killed. The people carrying out the repression were mainly Estonians. (Laur et al. 2002: 270)

The Nazis were quite secretive about their crimes. As Singer (2002) puts it, even after eight years of propaganda and unopposed rule in Germany, the Nazis "did not dare be open about what they were doing to the Jews. Himmler told a group of SS leaders that their work in exterminating the Jews was 'an unwritten, never-to-be written, glorious page of our history'" (128). In addition to the issue of secrecy, the Nazis also had many fewer ethnic Estonian victims. Finally, despite Nazi atrocities, Soviet propaganda focused on fascism rather than the Holocaust itself. As effective a propaganda tool as the Holocaust could have been, the Soviets' strict control over information prevented widespread knowledge of those events. As Estonia's education minister said, "In Soviet times objective research into the events of the Second World War was not possible. So we must undertake this now" (Education and Science Ministry, n.d.).

With research impossible and Western European historical narratives carefully kept out, the stories that did circulate stayed within circles of trust, most often families. While most families could claim a relative or ancestor lost to the Soviets or share stories of their own deportations to Siberia, fewer claim direct harm done by the Nazis. Remarkably, even in cases where people did lose ancestors to the Nazis or had Jewish relatives, the Holocaust is often still not held in different regard than the atrocities inflicted on other peoples. Perhaps this is because it is difficult to conclude that one crime is worse than others when each claimed relatives.

Laar (2004) tells his story this way:

> My grandfather was shot by the Nazis. Two of my great-uncles were sent to Siberian death camps by the Soviets. My father-in-law was deported to Siberia as a nine-year-old boy, where he struggled to survive against death by starvation. Unknown to him, his hopes of seeing his father alive again were in vain; his father was shot early in 1941 by the KGB in Moscow's Kirov prison.

A civics official, after explaining how her Jewish grandmother's family had not been betrayed at the end of the war, when all the residents of Narva were driven out by German forces, continued by adding, "My other bloodline is Estonian-Swede and Catherine II deported them to Ukraine." She concluded, "If we continue along this path [of commemorating other peoples' suffering like the Holocaust Day], we will have nothing left but memorial days, or . . . The [Anniversary of the Deportations] suffices, for sure"[10] (e-mail correspondence with the author).

The other deportation that she cites, the one conducted under Catherine II, again involves the Russians. Two related issues are at play here. One concerns whose suffering is most important and the other involves whose crimes are paramount. Operating in the background is an assumption that the Jews constitute a single, separate nation—even though they were not centered in one place. The Estonians' status as a nation is thus perceived to be no different than the Jews' status as a nation. This civics official cited a different case of national suffering: "I was in Armenia during the Karabach crisis and I don't think at all that the Armenian people's fate is any less worthy of memory." For many Estonians, the Jewish Holocaust is one atrocity among many. The question then becomes "whose suffering do we recognize?" The attempt to give special attention to one nation's suffering is taken to be an assertion that some other population is more important than they are. One of the curriculum specialists in civic education whom I interviewed is much more of a cosmopolitan than a nationalist. Enamored with travel and a fluent speaker of several languages, the specialist expressed it this way:

A lot of people really think that Syrians and Vietnamese and Chinese and Armenians have been very treated badly through history and now why Jews? It wasn't anti-Semitism or anything, but it wasn't clear and isn't clear for me as well . . . for me, the Estonians, I would compare it . . . it was tragic for Jewish people had their own holocaust, Latvians had, Lithuanians had, some were even worse; it is not logical that we should pick up one nation's misery among 100 or 200 people's miseries. (interview transcript, April 15, 2006)

If there is a hierarchy of crimes for the Estonians, there is little question that the Soviet crimes rank much higher than the Nazis'. As one Estonian friend remarked, "We must be the only people in the world who don't hate our former masters." (Estonians lived as serfs under German lords for centuries.) Not only is there little animus toward the Nazis, but it is not terribly unusual to encounter positive memories from the Nazi occupation.

A fellow American ethnographer who worked at one of the same schools that I did shared this account that she heard from a teacher there:

I was waiting at the bus stop, talking to the math teacher at the Oak school, and it was in the context of learning German at the school, and she was saying that they had always been pretty conversant in German. Because they knew German, it made things very different during World War II; they could talk to the German soldiers. That's when she said that, "I remember very clearly the Germans knocking at our door and asking for honey and cream." She remembered that there was one soldier in particular who would always come by and he said he had three children of his own in Germany and he missed them so much. "And that's just the way they were. And everything changed when the Russians came. They would sleep in the barns, and they were drunk and they would bang in the doors with their rifles. They demanded bread and milk, and they came in and raped and murdered." (personal correspondence with the author, April 26, 2006)

Polite and civil German soldiers constitute just one side of the complex attitudes toward the Germans and the Nazi era in particular.

Having a father or a grandfather who fought for Estonian independence alongside the German/Nazi forces further complicates the issue. One Estonian civics teacher had recently uncovered his grandfather's possessions, including some items he carried with him during World War II. "He fought with the German army," he explained. The choice of words was very important: he was not referred to as a Nazi or someone who served with the Nazi army. After the war, Estonians who served with the Nazi forces and remained in Estonia were ordered to report to the Soviets and were often deported. To descendants who have learned of their experiences and know them as elderly men and as family members, it is easier to see them as victims than as perpetrators of war crimes.

For Estonians, those who fought against the Soviets and the half-century occupation of Estonia are heroes. That they fought primarily with the Nazis is, for them, largely incidental. Conversely, for Russians and Russian speakers who served with the Soviet army during what they call the Great Fatherland War, nothing is more glorious or celebrated than the defeat of the Nazis, who are typically referred to as the "fascists." When anniversaries of the war come around, when the politics of memorials are debated, when attention is given to war crimes, one side's war dead are the other's war criminals who died in the service of the most evil regime in human history. These issues all evoke the opposition between sides, and this strains the tenuous bonds that permit some semblance of a common civic identity to reach beyond ethnic Estonians who speak fluent Estonian.

AN ESTONIAN HOLOCAUST?

Among those who resisted the Soviets were the Forest Brothers, a band of men who took to the woods to resist the Soviet occupation. While some went to the woods already during the first year of the Soviet occupation (and often enlisted with the German/Nazi forces to fight the Soviets), the Forest Brothers became increasingly important after the return of Soviet forces toward the end of the war. The story of one Forest Brother, Alfred Kaarmann, recently entered the global English-language media. "In a land tossed between one occupier or another," Mr. Kaarmann makes no secret of preferring the Germans. "The conquerors from the West tried to enslave us," he said. "The conquerors from the East had another approach. They tried to kill as many of us as possible—to wipe us off the face of the earth" (Wines 2003). Kaarmann thus makes a claim that is often unspoken but that has adherents. And it may have even more sympathizers. Kaarmann suggests that the Soviet approach to the Estonians was essentially genocidal.

The reporter who quoted him immediately adds, "This is, of course, an exaggeration" (Wines 2003). But it is not at all clear that the claim is obviously an exaggeration for many Estonians. Many Estonians feel that Russia was and is dedicated to the elimination of Estonia. Population data show that "between 1940 and 1945 the population seems to have declined by a minimum of 200,000" (Raun 1991: 181). For a country with barely a million Estonians, that loss constituted a large proportion of the population. It got worse, however: the "demographic consequences of Stalinism in peacetime proved even more devastating to the population of Estonia than the upheavals of World War II" (Raun 1991: 181).

Indeed, it is exactly this perception that what the Estonian nation suffered was not wholly dissimilar to what Jews suffered in the Holocaust that allows some to appropriate the language of the Holocaust or of genocide to describe what happened to them. One curriculum specialist who worked in citizenship education explained the resistance to accepting Holocaust Day. "We have two days like this already, for us the Holocaust was the deportation, when we had massive deportation in '41 and '49, and these are opportunities for us to talk about humanity" (interview transcript, April 16, 2006). While many fled and died during the war, in the postwar Stalin years the Soviets also deported or sent to labor camps more than fifty thousand Estonians (Raun 1991: 236). And while the crimes against Estonia's Jews by the Nazis could not be taken as targeting Estonians as a whole, the Soviets' deportations are understood to constitute a collective assault on Estonians. Additionally, so many Russians and Russian speakers were settled in Estonia that the native population dropped from approximately 94 percent to 76 percent between 1945 and 1950, prompting questions about whether "Moscow was following a purposeful long-range Russification policy" (Raun 1991: 182). As Budryte points out, the Baltic states' experiences of "the Stalinist deportations, planned immigration, and russification policies were remembered as an attempt at nation killing, or genocide" (Budryte 2005: 8).

For a small nation once pinned between the Nazis and the Soviets, the perceived threat to the language, culture, and people of Estonia was extreme. These conditions may explain why many there are reluctant to attribute unique status to the Holocaust or to accept that it constituted something qualitatively different than the targeting of Estonians. Kaarmann expanded on his remarks about the Nazis and Soviets in an interview with the BBC. "The difference between them was that the Germans enslaved us and took our land. But the Russians destroyed the Estonian nation. They opposed—and still oppose—Estonian independence" (Fish 2003). He did not speak about the Soviets or the Soviet Union or even Russia. He spoke of Russians, and the reference was contemporary. He certainly meant Russians in Russia, but he by no means excluded Russians within Estonia. This case reveals the ways that attention to history can reinforce the divisions between Russians and Estonians within Estonia.

Zuroff rejected the idea of a Baltic genocide just two days after Estonia announced the creation of Holocaust Day: "[W]hat happened in Estonia was not a Holocaust or even close to one. The suffering of Estonians was appalling, but it does not mean that historically-false symetries [*sic*] with other far worse suffering should be created" (*Online Intervjuud* 2002). U.S. Ambassador DeThomas (2002) also argued in his column that "the Holocaust is a crime of unique proportions." Zuroff (2005) elaborated in an article that "one of the most prevalent tendencies in post-Communist Eastern Europe has been the attempt to create a false symmetry between Nazi and Communist crimes, and the erroneous classification of the latter as genocide [the 'double genocide' theory]."

Debates over where to draw the line in the definition of genocide date back to drafting of the 1948 Convention on the Prevention and Punishment of Genocide. According to Article 2, "genocide means any of the following acts committed with intent to destroy, in whole or in part, a national, ethnic, racial or religious group, as such: . . . (c) Deliberately inflicting on the group conditions of life calculated to bring about its physical destruction in whole or in part." How big must a part be to meet the definition is not stated. The prevailing sentiment in Estonia holds that such intent existed, and that the deportations constituted element c.

Raphael Lemkin, who coined the term, conceived of genocide as a multifaceted assault that contains many elements familiar to Estonians. He saw *genocide* as

> a coordinated plan of different actions aiming at the destruction of essential foundations of the life of national groups, with the aim of annihilating the groups themselves. The objectives of such a plan would be disintegration of the political and social institutions, of culture, language, national feelings, religion, and the economic existence of national groups, and the destruction of the personal security, liberty, health, dignity, and even the lives of the individuals belonging to such groups. (Lemkin 1944, cited in Nersessian 2005)

This broader definition, which makes clear the cultural and linguistic elements of genocide, was initially included in the draft of the 1948 convention but omitted with the intention that it be left to separate conventions. Proponents of exclusion argued "forcefully that it defied both logic and proportion 'to include in the same convention both mass murders in gas chambers and the closing of libraries'" (Nersessian 2005). The problem raised "by limiting genocide to its physical and biological manifestations [is that] a group can be kept physically and biologically intact even as its collective identity suffers in a fundamental and irremediable manner. Put another way, the present understanding of genocide preserves the body of the group but allows its very soul to be destroyed" (Nersessian 2005).

The "false symmetry" question may be no more than a quest for recognition for the suffering and losses endured by long-occupied peoples. Attempts to link the Holocaust to the suffering of the Baltic nations may not imply that the Holocaust was in fact equivalent or identical to the Soviet crimes. By linking the crimes together, Estonians and the other Baltic nations are able to seek recognition for their own stories while offering recognition to the issue of the Holocaust. The long-term members of the European Union may have to open themselves up to new versions of the history of World War II, as this report from the BBC suggests:

> On 14 June 1941 more than 30,000 were deported from the Baltic countries to prison camps in Siberia. At a ceremony in Tallinn, the Estonian President,

Arnold Ruutel, said the victims of the Stalinist deportations would be remembered forever. But controversy surrounds a plan to put up a plaque at the European Parliament. Some Socialists in the European parliament are blocking the plan, saying that it would lead to a plethora of memorials. But Baltic MEPs say they feel it is important that older members of the EU learn about the history of new member countries, to understand them better. ("Baltic Victims of USSR Remembered," 2006)

The Baltic states may recognize better than most that there is value in allowing different understandings of history to stand side by side. Budryte (2005) notes that the "consequences of forced integration of Russians into the Estonian demos . . . would have been grave," particularly if it had involved the "imposition of Estonian commemorative practices, as well as one version of Estonian history" (9).

Difficulties seem to arise not from attempts to link these sets of crimes but in approaches that seem to differentiate between victims. American engagement in Estonia seemed to many Estonians not to promote evenhanded justice but rather ethnic favoritism. Proponents of this position felt that the foreign focus on the Holocaust inappropriately privileged one set of victims and one type of suffering over others, namely, their own victims and suffering. This view was articulated clearly to the ambassador in an anonymous, Internet based question-and-answer forum:

> Mr. Ambassador: while this writer fully acknowledges the horror of what the Nazis and their accomplices did to Jews, Gypsies and Estonians during the three years of German WW II occupation of Estonia, the number of lives lost and the duration of the combined Soviet occupations enormously eclipse the Nazi period. When will the US Embassy begin dedicating time to these dark chapters in proportion to their significance to the host country? When will the US begin funding an Office of Soviet Investigations or an Office of Communist Investigations designed to systematically condemn and bring to justice [*sic*] the few surviving communist war criminals, torturers and executioners who terrorized Central and Eastern Europe (and Cambodia and several other victim societies?). A few more years and it will be too late. Is this the objective? Surely it must be the gravity of the offenses and even-handed consistency of approach that interests the US government—a country that practices and advocates the rule of law—and not the ethnic origin or the religious orientation of the victims? Even-handedness is what we're asking for. Most Estonians are in agreement that German atrocities and Soviet Russian atrocities must be handled using the same legal yardsticks, and that the consequences for the perpetrators should be the same. (*Online Intervjuud* 2003)

Implicit is the idea that Soviet criminals should not be placed second in the quest for justice behind the Nazis in Estonia. An appropriate application of justice in Estonia, the reasoning goes, would not treat Estonians as inferior or less important victims than the Jewish victims, but would respect each victim's suffering and death equally by pursuing justice equally and pursuing each criminal with equal dedication.

DeThomas explained the U.S. focus on the Holocaust in this way when he was asked why a similar standard was not applied to other human rights atrocities, like those perpetrated by the Soviets:

> You are correct that there were many crimes against humanity. I have personally participated in events commemorating victims of Soviet crimes in Estonia. However, the legal structures the US government pursues regarding the Holocaust are unique to that particular set of crimes. In large part, this is because many survivors of the Holocaust fled to the US and are now U.S. citizens. They look to U.S. law for redress. (*Online Intervjuud* 2003)

The international effort to bring to justice those Estonians who were involved in war crimes related to the Holocaust is thus taken to reflect a lack of foreign understanding about the suffering endured by Estonians as a whole under the Soviets. Such an emphasis calls attention only to Estonian criminals with no acknowledgment that most Estonians were victims. Since most Estonians today have connections to victims of atrocities, and the number of war criminals is drastically smaller, this emphasis can feel like a collective accusation. For Estonians, the dominant story is of Estonians as victims, while a tiny minority, trapped between two powers, was complicit in the Holocaust. Furthermore, no foreign powers are seeking to bring Soviet war criminals who executed or deported Estonians to justice. The combination of these facts—the pursuit of Estonians who committed war crimes and the disregard for criminals who victimized Estonians—suggests that Estonians don't matter to the rest of the world. It is frequently taken to belittle Estonians' own suffering by implying that the one category of "other" victims is more important than their own. Worse, it replaces the Estonian nation's identity as a victim with an accusation that is perceived to imply collective guilt or criminality. Finally, it makes the United States appear to be more concerned with advancing the interests of one group than it is with principles of justice.

Estonians may cling to the notion that they survived a genocidal regime, that the Soviets had in mind to destroy the Estonian nation, whether through occupation, deportations, assimilation, executions, or any of the other tactics brought to bear on them. Families' memories of loss and suffering may never cede pride of place to victims of the Holocaust. And they may never accept the notion that Soviet criminals were any less terrible than Nazi criminals.

These experiences need not be set against each other. As Margaret Buber-Neumann wrote, after surviving Stalin's prisons only to be handed over to the Nazi camps,

"I asked myself which is really worse: the lice-infested corncob-walled cabins in Birma [Kazakhstan] or the nightmare-order of Ravensbruck. . . . It is hard to decide which is the least humane—to gas people in five minutes, or to strangle them slowly, over the course of three months, by hunger?" (in Ferguson 2002: 27).

Linking the horrors, which often shared time and space, need not imply equivalency or symmetry. The atrocities suffered by the Estonians at Soviet hands could be used as an entrée to the horrors of the Holocaust. This approach was used by the U.S. embassy, which supported the foundation of the Estonian International Commission for Investigation of Crimes against Humanity in 1998. The commission, which investigated the periods of occupation under both the Nazis and the Soviets, was able simultaneously to give recognition to Estonian victims of the Soviet occupation while at the same time confronting the events of the Holocaust on Estonian soil and perpetrated by Estonians. For foreigners concerned with the Holocaust, the fact that the commission placed those events in a larger context that did not single out Estonian criminals while ignoring Estonian victims allowed attention to be brought to the issue. For Estonians, the connection of the two in this context served to legitimize their attempts to link the Holocaust and the Soviet occupations.

A similar approach was taken by a museum in Tallinn. Because it is all but impossible to celebrate the ideology for which anyone fought, since combatants fought under the swastika or under the hammer and sickle, people's individual sacrifices are commemorated with respect to what they fought against. Families' fallen members are honored for defeating fascism or for resisting Soviet occupation. Honoring the fallen for defeating fascism or resisting the Soviets, however, is often taken as a dishonor to those who fought on the other side, if not a celebration of the cause for which they fought.

When the Soviet occupation was nearing its end and Gorbachev had declared a period of openness, the monuments to the Soviet Union in Estonia began to be removed. The exception to the rule was the preservation of monuments to those who died in World War II. One such Soviet-era monument, a memorial of a soldier with his head lowered, has been the site of rallies and of vandalism.[11] Across the square, with support from the foundation of a member of the Estonian diaspora who has lived for decades in the United States, Estonia built a Museum of Occupations. Locating the museum so close to the Soviet-era monument may be a way of challenging the Russian narrative of World War II. Russia certainly interpreted it that way:

The Russian Foreign Ministry released a statement . . . accusing the Estonian authorities of attempting to raise again the theme of Soviet occupation . . .

[and] called the opening of the Museum of Occupation in Tallinn and the unveiling of a monument to the forest brothers killed by the Red Army in May 1945 actions which cast doubt on the sincerity of the assurances of Estonian leaders that they are loyal to European principles. The statement further condemns the efforts of "Estonian nationalists to glorify Estonian Nazi henchmen as fighters for Estonia's freedom and against the Soviet occupation. ("Baltic States Report," 2003c)

In the museum, two large, dark, and identical trains stand together. One bears a swastika; the other the Soviet red star. "In Western and Central Europe, the image of the cattle wagon is immediately associated with the memory of the deportation and destruction of the European Jews by Nazi Germany. In the Baltic states, the image of a cattle wagon is a symbol of suffering during the Stalinist times and deportation to the *gulag*" (Budryte 2005: 187). The stories told by the trains honors the suffering of all of the victims of destructive ideologies during the Soviet and Nazi periods. The stories told by the trains narrow the gap between Estonians and their Western European and American allies. Locating Estonians' suffering among other crimes against humanity simultaneously seeks recognition while acknowledging what other peoples have endured. It may also facilitate Estonia's task of crafting a common civic identity that is not rooted in the narrow historic, binary opposition between Russians and Estonians.

NOTES

This research was made possible by the generous support of a predissertation grant from Indiana University's Office of International Programs, a Fulbright Fellowship, and a Professional Development Fellowship. A study of the policy and practice of civic education in Estonia, including its transnational elements, this research involved participation in and observations of a broad range of international events, seminars, teacher-training sessions, and classrooms over three years. Officials and teachers across the entire range of the policy process were interviewed as well. Because Estonia is a small country and the number of people involved in these issues was relatively small, it is a challenge to provide detailed information and anonymity at the same time. Individual participants in this study are therefore referred to in very general terms (an official, a textbook author, etc.), without, I hope, much loss to the overall arguments.

   1. This exhibit can be seen at www.muuseum.harju.ee/holokaust/.
   2. These projects are detailed at http://estonia.usembassy.gov./assist.php.
   3. This interview took place in 2003. Like all interviews conducted during my research, names would not be provided, even if the interviewees, as in this case, insisted that they stood by their statements publicly and such anonymity was unnecessary.

4. The source for this claim was never located. It is not inconsistent with the prevailing sentiments that I encountered.

5. See, for example, www.hm.ee/index.php?03122.

6. Last retrieved in November 2005, from www.hm.ee/uus/hm/client/index .php?035265513313142003. This link is no longer operative. Months after purging the website of most mentions of Holocaust Day, the entire press release archive has been removed from a revamped website.

7. This refers to a struggle against Germans that took place more than six centuries earlier, in 1343–1345.

8. *City Paper* assembled a page of "Zhirinovskyisms" up through 1996, including his claim that "I'm doing everything possible to liquidate the Baltic states. . . . You are directly on our path to the sea. Russia needs ports and therefore the occupation of the Baltic states is inevitable. . . . War is inevitable, and Estonia, Latvia and Lithuania will disappear completely and finally from the political map of world." See www.balticsworldwide.com/quotes/zhirinovskyisms.htm. More recently, in 2004, he threatened, "Latvia will be destroyed. . . . Absolutely nothing will remain from Latvia. Everybody will forget the words 'Latvia' and 'the Latvian language.' There will be nothing in Latvia, forever. We will destroy everything. If you touch Russians and Russian schools. I assure you. Nothing will remain." "Latvia Will Be Destroyed," *Pravda*, March 27, 2004, http://english.pravda.ru/world/20/92/372/ 12363_Latvia.html.

9. Estonia's leading newspaper, quoting the European Commission against Racism and Intolerance report, claims approximately 139,000 residents lack citizenship. "Euroopa Nõukogu komisjon kritiseeris Eestit," *Postimees*, February 21, 2006, www.postimees.ee/220206/esileht/siseuudised/192821.php.

10. June 14, now a national day of commemoration, represented both the first major deportation and the day with the largest number deported. Approximately ten thousand Estonians were deported on that one night in 1941 alone, about 1 percent of the population, while roughly four hundred Jews were deported as well, a sum that amounted to 10 percent of the entire Jewish population of Estonia. Jewish suffering at the hands of the Soviets was not limited to the deportations. (Information provided by the Estonia Institute and hosted by the Jewish Virtual Library, a division of the American-Israeli Cooperative Enterprise; "The Jewish Virtual History Tour: Estonia," www.jewishvirtuallibrary.org/jsource/vjw/Estonia.html). In July 1940, Jewish cultural autonomy was eliminated, and all Jewish institutions were eliminated. All organizations were eliminated in the same year. Soviet policy remained inhospitable to Jewish organizations; Soviet passports, which categorized people by citizenship (Soviet) and nationality, listed Estonian and Jewish as separate categories.

11. A spherical view of the monument during a rally is available for viewing at http://ww2panorama.org/panos/andrei_bordov_tallinn1.html.

REFERENCES

Baltic News Service (BNS). 2002. "Koolijuhid Taunivad Holokaustipäeva." *Õhtuleht*, August 26. www.sloleht.ee/index.aspx?id = 127279&r = 4.

"Baltic States Report." 2003a. *RFE/RL Reports* 4, no. 5 (February 10). www.rferl.org/ reports/balticreport/2003/02/5-100203.asp.
———. 2003b. *RFE/RL Reports* 4, no. 8 (March 4). www.rferl.org/reports/baltic report/2003/03/8-040303.asp.
———. 2003c. *RFE/RL Reports* 4, no. 23 (July 28). www.rferl.org/reports/baltic report/2003/07/23-280703.asp.
"Baltic Victims of USSR Remembered." 2006. *BBC News,* June 14. from http://news .bbc.co.uk/2/hi/europe/5081310.stm.
Budryte, D. 2005. *Taming Nationalism? Political Community Building in the Post-Soviet Baltic States.* Burlington, Vt.: Ashgate.
City Paper's Baltics Worldwide. 2002. "News Highlights from Lithuania, Latvia, and Estonia." November 18. www.balticsww.com/wkcrier/2002-05-12.htm.
———. 2003. "News Highlights from Lithuania, Latvia, and Estonia." January 28. www.balticsww.com/wkcrier/2003-01-12.htm.
DeThomas, J. M. 2002. *Past, Present, and Future.* May 28. http://estonia.usembassy .gov/holocaust_eng.php.
Education and Science Ministry. n.d. *Minister Maimets Jerusalemmas uue muuseumi avamisel.* www.hm.ee/index.php?045848.
Estonian Ministry of Foreign Affairs. 2006. *The Holocaust Day Was Commemorated in Estonia.* January 26. www.vm.ee/eng/kat_137/7304.html.
Embassy of the United States in Estonia. 2002. *Remarks by Heather Conley, U.S. Deputy Assistant Secretary of State for European and Eurasian Affairs at Stockholm Security Conference—The United States and Northern Europe: A Continuing Commitment.* April 24. www.usemb.ee/conley.php.
European Commission against Racism and Intolerance. 2006. *Third Report on Estonia.* February 21. www.coe.int/t/E/human_rights/ecri/1-ECRI/2-Country-by -country_approach/Estonia/Estoniapercent20thirdpercent20reportpercent20- percent20cri06-1.pdf.
Ferguson, N. 2002. "Introduction to Tzvetan Todorov." In *Human Rights, Human Wrongs,* ed. N. Owen. Oxford: Oxford University Press.
Fish, J. 2003. "Grim Reminder of Estonia's Soviet Past." *BBC News,* November 17. http://news.bbc.co.uk/1/hi/world/europe/3249737.stm.
Jewish Virtual Library, a division of the American-Israeli Cooperative Enterprise. 2006. *The Jewish Virtual History Tour: Estonia.* www.jewishvirtuallibrary.org/ jsource/vjw/Estonia.html.
Laar, M. 2004. "When Will Russia Say Sorry?" *Wall Street Journal,* August 20, p._A.12
Laur, M., T. Lukas, A. Mäesalu, A. Pajur, and T. Tannberg. 2002. *The History of Estonia.* 2nd ed. Tallinn, Estonia: Avita.
mauri [*sic*]. 2003. *Holokaustipäev kui NATO pileti konts.* April 10. www.minut.ee/arti cle.pl?sid = 03/04/10/2249239&mode = nested.
Mudde, C., ed. 2005. *Racist Extremism in Central and Eastern Europe.* London: Routledge.
Nersessian, D. 2005. "Rethinking Cultural Genocide Under International Law." *Carnegie Council on Ethics and International Affairs.* www.cceia.org/viewMedia.php/ prmID/5139.
Nielson, I. 2003. "Holokaustipäev jätab koolid ükskõikseks." *Pärnu Postimees,* Janu-

ary 25. http://vana.www.parnupostimees.ee/index.html?op = lugu&rubriik = 77& id = 15996&number = 457.

Online Intervjuud. 2002. "Eesti Päevaleht." August 8. www.epl.ee/artikkel _211663.html&P = 1.

———. 2003. "Eesti Päevaleht." April 9. www.epl.ee/artikkel_232604.html.

Pettai, I. 2002. "Estonians and Non-Estonians: A Typology of Tolerance." Non-Estonians' Integration Foundation. www.meis.ee/pictures/PETTEXT.pdf.

Poleshchuk, V. 2005. "Estonia." In *Racist Extremism in Central and Eastern Europe*, ed. C. Muddle. London: Routledge

Raun, T. 1991. *Estonia and the Estonians.* 2nd ed. Stanford, Calif.: Hoover Institution.

Simon Wiesenthal Center. 2004. "Wiesenthal Center Protests Erection of Monument Commemorating Estonian SS-Division Which Fought with Nazis in World War II." August 25. www.wiesenthal.com/site/apps/s/content.asp?c = fwLYKnN8 LzH&b = 253162&ct = 285196.

———. n.d. "About Us." www.wiesenthal.com/site/pp.asp?c = fwLYKnN8LzH& b = 242501.

Singer, P. 2002. "How Can We Prevent Crimes against Humanity?" In *Human Rights, Human Wrongs*, ed. N. Owen. Oxford: Oxford University Press.

Wines, M. 2003. "A 'Forest Brother' Remembers a Life on the Run." *New York Times*, August 23, p. A4.

Zuroff, E. 2005. "Eastern Europe: Anti-Semitism in the Wake of Holocaust-Related Issues." *Jewish Political Studies Review* 17, no. 1–2 (Spring). www.jcpa.org/phas/ phas-zuroff-s05.htm.

10

Forming and Implementing a New Secondary Civic Education Program in Mexico: Toward a Democratic Citizen without Adjectives

Bradley A. U. Levinson

For at least two decades now, Mexico has been in the throes of a fitful transition from a long history of corrupt authoritarian rule to a more fully democratic regime. Yet changes in civil society have not always kept pace with changes in the formal political-electoral sphere. Like so many other countries currently experiencing democratic transition, Mexico has looked to its school system to undertake the daunting task of cultivating democratic attitudes and dispositions among the new generation. There is both great enthusiasm for this project, and great skepticism that schools can accomplish it.

Civic education in Mexico is back—sort of. After twenty-five years of nearly invisible incorporation into the cross-disciplinary subject of "social studies" in the national secondary school (*secundaria*), civic education in 1999 was reconceived as a separate course of study that might invigorate the entire secondary curriculum. Renamed "Civic and Ethical Formation" (*Formación Cívica y Etica*, or FCE), this new course had been implemented in virtually all secundarias by 2001. A great deal of hope had been invested in this new school subject, which encompassed everything from citizenship and government studies to "values" and sex education. With its emphasis on student-centered pedagogy and critical thinking, FCE teachers were envisioned as the catalysts of a new educational culture in the schools. Students, meanwhile, had become the new democratic subjects of schooling.

While the reform of civic education began in the mid-1990s, what gave it renewed impetus, and special interest, was its convergence since 2000 with more robust democratic openings in the Mexican political and policy-making process. In that year, long-standing single-party rule effectively ended in Mexico with the election of the opposition candidate, Vicente Fox, and with the achievement of an opposition majority in the bicameral congress. Fox's party, *Partido de Acción Nacional* (PAN), has made inroads into all major ministries, and he has made significant new appointments within the national education ministry, the Secretaría de Educación Pública (SEP). While most Mexicans hailed these new developments as important steps on the road to full democracy, many worried that the rightist PAN, historically allied with the Catholic Church, would use its power to erode the strong separation of church and state that had characterized public education since the Revolution ended, in 1921. Because it centrally addressed questions of ethics, morality, and citizenship, the FCE program was feared to be a beachhead from which the PAN might seek to introduce religion back into the schools. Yet most policymakers and curriculum experts in the education ministry remained nonpartisan and, like the vast majority of schoolteachers themselves, strongly upheld the principle of "*laicidad*" (secularism) in schools.

The new course for civic and ethical education in Mexican secondary schools is ambitious, complex, and compulsory. For roughly three hours a week, during all three years of secundaria, Mexican students examine a number of social and civic issues. The new program not only covers the traditional themes of civic education (constitution, structure of government, laws, electoral processes, etc.) but also entails a variety of "ethical" considerations, including prevention of drug addiction and gang membership, sex education, multicultural awareness and tolerance, gender relations, and environmental awareness.

During my initial research on the new Mexican program,[1] I spoke with a number of policymakers, scholars, administrators, and teachers. Many were understandably excited about the prospects for the FCE course. They thought it could serve as the axis of a new "democratic" culture in the schools, where teachers and school authorities would come to model a spirit of participation, dialogue, respect, and open inquiry; they hoped it would pave the way for a Mexican democracy "without adjectives."[2] Yet many expressed skepticism about whether the reform could meaningfully take hold. Skepticism, as I will discuss further, seemed to turn around two areas of concern: (1) teacher subjectivities,[3] teacher training, and teacher hiring, all mired in older structures of tradition, convenience, economic opportunism, and even union favoritism and corruption, and (2) the cultural and political immaturity of the broader society to sustain whatever democratic habits and attitudes the school manages to develop in students.

In this chapter, I present the main goals and themes of the new Mexican program and highlight some of the challenges that national and local actors have identified for its implementation. I begin with a brief historical review of civic education in the modern Mexican secundaria, follow with an account of how the FCE was created, and then turn to a thematic analysis of the new published curriculum and study program. From there I consider what Mexicans themselves have told me about the program, summarizing the challenges that they articulate.

THE VICISSITUDES OF CIVIC AND ETHICAL EDUCATION IN THE MEXICAN SECUNDARIA

Though the public secundaria was officially created by law in 1915, it was not until 1923, shortly after the first federal rural primary schools (*primarias*) were brought into being, that the secundaria received serious attention. Until that time, Mexico had followed the classical European tradition of combining secondary education with college preparatory studies, thereby emphasizing specialization and encyclopedic knowledge. In 1923, Bernardo Gastélum, Subsecretary of Education, proposed a reorganization of college preparatory studies by clearly distinguishing a phase of secondary education as an extension of the primary school. In this manner, the secundaria would still retain some of the subject matter and specialization characteristic of preparatory studies, but it would now continue the "basic" cultural and ideological functions of the primaria. Following the liberal imperative to wrest power from the church and assign the task of moral socialization to the state, the secundaria would now focus on a formative *education* of the character rather than the instruction of specialized knowledge.[4]

It was not until 1928 and the creation of a separate Office of Secondary Education that the secundaria became more explicitly guided by methods and principles appropriate to the "adolescent" life stage (Meneses Morales 1986: 479, 603). Moisés Sáenz, considered by most the founder of the secundaria, had studied at Columbia University with John Dewey. Yet while the U.S. junior high school advocated by Dewey had been developed in part to foster individual identity formation and critical thinking, the Mexican secundaria emphasized the importance of curtailing selfish individualism and creating a sense of social solidarity. The goal of the secundaria was to balance the desire for a curriculum more specialized than the primaria—a curriculum that would offer students the chance to explore their vocational options—with the themes of integration and national unity. The goal, in other words, was to accommodate the "individual differences" of the students while still subordinating individual interests to the imperatives of "solidarity," "cooperation," and so-called social values (Meneses Morales 1986: 486).

The presidency of Lázaro Cárdenas (1934–1940), the great populist reformer, oversaw a significant growth in secondary enrollments. Now with an avowedly socialist educational program, children of workers were more strongly encouraged to continue their schooling as the secundaria turned more "technical," and the curriculum included more hours devoted to practical, productive activities. It was at this time that "vocational counseling" (*orientación*) first appeared in the secundaria. Also at this time, the teaching of history and civics was given new emphasis. In 1932, the curriculum added a course in "civic culture" to the required courses of Spanish, foreign language, mathematics, science (biology, chemistry, and physics), geography, and history for each of the three years. This course added an important critical element to the curriculum, as it focused on political, economic, and legal "problems" in Mexico. By 1937, the course in civic culture had been changed to "socialist information and practice," and students increasingly learned about class conflict and imperialism as a way of understanding Mexican history. They participated in student government and mutual aid societies to practice cooperative social work. Finally, students made frequent trips to shops and factories in order to gain a fuller appreciation of working-class life.

The short-lived socialist experiment ended abruptly in 1940, as the reins of presidential power swung over to the more conservative Avila Camacho. If the school under Cárdenas had given preference to workers and become the school of struggle, under Camacho's first education secretary, Véjar Vázquez, it would become the "school of love," and under his second secretary, Torres Bodet, the school of unity. Official educational discourse thus reinstated the signal importance of "national unity" and reconciliation above class struggle.

The secundaria expanded under Camacho at an even greater rate than under Cárdenas. Once again, the uniquely "adolescent" character of the institution was proclaimed, and reformers sought to protect the secundaria from the "threat of two contradictory invasions:" the primaria and higher education (Meneses Morales 1988: 283). The secundaria was to have its own personality, its own agenda. As the Mexican state entered into a period of more comfortable alliance with national and transnational capital, the official discourse of this period constructed the interests of the nation, of subordinated classes, and of capital as convergent; each could win in the formula for national development, modernization, and the stabilization of a "revolutionary" regime. This formula then provided the basic continuity in policy and practice around the secundaria at least until 1974, perhaps even until 1992 (see the later discussion here). In the period from 1950 to 1970, there was a 1,000 percent increase in secundaria enrollments, mainly due to the growing participation of female students, who came to form half the student body in most secundarias by the late 1970s.

Before 1974, then, civic education had always been present in the secundaria, though it was oriented more toward unity and solidarity (of class, of nation) than to the construction of a democratic citizen. In 1974, after a major national reform law and a national conference held in Chetumal, Quintana Roo, there was another significant modification of the secundaria curriculum. Among other things, the so-called Chetumal Reforms brought together previously separate subjects (*asignaturas*) into multidisciplinary fields of inquiry, called *áreas*. Thus, for instance, biology, chemistry, and physics came together as "natural sciences," and were given a combined seven hours per week in the national curriculum. For our interests here, history, geography, and civics were combined into "social sciences" and also given seven hours of the weekly study program. Teachers who had previously been more strongly specialized in, and identified with, one of three subjects, now had to cover a broader field of social sciences. The teaching of civics was folded into the new social science curriculum, and not always in a wholly coherent fashion.[5]

From 1992 to 1993, a series of educational "modernization" measures included an important amendment to the constitutional article mandating public education and a new "general law" of education. The amendment now made secundaria attendance compulsory, thereby raising the stakes of civic education at that level; the new law stipulated values of critical reflection, democratic participation, and human rights. From 1993 to 1999, the older asignaturas returned to all secundarias in Mexico, with civics accorded just three hours during the first and second year. A brand new subject, Educational Orientation (*Orientación Educativa*), was added to the third year of studies, along with a three-hour elective course that the states and localities could determine according to their own needs and interests. It was during this time that many social workers, psychologists, and "vocational counselors" made their first regular appearance in classrooms. Previously, such school personnel had been limited to occasional classroom visits to conduct vocational aptitude tests or to lead discussions about sexual development. After 1993, however, many of these personnel became regular classroom instructors, charged with teaching a new subject that combined vocational orientation with elements of self-exploration, sex education, and drug and crime prevention.

INFLUENCES AND INSTITUTIONAL DYNAMICS
IN THE CREATION OF THE FCE

The next serious reform of Mexican civic education, which most concerns us here, began in the mid-1990s. During the last PRI presidential administration (1994–2000), the Secretary of Education gave a team the charge to create what would eventually become the FCE. The policy process for the reform of civic education in Mexico received a strong impulse, according to many, from then-president Ernesto Zedillo (1994–2000), who had actually served as Secretary of Education during the prior presidential administration, from 1988 to 1994. Zedillo had been the primary architect of the modernization reforms of 1992 and 1993, which among other things enshrined new language in the Federal Education Law that made participatory and "pertinent" education a cornerstone of national development. Such emphases were reiterated in the national Program for Educational Development 1995–2000 under Zedillo's presidency, which highlighted the goals of achieving educational "equity, quality, and relevance" (*pertinencia*).

There is good evidence that Zedillo was reading and channeling a variety of social concerns that had been brewing for over a decade. Based on my previous fieldwork, my reading of popular and scholarly literatures, and my ongoing trips to Mexico, I have identified at least three powerful societal discourses that formed and expanded throughout the 1980s and 1990s. Each one of these discourses expressed certain understandings of democracy, and each one, I argue, would impact the eventual formation of this new program for citizenship education. Such discourses emerged out of rather different social sectors and movements, but each one articulated a set of existential concerns that cut across broad sectors of Mexican society. Each one also highlighted a different set of "values" that needed to be recovered or constructed.

Finally, if there is one theme that cuts across all the discourses it is the concern with human rights and the creation of a culture of "tolerance." Fed up with political violence and economic misery, and disgusted by the impunity accorded to most perpetrators, many Mexicans by the 1990s had seized on human rights as a crucial value. The notion of human rights, in turn, was often vitally linked to the attainment of democracy. However, human rights could also become a kind of Rorschach of cultural projection: the place of human rights and the route to achieving a regime respectful of such rights, would vary by discourse and social sector.

One discourse, which I call "lost values" (*valores perdidos*), drew attention to the signs of what many observers call "social disintegration," such as increased violence, corruption, divorce, and disregard for adult authority. The assumption made by this discourse was that traditional values of respect, honesty, and obedience had once effectively ordered society, but had since fallen into disuse. There was a strong sense of proper social hierarchy having become challenged and turned upside-down. Most strongly articulated through conservative Catholic organizations such as the national "Parents' Union" (UNPF), the discourse on lost values nevertheless resonated with a much broader public. The often explicit solution proposed by the very same discourse was the recovery of values that had been "lost" in recent years—typically through religious education or other kinds of catechistic instruction, and the reassertion of paternal control.

Another discourse, which I call the active and "critical citizen" (*el ciudadano crítico*), highlighted the importance of creating deeper democratic habits and a political culture that would support a democratic transition over the longer term. Most strongly articulated by a generation of left-leaning Mexican intellectuals and leaders who'd come of age in the political opposition to the PRI-dominated state, the discourse of the "critical citizen" called for a new participatory sensibility among citizens, most of whom were seen as having grown complacent, fatalistic, or too accustomed to state largesse. This form of participation presupposed an ethos of respectful dialogue but also critical questioning, in which existing social hierarchies and received norms would be subject to constant critique. The new citizen would actively consider different social and political options through a critical discursive process, and arrive at independent stances. The discourse of the critical citizen implicitly valued equality over hierarchy—gender equity was often prominently touted as a goal. Although it originated in the more highly schooled sectors of society, this discourse, too, found resonance across broad sectors of society that had been irrevocably changed by experiences of immigration and/or consumption of cultural media such as television, movies, popular music, and the Internet.

The third discourse, which I call "accountability" (*rendición de cuentas*), virtually created a new phrase in Mexican Spanish overnight, since there had been no adequate predecessor to this cultural import. Even more clearly influenced from abroad than the others, the discourse on accountability called for greater transparency in public management and more valid and neutral forms of evaluation in assessing educational "quality." One of the important assumptions of this discourse was that the goals of transparency and quality called for both institutional and personal transformations. On the one hand, new kinds of institutional arrangements, such as the creation of a quasi-independent National Institute for Educational Evaluation, or the implementation of a merit-based assessment of teacher performance, would leverage higher quality and greater public accountability. On the other hand, the discourse called for the cultivation of a new subjectivity which placed responsibility for public outcomes—such as students' learning—on individuals as well as institutions. In this sense, the new democratic citizen had to learn to become more responsible—that is, accountable—for his or her actions.

The growth of these societal discourses clearly put the need for some kind of citizenship education on the national agenda. Time and time again, people who were involved in some way with the creation of the FCE program alluded to aspects of these societal discourses and the social pressures that accompanied them. Usually the pressures were characterized in rather general terms, with reference to "values," above all (Latapí 2003). As the main author of the FCE program put it in an interview, for instance, "There was an urgent social demand, expressed in many different venues, that values be taught, that there was a lack of values [in the current generation]." Such social pressures, of course, would have to be channeled and mediated in specific ways through the bureaucracy of the education ministry (SEP), which is relatively impervious to the demands of particular social movements. Indeed, as I highlight here, the final impetus for development of a program like FCE would come from the personal initiative of key actors— the president, the secretary of education, and, perhaps most decisively, the secretary's wife.

The secretary of education who took over shortly after the beginning of the Zedillo administration, Miguel Limón, is a professor of constitutional law with a long trajectory of civil service. After having served as dean of social sciences at the Autonomous Metropolitan University in Mexico City and academic secretary at the National Pedagogical University, Limón went on to serve for a number of years as director of the National Institute for Indigenous Affairs (INI), as subsecretary of the interior (*Gobernación*) for issues of corruption and extortion, and finally as attorney general for environmental protection. This list of positions covers a remarkable range of issues and concerns that were eventually encompassed by the FCE program; indeed, the former secretary himself pointed out that each of these former positions had a strong "ethical" dimension (*contenido ético*), and that he saw his appointment as secretary a grand opportunity to bring this ethical dimension to public education. Yet why did Limón give the development of citizenship education such a high priority among the many pressing educational problems confronting him at the outset of his administration?

On this point, the former secretary revealed the influence of his wife. When I asked him to reflect on how his biography influenced his interest in the FCE program, he started in with a chuckle:

> Look, in the first place let me tell you something: I'm married to a teacher, an educator, and she has had a lot of influence on my education as an adult. . . . She has been very important in all of this, she really insisted and persevered with me so I wouldn't lose sight [of civic and ethical education] beyond all the fog that is created as part of bureaucratic routine. Her insistence was in that sense very, very important.

The Secretary then went on to describe how his wife eventually formed the crucial authorship team for FCE. She became a member of the team and an active contributor to the development of the program.

For her part, the Secretary's wife, Maestra Campillo, placed the highest emphasis on the multiplicity of perspectives and materials that shaped the program. As she traveled with her husband to numerous international meetings during the early part of his tenure, she took advantage of each site to gather materials on civic education. Among the sites she mentioned most prominently were Switzerland (for UNESCO), France (where her husband had studied many years before), Spain, England, the United States, various countries of South America, and, perhaps most intriguingly, Japan. As she put it in response to my question about whether foreign influences had shaped FCE:

> I had the advantage that my husband was speaking regularly with the minis-
> ters, the policymakers, so the obligatory question on my part was always,
> "Please, ask them what they're doing in this area [of civic education]." . . .
> There's no influence from a single place but we are certainly, and necessarily,
> influenced by the materials that we have read.

Societal discourses, as I have discussed then, created impetus and formed an important backdrop for the work of the FCE team. They provided a critical "problem diagnosis" for policy reform (Sutton and Levinson 2001). Public concerns about values were often expressed through the media or directly to the President's office, and then channeled to Limón. Such discourses also established a set of implicit parameters within which the FCE team would have to conduct its work.

Legitimated by public discourse, supported by the President, and bolstered by the general goals of the Plan for Educational Development 1995–2000, by 1995 Limón felt a clear mandate to begin the reform of civic education to include a stronger component of "values formation" as well as participatory pedagogy. Ordinarily, proposals for curricular reform within the SEP would have been routed through the appropriate content "team" in the General Directorate of Educational Methods and Materials, under the Subsecretary of Basic Education. The Secretary, in consultation with the President, would provide a policy mandate to reform curriculum, and would instruct the Subsecretary to put the reform into motion through the appropriate content team. However, Limón proceeded differently. First, he convened a prominent group of educational researchers to produce a white paper on the topic of citizenship and values education. This group was coordinated by one of the foremost education scholars in modern Mexican history, a man whose principled and pointed criticism had often caused problems for previous PRI administrations. When the white paper was delivered, the discussion about how to create a program in civic education was really just beginning. The subsecretary for basic education took a less active role in these discussions. In his mind, there were more pressing matters requiring resources and attention, and he also worried about giving teachers too much latitude to teach civic "values." This is apparently why Limón took the unprecedented step of convening a separate team of advisers to draft the new program in civic education. The team was literally housed in Limón's private offices and figuratively taken under his wing. His wife would come to form the symbolic heart of the team, and a Harvard-trained educational philosopher was selected to head it up. Then two more members were added—one a classical musician and music professor of broad reputation, another a writer of fiction and social commentary.

This team took the draft white paper produced by the specially convened research team and went about seeking additional input from a variety of organizations and government agencies that had rarely been consulted in the past. Clearly, this was going to be a new, more collaborative process for curriculum and program design. Technical curriculum teams from all the states of the Mexican republic were invited to participate in early discussions, comment on drafts, and propose their own ideas. Then, among the organizations external to the SEP that were invited to submit proposals for content, and to vet the early drafts of the program, were the Catholic Church, the National Autonomous University of Mexico, the National Pedagogical University, the National Youth Institute, the Human Rights Commission of the Federal District, the Ministry of Health, and the Council on Addictions. Particularly important was a burgeoning collaboration with the Federal Electoral Institute (IFE), which had its own parallel program in citizenship education for a democratic political culture.[6] For nearly two years, there were numerous discussions and numerous drafts of the curriculum. All those involved characterized this time as one of intensive study and intensive discussion.

In the end, the four-member FCE team delivered a comprehensive three-year program for the consideration of the civic education team in the General Directorate of Educational Methods and Materials—the team that would have ordinarily been charged to produce the program itself. It had been made clear to this team, with all due discretion, that their expert input would be valued, but that all final decisions belonged to the FCE authoring team and Limón, for whom that team directly worked. The civic education team was in accord with the basic orientation of the program and its pedagogical focus. Their greatest concern was with the overabundance and sequencing of themes; they made some observations that were heeded, and others that weren't. In any case, the final product was judged sufficiently cogent and viable for the subsecretary of basic education, Olac Fuentes, to give it his full support. Despite his earlier reservations, Fuentes provided the full support of his office to launch the new program, and he even proved an articulate defender of its core principles.

Thus, combining civics, ethics, and orientation into one subject, *Formación Cívica y Etica* went into partial effect in 1999, with three hours a week in the first year. By 2001, it was operating in virtually every *secundaria* in the country, public and private alike, for all three grades.

MAJOR ORGANIZING THEMES AND PRINCIPLES OF THE NEW FCE

When I first heard of the FCE, in 1998, I would not have predicted its progressive orientation. After all, since the early 1980s a succession of neoliberal political regimes had shrunk the populist welfare state constructed throughout the 1970s and emphasized the benefits of technical and vocational education. The right was becoming more politically cohesive and making inroads into social policy, while the left, despite some significant electoral gains, was in disarray. Thus, I expected that any new program in civic or ethical education would largely avoid critical thinking and instead emphasize the reinforcement of conservative moral truths along with a spirit of social adjustment. What I learned surprised me.

An analysis of two key documents—the *Annotated Program of Studies* (SEP 2000) and the *Teachers' Guide* (SEP, 2001)—provides us with the major organizing themes and principles of the new course in civic and ethical education. After affirming the special importance of citizenship education (*formación ciudadana*), the opening pages of the *Program of Studies* (2000: 12–13) go on to emphasize that the new subject adopts a focus that is "formative, secular, democratizing, nationalist, universalist, preventive, and communicative." Each of these terms, of course, encompasses a broad domain of meanings, yet they can be fairly glossed as follows.

The first term, *formativo*, points to the widest educative intent of Mexican schooling: to mold the habits, values, and attitudes of future citizens. In the Mexican lexicon, *educación* has always had a broader meaning than mere *instrucción*, and *formación* indicates a fuller approach than *educación*. While instruction, and even education, can refer to the transmission and acquisition of facts and knowledge through mental processes, formation points to habit and affect, with the intention of shaping forms of perception and conduct in everyday life. The Mexican *secundaria* has always presumed to be *formativo* and *integral* (holistic), thus the new FCE program does not so much propose a new focus as recover and reinforce one of the *secundaria's* perennial goals.

The next four terms point to foundational concepts of the Mexican constitution. Rooted in the Liberal constitution of 1857 but reformulated during the Revolution (1917), the current Mexican constitution gives the federal state a broad tutelary role through public education. Because of the historical struggle against the power of the Catholic Church, the constitution stipulates that public education will be secular (*laica*) and shall not be used to propagate the beliefs of specific religions. It also provides the foundation for a democratic form of governance, so civic education should contribute to the formation of democratic habits. Although the democratic promises of its constitution were rarely fulfilled in the past century, the rise in recent years of a more truly pluralistic political system, and the growth of a more vibrant civil society, have given renewed meaning to a democratic education.[7] Perhaps for the first time ever, Mexicans can now debate and vote in ways that may really make a difference.

An emphasis on both nationalism and universalism might seem a naked contradiction to some, but throughout its modern history Mexico has tried to couple a strong sense of national identity with gestures of international solidarity for peace and justice. Because of its troubled history with the great U.S. colossus to the north, and because of its own regional, class, and ethnic diversity, Mexican basic education has always attempted to form strong allegiance to the nation. Civic ceremonies and the celebration of national holidays and heroes figure prominently in the lives of all Mexican schoolchildren. Yet for all this nationalist pride, Mexican schools have also tried to inculcate in their children an appreciation for world history and the contributions of different national cultures.

The new FCE subject establishes a "preventive" focus in relation to certain growing problems in Mexican society, such as drug addiction, early, unwed pregnancy, and organized crime. Students learn about the causes and consequences of such activities in order to "prevent" their own participation in them. Finally, and very importantly, FCE highlights a "communicative" rationale. Instead of merely digesting received opinion and fact, students in FCE are to learn to dialogue and question received wisdom, expressing their doubts and opinions openly. In this way, knowledge and value can be constructed through communication, not imposition.

This latter point seems especially important when one glances over the remainder of the *Program of Studies* and *Teachers' Guide*. Throughout the text, the authors of these documents place emphasis on a communicative pedagogical stance, and a new role for the teacher as facilitator rather than provider of information. As in the educational philosophy of John Dewey, such communication is intimately linked to the urgent need for students to take control of their learning and to begin practicing democratic virtues:

> [The program] seeks to strengthen the student's capacity for critical analysis, for group work and participation in both individual and collective decision-making processes based on the values of a democratic life. . . . It's important

that students understand the vital importance of this subject and that they come to recognize themselves as the center of the curriculum. (SEP 2000: 14, 20)

The documents go on to criticize the heavy emphasis on information in the previous curriculum, saying, for instance, that

in [the old civics] the contents were dominated by detailed description of our public institutions and the recital of human rights, to the detriment of a more systematic development of abilities and attitudes that might lead to greater citizenship participation. In the new subject (FCE), we seek to make the connections between civics and students' lives more apparent. (SEP 2001: 3)

Correspondingly, the new plan establishes a number of "pedagogical and didactic guidelines" for teachers. Such guidelines include, among other things, clear directions to

- relate themes to students' lives.
- deepen themes through inquiry activities.
- foment . . . attitudes of respect and acceptance that encourage freedom of expression for all, taking special care to promote gender equity.
- encourage the practice of values, attitudes, and habits related to democratic life, to group work and collective organization.

Clearly, these new guidelines create a significant break with the older, teacher-centered approach to civics instruction.

While civics has a long and illustrious history in Mexican schools, the term *ethical* in a school context is less familiar to the current generation of Mexicans. It also raises more eyebrows. This is because of its possible connection to specific moral values derived from Catholicism. Steeped in the tradition of "lay" education, schoolteachers are especially vigilant about the introduction of religion to the public classroom. However, a close analysis of the new FCE program reveals strict adherence to a secular conception of ethical values, one that allows, but does not promote, the adoption of specific moralities (see Latapí 2003 for a critique). Still, what exactly is the difference between "civic" and "ethical" education, and how do they mesh? The *Teachers' Guide* explains it this way:

Formación cívica can be defined as a process of personal development through which individuals articulate values and form conceptions . . . that lead them to conceive of themselves as members of a political and social community, and to thereby exercise . . . the qualities of citizenship that the Constitution grants them. . . .

Formación ética can be defined as a process of human development in which the individual acquires and forms a set of abilities, attitudes, values, and knowledge that enables her to know herself and to recognize others as equal in dignity and rights. (SEP 2001: 9; my translation provides the female pronoun)

Each of these formative goals, in turn, is linked to the overarching concept and goal of democracy. Civic education can make students aware of their rights and responsibilities as democratic citizens, the guide suggests, but only ethical education can deepen the attitudes that make respectful participation possible.

The three years of secundaria study have been organized around three main themes that run throughout the FCE program. Such themes are interspersed through a variety of curriculum units. The first theme, focused on ethics, consists of "reflection about human nature and human values." The second theme, unusually reflexive with regard to their life stage, considers both "problems and possibilities for adolescents and youth." The third and final theme centers on traditional civics concepts: "social organization, democracy, citizenship participation, and forms of government in Mexico."

The first year course of study opens with a broad exploration of human nature and values. Students consider the evolution of culture and the characteristics of *Homo sapiens* as a species. Before long, the course centers on the perennial issue of gender relations, and invites students to discuss what it means to "be a woman and be a man." This is just one of many points where gender becomes salient. Even here, at this early stage in the program, students are encouraged to explicitly reflect on the goals of equity, the economic and educational disadvantages women typically face, and so on (SEP 2000: 39).

A major section of the first year, called "youth and goals," opens an explicit reflection about the promises of adolescence. Students are encouraged to project their aspirations into the future, to imagine their possibilities. There is a good deal of language here seemingly borrowed from humanistic psychology: "personal realization," "life cycle and life goals," and "human potential." There is also the first opening toward vocational orientation, as students are encouraged to "identify tastes, aspirations, and goals during the stage of adolescence" (SEP 2000: 46*ff.*). Finally, the first year ends with forty hours of instructional time spent exploring how to "live in society." Concepts include interdependence, communication, emotional connection (*afectividad*), enjoyment, solidarity, and reciprocity, as well as the "spirit of service, creativity, and work." Activities direct students to pose examples of such concepts in everyday life (SEP 2000: 50*ff.*).

The second year of the program picks up at the same point but gives a different twist to "living in society." Under the rubric of democracy now, students learn about the "values of living together" (*valores de la convivencia*), as well as the more specific "civic values and citizenship formation."

What are considered the key values of democracy are imparted to students: liberty, equality, equity, justice, respect, tolerance, solidarity, and responsibility (SEP 2000: 55*ff.*).

As if to give concrete and immediate meaning to these values, the second year moves on to consider students' relation to the secundaria itself. In an interesting example of institutional self-reflection, students are encouraged to explore their "reasons for attending the secundaria," and to ask themselves, "How do I take advantage of what the secundaria has to offer?" The goal here is to urge students to "acquire the elements for actively participating in society," by taking the secundaria as a microcosm of the broader society (SEP 2000: 79*ff.*). From the secundaria, teachers and students make the leap to the nation, exploring concepts such as "nationalism, love of country, and national pride," as well as "unity and cultural pluralism." Students are even asked to examine the "possibility of participating in, and influencing, matters of national interest" (SEP 2000: 85*ff.*). Finally, the second year ends with a further opening out to the study of "humanity." It is here, for the first (and perhaps only) time, that students explicitly consider their relationship to the environment (SEP 2000: 89*ff.*). This relationship is framed not only by a national interest, but with reference to worldwide environmental issues and problems. Here is one of the few moments where the curriculum opens explicitly to consider a global perspective.

The third year of the FCE course turns to focus a good deal on the traditional subject matter of civics: study of the constitution, the political structure (elections, parties, etc.), the governance structure (federal, state, and municipal agencies), and the separation of powers (executive, legislative, and judicial). Yet toward the middle of the year, the program of study returns to refocus some themes that have already been introduced in previous years. These themes are considered now under the rubric of "responsibility and individual decision-making." References to gender inequality pepper the consideration of sexuality, addiction prevention, and "study, work, and personal realization" (SEP 2000: 97*ff.*).

The FCE program includes an ambitious final project meant to foster "responsibility, collective decision-making, and participation." Either in small groups, or as a whole class, students must "demonstrate that they are capable of making change in some aspect of their school or immediate environment. For this the youth must identify an improvable aspect of one of the broad fields that they've studied throughout the course: education, work, health, environment, and free time." Through this project, students should learn how to arrive at decisions through consensus, how to conduct an empirical investigation and divide the work fairly among themselves, and how to present the results of an investigation to authorities and peers in order to effect positive change. The program description ends with a final observation of the anticipated "formative" benefits of this group project, in which "the students will discover that they're capable of cooperating, joining a team, finding a problem and proposing viable solutions, coming to an agreement, respecting one another, and researching" (SEP 2000: 103–4).

This brief analytic summary of the FCE program's major themes and activities should make one thing apparent: the program is ambitious, comprehensive, and, in relation to previous Mexican civic education, even revolutionary. Yet the success of any program lies in the conditions that make implementation possible and effective pedagogy enduring. I turn to these conditions in the final three sections.

"*YA PASÓ EL TIEMPO DE LOS DICTADORES*": THE CHALLENGE OF CHANGING INSTITUTIONAL STRUCTURES AND TEACHER PRACTICES

One fall afternoon in 2002, I was chatting with a regional pedagogical adviser (*jefe de enseñanza*) in the Mexican state of Morelos. Jefes de enseñanza typically work for the state education ministries; they are assigned a subject and a region, and they have primary responsibility for supervising the teaching of that subject in the region and for providing materials and in-service training opportunities. On this occasion, I was asking the jefa de ensenañza, a sixty-something former history teacher who was now in charge of disseminating the program in FCE, what she thought of the way the new subject was being taught in schools. She expressed some exasperation and said that many teachers were simply not grasping the new pedagogical focus of the program. She described how some teachers were still relying too heavily on the textbook and dictating passages for their students to copy. In an irritated tone, she finished her lament: "*Ya pasó el tiempo de los dictadores, pues*" (The reign of the dictators is over, come on!).

I am not sure whether the adviser deliberately intended the double meaning of this phrase, but I have taken it as a telling epigram for the challenges of creating a new democratic citizen in Mexico. The word *dictator* in this phrase can refer either to a tyrannical political leader or to the type of teacher who dictates notes and generally leads an authoritarian classroom, where only one correct response is possible. Her phrase suggests that in order to rid themselves of dictators at the political level,[8] Mexicans would also have to eventually rid themselves of classroom dictators. In other words, the way to create a more active, participatory Mexican citizen who would no longer accept undemocratic regimes was through a more active, participatory pedagogy. Only teachers who could develop such a pedagogical style would be appropriate for modeling and thereby encouraging democratic conduct.

It was no coincidence, then, that when I posed the question "What is the greatest challenge to the successful implementation of the new FCE program?" the almost unanimous response of policymakers, administrators, and teachers alike was some version of "teacher training." Teachers themselves, when discussing their experiences with FCE, often called for more training and more in-service "courses." With few exceptions, they recognized that their own training did not adequately prepare them to teach the subject. They even noted that the new programs explicitly called for teachers to "change," to adopt a new "stance" in relation to their students, but that the guidance and resources needed to effect such a change were rarely forthcoming. Few incentives existed to encourage reticent teachers to examine and change their old teaching habits.

Those teachers who'd conscientiously adopted the new program's progressive pedagogy and sought to improve themselves further in this regard, were often dismayed by some of their colleagues' techniques. In my talk with an FCE teacher in the capital city of Morelos, she related how she had come to learn about one of her colleague's methods. Apparently a clerk at one of the local stationery stores, with whom she maintained a friendship, had asked her whether she was the civics teacher requiring her students to buy a values chart (*lámina*). The clerk could not provide the chart the students requested, because, in effect, it didn't exist. This teacher told her no, of course she hadn't made that request, but then she asked around the school to find out who in fact it was. The culprit—a former history and geography teacher—had fallen back on one of the time-honored methods used by the "dictators": have children go and purchase a chart, as if it were a worksheet, and then copy it into their notebooks. My interviewee, noting the irony of a new "dialogical" subject being taught in this way, finished with an exasperated chuckle, "What's up with that—buying a 'values chart'?" (*¿Cómo es eso de comprar una "lámina de valores"?*).

Finally, some teachers, and even some of the administrators and policymakers at higher levels, called attention to the political and structural challenges contained in the FCE. The new program espoused a more democratic approach to instruction and a more collegial dialogue about how to teach values and democratize instruction across the curriculum. Yet this program, more than one actor noted, had still been foisted upon the states by a "higher decision," and it appeared that little popular consultation had gone into it. Moreover, as one regional *jefe de enseñanza* put it, the notion of "democratic education" involves a different, more collegial role for school administration, yet current administrators are resistant:

> The principals in general have been reinforcing their defenses because their position, their role as principal is the equivalent of the function of a governor, of a president, and that's what we're generally questioning in Mexico right

now. . . . So the principals see their position as being very threatened, in fact they've said as much, they say, "The respect for our office has been lost" (*Se ha perdido el respeto a nuestra investidura*). . . . Go ask any principal and he will tell you, "Well yes, of course, respect and democracy . . ."; they know the rhetoric well, the problem is in their attitude.

Yet others drew attention to the structural problem of school organization. Mexican scholars like Rafael Quiroz have been analyzing this problem for years (Quiroz 1991, 1992, 1993, 1996). The secundaria curriculum is highly fragmented, with students taking up to eleven different subjects at a time—ranging from one to five hours per week. They may have as many different teachers as subjects, and class periods typically last less than an hour. To paste together sufficient hours for a full-time position, teachers must often teach a number of disparate classes throughout the day, even at different schools within the same city or region. It is not uncommon for secundaria teachers of FCE to give ten hours of the class to five different groups in the morning shift, ten hours to five other groups in the afternoon, and yet another ten to twenty hours in a different school altogether. And those are the full-time teachers, often trained in normal schools. Perhaps more often than not, FCE teachers were first trained as "professionals" (lawyers, psychologists, etc.) and then acquired some teaching hours in the secundaria. They typically pursue a parallel career outside the school. The effect of all of this is for FCE teachers to have little chance to get to know their students in any real depth. The trust and familiarity that the new FCE program postulates for its success are structurally obviated by secundaria curriculum and hiring practices.

One last aspect of school organization and governance involves the bureaucratic infrastructure created to monitor student attendance and report their grades. As several supervisors and policymakers pointed out, this infrastructure had developed a sort of life of its own, often divorced from the practical exigencies of school life—and certainly counterproductive to good pedagogy. Teachers and support personnel had to spend an inordinate amount of time on paperwork, and this took away from time they might spend on more productive or engaging activities with the students. The "logic of evaluation," as Rafael Quiroz calls it, often led teachers to objectify knowledge and seek shortcuts for assessing learning. In sum, as another jefe de enseñanza put it, "We experience a daily conflict between administrative needs and pedagogical needs, and it's almost always the pedagogical needs that come out losing."

"UNA MERA SIMULACIÓN": STAFFING, RESOURCES, AND TEACHER SKEPTICISM

As already intimated, among the institutional challenges to effective implementation of FCE have been the policies and practices around school staffing and teacher hiring. The FCE course was launched in 1999, and it was only that same year that normal schools in the country began offering the subject for credential specialization. Thus, schools had to assign existing teachers—of civics and of educational orientation, but also of geography and history—to the teaching of FCE. Moreover, even as new FCE-trained graduates become available to teach in the future, rules of seniority as well as teachers' union politics will assure that existing teachers retain their positions for many years still. In most cases, once teachers have acquired a certain number of "hours" at a school, or a full-time position (*plaza*), they are entitled to maintain the same level of work. Since schools must honor the hours of existing teachers, they have tended to transfer previous civics and history teachers into the first and second year of FCE, and the *orientadores* into the third year of FCE. These teachers can be encouraged, but generally not required, to take FCE training courses or pursue a specialized teaching degree in FCE.

Administrators commented to me that the old civics and social studies teachers—many of them originally lawyers by training—seemed to do well enough with the civics elements of the new FCE course, but they had a hard time with the "ethical" dimensions of the curriculum. Accustomed to teaching in rote fashion about the Constitution and government structures, they tended to have a poor grasp of dialogical, student-centered pedagogy. Conversely, the old orientadores—mostly psychologists and social workers by training—seemed to do well enough with the ethical part of FCE. After all, the old stand-alone course in "educational orientation" had become popular with students because it spoke directly to their concerns and interests and allowed for a degree of "free expression" lacking in most other classes. Yet the orientadores now struggled with the civic and legal elements of the FCE program.

Thus, most policymakers were realistic in preaching patience for the successful implementation of FCE. It would take many years for older teachers to retire or retrain themselves, and for schools to begin hiring the new FCE teachers. To make matters worse, there is some evidence that normal schools may be having a hard time attracting students to the new subject. It seems that few students want to take a risk on it. The new director of normal schools for the Mexico City district reported to me that many students who'd initially signed up to major in FCE in 1999 were now switching to other specializations because of doubt about the subject's future. Knowing Mexico's history of volatile change, these students were hedging their bets—better to study a long-standing subject, like history or Spanish, which stood little chance of being crushed by the next wave of educational reform.

Another problem that the teachers and administrators in the states emphasized was the uneven provision of training and resources. Some schools have ready access to computers and Internet connections, through which they can research topics related to civics. Some schools and regions also have ready access to supplementary curriculum materials, teaching guides, videos, and the like. Yet other schools are far removed from such resources. One poor rural secundaria I visited in the state of Michoacán had, by early October, only recently received a shipment of textbooks for the FCE subject. Even more disconcerting, neither of the two FCE teachers at this school had ever seen nor been issued the official *Teachers' Guide* for the subject; they had planned their classes and curriculum according to the themes that were laid out in the textbook sent to the school.

Policymakers and functionaries involved with the FCE program also made it clear that the quality of teacher training and FCE implementation in the states depends a good deal on the energy and focus accorded the program by state "technical teams" and, perhaps most importantly, by regional jefes de enseñanza. Some states had clearly decided to devote more resources to augment the sparse training modules offered by the national directorate of teacher training. Many states also took full advantage of an array of "complementary" programs developed by nongovernmental organizations to bolster the official FCE curriculum (e.g., Movimiento por la Democracia and Amnistía Internacional [MCD/AI] 2001). Technical teams in such states could thus feel empowered to pursue a more aggressive program of teacher training and supervision. Even in the absence of strong support at the state level, though, some jefes de enseñanza clearly threw themselves into their work and felt passionately about the new subject. They made the FCE program into a kind of personal crusade, often attempting to leverage resources in the face of official indifference.

Lying behind all of these more concrete challenges of staffing, training, and resource provision is a deeper problem of skepticism, even cynicism that informs many teachers' understanding of the new program. Because educational policymaking has always been subject to the vicissitudes of the six-year presidential administrations known as *sexenios*, continuity has often been difficult to achieve. Teachers that have been in schools for a number of years will note the grand rhetoric that accompanies the inauguration of a new sexenio; they observe the arrival and departure of educational reforms, and they see that very little changes in the end. Mixed with this sense of inertia is often a more active critique of the duplicity of the state. Many teachers have developed a profound suspicion of educational authorities, seeing them as willfully complicit with an agenda of obfuscation, projecting polished surfaces that have little substance behind them. As one teacher at a rural secundaria put it:

> What's always existed in Mexico has been a mere simulation (*una mera simulación*), and I think that today it's even more urgent that we see critically what's

happening with our schools. . . . Where's the seriousness, the coherence between what's said and what's done? There's a lot of interest [among teachers] in self-improvement, in updating knowledge, in taking challenging courses, but unfortunately the courses they offer us, the meetings are just two or three people, or all the teachers from the FCE area, getting together, and they tell us, "How's it been going in your classes? Tell us about your experiences?" And supposedly those are the courses [said in a tone of disgust].

The implication here is that the provision of teacher-training courses is not taken seriously enough, that it is only half-hearted, a "mere simulation" to show institutional compliance. Many teachers see the federal government as responsible for this situation.

"COMO ECHAR UNA SEMILLA AL PURO DESIERTO": THE SCHOOL'S DIFFICULT ATTEMPT TO CREATE LASTING CHANGES IN STUDENTS

The female principal of a secundaria in the state of Morelos had been praising the qualities of the new FCE course, but then she began to acknowledge its limitations. She focused on the challenges of creating a new student sensibility when the broader society would not nurture it. She even said that family and community life, not to mention the media, often directly contradicted the positive messages of the program. "What are we supposed to do when we teach about the peaceful resolution of conflicts, or about respectful dialogue, and [the students] go home to watch so much violence on television, or they see their fathers bossing everyone around? It's like tossing a seed into the middle of the desert" (Es como echar una semilla al puro desierto).

In my discussions with teachers and administrators, optimism about the program's possible success was especially guarded. Optimism was generated by a common feeling that many of the current problems in student attitude and conduct—increased selfishness, violence, use of obscenity, apathy, and so on—could be traced to the dissolution of civic education in 1974. More than one teacher identified the early 1970s—when civics was folded into the new "area" of social sciences—as the origin of contemporary "social disorganization." Students were now generally thought to lack the "values" that previous generations had demonstrated. The remarks of this FCE teacher from Morelos, a male about sixty years old, were fairly typical:

The kids who were prepared according to these new "areas" [e.g., social sciences] no longer practiced the values that had been practiced for many years

before 1972 [*sic*], at which time there was, in the first place, the important fact
that the father, from within the heart of the family, saw to it that from the time
they were born to the time they arrived at school . . . the child already *had*
values. And not just in the head, but in conduct (*demostrables*). So all this gets
cut off, and these kids from 1972 [*sic*] onward, until 1999, are the product of
this societal disorganization. But, who provoked it? The educational policy of
the state, you see?

This teacher begins by attributing current problems to the abolition of the
self-contained civics course in the early 1970s, but he then quickly points
to the role of the family, especially the father, in forming solid values before
school attendance. After a few sentences, though, he returns to blaming the
curriculum change in the 1970s, and the state that promoted this change,
for today's "disorganization." After further prompting, the teacher tried to
clarify the link: "[The creation of so-called areas like social sciences] created
a movement contrary to what had been in place before, which was exactly
about nurturing that value of responsibility, of honesty, of tolerance, of solidarity, that was in the family. . . . These were also the values in civics."
Aside from the gender prejudice of his comments, what strikes me is the
attempt to link school-based curriculum with social changes beyond the
school. In his mind, the lack of a civics course after 1974 created a deficit
of values formation in the school. The school no longer reinforced positive
values taught previously (by the father!) in the family. In effect, this teacher,
like many others, felt that as long as school curriculum provided a space for
the reinforcement and extension of "values," teachers could sustain a
guarded optimism about the new program.

As the principal quoted at the start of this section suggests, teachers have
to contend daily with the apathy, even the opposition, of many parents
regarding school-based values formation. In the state of Michoacán, nearly
every teacher I interviewed mentioned this challenge. Parental opposition,
though, did not always fall along ideological lines. Many parents appeared
to resent the school's incursion into their lives, signified by the teachers'
often paternalistic assumption of a tutelary role. One teacher cited a dis-
gruntled parent who, in response to a suggestion that his child was learning
inappropriate language in the home, retorted, "If I tell my kids vulgarities
or curses it's OK with me. That's got nothing to do with them here in
school; for me it's something normal." And even if parents did not explicitly oppose themselves to the school's angle on values, teachers still
lamented the discrepancy between what students might learn in school and
what they learned, by example, in the home. As one teacher lamented, "We
[teachers] give one meaning or understanding of a value, and the students
are living a different kind of value in their homes, right? So there's probably
confusion. There's confusion in our students because we speak of values

and their meanings, and sometimes they don't put it into practice because they're not living it."

CONCLUSION

Exciting changes have been occurring in Mexican secondary education, and the new program for civic and ethical education lies at the heart of many of these changes.[9] A progressive curriculum and pedagogy may indeed point the way to a flowering of civic awareness and participation amongst youth, and a corresponding diminution of social problems. Mexicans are looking to the school to help create a new democratic sensibility amongst youth, to form a new democratic citizen "without adjectives." Hope is running high in many quarters, and some teachers and administrators point to the program as the main contributor to positive changes they have already seen in their students.

Yet the challenges that remain are great. The new program must contend with an aging and ill-prepared teaching corps, undemocratic school governance, a prevailing emphasis on specialization and testing, and an entrenched bureaucratic structure that provides few incentives for teachers to change or improve. The new program must also overcome a pervasive society-wide cynicism about reforms initiated by the federal government, as well as disillusionment about resource inequities. It is indeed unfortunate that the central ministry takes a too-passive stance in compensating for geographic and economic conditions that translate into unequal quality of materials and instruction. And even as the state might begin to address imbalances in resource provision and challenge the union's dominance over hiring, it will have a much longer term problem to address: the creation of confidence through transparent and consistent actions. It is no coincidence that "accountability" (*rendición de cuentas*) recently has become a watchword in many quarters of the Mexican education system or that a National Institute for Educational Evaluation was recently established in Mexico to monitor its educational progress.

Finally, and perhaps most importantly, the new civics education cannot contribute to lasting change if it is not complemented by similar efforts in other spheres of contemporary society. The school, of course, is only one socializing institution among many, and the secundaria is only one transitory stage in Mexican youth's development. Only if like-minded reforms are made in family socialization, in community and municipal life, in religious education, in the media, and perhaps most importantly, in the provision of meaningful economic opportunities for young adults, can the new civics education come to fruition.

NOTES

Much of this chapter first appeared in the *International Journal of Educational Development* 24 (2003): 269–82. Reprinted with permission of Elsevier Scientific. Some sections first appeared in "Programs for Democratic Citizenship in Mexico's Ministry of Education: Local Appropriations of Global Cultural Flows," *Indiana Journal of Global Legal Studies* 12, no. 1 (2005): 251–84. Reprinted with permission of Indiana University Press.

1. This chapter is based on approximately five weeks of fieldwork in Mexico, followed by several long-distance telephone interviews. Fieldwork conducted in December 2001 and September–October 2002 consisted of interviewing national-level researchers, policymakers, and education ministry workers, as well as state- and local-level administrators and teachers; collecting documents (textbooks, official study plans, teacher training materials, newspaper articles, etc.); and observing classrooms in seven different secondary schools in two different Mexican states.

2. The reference is to a well-known argument by Enrique Krauze (1988) against all "qualified" forms of democracy (e.g., "presidential" democracy; "populist" democracy) that had been said to exist in Mexico. He argues for a "democracy without adjectives" or, as we might say, "democracy, period."

3. The term *subjectivity* is used here to encompass the whole assemblage of attitudes, perceptions, and forms of self-awareness teachers may manifest in their behavior. I define *subjectivity* as "those forms of awareness, mostly but not exclusively embodied and sensual, that are given by personal and social history yet transmutable by context and contingency." See Levinson (2001: 343–44) for a fuller discussion of this term's meanings and usage in contemporary scholarship.

4. The debate over "education" versus "instruction" apparently dates from the late nineteenth century (Hale 1989: 162). In Spanish, *educación* implies a broad formation of character, manners, and morals, while *instrucción* implies the transmission of specialized knowledge. The Catholic Church, along with the family, had traditionally held a monopoly over the "education" of children. Liberals at the end of the century argued amongst themselves over whether the displacement of church power should include the state's assumption of an educative role. Many argued that education should remain a family affair, with instruction the domain of the state. But by 1890, the Mexican state had begun to provide primary schooling with important educational functions. After the Revolution, the state expanded this formative quality of public education, and, modeling the German system, extended it to the secundaria. See also Zúñiga (1981: 223).

5. Although the Chetumal Reforms were adopted widely throughout the country, they were not legally required of all schools. Therefore, throughout the remainder of the 1970s and 1980s a number of localities, most notoriously Mexico City, continued to operate according to the older asignaturas. This created in effect a dual national system of secundaria curriculum.

6. The IFE is a government-funded yet independent agency created in the late 1980s mainly to administer fair and clean elections. However, a significant part of its work also includes fomenting civic education and the creation of a new democratic political culture. Through its Department of Electoral Certification, Civic Edu-

cation, and Citizenship Participation, the IFE has run several educational programs that complement the school-based FCE curriculum: these include the Jornadas Cívicas Infantiles y Juveniles, day-long programs of activity that range from mock elections to drawing and role-playing; "Project-Citizen," a program adapted from the U.S.-based Center for Civic Education that fosters community involvement and problem solving among adolescents; and the elementary program "Rights and Values for Mexican Children." See Salazar Ugarte (2001).

7. Although the Mexican Constitution provides for multiple parties, a bicameral Congress, and a system of checks and balances similar to the U.S. system, the reality until 2000 was distinct. After the rise to power of the Partido Revolucionario Institucional (PRI), which since 1929, in one guise or another, had maintained the presidency until 2000, electoral and civic participation was manipulated through corporatist networks. The presidency assumed preponderant weight, and Congress, controlled by the PRI as well, served as a rubber stamp for presidential initiatives. Citizens were encouraged to look to the paternalist state for solutions and largesse. This scenario only began to change in the 1980s when opposition parties scored important victories in governors' and mayors' races and began to redress the imbalance in the federal Congress. By 2000, when the opposition candidate Vicente Fox finally won the presidency, the PRI only controlled a slim majority of governors' seats and senator positions. They maintained only a plurality of seats in the "House" (Cámara de Diputados). See Levy and Bruhn (2001) for a fine overview of recent Mexican politics.

8. The Mexican political regime, characterized by many political scientists as authoritarian and, until 2000, ruled by a single party for some seventy years, was once called "the perfect dictatorship" by the Peruvian author Mario Vargas Llosa.

9. Since the original drafting of this chapter, the Mexican Ministry of Education has undertaken a major reform of secondary education. The FCE program has remained intact, though its contents have been reordered and the number of student-teacher contact hours diminished. The new version of FCE was implemented with the 2006 school year.

REFERENCES

Hale, C. 1989. *The Transformation of Liberalism in Late Nineteenth-Century Mexico.* Princeton, N.J.: Princeton University Press.

Krauze, E. 1988. *Por una democracia sin adjetivos.* Mexico City: Cal y Arena.

Latapí, P. 2003. *El debate sobre los valores en la escuela mexicana.* Mexico City: Fondo de Cultura Económica.

Levinson, B. A. U. 2001. *We Are All Equal: Student Culture and Identity at a Mexican Secondary School, 1988–1998.* Durham, N.C.: Duke University Press.

Levy, D., and K. Bruhn. 2001. *Mexico: The Struggle for Democratic Development.* Berkeley: University of California Press.

Meneses Morales, E. 1986. *Tendencias educativas oficiales en México, 1911–1934.* Mexico City: Centro de Estudios Educativos.

———. 1988. *Tendencias educativas oficiales en México, 1934–1964.* Mexico City: Centro de Estudios Educativos.

Chapter 10

Movimiento for la Democracia and Amnistía Internacional. 2001. *Formación cívica y ética ciudadana: Manual de actualización docente.* Mexico City: Author.

Quiroz, R. 1991. "Obstáculos para la apropiación de los contenidos académicos en la escuela secundaria." *Infancia y Aprendizaje* 55: 45–58.

———. 1992. "El tiempo cotidiano en la escuela secundaria." *Nueva Antropología* 12, no. 42: 89–100.

———. 1993. "La reforma curricular de la escuela secundaria en México." In *Educación, ciencia y tecnología: Los nuevos desafíos para América Latina,* ed. J. Labastida Martín, G. Valenti, and L. Villa. Mexico City: Universidad Nacional Autónoma de México.

———. 1996. Del plan de estudios a los aulas. In *La educación secundaria: cambios y perspectivas,* ed. Estatal de Educación Pública de Oaxaca. Oaxaca: Author, 89–109.

Salazar Ugarte, S. 2001. "El IFE ante la educación cívica." *Educación 2001* 1, no. 7 (July).

Secretaría de Educación Pública. 2000. *Formación Cívica y Etica, Educación Secundaria: Programas de estudio comentados.* Mexico City: Secretaría de Educación Pública.

———. 2001. *Formación Cívica y Etica, Educación Secundaria: Libro para el maestro.* Mexico City: Secretaría de Educación Pública

Sutton, M., and B. A. U. Levinson, eds. 2001. *Policy as Practice: Toward a Comparative Sociocultural Analysis of Education Policy.* Westport, Conn.: Ablex.

Zuñiga, R. M. 1981. "La escuela que surge de la revolución." In *Historia de la educación pública en México,* ed. F. Solana, R. Cardiel, and R. Bolaños. Mexico City: Secretaría de Educación Pública.

11

The Emergence of Global Citizenship Education in Japan

Yoko Motani

This chapter focuses on one of the most recent progressive educational movements in Japan, called *global citizenship education*. The progressive educators in Japan have been relatively unknown outside Japan, except for the longtime progressive educators' group, Japan Teachers Union (JTU). Since its establishment of 1947, immediately after Japan's defeat in World War II, JTU has always been an oppositional force to the conservative Japanese government and the Ministry of Education.[1] Conflicts between JTU and the conservatives had sometimes been quite intense, but the conservatives had almost always dominated the educational policymaking process. As globalization accelerated during the 1980s and early 1990s, however, this relatively static field of progressive education diversified, as new developments of progressive educational movements such as development education, global education, environmental education, and human rights education are introduced to Japan. The actual names of such "educations" may vary, depending on who their advocates are. Japanese society underwent fundamental social changes during the 1990s as it experienced such challenges as the Hanshin earthquake, a sarin gas attack of a religious cult, and more than a decade of economic stagnation. This chapter shows that the analysis of small but powerful global citizenship education movement illuminates the sociopolitical changes the Japanese society has been experiencing since the mid-1990s.

The analysis of global citizenship education is important because it is a new development of progressive education that has been promoted in the official school curriculum. This was possible in the educational reform of 2002, when the intentions of the conservatives for more cost-effective and flexible educational policies and the progressive educators' call for more democratic school culture coincided. The Ministry of Education introduced a new subject called integrated studies (discussed later) in the New National Curriculum of 2002. It is a new subject area designed to encourage more student-centered, problem-solving pedagogy; there are no recommended textbooks from the Ministry of Education. This is exciting news for progressive educators in Japan because this class period can be utilized as a laboratory for experimental learning that prepares students to become active citizens in our increasingly global society. Many contemporary progressive educators in Japan are promoting global citizenship education under the auspices of integrated studies.

The emergence of global citizenship education is remarkable considering that the role of citizenship education in developing active citizens for democratic society has not been well articulated in contemporary Japanese educational discourse. Until recently, *citizen (shimin/kokumin)* was not a widely used term in daily life, except when it is used to refer to Japanese nationals. "Citizens' groups" exist in Japan, but have a connotation of general opposition to what the government is planning. In the field of education, the subject area of civic education (civics) is called *komin*. This is a special term used by the Ministry of Education and is rarely used in ordinary conversation outside school (Otsu 1998). *Komin* can be used in describing citizens, but only in specific contexts, and it cannot be used interchangeably with *shimin*, which also means citizen.

Since the mid-1990s, however, there is a change emerging in this trend. Terms such as *global citizen* and *global citizenship* came to be used more frequently. *Citizen* also became a more common word. Global citizenship education and "education for living together" gained much broader acceptance, and not just among the progressive educators who traditionally advocate for these issues.

How did all these changes emerge? Do they indicate that a structural shift has occurred and that the country has decided to address the issues of citizenship, democracy, and justice through public education in order to prepare Japanese children for an increasingly interdependent, global, and multicultural world? How are these changes affecting citizenship education in social studies and beyond? To seek answers to these questions, first, the outline and origin of the 2002 educational reform will be presented, followed by an analysis of the sociopolitical factors related to the educational reform. The analysis, which draws on recent scholarship on Japan and Japanese education, is rooted in interview data obtained from 2002 through 2004.[2]

THE OUTLINE OF THE 2002
EDUCATIONAL REFORM

The educational reform of 2002 is part of the third major educational reform period in modern Japanese history. The first reform occurred during the Meiji Restoration (1866–1869), which laid the foundation of Japan as a modern nation-state. The second took place immediately after the country's defeat in World War II (1945–1952), and it aimed to rebuild the country by promoting democracy and peace (Fujita 2000b). The origins of 2002 initiatives can be traced back to the report of the Central Educational Council of the Ministry of Education, *The Model for Japanese Education in the Perspective of the Twenty-first Century*, which was released in 1996 (Ministry of Education 1996). This report set the framework for the current educational reform. It argued that there was a need to encourage "zest [power] for living" (*ikiru chikara*) and to provide "relaxed education" (*yutori*) for students. The Ministry of Education explains that zest for living is

> a capacity to identify a problem, learn and think by herself/himself, make judgment assertively, take action, and find better ways to solve a problem, no matter how much the society changes; it is also a rich humanity, that knows her/his boundaries, co-operates with others, whose heart empathizes with others and is moved by various things. (Oride 1996: 148–49)

Relaxed education is perceived as necessary to cultivate zest for living; it refers to a relaxed, humane state, as opposed to a competitive, stratifying environment.

The official reasoning behind these slogans is that the Ministry of Education came to recognize that children in Japan were suffering from undue competition because of the fierce entrance examination system, which accelerated over the years as higher education became more accessible. In this context, it is no wonder that most schools failed to encourage children to discover the joy of learning; rather, schools were a place where they had to hide their true sense of self and conform. The Ministry of Education also recognized that thus far it has have put too much emphasis on the memorization of knowledge. Ministry officials believed more emphasis should be placed on how to analyze and critically reflect on various issues in this increasingly complex world. The major reform initiatives proposed by the Ministry of Education in order to realize these goals included the reduction of school days to five days per week, the reduction of curriculum content (so that children could concentrate on the basics and processes of problem solving), and the introduction of the period for integrated studies from grades 3 to 12.

Although the idea of integrated curriculum is not totally new to Japan, the fact that integrated studies comes from the Ministry of Education is quite novel (Tanaka 1998; Hidai 1999). In general, the Ministry of Education sets specific rules about how and what students should be taught. In the case of integrated studies, however, it sets only the framework and aims of the curriculum so that each school and teacher can come up with unique interdisciplinary and comprehensive studies of their own, which will captivate the children's interest in self-learning and discovery. The aims are "to develop in students the capability and ability to discover problems by themselves and solve those problems properly" as well as "to help children learn how to learn and reason, to develop their minds for independently and creatively coping with problem-solving activities and/or enquiry, and deepen their understanding of their own way of life" (*Curriculum Guidelines*, 1998, cited in Hidai 1999: 35). Suggested themes of inquiry in the integrated studies are international understanding, information technology, environment, welfare and health, and subjects in which children are interested and those related to the unique characteristics of the community and school (Hidai 1999: 35).

Although the time allocated to integrated studies is limited to two to three units per week many progressive educators are quite excited about this opportunity because they are able to promote their philosophy and pedagogy more rigorously than ever before. Although a consensus emerged during the 1990s that the ministry's control over curriculum content and method was excessive (Cave 2001), these educators had never enjoyed this kind of opportunity. Indeed, conservatives criticize this program specifically because its underlying philosophy is child centered and experiential. But does the 2002 educational reform truly indicate the "progressive turn" in Japanese education? The answer to this question is sought here through the analysis of the origin and sociopolitical contexts surrounding it.

THE ORIGIN OF THE 2002 EDUCATIONAL REFORM

All educational policies affecting both public and, to a certain extent, private schools, are issued by the Ministry of Education. As mentioned, the origins of the current initiatives can be traced to the *The Model of Japanese Education in the Perspective of the Twenty-first Century* (Ministry of Education 1996). Although it is clear that the educational policies and guidelines are formulated by the Ministry of Education, how these new reform initiatives evolve is not always as clear, as policymaking is a complex sociopolitical process.

Some suggest two primary actors influence educational policy in Japan: the conservatives and the progressives (Schoppa 1991). The conservatives include many of the Ministry of Education bureaucrats and the Liberal Democratic Party (LDP) politicians. These two dominant groups share a basic perspective that they have to "restore" more traditional Japanese values by revising the constitution and the Fundamental Law of Education and "rescuing" Japan, which was "excessively" democratized and westernized by the occupying authorities (Schoppa 1991). The progressives, on the other hand, think democratization of the occupying authorities was good and seek to promote a more egalitarian, democratic educational system. The most prominent group on this side is Nikkyoso, the Japan Teachers Union (JTU). The politics of education in Japan has often been understood as a struggle between these two ideological perspectives, manifested in the conflict between the Ministry of Education and the JTU (Thurston 1973; Kumagai 1983; Duke 1989).

Historically, the conservatives dominated educational policy, although progressive forces resisted the status quo, a pattern which has continued at the start of the new millennium. The Ministry of Education promulgates all policies affecting the entire educational system, which are based on reports (called *toshin*) issued by its councils. The members of these councils include famous novelists, poets, athletes, business executives, as well as a variety of educators, but are chosen by the Ministry of Education. While the LDP has lost dominance as a single party since 1993, it continues to control the current Japanese political system.

During the 1980s, however, a new trend emerged in this somewhat rigid picture. Zaikai, a special interest group of business executives, created educational reform ideas and began influencing educational policies (Horio 1986, 1997; Schoppa 1991; Koyasu 1999; Fujita 2000a, 2000b). From 1984 to 1987, four reports were published by the Ad-Hoc Council of Education under the direction of then–prime minister Nakasone, which clearly reflect Zaikai's demands for educational reforms. Calling for "internationalization" and "individualization," Nakasone wanted to create a more cost-effective, flexible education system through decentralization, deregulation, and privatization, in order to produce more assertive and creative Japanese workers for the economic development of the country in an increasingly competitive world economy. More precisely, they were interested in producing a new type of elite business person, who has practical English skills, is aware of global issues, and is able to lead the profitable industries of the next generation (Schoppa 1991; Koyasu 1999). Nakasone's vision of internationalization was intended to raise the status of Japan in the international community and not to promote understanding among the Japanese about global problems such as the environment and poverty (Lincicome 1993). With this vision of internationalization and individualization, the conservatives' "love for the country and its tradition" was emphasized without any contradiction. Thus, the direction of educational reform was set within the neoliberal/conservative framework.

While the Ad-Hoc Council of Education did not release concrete educational reform initiatives, they can be found in reports published by various business executives' associations that followed its lead. For instance, the report titled *From Schools to "The Place of Integration,"* published by Keizai Doyukai (Japan Association of Corporate Executives) in 1995, suggests the "downsizing" of public education, limiting its role to the very basics and utilizing the resources of communities, families, and private sectors (Horio 1997: 190). This report clearly indicates that the educational reform ideas that the Ministry of Education prepared—the reduction of curriculum content and focus on the basics, cultivation of abilities to meet the rapidly changing social needs and creativity, and encouragement of each individual's unique ability—all coincide with their ideas. Another example is the report published by Keidanren (Japan Federation of Economic Organizations) in 1996, entitled *Developing Japan's Creative Human Resources: An Action Agenda for Reform in Education and Corporate Conduct.* This report also gives more clear proposals for educational reform: the introduction of competition through deregulation, as opposed to the currently available uniform, standardized education; more choices and varieties of curricula; and emphasis on creative thinking and experiential learning. Underlying these proposals is their belief that Japanese society needs "creative individuals who act independently and possess a strong sense of individual responsibility" (Keidanren 1996: 2). These images of the future Japanese echo the ones presented by the Ministry of Education in its report (Koyasu 1999). Furthermore, the Ministry of Education (1999) also notes that its current reform ideas are largely based on the reports prepared by the Ad-Hoc Council of Education.

Clearly, the direction of 2002 educational reform initiatives is largely influenced by the ideas from Zaikai: demanding more cost effective education, preparing independent and creative students for an increasingly competitive world market economy, and meeting the interest of their own country. While the philosophy behind curriculum content reduction and the introduction of integrated studies may be described as a progressive, child-centered educational approach, and while they could be utilized to promote progressive education, the origin of these initiatives is not egalitarian or democratic.

Even if these neoliberal/conservative forces—business executive groups, politicians, and bureaucrats—have direct influence on the educational policy formation process, they cannot be finalized and implemented if they are largely unacceptable to external forces, including progressive educators and the public opinion. Indeed, the rapidly changing sociopolitical landscape surrounding Japan laid the groundwork for progressive education movements to expand. By examining the sociopolitical background leading to the 2002 educational reform, we will see how progressive educators came to advocate ideas that formed an educational discourse and perhaps influenced indirectly the direction of educational reform.

SOCIOPOLITICAL BACKGROUND LEADING TO THE 2002 EDUCATIONAL REFORM

After Japan reached its economic height in the late 1980s, the economy plunged drastically, usually described as the burst of the bubble economy. In the heyday of economic affluence in the 1980s, the need for educational reform from Japanese citizens grew stronger, especially because of the following educational problems: bullying, truancy, violence, and "classroom collapse," or teachers' loss of control. Bullying (*ijime*) has become a national concern since the 1980s, when some victims found suicide the only way out. The number of children who refuse to go to school for a prolonged period of time (thirty days or more) for reasons other than illness (*futoko*) has started to increase drastically. More incidents of violent outbursts (*are/kire*) are reported, and many teachers are losing control over children to the point that they cannot teach their classes (*gakkyu-hokai*). While various factors could contribute to each of these incidents, these "pathological phenomena" at school indicate that too much stress is put on children, pressuring them to succeed at exams, get into good high schools and universities, and eventually work for Japan's major corporations, to become elite business*men*. Because the country's priority was almost exclusively targeted at its economic success in the world, this scenario has been, and still is for many in Japan, the "good life" (Asano 2000, 2002). Fueled by sensational coverage by the media, these problems prompted progressive educators and the general public to highlight the need for educational reform. The perception is that traditional Japanese schooling is not working anymore and is even hurting the future of its own citizens. Partly because the economy was booming, however, radical reform initiatives were not implemented during the 1980s. Since then, however, the Ministry of Education began suggesting the need for more "relaxed education" and reduced curriculum content (Kariya 2002: 48).

In the 1990s, then, the country went through a series of shocking events that raised fundamental questions about Japanese values, life goals, and the purpose of education. The Ministry of Education had to develop innovative and concrete proposals for educational change. As the economy plunged into a long-term recession, what were known as the "Japanese models" collapsed. The Japanese realized that there was no more guarantee of lifelong employment, since even major corporations go bankrupt. The unemployment rate started to rise, and Japanese corporations started to slip in the global markets.

Then, in 1995, two catastrophes hit the nation. On January 17, a major earthquake hit Kobe/Awaji area, killing more than six thousand people and injuring more than forty thousand. Japanese citizens were not only devastated by the loss of lives but also by the fact that the Japanese government, both local and central, was slow in responding to the crisis. The Japanese became suspicious about their own government's ability to protect its citizens. Then on March 20, 1995, there was a sarin gas attack by a religious cult called Aum Shinrikyo during the peak rush hour on crowded Tokyo subway lines. Tokyo was supposed to be one of the safest big cities on Earth, but in this incident, twelve people were killed, and approximately five thousand others were affected. The Japanese were greatly disturbed because this new religious cult recruited followers among the most well-educated people in Japan.

In addition to these national catastrophes, in 1997, Japan was shocked to learn that a fourteen-year-old boy murdered an elementary school boy, as well as another younger girl previously. Even more shocking was that he had put the dead boy's head in front of his school's gate, "trying to disturb" the police. He also sent a letter to the local newspaper that seemed to suggest that he had committed these crimes because he was a victim of the Japanese educational system.

This series of events disturbed the Japanese people in general. The report prepared by the Prime Minister's Commission on Japan's Goals in the Twenty-first Century, entitled *The Frontier Within: Individual Empowerment and Better Governance in the New Millennium*, summarizes this unsettling Japanese social and political climate as follows:

> All this left people with the impression that core attributes of Japanese society on which they had prided themselves—family solidarity, the quality of education (especially primary and lower secondary education), and social stability and safety—were crumbling. It could be said that these episodes revealed a brittleness and inflexibility of Japan's economy and society that had been building up gradually. Perhaps all this represented the price of success. (Prime Minister's Commission 1999: 1)

It was no longer possible to ignore the need for a radical educational reform.

Situated in this discourse, the current educational reform ideas seem to have emerged at least partly as a result of Japanese citizens' egalitarian hope to use education to reconstruct the country into a more democratic and just society for children. Indeed, there have been apparent shifts suggesting that Japan is beginning to promote broader participation in social and political processes. In particular, after the Hanshin earthquake, Japanese citizens sought a greater voice in the political process. As the local and central governments' response to the emergency was quite slow, nearly 1.3 million people of all ages volunteered, thereby forming one of the most active resources for helping the victims. Volunteerism, once considered a practice of Christian origin that had not taken root among the Japanese, has become more widely accepted. As a result, 1995 was recognized as the Year of Volunteers (*borantia gannen*).

Following this event, in March 1998, the so-called NPO Law, the "law to promote specified nonprofit activities," was promulgated. This law enabled small voluntary organizations and citizens' groups to incorporate for the first time, with limited control by the government. The legislative process was quite unique as these small-scale organizations had opportunities to influence the making of the law (Yamaoka 1998; Japan Centre for International Exchange 1999). As of late November 2001, 5,369 of the 6,228 organizations that applied to obtain NPO (nonprofit organization) status had been approved (Pharr 2003).

Increasingly, concepts such as citizen and citizenship, which were foreign to Japanese, have become more commonly used. As one global citizenship educator noted:

In the past 10 years or so, the term citizen (*shimin*) has become acceptable to Japanese government officials. Before, *shimin* meant a group of people simply protesting whatever *okami* (the authoritative central government) is doing. Literally, I have witnessed that the term citizen is gaining citizenship. (interview, May 2002)

Susan J. Pharr (2003), the acting director of the Edwin O. Reischauer Institute of Japanese Studies in 2002–2003, confirms this trend:

There is no question that civil society in Japan is expanding and becoming more pluralistic. . . . Coinciding with a decline in popular confidence in government found until recently in virtually all the advanced industrial democracies, the general public—and some leaders—in Japan have concluded that the state lacks the flexibility and resources to cope with increasingly complex socio-economic issues, and more and more citizens have responded with their own initiatives. (2)

Although their motives are quite different, the demand for more government flexibility and the citizens' desire to increase their initiative happen to match closely the ones from neoliberal and neoconservative business leaders who have advocated deregulation, privatization, and decentralization. Indeed, as Fujita (2000a) points out, the key characteristic of the dominant discourse on the current educational reform is that, by and large, progressives, neoliberals, and neoconservatives agree with each other on reform ideas.

> Many educational critics committed to progressive ideas have emphasized individuality, self-realization, self-cultivation and freedom in learning, and argued that the "cramming" education, standardized curriculum, uniform teaching, and strict school management obstruct authentic learning, a stress-free life, and the development of individuality and creativity. (7)

This list of reform ideas is indeed similar to the ones coming from Zaikai.

How can we interpret this convergence of progressive educators and neoliberal and neoconservative business leaders and politicians? One could conclude that all educational interest groups in Japan were forced to come together when faced with a series of serious educational and social crises. In 1995, the JTU announced it was no longer opposed to the Ministry of Education. National newspapers reported this incident as a "historical reconciliation between the Ministry of Education and JTU" (*Asahi Shinbun*, 2003). Another possible interpretation is that progressive educational forces in Japan have further weakened in the midst of sociopolitical changes. In recent years, the JTU has been having trouble recruiting new teachers to join the union and has been losing influence. In the past, as many as 80 percent of teachers belonged to the JTU, while the current rate is only about 30 percent; the rate for new teachers is less than 20 percent (Ministry of Education 2002).

Of course, "reconciliation" between the Ministry of Education and JTU does not necessarily mean that their current vision and strategies for educational reforms are the same. As a matter of fact, many progressive educators, whether or not they are affiliated with the JTU, are quite critical of many of the current educational reforms. The traditional rigid structure of educational policies and practices that characterized the conflicts between the Ministry of Education and JTU is changing, and more constructive dialogue between them is anticipated to improve education. But their distinct histories and philosophies are likely to keep them apart.

The apparently weakening role of JTU does not necessarily imply that progressivism has also weakened. As the JTU lost its unifying power, the progressive educators in Japan diversified. New trends that were developing outside the country during the 1960s and 1970s—development education, world studies, global education, and environmental education—were introduced to Japan "like a storm" during the 1980s and 1990s. One teacher/educator/researcher who has devoted his thirty years of teaching life to promoting education for international understanding stated in a research interview that these new progressive educational theories and practices outside Japan helped set off new initiatives all over Japan. During the 1980s and early 1990s, Japanese education was filled with "pathological phenomena," as mentioned earlier. Many educators in Japan looked at new educational developments abroad while trying to find ways to solve their educational problems. As people's interest in developing civil society grows, various progressive educational movements in Japan also found "global citizenship education" as their new slogan.

Although there is no evidence suggesting that these emerging progressive educators have ever had any influence on the actual educational policymaking process, they are clearly making their presence felt, as particularly indicated by the introduction of integrated studies and the increased interest among the general public in realizing a civil society. Sutton and Levinson's (2001) argument that educational policy analysis extends to the level of appropriation applies here. They write that appropriation is "the way creative agents 'take in' elements of policy, thereby incorporating these discursive and institutional resources into their own schemes of interest, motivation, and action" (3). The progressive educational movements in Japan should be viewed as a significant influence upon the dominant educational discourse.

Considering its relatively recent emergence and lack of institutional support, citizen- and global-oriented progressive educators in Japan have achieved something quite remarkable. Some of the strongest promoters of global citizenship education will be presented after a discussion of its definition.

GLOBAL CITIZENSHIP EDUCATION AND ITS RELATED FIELDS

Definition

The conceptualization of global citizenship education is still in the process of development, and various definitions of it exist. To clarify what is meant by this term in Japan, we consider the concepts of world-mindedness and child-centeredness suggested by Pike and Selby (1998: 11). These concepts are quite useful since they have been adopted by global citizenship educators in Japan. Pike and Selby (1998) propose that world-mindedness has to be cultivated in education in order to develop "young citizens who demonstrate tolerance of, and respect for, people of other cultures, faiths and worldviews, and who have an understanding of global issues and trends in our 'one world,' in which the interests of individual nations must be viewed in light of the overall needs of the planet" (11).

This emphasis on respect for diversity for any organism of this planet, not just "an understanding of global issues and trends," is quite important, and many global citizenship educators in Japan acknowledge this point.

For instance, Otsu (1992), a leading scholar in education for international understanding and development education in Japan, states that global citizenship refers to "knowledge, attitudes, and skills necessary as a responsible citizen in the world where diverse cultures coexist and people are mutually interdependent" (198). The importance of understanding "interconnectedness" of our "one world" through holistic, systemic thinking is also recognized (Otsu 1997). Uozumi (1995) emphasizes that global citizens have to consider various contemporary trends of "globalized society," particularly the ideas that we are becoming more and more interdependent due to the development of information technology and that we need to realize global common good as a member of Spaceship Earth.

Global citizenship educators in Japan are careful about the historical context facing Japan when they speak about world-mindedness and the goals of global citizenship education in general. For example, they are keen to emphasize that respect for cultural diversity within the country needs to be fostered, not merely the respect for "other cultures" (Minoura 1997; Yoneda et al. 1997). Otsu's (1997) rationales of global education in Japan also include special attention to Japan's unique political-historical contexts. She reminds us that Japan is committed to promoting peace and developing global citizens because they are written in the Fundamental Law of Education and other governmental documents. Global education is necessary, she argues, in order to realize these ideals as well as not to repeat the past mistake of World War II. Otsu explains that "internationalization" before the war meant to be "westernized," looking down on other Asian countries. She also notes that although Japan is experiencing globalization of its economy, commodities, and people, the consciousness of ordinary people in Japan is quite ethnocentric and biased, especially toward other Asian peoples and countries. Japan needs education that promotes a better understanding of different cultures, inside and outside Japan (Otsu 1997: 18–21).

Bearing in mind that these rationales are unique to Japan, Otsu believes that global education there must strive to foster values that have been absent historically and that are necessary in today's world. She states:

> The characteristics of Japanese which are required in the global age are, cooperation and collaboration with other ethnicities and nations, derived from the deep, sincere, and critical reflections on the past deeds of Japan to other Asian countries after the establishment of modern Japan. Further, we need to overcome our continued tendency to marginalize diversity in pursuit of homogeneity and to respect diverse perspectives. (22)

These critical perspectives about Japan's past and present sociopolitical conditions are what differentiate global citizenship educators from other advocates of the concept similar to world-mindedness but actually quite different (e.g., an "international" or "cosmopolitan" person).

Child-centeredness is the "idea that children learn best when encouraged to explore and discover for themselves and when addressed as individuals with a unique set of beliefs, experiences and talents." This position has been promoted by notable progressive educators such as "John Dewey, Friedrich Froebel, Maria Montessori, A. S. Neill and Leo Tolstoy" (Pike and Selby 1998: 11). These progressive educational theories are quite well-known among Japanese educators and researchers, although the actual practice has not been vigorously promoted by the Ministry of Education. Under the reform of 2002, however, some argue that the philosophy behind integrated studies is child-centered pedagogy (e.g., Kariya 2002).

The recent call for child-centered pedagogy also stems from Japanese educators who are concerned with their children's stressful school lives in an increasingly competitive society. This view, identified as the "recovery of selves," is considered by Tada (2000) as one of the main concepts within global citizenship education. This is by no means mere promotion of "Western" individualism but was drawn from Tada's hope to foster assertive and responsible children who can respect differences and thereby overcome the ongoing stressful and competitive school environment that has been depriving children of their opportunities to develop their full potential as human beings (Tada 2000: 19–27).

The need to develop individuals who are assertive and can find problems and solutions for themselves was frequently mentioned by interviewees. In this sense, an interest in child-centeredness is rooted in the uniquely Japanese contexts where respect for diverse individuals and cultures has been undermined before. Two interviewees, who belong to Zenseiken,[3] also commented that their commitment to encouraging children's participation to create a more democratic school culture is the same as that of global educators within and outside of Japan. One global citizenship educator explained that he is promoting the usage of the term *studies* as opposed to *education* in his work in order to emphasize his learner-centered pedagogy (interview, May 2002).

In addition to world-mindedness and child-centeredness, global citizenship educators in Japan stress the importance of developing attitudes and skills rather than knowledge necessary as global citizens among their children (Minoura 1997; Otsu 1992, 1997). This might be too obvious for global educators in other countries, but in Japan, this aspect is important since it is relatively recent that the criticisms against the "cramming" of knowledge have come to be accepted.

In summary, global citizenship education in Japan is a new paradigm of education that encourages holistic and systemic thinking (which supports world-mindedness) and the development of the attitudes, skills, and knowledge necessary for global citizenship. Global citizens are not only aware of global issues but are assertive individuals actively participating in community developments at various levels of Spaceship Earth in order to promote social justice and peace for future generations (which, it is held, can be achieved through child-centered learning).

Related Fields of Global Citizenship Education

Education for International Understanding

The field of education that is most closely related to global citizenship education is education for international understanding (EIU) (*kokusai rikai kyoiku*). The term was first introduced to Japan by UNESCO in 1974. Since then, it has been well accepted in Japan, but it often means different education for different people. To clarify this confusing term, I would like to distinguish two strands of EIU: narrowly conceptualized, government-led EIU and more progressive, globally oriented EIU, or "new" EIU.

Originally, EIU had some progressive, egalitarian perspectives and was informed by the progressive international educational movement, in particular the initiatives of UNESCO. However, during the 1980s, EIU promoted by the Ministry of Education started to show wider and wider differences from the UNESCO recommendation of 1974. The "official" EIU started to stress that national identity needed to be cultivated *before* one is able to understand foreign cultures and nations (Minei 1996). UNESCO itself became the field of political power struggles in the 1980s, leading the United States and United Kingdom to withdraw. This change may have contributed to the subsequent decrease of UNESCO influence on the Japanese educational system (Minei 1996; Nagai 1989). The Ministry of Education's initiatives in EIU were limited to following areas: (1) international and/intercultural exchange activities, (2) English conversation classes with native English speaking instructors, (3) establishment of International and English departments at high schools (especially private ones), and (4) accommodation of returnee students (*kikokushijo*)[4] (Watanabe 1998).

The new EIU became a more unified, significant educational trend during the 1990s. Educators and researchers in Japan, as well as the Ministry of Education, were exposed to new movements and ideas such as development education and global education. New EIU advocates have come to be influenced more by global education (Hanvey 1982; Kniep 1987; Pike and Selby 1988) and world studies abroad (Fisher and Hicks 1985; Hicks and Steiner 1989). As a result, more educators and researchers started to emphasize their commitment to cultivating global citizens since the mid-1990s (e.g., Minoura 1997; Otsu 1992; Tada and Sakurabashi 1997).

For this new EIU movement, the Japan Association for International Education (www.kokusaiken/hyoshi-e.htm), which was established in 1991 with 290 members, has played a significant role in leading the direction of the entire field of EIU. As explained in a May 2002 interview by an educator and researcher who has been in this field for more than thirty years, the association has attracted more than five hundred members during its first decade. There is no denying that voices promoting global citizenship education are becoming mainstream within EIU as the conceptualization of the field "expanded and became closely related to the field of global education."

Another important organization in "new" EIU/international education is the Institute for International Understanding (www.tezuka-gu.ac.jp/from_ toppage/kokuri/top.html), associated with Tezukayama Gakuin University in Osaka since 1993 but existing for more than twenty years before then as a private organization. Its journal, *Kokusai-rikai* (*International Understanding*), published annually, and the annual article contest for the International Education Award, now in its thirty-second year, have had a significant influence on the development of EIU in Japan. In recent years, their central themes of articles selected for special recognition include "the concept of global citizen," "international understanding and globalization," and "multiculturalism." The new EIU/international education movement, then, is one of the leading initiatives in the field of global citizenship education in Japan.

Development Education

Development education (*kaihatsu kyoiku*) was formally introduced to Japan in 1979, when the Symposium on Development Education was held in Tokyo, with the collaboration of the Public Centre of United Nations, UNICEF office in Japan, and the United Nations University (Amemori 1998). In 1982 the Development Education Council of Japan (DECJ), currently known as Development Education Association and Resource Center (DEAR; http://decj.on.arena.ne.jp/), was founded by the effort of individuals and organizations, many of whom had experienced volunteer work with the Japan Overseas Cooperation Volunteers and other organizations. At present, the number of members (including individuals and organizations) is about nine hundred, and the association's newsletter reaches about two thousand individuals and organizations.

In Japan, development education is, in general, recognized as a relatively new educational field that started in the 1960s among the young people in European and North American countries who were involved in NGO or volunteer activities in developing countries (Miyazaki 1998). According to Miyazaki (1998), in the beginning, the aims of development education were narrow; they were initially intended to let the people in the North (developed) countries know about the problems and cultures of the South (underdeveloped) countries and to promote more support for the South. As the field grew, development education came to cover a wider range of issues, including so-called North-South problems, the environment, gender, human rights, and economics generally, and to promote people's understanding of these issues and inspire them to become active agents for change toward a just and peaceful world (Miyazaki 1998). According to Minoura (1997), the major characteristics of development education lie in its participatory learning approach and problem-solving method. These aspects are significant in that they clearly distinguish themselves from mainstream, traditional learning styles in Japanese schools that generally expect students to find the right answer, absorbing knowledge as much as possible. In development education, there is no single right answer, and the learning process is more important than reaching answers. There have also been efforts to conceptualize development education from global and holistic perspectives (Iwama and Yamanishi 1996). With their emphasis on interconnectedness; issues of the environment, human rights, gender, and economy; and participatory learning, development education is one of the most active fields of education promoting global citizenship education in Japan.

DEAR has been making a great effort in promoting development education in integrated studies (Tanaka 1998). It has been organizing workshops for teachers about how to use development education approaches in the period for integrated studies. DEAR has also has published a series of booklets promoting development education in integrated studies, introducing examples of participatory learning in development education (March 1999), and discussing curriculum examples and resources of development education in integrated studies (May 2000), and ways to build partnerships between resources of local communities (NGOs, volunteers, other community organizations, etc.) and schools (March 2001). Its annual meetings, which attract hundreds of participants, allow member teachers to share their ideas and practices. The annual meeting of 2003 marked a record number of participants: about one thousand. This group's work has made Japan one of the world's leading countries in the quality and acceptance of development education (Tanaka 2003).

Guidance Education

Development, human rights, and global and global citizenship education abroad have had a considerable impact on guidance education in Japan as well. This is a progressive educational movement situated in a uniquely Japanese context. "Life Guidance for Students" is an initiative set forth by the nongovernmental educator research group called the National

Guidance Education Research Council (Zenkoku seikatsu shido kenkyu kyogikai, Zenseiken). This counseling does not refer to helping students with social problems or career options; rather, it concerns all areas of each student's life outside the nonacademic realm of school. Zenseiken was established in 1959 when the Japanese government started to discourage the democratization of the country by implementing authoritarian educational policies that revoked those promoted by Imperial Japan. Zenseiken was concerned with the formation of democratic schooling based on civilian morality and children's participation, not the moral education imposed by the Ministry of Education. Since the mid-1990s, guidance education advocates came to realize that their mission is closely linked to the progressive educational movements abroad and incorporated educational materials from development and global education. This approach was well accepted among the group and also promoted more interactions with other progressive educators in Japan, such as development education and global education advocates.

CONCLUSION: IMMOBILIZED CITIZENSHIP EDUCATION

Considering that citizenship education has been marginalized in post–World War II education in Japan, it is quite significant that global citizenship education has emerged and become accepted beyond the circle of progressive educators. This acceptance became possible because the discourse envisioning Japan as a more civil society emerged after the mid-1990s, as people's interest in volunteerism and civic participation increased dramatically following the slowdown of the economy and the Hanshin earthquake. Neoliberal and neoconservative business leaders increased their influence on educational policies in the strong Japanese economy in the 1980s, and their ideas for educational reforms based on the principle of more cost-effective education through decentralization, deregulation, and privatization, clearly influenced the direction of the 2002 educational reform.

Nevertheless, radical reform ideas, such as drastic reduction of the curriculum content and the introduction of integrated studies, would not have been implemented if people's genuine desire to create a more civil-based Japanese society through education had not existed. The fact that the role of NGOs and NPOs is increasing in Japan might only indicate that both central and local governments in Japan were forced to invite elements from the private sector, including NGO/NPOs, to replace their traditional roles in social and political administration. However, without dedicated individ-

uals working toward the goal of creating a more civil-based Japan, NGO/
NPOs would not have increased so dramatically.

In this sociopolitical context, even though the 2002 educational reform
ideas originated from neoliberal and neoconservative business leaders and
politicians, progressive educators in Japan were given the greatest opportunity to promote their education, in particular in integrated studies. Indeed,
progressive educators in Japan have diversified and become energized in
the late 1970s and 1980s, partly under the influence of various progressive
educational movements abroad. They attracted attention because they were
able to provide an alternative response to the increasing number of problems facing schools.

Citizenship education in social studies, however, has escaped the influences of sociopolitical factors which helped the rise of progressive educational movements. Civics remains immobilized, committed to fostering
love of country, tradition, and culture among the young Japanese. Japan is
not unique, of course, in promoting such nationalism through citizenship
education. How to balance tensions between nationalism and internation-
alism in education is still a topic of debate in many democratic societies.
Nevertheless, what characterizes the Japanese case is the fact that global citizenship education is almost exclusively promoted in integrated studies
while more traditional citizenship education is escaping from global influences. This situation is problematic because integrated studies is still quite
controversial. As a matter of fact, criticism of integrated studies has
increased in recent years.

Advocates of global citizenship education need to consider how they can
relate to more traditional civic education. Some efforts are already under-
way. For example, influenced by the new compulsory citizenship education
subject in the United Kingdom's new curriculum of 2003, some educators
and researchers in Japan have started to explore new direction of citizenship education. They emphasize that education plays an important role in
raising citizens who can contribute to the development of democratic society (Okada 2005: 24). For citizenship today, the ability to make judgments
of social values in a rapidly changing society and to take an initiative in
such circumstances is greatly needed (Okada 2005: 24).

Such new "citizenship education," as well as global citizenship education, has just started. Their impact on younger generations of Japan in fostering global, democratic citizenship remains to be seen. What is certain is
that, in the context of a society where a civil movement has taken off since
the mid-1990s, progressive educators have become a significant element in
influencing educational practices and discourse. The further development
of progressive educators will be the key to developing global, democratic
citizenship education in Japan.

NOTES

1. Currently, the Ministry of Education in Japan is called the Ministry of Education, Culture, Sports, Science, and Technology (MEXT, *Monbukagakusho*). Until 2000, it was known as the Ministry of Education, Culture, Sports, and Science (MOE, *Monbusho*). To avoid confusion, in this chapter, "the Ministry of Education" will be used to refer to both MEXT and MOE.

2. More than thirty people were interviewed, either as individuals or as part of focus groups. The interview data used were collected for the Japanese case study of the Global Citizenship Education Research Project, led by David Selby, then a professor at the Ontario Institute for Studies in Education of the University of Toronto and director for the International Institute for Global Education. This project, funded by the Ford Foundation, was intended to examine the origin, development, and impact of the emerging global citizenship education movement in ten countries: Albania, Brazil, Canada (Ontario), the Czech Republic, Japan, Jordan, Poland, South Africa, the United Kingdom, and the United States. The final report of the project is currently being prepared. The analysis given in this chapter is fully extended and rewritten from the draft report of the project.

3. The educational group practicing and researching guidance education, which is also examined here.

4. *Returnees* are children who returned to the Japanese school system after spending substantial amount of time outside of Japan, usually more than two years. The special treatment of returnee students may sound more like a privilege than a fair treatment to some. The difficulties of returnees' adjustment to schools of their own home country have been quite stressful, often involving bullying from their peers who have never been abroad. These problems have been well documented and raise questions about Japanese school culture in general, because it has tended to promote homogeneity rather than respect for diversity.

REFERENCES

Amemori, T. 1998. "Itsu, donoyouni hajimatta no?" ("How and When Did Development Education Start?"). In *Kaihatsu kyoiku tte naani? (What Is "Development Education"?)* Tokyo: Development Education Council of Japan.

Asahi Shinbun. 2003. "Tabo sensei oikomu" ("Teachers under Pressure Because They Are 'Extremely Busy'"). April 22.

Asano, M. 2000. "School Reform, Human Rights, and Global Education." *Theory into Practice* 39, no. 2: 104–10.

———. 2002. "Ikikata/seikatsu no tenkan wo motomeru mirai kyoiku" ("Future Education Pursuing the Transformation of Our Ways of Life"). In *Global kyoiku kara no teian: Seikatsu shido/sogogakushu no sozo (New Century, New Belongings: Essays in Global Education)*, ed. M. Asano and D. Selby. Tokyo: Nihon Hyoronsha.

Cave, P. 2001. "Educational Reform in Japan in the 1990s: 'Individuality' and Other Uncertainties." *Comparative Education* 37, no. 2: 173–91.

Duke, B. 1989. "Variations on Democratic Education: Divergent Patterns in Japan and the United States. In *Japanese Schooling: Patterns of Socialization, Equality, and*

Political Control, ed. J. Shields. University Park: Pennsylvania State University Press.

Fujita, H. 2000a. "Choice, Quality, and Democracy in Education: A Comparison of Current Educational Reforms in the United States, the United Kingdom, and Japan." www.childresearch.net/cybrary/evision/index.html.

———. 2000b. "Crossroads in Japanese Education." *Japan Quarterly* 47, no. 1: 49–55.

Hidai, T. 1999. *Sogo gakush no susume kata: Kiso/kihon (How to Plan and Practice the Period for Integrated Studies: The Basic Foundations and Principles).* Tokyo: Toyokan Shuppansha.

Horio, T. 1986. "Toward Reform in Japanese Education: A Critique of Privatization and a Proposal for the Re-creation of Public Education." *Comparative Education* 22, no. 1: 31–36.

———. 1997. *Gendai shakai to kyoiku (Contemporary Society and Education).* Tokyo: Iwanami shoten.

Iwama, H., and Y. Yamanishi. 1996. *Wakachiai no kyoiku: Chikyu jidai no "atarashii" kyoiku no genri wo motomete (Education for Sharing: Toward the Principles of Education for the Global Era).* Tokyo: Kindaibungei sha.

Kariya, T. 2002. *Kyoiku kaikaku no genso (The Illusion of Educational Reform).* Tokyo: Chikuma shinsho.

Keidanren. 1996. *Developing Japan's Creative Human Resources: An Action Agenda for Reform in Education and Corporate Conduct.* Tokyo.

Keizai Doyukai. 1995. *Gakko kara "gakko" e (From School to "The Place of Integration").* Tokyo.

Koyasu, J. (1999). *"Manabi" no gakko: Jiyu to kokyosei wo hosho suru gakkou/jyugyo zukuri (Schools for "Learning": Creating Schools/Lessons that Guarantee Freedom and Common Good).* Kyoto: Minerva shobo.

Kumagai, I. 1983. "Gendai kyoiku seisaku no rikigaku to Nikkyoso" ("The Dynamics of Contemporary Educational Policies and Japan Teachers' Union"). In *Nihon kyoiku no rikigaku (The Dynamics of Japanese Education),* ed. A. Kazuo and S. Michiya. Tokyo: Yushindo kobunsha.

Lincicome, M. 1993. "Nationalism, Internationalisation, and the Dilemma of Educational Reform in Japan. *Comparative Educational Review* 37, no. 2: 123–51.

Minei, A. 1996. "The Task of International Education in Japan Related to the Recommendation of UNESCO (1974)." *Kokusai Rikai Kyoiku* 2: 26–42.

Ministry of Education. 1996. "Goals of Our Country's Education Prospecting in the 21st Century." www.mext.go.jp/b_menu/shingi/index.htm.

———. 1999. "White Paper on Educational Policy." www.mext.go.jp/b_menu/shuppan/index.htm

———. 2002. "Kyoshokuin no soshiki suru kyoshokuindantai ni kansuru chosa-kekka no gaiyo nitsuite" ("Summary of the Survey Results on Teachers' Organizations"). Tokyo.

Minoura, Y. 1997. *Chikyu shimin wo sodateru kyoiku (Education for Raising Global Citizens).* Tokyo: Iwanami shoten.

Miyazaki, Y. 1998. "Kaihatsu kyoiku tte naani?" ("What Is Development Education?"). In *Kaihatsu kyoiku tte naani? (What Is Development Education?),* ed. Development Education Council of Japan. Tokyo: Development Education Council of Japan.

Nagai, J. 1989. *Kokusai rikai kyoiku: Chikyu teki na kyoryoku no tame ni* (*Education for International Understanding: For Global Cooperation*). Tokyo: Daiichi gakushu sha.

Okada, Y. 2005. "Shichizunshippu kyoiku wo megutte ima dokode donna ugoki ga arunoka: Ochanomizujoshidaigakufuzokushogakko no "shichizunshippu" no koso" ("What Is Happening in Citizenship Education—Now, Where, and What: The Idea of 'Citizenship' at the Ochanomizu University Elementary School"). *Shakaikakyoiku* 42, no. 1: 24–26.

Oride, K. 1996. *Kosodate, kyoiku, tomo sodachi: Ijime kokufuku to jiritsu* (*Child Rearing and Education as Growing Together: Overcoming Bullying Problems and Helping to Become Self Reliant*). Nagoya, Japan: Chunichi shinbun honsha.

Otsu, K. 1992. *Kokusai rikai kyoiku* (*Education for International Understanding*). Tokyo: Kokudo sha.

———. 1997. "Chikyu shimin wo sodateru tameni: Atarashii kaihatsu kyoiku to shite no gurobaru kyoiku" ("To Raise Global Citizens: Global Education as New Development Education"). In *Atarashii kaihatsu kyoiku no susumekata: Chikyu shimin wo sodateru genba kara* (*How to Promote New Development Education: From the School Field Raising Global Citizens*), ed. Seminar for the Promotion of Development Education. Tokyo: Kokon shoin.

Otsu, K. 1998. "Japan." In *Citizenship for the Twenty-first Century: An International Perspective on Education*, ed. J. J. Cogan and R. Derricott. London: Kogan Page.

Pharr, S. J. 2003. "Japan's Civil Society Today." www.fas.harvard.edu/~rijs/Pharr_CivilSoc2_v9n1_2003.html.

Pike, G., and D. Selby. 1988. *Global Teacher, Global Learner*. London: Hodder & Stoughton.

Prime Minister's Commission on Japan's Goals in the Twenty-first Century. 1999. *The Frontier Within: Individual Empowerment and Better Governance in the New Millennium*. Tokyo.

Schoppa, L. J. 1991. *Education Reform in Japan: A Case of Immobilist Politics*. London: Routledge.

Sutton, M., and B. A. U. Levinson. 2001. "Introduction: Policy as/in Practice—A Sociocultural Approach to the Study of Educational Policy. In *Policy as Practice: Toward a Comparative Sociocultural Analysis of Educational Policy*, ed. B. A. U. Levinson and M. Sutton. Westport, Conn.: Ablex.

Tada, T. (2000). "Chikyu jidai" no kyoiku towa? (*What Is Education "in the Age of Globalism"?*). Tokyo: Iwanami shoten.

Tanaka, H. 1998. "Sogo gakushu to kaihatsu kyoiku" ("Integrated Studies and Development Education"). *Kaihatsu Kyoiku* (*Development Education*) 38, no. 8.

———. 2003. "Ajia taiheiyo no nettowaku ("Network in Asia-Pacific"). *Kyoiku no yume kikin nyusu* (*Foundation for Education for Dream News*) 5 (October 1).

Thurston, D. 1973. *Teachers and Politics in Japan*. Princeton, N.J.: Princeton University Press.

Uozumi, T. 1995. *Gurobaru kyoiku: Chikyu jin/chikyu shimin wo sodateru* (*Global Education: Raising Global People and Citizens*). Nagoya: Reimei shobo.

Watanabe, J. 1998. "Ima motomerareru kokusai rikai kyoiku towa" ("Global Education in Need Now"). www.acejapan.or.jp/exchg/globaled/seminar.html.

Yoneda, S., K. Otsu, I. Tabuchi, T. Fujiwara, and Y. Tanaka. 1997. Tekisuto kokusai rikai (*Textbook of International Understanding*). Tokyo: Kokudo sha.

12

Intercultural Meanings of Citizenship in the Australian Secondary Curriculum: Between Critical Contestations and Minimal Constructions

Joan G. DeJaeghere

Australia is a former British colony and an established democracy with more than one hundred years of statehood. In recent decades, however, Australia has been undergoing two simultaneous transformations: (1) an internal shift in the diverse composition of its population and (2) changing economic, political, and social relations influenced by globalization. Internally, immigration has changed the composition of Australia's population, forming a more diverse multicultural society. Nearly 24 percent of Australians are born overseas (Australian Bureau of Statistics 2005). In the 1990s, immigrants from non-English-speaking countries constituted 14 percent of the population (Jupp 1997). Aborigines comprise approximately 2 percent of the population, speaking 170 different Aboriginal and Torres Strait Islander languages (Ainley, Malley, and Lamb 1997).

Several political and social events illustrate the Australian society's response to and debate with this internal change. In 1999, a referendum was put before Australian citizens to determine whether they would establish a republic or maintain their constitutional monarchy affiliated with the British Crown. This referendum was, in part, reflective of the changing nature of the people who live in Australia and the changing allegiances of the government. While the vote for a republic was narrowly defeated, the discourse prior to the referendum and the symbolism of this political change brought new thinking and public contestation about what it means to be an Australian (Warhurst 1999). Similarly, the legislative acts and societal discourse related to indigenous rights, including land rights, have affected the policies and practices of citizenship and citizenship education (Chesterman and Galligan 1997; Peterson and Sanders 1998).

Externally, Australia has directed its political and economic relations with countries in addition to the United Kingdom, United States, and Europe. Australia's economic policies and trade have begun to look more toward Asian countries, affecting the orientation Australians have to their geopolitical reality (Dobell 2000). For example, data from July 2004 to July 2005 show that both exports and imports with Asia comprise nearly half of all exports and imports for Australia (Department of Foreign Affairs and Trade, Government of Australia 2005). Furthermore, Australia has realigned its political and economic alliances, including becoming a member of the Asian-Pacific Economic Cooperation (APEC) and a dialogue partner in the Association of South East Asian Nations (ASEAN). Such shifts suggest new political and economic orientations within the geographic area in which Australia lies. These external and internal changes indicate that Australia is a changing society grappling with new ways to imagine and enact citizenship that appropriately accommodate its dynamic multicultural nature.

This chapter analyzes how ideas of citizenship are constructed and contested in Australia's secondary education curriculum in this context of globalization and the changing multicultural nature of Australian society. It begins with a theoretical framework of minimal and critical forms of citizenship education, used to interpret the meanings of citizenship in curriculum documents. The second section briefly describes civics and citizenship education in the Australian school curriculum. An interpretive analysis of the civic and citizenship education curricula, including curriculum documents, textbooks, and interviews with educators, illustrates the contested meanings of the intercultural relations dimension of citizenship. This interpretation draws on historical and sociocultural analyses of the changing meanings of citizenship in the Australian society. Finally, I argue that critical forms of constructing and contesting citizenship are needed to address the issues and dilemmas facing a democracy in a changing multicultural society.

MINIMAL AND CRITICAL FRAMEWORK FOR CITIZENSHIP EDUCATION

Scholars of citizenship education debate the nature of citizenship in a democracy and, in turn, the purposes and goals of citizenship education.

One perspective is that citizenship is a legal status of rights and responsibilities in a democratic system, and that citizenship education should prepare people to understand and act on these rights and responsibilities. Such an education requires a thorough understanding of a country's history and government. Another perspective is that citizenship is participation within societal structures and processes, such as voting or lobbying for policies. Education for this type of citizenship requires active participation in both government and community issues. It also includes the acquisition of knowledge and skills in a variety of subjects, including environmental sciences and global studies. Finally, some scholars and educators advocate that citizenship is about creating and changing democratic structures and processes so they support the full participation of all people. Education for this type of citizenship would address issues of discrimination and oppression, and aim to help students be agents of social change (Print, Kennedy, and Hughes 1999; Gutmann 2004; Parker 1996; Torney-Purta, Schwille, and Amadeo 1999). The following framework of minimal and critical forms of citizenship and citizenship education is grounded in this debate. Furthermore, an analysis of citizenship education suggests that minimal and critical forms of citizenship may exist simultaneously or on a continuum within the curricula.

While I use the term *minimal forms of citizenship education*, other related terms used in the literature include *traditional citizenship* (Parker 1996), *personally responsible citizenship*, and *participatory citizenship* (Westheimer and Kahne 2004). Minimal forms of citizenship education refer to a minimum set of educational standards, including knowledge, values, and skills (Gutmann 2004). Minimal citizenship education tends to focus on knowledge about citizenship, governance, rights, and responsibilities (McLaughlin 1992; Kerr 1999; Kymlicka 1995). Testing, and particularly high-stakes testing, may pressure teachers to teach minimalist forms, emphasizing content and knowledge of citizenship topics more so than processes of learning to be and participate as a citizen.

A minimalist approach to citizenship education also suggests preconceived notions of what citizenship is, often denoted in exclusive or elitists terms (McLaughlin 1992; Kerr 1999), without the possibility of public debate and discourse (Gutmann 2004). Citizenship education in these forms promotes values, attitudes, and behaviors related to democracy and citizenship, but the aim is for students to acquire these values and behaviors without a larger understanding of the tensions in these values and behaviors in society. Citizenship education in minimalist forms tends to promote the "good" citizen, who is law-abiding, works hard, and possesses a good character. Furthermore, minimal forms of citizenship education do not problematize the societal processes and structures that create inequalities among citizens. Participation is often included in these forms of citizenship education; however, such participation tends to occur in established systems and structures, often for the good of one's own interests (Westheimer and Kahne 2004).

Critical forms of citizenship education, informed by Giroux and McLaren's (1996) education for critical citizenship, Merryfield's (2001) world-centered global education, and Westheimer and Kahne's (2004) justice-oriented citizenship education, promote critical assessment of discourse, knowledge, and experience through the lenses of power, decolonization, and hybridity of perspectives and identity.[1]

Beyond mere participation, critical citizenship education aims to solve societal problems and to create social change. To create societal change, critical citizenship education empowers and emancipates learners, and it helps them to understand the causes that underlie problems. Students and teachers are proactive agents of change. They participate in decision-making processes, and they critically analyze knowledge and the outcomes of applying knowledge (Giroux and McLaren 1996).

Education for critical citizenship allows for critical and structural social analysis. In addition to knowledge about social issues, it seeks to analyze the causes and consequences of social issues and how they affect different groups in society. Beyond a focus on personal responsibility and duties to society, critical forms of citizenship education examine the relationships between the individual's behavior in society and structures of social injustice. The aim is to enhance an understanding of and ability to change society, rather than the mere adoption of citizenship values or behaviors. Finally, critical forms of citizenship education help students and teachers understand their personal responsibility and place in society as part of a collective effort. Critical citizenship is not only individual action but also collective social change (Westheimer and Kahne 2004: 257–60).

Merryfield (2001) suggests three pedagogical practices that promote the teaching and learning of global dimensions of critical citizenship. The first is the examination of the pedagogy of imperialism in which students and teachers inquire about and understand how imperialism shapes mainstream knowledge. A pedagogy of imperialism asks, How does this imperialist, mainstream knowledge affect our understanding of the world's people, issues, and conflicts? The second critical pedagogical practice is using marginalized or misrepresented views of people in teaching and learning so that students learn from the perspectives of people who are poor, oppressed, or not in power. The third pedagogical process is cross-cultural experiential learning within different contexts of power. This learning goes beyond the usual intercultural learning experience to live, understand, and address issues of power and marginalization.

Westheimer and Kahne (2004) argue that minimal forms of citizenship are not inherently democratic, nor are they adequate to advance democracy in multicultural countries. Gutmann (2004) and Kymlicka (1995) suggest that elitist and exclusionary forms of minimal citizenship are undemocratic because they fail to address inequality or to seek equality as a foundation of democracy. The complex nature of democracy in multicultural societies, such as Australia, in which identity, values, rights, and participation are contested, warrants a critical approach to citizenship education.

CIVICS AND CITIZENSHIP EDUCATION (CCE) IN THE AUSTRALIAN CURRICULUM

Schools, including teachers, students, and the curriculum, constitute an important link in the creation of citizens in a democratic society (Cogan and Derricott 2000; Cogan, Morris, and Print 2002; Nie, Junn, and Sthlik-Barry 1996; Gutmann 1987, 2004; Torney-Purta et al. 2001). Citizenship and citizenship education, however, have been contested ideas and practices for much of Australia's history (Curtin 2000). In the early years of the Australian nation, civic education was an important component of the education curriculum (Marginson 1993; Print, Kennedy, and Hughes 1999; Print and Gray 2000). Civic education had varied and multiple purposes, including creating an awareness of the values and practices of democracy, preparing individuals to contribute to the development of the nation-state and its economy, and developing young people's identity as Australians and as British subjects (Ling 1984; Musgrave 1979). This civic education, however, might be interpreted as a minimal form, constructing citizenship in predefined ways for the new Australian state. In the following decades, civic education became diffused in the curriculum. From the 1960s until the past decade, civic education received little attention in the education system (Thomas 1994).

In the 1990s, Civics and Citizenship Education (CCE)[2] reemerged in the national curriculum, with the support of several commonwealth initiatives (Kemp 1997; Kennedy 1993; Print 1996; Print et al. 1999). This national CCE initiative attempted to include more critical elements of citizenship, though this analysis will illustrate the extent to which more critical perspectives have been incorporated into civics curricula. The reports and initiatives that led to the development of this new civics and citizenship education are discussed in detail by other scholars (Kennedy 1993; Print 1996; Print et al. 1999). Table 12.1 provides a summary of these initiatives, including an overview of these initiatives, their purposes, and the acronyms of important groups and legislation.

As a result of the Civics Expert Group (CEG) report, civics and citizenship education has been integrated into the Studies of Society and Environment (SOSE) curriculum at all grade levels. The *National Statement* and *National Profile for SOSE* (Australian Education Council [AEC] 1994a, 1994b) pro-

Table 12.1.   Key Legislation in Australian Civics and Citizenship Education (CCE)

Date	Legislation	Governmental Authority
1989	*Active Participation in Citizenship Education* National report that assessed schools' roles in preparing young citizens Recommendations to strengthen civics and citizenship education	Senate Standing Committee on Employment, Education, and Training
1989	*Hobart Declaration: Ten Common and Agreed National Goals for Schooling in Australia* Goal 7: To develop knowledge, skills, attitudes, and values which will enable students to participate as active and informed citizens in our democratic Australian society within an international context	Ministerial Council on Education, Employment, Training, and Youth Affairs (MCEETYA)
1999	*Adelaide Declaration: National Goals for Schooling in the 21st Century* (reevaluation of Hobart Declaration) "The national goals for schooling will assist young people to contribute to Australia's social, cultural and economic development in local and global contexts. Their achievement will also assist young people to develop a disposition towards learning throughout their lives so that they can exercise their rights and responsibilities as citizens of Australia."	Ministerial Council (MCEETYA)
1990	*National Aboriginal and Torres Strait Islander Education Policy* Educational goals and strategies to address curriculum reform, professional development, and community education initiatives for and about indigenous peoples	Commonwealth Task Force and Ministerial Council (MCEETYA)
1994	*Whereas the People: Civics and Citizenship Education Report* Strategic plan for public education programs, including the integration of Civics and Citizenship education (CCE) in the Studies of Society and Environment Learning Area (SOSE)	Civics Expert Group (CEG)

1994	*National Statement and National Profile, Studies of Society and Environment (SOSE)*	Australian Education Council (AEC)
	New learning area statements; includes Civics and Citizenship Education (CCE) goals and content, as well as multicultural education, indigenous education, global education, and environmental education	
1997	*Discovering Democracy: Civics and Citizenship Education*	Ministry of Schools, Vocational Education, and Training (now Department of Education, Science, and Training (DEST)
	Materials for primary, lower, and upper secondary levels distributed nationally to all teachers	

vide the rationale and goals as well as suggest content, outcomes, and assessment methods. While each state and territory has developed its own SOSE framework or curriculum, they are guided by the *National Statement* and *National Profile*.

Several other areas of study are also integrated into SOSE or across the curriculum; these include global education, environmental education, multicultural education, and indigenous education.[3] For purposes of this analysis of the meanings of the intercultural relations dimension of citizenship, the multicultural education and indigenous education perspectives in the SOSE curriculum are important curriculum domains that bring new meanings to citizenship. One of the seven perspectives included in the SOSE *National Statement* is multicultural perspectives (AEC 1994a). In the SOSE *National Statement*, multicultural education includes an awareness of Australia's diversity and the various perspectives people of different backgrounds bring to society and issues. A multicultural perspective also means having an understanding of the history of migration to Australia, the ways in which groups experience discrimination, and the social and institutional structures that can be improved to promote social justice (Parry 1998). Indigenous education seeks to bring equity in educational outcomes for indigenous peoples. In the SOSE curriculum, indigenous education has sought to recognize how citizenship and its rights and responsibilities have not been granted to Aboriginal peoples in Australia and other countries. Indigenous education also aims to bring an appreciation and understanding of the culture of people living within Australia, and as such, it has brought intercultural perspectives to the curriculum. Within most states' curriculum and in many curriculum texts on civics and citizenship education, topics address citizenship, reconciliation, and rights of Aborigines (see, e.g., Bereson and McDonald 1997 or the *Discovering Democracy* materials in Curriculum Corporation 1998a).

USING HERMENEUTIC INTERPRETATION TO
ILLUMINATE NEW MEANINGS OF CITIZENSHIP

A hermeneutic interpretive approach (Dahlberg, Drew, and Nystrom 2001) was used to analyze and understand the meanings of the intercultural relations dimension of citizenship in the SOSE curriculum. Hermeneutics reveals new and implicit meanings that may not otherwise become evident if other text analysis approaches are used (Crotty 1998).

Hermeneutics was chosen as a methodology for this study based on several assumptions about citizenship and citizenship education. First, citizenship is about how we live our daily lives and engage in the communities around us (Boulding 1987; Heater 1990). Second, effective learning processes connect citizenship education with citizens' (teachers' and students') daily lives by making sense of complex issues in the context of their lives (Engle and Ochoa 1988; Torney-Purta et al. 2001). Finally, societies are changing, because of globalization; in turn, meanings of citizenship are shifting. Hermeneutics allows for these constructed and changing meanings to be understood, particularly in relation to the social-cultural environment within which citizens live.

Three methodological components guided the interpretive approach used in this study: (1) dialogical relationship between the researcher and the texts; (2) hermeneutic circle, or interpreting the interrelationships of the parts and the whole of the texts; and (3) a fusion of horizons, which involves the framing of interpretations within a larger historical and cultural context and literature (Gadamer 1989). To interpret a particular text—in this case, the curriculum documents—I entered into a dialogical relationship with the text that was characterized by my sustained openness to the text's meanings and intents, while at the same time I consciously utilized the knowledge from the disciplines and my own experiences to frame the interpretation within a cultural-historical context. In this interpretive process, I returned again and again to the parts and the whole of the texts in an iterative process, the hermeneutic circle (Dilthey 1988; Gadamer 1989). Within a delicate balance, I also turned to external sources for further comparison of ideas. This process of interpreting the curriculum text in relation to external sources is the "fusion of horizons" (Gadamer 1989). In this chapter, a "fusion of horizons" is achieved by bringing theories about citizenship, intercultural relations, multiculturalism, and democracy to the interpretations of the written text, as well as the experiences of educators based on my interviews with them. This process reveals new understanding of the intercultural meanings of citizenship that are conceptualized and contested in the Australia curriculum.

The primary documents used for this interpretation were Studies of Society and Environment (SOSE)[4] curriculum documents[5] from five states and territories within Australia.[6] The interpretations of these curriculum documents focused on the secondary school compulsory years.[7] SOSE curriculum documents constitute the primary framework from which all teachers have to teach civics and citizenship education. For teachers who have not been formally trained to teach civics and citizenship education,[8] the written curriculum is a powerful tool to construct and communicate the content that teachers are to know, understand, and teach. "A curriculum is not a neutral document"; it is permeated with intentions, objectives, and values (Ross 2002: 45). The *National Statement* (AEC 1994a) and *National Profile* (AEC 1994b) for SOSE were written by educators and policymakers and distributed to all teachers and schools for their use in teaching civics and citizenship education. These documents represent and transmit particular messages to teachers about the content, skills, values, and meanings that policymakers, departments of education, and educators perceive to be important to teach students.

The interpretation of the intercultural meanings of citizenship in the curriculum were also informed by interviews with twenty-two educators from these five states in Australia, as well as literature on the social, cultural, political, and economic issues within the Australian context.

An example illustrates how the hermeneutic interpretive approach was used to understand the meanings of intercultural relations in the curriculum. In an initial interpretation of the curriculum documents, statements referring to content and outcomes about intercultural relations were identified. For example, one state's curriculum document refers to content that should address "diversity within Australian cultural groups" (ACT, SOSE Framework: 59). To understand the meaning of this statement, it must be considered within the larger context of the curriculum document (the parts and the whole), which includes many other references to cultural groups. For example, additional content included in this curriculum are: comparisons of beliefs and culture of other indigenous peoples, similarities with the dominant Australian culture, and effects of racism and prejudice, and ways to counter it (59). This state's framework aims to "challenge students to make creative responses both as individuals and with others, to important issues. Students are equipped to seek change, and helped to find the confidence to manage the future. . . . [It] focuses on the need to live in peace and harmony" (4). These statements allow for a deeper interpretation of how the study of diverse groups in Australia should be undertaken. The merging of the meaning of these statements suggests that learning about cultural groups has an aim of understanding societal issues, such as racism; the curriculum also attempts to help students create change.

THE CURRICULUM: MINIMAL AND CRITICAL
FORMS OF CITIZENSHIP

In the following sections, minimal and critical meanings of the intercultural relations[9] dimension of citizenship are interpreted.

The intercultural relations dimension in the SOSE curriculum constructs and contests issues of who a citizen is, what the identity of a citizen is, what rights a citizen has, and what the relations are among citizen groups and between citizens and the government. This dimension addresses the diverse constructions of citizenship in response to a changing multicultural society. Not only is the Australian society more diverse due to increasing immigration, but the growing awareness among the populace about the indigenous history of the country is resulting in contested meanings of citizenship in a multicultural democratic society.

Two themes illustrate the intercultural relations dimension: (1) cultural identity of citizens and (2) cultural groups' struggle for citizenship rights. The intentions, values, perspectives, and outcomes of these themes vary greatly in the different curriculum documents across the states. This sociocultural interpretation draws on several examples across curriculum documents to illustrate the meaning of intercultural relations from minimal and critical approaches (see table 12.2).

Cultural Identity of Citizens

One approach in the curriculum is to construct the cultural identity of citizens in relation to predefined groups, such as national or ethnic groups.

Table 12.2.   Examples of Minimal and Critical Forms of the Intercultural Relations Dimension in the SOSE Curriculum

Dimension	Minimal	Critical
Intercultural relations (indigenous peoples, immigrants)	• Creating awareness of and examining multiple perspectives related to issues • Understanding values and beliefs within and among groups/societies • Understanding the construction of cultural identity • Understanding cultural and ethnic groups' struggle for rights	• Analyzing cultural groups' perceptions of advantage and disadvantage in society • Devising strategies to effect social change for different groups in society • Proposing resolutions to conflicts among intercultural groups

For example, one curriculum document states that students learn how different Australian communities and the factors (e.g., ethnicity, culture, religion, Aboriginality) contribute to a sense of identity (New South Wales [NSW] 1998, Geography Syllabus: 28–29). An outcome in this curriculum is that students are able to account for differences within and between Australian communities (NSW, Geography Syllabus: 28). In a related curriculum document, students must be able to "describe people's differing experiences of citizenship" (NSW 1998, History Syllabus: 14). One of the questions for students to understand related to the identity of citizens is "How have images of being 'Australian' changed?" (25).

An understanding of the historical and sociocultural perspectives of citizenship in Australian society assists in interpreting the constructions of citizenship identity in the present curriculum. Historically, the Australian state constructed the identity and rights of citizens based on overlapping yet differentiated identities, including "native," "citizen," "subject," and "Australian." The term *citizen* was not used in the Australian constitution or laws until 1948, when the Nationality and Citizenship Act revised naturalization processes for people living in Australia and granted them the title of citizen (Chesterman and Galligan 1997). Historically, and even today, the term *citizen* implies various meanings. Its informal use often refers to someone who lives in a particular place; being a citizen also suggests someone who has particular rights and responsibilities in that place. Historically, *citizen* described people's relation to states within Australia (Davidson 2001; Irving 1997). Furthermore, a legal definition of *citizen* was confounded by Australians' status as subjects of the queen, although this status does not have any particular meaning in relation to rights within the Commonwealth of Australia (Chesterman and Galligan 1997). Davidson (2001) concludes that because there is no reference to citizenship in the constitution and there is no bill of rights, a false sense of democratic citizenship continues to be perpetuated.

In the period prior to federation, or the founding of the Australian state in 1901, and for some time thereafter, people born in Australia were considered "native," although this term commonly referred to those of Anglo-Celtic background and not Aboriginal peoples. The "natives" regarded themselves as distinct from the British because Australian natives had ascribed traits that connected them to the social and geographical environment of Australia, in effect an Australian identity. At the same time, these Anglo-Celtic "natives" wished to be associated with the "home" country, Great Britain, to retain a British identity (Chesterman and Galligan 1997; Irving 1997).[10] Curriculum documents and texts reference this historical identity and the traits that tended to define Australians.

Prior to and during the federation period, the Aborigines were not considered "natives." They were regarded as a distinct racial group of inferior status. As legislation developed in the early years of the Commonwealth, a term emerged to define the indigenous peoples of Australia: *Aboriginal native*. *Aboriginal* refers to "an original inhabitant or descendent thereof," and *native* refers to a specific place of birth (Chesterman and Galligan 1997: 88).

The first members of Parliament and the creators of the constitution and democratic institutions were, in the main, white, male Anglo-Celtic "natives." Women were not involved in the formal process of developing the constitution. Even after the Franchise Act of 1902 was enacted for white women, they did not have other economic and social rights associated with the status of citizen. For example, it was not until 1967 that married women were no longer legally excluded from public service (Curtin 2000). Furthermore, nonwhite women or women married to nonwhite men were not granted similar social rights, such as the benefits conferred to white women in the Maternity Act of 1912 (Lake 1997). Thus, the imagined identity of "the community" (Anderson 1991) of the Commonwealth of Australia in the early twentieth century became associated with being white, male, and culturally Australian of British/Celtic origin, not black (Australian Aborigine) or any other racial or national group.

The 1960s and 1970s marked a change in these long-held notions of Australian identity and citizenship. An influx of immigrants from non-European countries caused a reaction to the "White Australia" policy, the immigration and naturalization laws that had prohibited immigration of people who were not "white" and European. In 1974, a Commonwealth multicultural policy was enacted to counter the effects of the White Australia policy. Following the war between the United States and Vietnam, more than seventy thousand refugees from Vietnam, Laos, and Cambodia entered Australia (Dobell 2000: 301). This growing population of non-European immigrants further marked a change in the identity of Australians.

The changing identity of people who live in Australia and the meanings of citizenship are reflected in the current curricula. For example, in one civics and citizenship education text, students learn about different cultural groups in a unit on immigration (Bereson and McDonald 1997: 148–64). The activities in the text tend to focus on knowledge about cultural groups. For example, key learning questions for students include "When did the first Asian immigrants come to the colonies, and why did they come?" (150) and, referring to a chart on recent data on migrants, "What was the main category of migrant arrivals?" (157).

These examples of curriculum outcomes and content create minimal constructions of citizenship in relation to cultural groups' identity. The civics and citizenship education textbooks tend to focus on the legal and political documents that create identity as a citizen, while less attention is given to individual's and groups' perceptions of their identity as citizens and as being Australian. Curriculum documents and texts that concentrate on how specific cultural groups came to Australia, and what their contributions have been, emphasize knowledge and use predefined constructs of citizenship, without little contestation regarding the experiences of these cultural groups as citizens.

What it means to be a multicultural society is not often contested in these curriculum documents or texts. As one educator noted, "For a long time in this country, you were only ethnic if you weren't Anglo-Celtic. The whole concept of multicultural was about other cultures." When multiculturalism is addressed in textbooks, students are often asked to understand the issues supporting and opposing this policy and value in society (see Bereson and MacDonald 1997: 160). For example, students are asked to debate issues related to immigration, such as, "Do you agree with the statement that immigrants changed Australia more than Australia changed the immigrants?" (155). Some curriculum documents also attempt to promote positive attitudes about multiculturalism, without critical analysis. For example, a curriculum document states an outcome for students is "respect for, and acceptance of, cultural diversity" (NSW 1998, History Syllabus). The content and outcomes that are not included are as important to this analysis as those curriculum content and outcomes that are stated. Throughout this curriculum document, there is no mention of prejudice or intolerance, nor does it include a component on helping students deal with and respond to these issues.

This approach of studying facts about cultural groups often has the goal of learning about the "Other," without a critical examination of what "Other" means and how one relates to the "Other" (Said 1978; Merryfield 2001). Furthermore, minimal constructions of citizen identity do not recognize the asymmetries of power that occur with one's identification with different groups. Mouffe (1993) argues that the multiple identities of an individual create different "positionalities." For example, an Aboriginal man may experience certain privileges and power based on one identity, such as male, but not experience privilege in relation to another identity, such as indigenous. These aspects of power and relations between individuals of different cultural groups are not addressed by the content and outcomes suggested in the curriculum statements cited earlier.

One teacher from Western Australia captured the tension in the curriculum and for teachers in the classroom to address citizenship identity and cultural groups in a critical way.

We haven't taken advantage of the [curriculum] material . . . particularly the social aspects and the incorporation of different values and groups. . . . If I can give the reason, it's probably because the teachers are from my generation and we have been trained and brought up to not dwell on these more sensitive social issues like racism and cultural things and ethnicity because that was not seen as being acceptable for teachers to open those issues up for discussion. . . . The political and legal [aspects of the curriculum] are seen as much more acceptable . . . and because the [curriculum materials] have been inspired by politicians who want better educated citizens, . . . but politicians are not interested in opening up debates about equality or the rights and wrongs of what's been done to the aboriginal people. . . . They don't want the issues discussed too much, but they do want people to be able to participate more fully in the systemic side . . . so it's a bit of a paradox. . . . [The new curriculum] opens up the opportunity to enter into these wider social issues and discuss how the political system is accommodating and reacting to these differences, . . . but there's a reluctance amongst us to go behind into a lot of these issues.

A critical approach to citizenship education links citizenship identity and behaviors to social structures and the examination of power asymmetries and discrimination within those social structures (Westheimer and Kahne 2004). In addition, critical approaches also encourage exploration, debate, and understanding of the various facets of identity and how they are affected by the larger society. An example of a critical approach in one curriculum document states that "student understands that factors such as gender, race, and socioeconomic status may influence personal, group and cultural identity" (Western Australia 1998, Cultural Strand). While this statement does not vary greatly in its intent, at the surface, from the previous minimally constructed statements, additional curriculum processes and outcomes clarify the meaning of what students are to learn and understand. The curriculum document further elaborates:

this is evident when students can . . . identify discrimination and/or disadvantage (acceptance in society, treatment by the legal system) resulting from difference in gender, race, disability, ethnic group membership or socioeconomic status; examine the ways in which groups, such as musicians, managers, young women, elderly people or Aboriginal people are presented in the mass media. (Western Australia, Society and Environment [WA, S and E], Culture Strand)

A critical approach exemplified in this curriculum document allows for discussion and examination of critical issues, sharing of perspectives among groups, and social action "to contribute to the achievement of more desirable futures for all" (WA, S and E Statement). An overall goal of this curriculum is that "students actively seek opportunities to address inequality . . . and address prejudice and discriminatory behavior in peaceful ways (WA, Active Citizenship Outcome Statement).

In another curriculum document, an understanding of "Other" cultural groups is explored in relation to oneself. "[Students learn about] impacts of particular perceptions of cultural groups held by a community (positive and negative impacts, social codes and creeds, marginalization, power distribution, advantage, disadvantage) (State of Queensland 2000: 39). This document goes beyond learning about perceptions of cultural groups to address social action. One of its objectives is for students to devise strategies to respond to negative perceptions of cultural groups.

These latter examples from curriculum documents illustrate how the content and concepts reflect a critical approach to citizenship education by directly addressing perceptions of those who have been marginalized, understanding power and discrimination, and empowering students to take social action.

Cultural Groups' Struggle for Rights

Another construction of the intercultural relations dimension of citizenship in the SOSE curriculum is the struggle for rights for certain cultural groups (i.e., Aborigines). Educational policymakers have included this topic, in part, to reflect the political and social changes and debates in the larger society, and to develop an understanding of historical interpretations of citizenship in Australian society.

The term *Aboriginal native* was used during the federation years, and for many years thereafter, to exclude Aborigines from political and social rights, such as voting and pensions (Read 1998). Both during colonization and after federation, policies and practices denied Aborigines of their rights, human dignity, and cultural practices. For example, the "stolen generation" refers to the generations of Aborigines who were stolen from their homes and placed with "white folk" to be educated and assimilated into Australian society. An official policy of assimilation for indigenous peoples existed between the 1930s and the 1960s (Read 1998). Years of colonization have resulted in dispossession by Aborigines of their land rights. The commonwealth constitution did not officially grant Aborigines political rights; furthermore, federal and state legislative acts specifically denied Aborigines of economic and social rights (Chesterman and Galligan 1997).

The 1960s saw the beginning of an era of change in ideas and practices surrounding the construction of citizenship rights in Australia. In a reversal of past legislative franchise acts, all adult Aborigines were given the franchise in 1962 (Chesterman and Galligan 1997). Over the course of the next several years, legislative acts granting Aborigines social rights and benefits were enacted on a state by state basis. These and other legislative changes led to the passage of a referendum in 1967 that has become known in practice as the Citizenship-Granting Referendum for Aborigines (Chesterman and Galligan 1997).

While political rights were granted in 1962, indigenous peoples continue to not have equal access or opportunity to social rights, such as education, jobs, and reasonable wages (Welch 1997). An agenda of "indigenous rights" began to take hold in the 1980s, and in 1992, the Mabo decision, in which the court ruled that Aborigines and Torres Strait Islanders held native title to the land, was a landmark case that upheld indigenous rights (Chesterman and Galligan 1997). In addition, a process of reconciliation between Aborigines and non-Aboriginal peoples has been a societal debate in the last decades. This process aims to find ways for the cultural groups within Australia to coexist in one nation-state (Mulgan 1998).

The inclusion of indigenous peoples' rights in the SOSE curricula takes both minimal and critical approaches in the different curriculum documents. One document states that students need to be able to "identify various marginalised groups who have struggled for rights and freedom" and "account for how and why the rights and freedom of various groups in Australian society have changed" (NSW 1998, History Syllabus: 15). The content included to achieve these outcomes may be a study of the Aboriginal experience in the early years of the Australian federation and issues related to indigenous rights that arose in the 1970s to 1990s (23, 25). Several questions guide the themes to be discussed and learned in this curriculum: "What forms of dispossession were carried out against Aboriginal people? What steps took place leading to the recognition of land rights and native title? How have traditional views about Australia's history been challenged by the end of terra nullius?" (23, 25). While these statements may suggest some attention to marginalization and oppression, in part because legislative acts and educational policy statements use these terms, the content and outcomes in this document primarily focus on understanding these historical events. The curriculum gives little attention to the processes and effects of colonization and discrimination or ways to address these issues to create societal change, as is important from a critical approach.

Minimal constructions of citizenship rights in some curriculum documents tend to use noncritical language in describing the outcomes, content, and topics related to citizenship rights and Aborigines. For example, "students learn about the way in which Aboriginal and Torres Strait Islander peoples of Australia's lifestyles have changed and adapted as a result of European occupation" (State of Victoria 2000, SOSE, History, Level 4). Furthermore, the outcomes state that a student at this level (grade 7) is able to "demonstrate knowledge about how the organization and lifestyle of Aboriginal and Torres Strait Islander communities have changed over time . . . [by] describing the diversity of Aboriginal and Torres Strait Islander communities" (Level 4, History outcomes and indicators). By level 6 (grades 9–10), students learn about "the movement of Aboriginal and Torres Strait Islander communities toward self-determination, including the recognition of native title." These outcomes are achieved when students can "identify which civil and political rights were denied the Aboriginal and Torres Strait Islander communities, analyse the reasons why they were denied, outline the different ways the Aborigines campaigned for rights, and evaluate the degree to which they have been successful" (State of Victoria 2000, SOSE, History Level 6 Outcomes and Indicators). While the curriculum documents attend to the denial and later granting of rights to indigenous peoples, the language and concepts used in this framework do not address power and discrimination, nor do they seek to empower students to take individual and collective social action. Furthermore, this curriculum does not address how social structures continue to affect Aborigines' way of life.

Some textbooks, like the state curriculum documents, tend to avoid larger critical debate and promotion of societal change through citizenship action. In a section of a textbook chapter, the struggle for reconciliation is addressed (Darlington and Hospodaryk 1999: 218–21). It clarifies what the Reconciliation Act is; how it was passed; and the continuing debate over "native title," the right of indigenous peoples' ownership to land. Perspectives of indigenous peoples are included, but the questions and activities for student learning remain focused on knowledge: "What is meant by self-determination and reconciliation?" In response to a speech by Prime Minister Keating, students are asked, "What makes Keating's remarks an act of reconciliation?" When students are expected to recite what these concepts mean, by providing statements from sources, little opportunity for debate or alternative perspectives exists.

Some curricula address these issues with a critical approach. For example, one curriculum document includes the topic of equity in relation to rights in these terms:

> [SOSE curriculum] encourages students to demonstrate an understanding of human rights in local and global contexts, and . . . to participate actively in the enhancement of human rights; enables students, teachers and the broader school community to be critically informed about privilege and injustice and enable to effect change through participatory and consultative processes, particularly with those experiencing these injustices. (State of Queensland SOSE Syllabus: 9)

This document, in contrast to those constructed from a minimal approach, specifically uses an approach to address privilege and injustice, and attempts to help students understand how they can create change to promote justice.

One educator who had taught for several years in an indigenous community, described how his experiences interacting with Aboriginal children, their families, and the larger community caused him to take a more active role in teaching all children about issues and rights of Aborigines. His approach was to bring the daily experiences of Aborigines into the classroom, such as their struggles to live in traditional communities and urban areas, and to help both Aborigines and non-Aborigines learn from these experiences and become actively involved in creating change in society. This approach is distinct from that of some other educators. All educators interviewed for this study recognized the importance of addressing indigenous peoples' history and present day issues. Many teachers found it difficult, however, to teach about social discrimination and problems facing indigenous peoples, in part because of a lack of knowledge and experience with these issues. A lack of openness among students to discuss social issues and be involved in community issues also inhibited teachers from taking a critical approach. Findings from the International Association for the Evaluation of Educational Achievement (IEA) study on civic education in Australia also support this interpretation. While students were not asked explicitly about indigenous peoples and issues, only half of the respondents indicated that they felt they could talk in an open way about certain political or social issues (Mellor, Kennedy, and Greenwood 2002: 99). In addition, teachers generally held the view that school is not the venue for engaging students in community and political activities; rather they felt that emphasis in citizenship education should be placed on knowledge about society (110). Given these perspectives from students and teachers, a critical approach, even when explicit in the curriculum documents, may be difficult to implement when addressing difficult societal issues about citizens' rights.

CONCLUSION

Several conclusions can be made from these interpretations of minimal and critical constructions of citizenship in curriculum documents. First, the meanings of intercultural relations are constructed from both minimal and critical approaches. Tensions exist among the meanings that educational policymakers, educators, and textbook writers wish to convey to students about these topics. While some curriculum documents take a critical approach, some educators and students may not feel comfortable with this approach. In addition, the system of national assessments seems to influence what and how teachers teach, and a critical approach seems not to be encouraged in these exams. One teacher's response to the analysis presented in this chapter was that although he agreed that a critical approach to citizenship was important, he felt that the curriculum and testing pushed him to teach in noncritical ways. The larger societal discourse also influences teachers' and students' ways of constructing these topics from a minimal or critical perspective.

Curriculum documents created in a disciplinary structure tend to emphasize minimal forms of citizenship, such as acquiring knowledge about citizens' rights, or skills necessary to act as a participatory citizen. These disciplinary focused curriculum documents tend not to develop a sense of agency to question knowledge, to reconstruct concepts, and to solve problems related to citizens. Curriculum documents that have an explicitly stated critical approach to citizenship education in their goals or rationale section tend to infuse critical contestation throughout the documents. For example, the Queensland syllabus states in the rationale section that it takes a "socially critical approach" with the goal of "deconstruct[ing] dominant views of society" (8). If a critical approach to citizenship education is not stated at the outset to guide the overall written curriculum, it appears that critical constructions and contestations of citizenship are intermittently interjected or arbitrarily included. Furthermore, when emphasis is placed on minimal approaches to citizenship education, efforts to foster critical constructions of citizenship are undermined (Westheimer and Kahne 2004).

Another conclusion is that critical contestations of citizenship seem most associated with current issues debated in Australian society, although even these current issues are constructed differently depending on policymakers' and educators' perspectives. Educators' responses and this interpretation of curriculum texts suggest that issues internal to Australia, which affect the nation's identity and development of social cohesion, such as citizen's rights and identity, are more difficult to address from a critical approach. Current debated issues that are externally driven or focused, such as immigration, the environment, or globalization, may be easier to approach from a critical perspective. Policymakers, as one educator stated, may have more to lose if internal issues are contested.

It has been suggested that the citizenship education curriculum in Australia is in a transitional phase moving from minimal approaches to maximal approaches (Morris and Cogan 2001). This interpretation of the intercultural relations dimension of citizenship in the curriculum indicates, however, that critical constructions are not thoroughly included in the curriculum. Given that creating and sustaining democracy is an ongoing development process (Przeworski 1995), critical forms of citizenship education play an important role in the deliberation, contestation, and reconstruction of new ways of conceptualizing and enacting citizenship (Gutmann 2004). While minimal constructions are necessary for knowledge about citizenship and participation in society, in the sense of voting and community obligations, critical constructions are important for enacting the complex nature of citizenship in a changing society and in a globalizing world.

NOTES

1. The term *minimal citizenship education* is contrasted with *maximal* in Kerr's (1999) and McLaughlin's (1992) work. The term *critical* used here goes beyond maximal forms of citizenship and includes a specific lens of power differences and societal change.

2. The term *civic education* is used because the curriculum was generally regarded as focusing on traditional subjects, such as history and government. In the 1990s, with the new initiatives, the term was reconceptualized to include civics and citizenship education, in attempt to integrate traditional forms of civic education and the active participation components of citizenship education.

3. Indigenous education was previously called "Aboriginal education," which referred to Aboriginal and Torres Strait Islander perspectives in the *National State-ments* and *National Profiles,* and particularly the SOSE learning area. Several other forms of Aboriginal education exist, including bilingual education and traditional aboriginal educational methods. See Hollihan (1993) for a description of bilingual education as a component of Aboriginal education; see also Welch (1997) for descriptions and analysis of Aboriginal education in its traditional forms, as well as initiatives that have aimed to improve education for Aborigines.

4. Studies of Society and Environment is the term used in the *National Profile* and *National Statement,* and it is the name of the course in which CCE is incorpo-rated in most of the states and territories. The course has different names in two states. In New South Wales, is called Human Society and Its Environment (HSIE), and in Western Australia, it is called Society and Environment (S and E).

5. These curriculum documents included "frameworks" and "syllabi," used dif-ferently in the different states. *Frameworks* are guides for teachers and schools to use in developing their own syllabus, whereas a *syllabus,* particularly in the case of NSW and to a lesser extent in Queensland, is more prescriptive in terms of the content to be taught. Throughout the remainder of this chapter, the term *curriculum documents* is used to refer to both curriculum formats and other curriculum materials.

6. The five states and territories included New South Wales, Australian Capital Territory, Victoria, Western Australia, and Queensland. These states were selected among the eight because they are the most populated and include the major urban cities.

7. Compulsory secondary school, also called lower secondary school, is gener-ally years 7 to 10. In Queensland, and in some other exceptions, such as private schools, compulsory secondary school is years 8 to 10.

8. See Craven, Print, and Moroz (1999) for research regarding the extent of teacher professional development in civics and citizenship education. This study found that at least 54 percent of teachers who responded to the survey had not had any CCE coursework.

9. The dimension "intercultural relations" represents a variety of concepts or themes in the curriculum related to cultural groups. This term expresses a meaning beyond "cultural groups," however, in that it addresses the interpersonal role of citi-zens to relate to and understand others who may be culturally different from them-selves. The term is also a variation on the concept of intercultural perspective used in the SOSE curriculum.

10. Irving (1997) notes that people of other ethnic and national backgrounds also saw themselves in terms of their prior national identity and as Australians. For example, people who were Chinese printed documents during federation that called themselves the "Chinese Australians."

REFERENCES AND ADDITIONAL CURRICULUM DOCUMENTS

Ainley, J., J. Malley, and S. Lamb. 1997. *Thematic Review of the Transition from Initial Education to Working Life: Australian Background Report*. Canberra: Department of Employment, Education, Training and Youth Affairs, Vocational Education and Training Division.

Anderson, B. 1991. *Imagined Communities: Reflections on the Origin and Spread of Nationalism*. London: Verso.

Australian Bureau of Statistics. 2005. *Australian Social Trends 2002*. www.abs.gov.au.

Australian Capital Territory. 1993. *Studies of Society and Environment Curriculum Framework*. Canberra: Department of Education and Training

Australian Education Council. 1994a. *A Statement on Studies of Society and Environment for Australian Schools*. Carlton, Australia: Curriculum Corporation.

———. 1994b. *Studies of Society and Environment: A Curriculum Profile for Australian Schools*. Carlton, Australia: Curriculum Corporation.

Bereson, I., and D. Macdonald. 1997. *Civics and Citizenship in Australia*. South Melbourne: Nelson.

Board of Studies, New South Wales. 1998a. *Geography Stages 4–5 Syllabus*. Sydney: Author.

———. 1998b. *History Stages 4–5 Syllabus*. Sydney: Author.

Boulding, E. 1988. *Building a Global Civic Culture: Education for an Interdependent World*. New York: Teachers College Press.

Chesterman, J., and B. Galligan. 1997. *Citizens without Rights: Aborigines and Australian Citizenship*. Cambridge: Cambridge University Press.

Cogan, J., and R. Derricott, eds. 2000. *Citizenship for the Twenty-first Century: An International Perspective on Education*. London: Kogan Page.

Cogan, J. C., P. Morris, and M. Print, eds. 2002. *Civic Education in the Asia-Pacific Region: Case Studies across Six Societies*. New York: Routledge Falmer.

Civics Education Group. 1994. *Whereas the People: Civics and Citizenship Education*. Canberra: Australian Government Publishing Service.

Craven, R., M. Print, and W. Moroz. 1999. "Civics and Citizenship Education in Australian Schools: The Challenge for the Twenty-first Century." *The Social Educator: Journal of the Social Education Association of Australia* 17, no. 3: 6–16.

Crotty, M. 1998. *The Foundations of Social Research: Meaning and Perspective in the Research Process*. London: Sage.

Curriculum Corporation. 1998. *Discovering Democracy: Lower Secondary Units*. Carlton, Australia: Author.

———. 2002. *Global Perspectives: A Statement on Global Education for Australian Schools*. Carlton, Australia: Author.

Curtin, J. 2000. "The Gendering of Citizenship in Australia." In *Citizenship and Democracy in a Global Era*, ed. A. Vandenberg. New York: St. Martin's.

Dahlberg, K., N. Drew, and M. Nystrom. 2001. *Reflective Lifeworld Research*. Lund, Sweden: Studentlitteratur.

Darlington, R., and J. Hospodaryk. 1999. *A History of Australia since 1901*. Melbourne: Heinemann.

Davidson, A. 2001. "The State, Democracy and Citizenship in Australia." In *Balancing Democracy*, ed. R. Axtmann. London: Continuum.

Department of Foreign Affairs and Trade, Government of Australia. *Monthly Trade Data 2004–2005*. www.dfat.au.gov.

Dilthey, W. 1988. *Introduction to the Human Sciences*. Trans. R. J. Betranzos. Detroit, Mich.: Wayne State University Press.

Dobell, G. 2000. *Australia Finds Home: The Choices and Changes of an Asia Pacific Journey*. Sydney: Australian Broadcasting Corporation.

Engle, S. H., and A. S. Ochoa. 1988. *Education for Democratic Citizenship: Decision Making in the Social Studies*. New York: Teachers College Press.

Gadamer, H.-G. 1989. *Truth and Method*. Trans. J. Weinsheimer and D. G. Marshall, 2nd ed. New York: Continuum.

Giroux, H., and P. McLaren. 1996. "Teacher Education and the Politics of Engagement." In *Breaking Free: The Transformative Power of Critical Pedagogy*, ed. P. Leistyna, A. Woodrum and S. Sherblom. Cambridge, Mass.: Harvard Educational Review.

Government of Western Australia. 1998a. *Society and Environment Curriculum Framework*. www.curriculum.wa.edu.au/.

———. 1998b. *Society and Environment Student Outcome Statements*. www.eddept. wa.edu.au/centoff/outcomes/.

Gutmann, A 1987. *Democratic Education*. Princeton, N.J.: Princeton University Press.

———. 2004. "Unity and Diversity in Democratic Multicultural Education." In *Diversity and Citizenship Education: Global Perspectives*, ed. J. A. Banks. San Francisco: Jossey-Bass.

Heater, D. 1990. *Citizenship: The Civic Ideal in World History, Politics and Education*. London: Longman.

Hollihan, K. T. 1993. "The Search in Australian Aboriginal Education: Recent Developments and Bilingual Education." *Canadian Journal of Native Education* 20, no. 1: 136–47.

Irving, H. 1997. *To Constitute a Nation: A Cultural History of Australia's Constitution*. Cambridge: Cambridge University Press.

Jupp, J. 1997. "Immigration and National Identity: Multiculturalism." In *The Politics of Identity in Australia*, ed. G. Stokes. Cambridge: Cambridge University Press.

Kemp, D. 1997. *Discovering Democracy: Civics and Citizenship Education*. Canberra: Ministry of Schools, Vocational Education, and Training.

Kennedy, K. J. 1993. "National Curriculum Policy Development in Australia: A Review and Analysis of Commonwealth Government Involvement in the School Curriculum." In *Citizenship Education for a New Age*, ed. K. J. Kennedy, O. Watts, and G. McDonald. Toowoomba, Australia: USQ Press.

Kerr, D. 1999. *Citizenship Education: An International Comparison*. London: QCA/ NFER.

Kymlicka, W. 1995. *Multicultural Citizenship.* New York: Oxford University Press.

Lake, M. 1997. "Stirring Tales: Australian Feminism and National Identity 1900–1940." In *The Politics of Identity in Australia,* ed. G. Stokes. Cambridge: Cambridge University Press.

Ling, P. 1984. *Education Policy in Australia 1880–1914.* Melbourne: Philips Institute of Technology Centre for Youth and Community Studies.

Marginson, S. 1993. *Education and Public Policy in Australia.* Cambridge: Cambridge University Press.

McLaughlin, T. H. 1992. "Citizenship, Diversity and Education: A Philosophical Perspective." *Journal of Moral Education* 21, no. 3: 235–50.

Mellor, S., K. Kennedy, and L. Greenwood. 2002. *Citizenship and Democracy: Australian Students' Knowledge and Beliefs: The IEA Civic Education Study of 14-Year-Olds.* Camberwell: Australian Council for Educational Research.

Merryfield, M. 2001. "Moving the Center of Global Education: From Imperial World Views That Divide the World to Double Consciousness, Contrapuntal Pedagogy, Hybridity, and Cross-cultural Competence." In *Social Studies Research for the 21st Century,* ed. W. B. Stanley. Greenwich, Conn.: Information Age.

Ministerial Council for Employment, Educational Training, and Youth Affairs. 1989. *The Hobart Declaration on Schooling.* Canberra: Department of Employment, Educational Training, and Youth Affairs.

———. 1995. *A National Strategy for the Education of Aboriginal and Torres Strait Islander Peoples 1996–2002.* Canberra: Department of Employment, Educational Training, and Youth Affairs.

———. 1999. *The Adelaide Declaration on National Goals for Schooling in the Twenty-first Century.* Canberra: Department of Employment, Educational Training, and Youth Affairs.

Morris, P., and J. Cogan. 2001. "A Comparative Overview: Civic Education across Six Societies." *International Journal of Educational Research* 35, no. 1: 109–23.

Mouffe, C. 1993. *The Return of the Political.* London: Verso.

Mulgan, R. 1998. "Citizenship and Legitimacy in Post-colonial Australia." In *Citizenship and Indigenous Australians: Changing Conceptions and Possibilities,* ed. N. P. W. Sanders. Cambridge: Cambridge University Press.

Musgrave, P. W. 1979. *Society and the Curriculum in Australia.* Sydney: Allen & Unwin.

Nie, N. H., J. Junn, and K. Sthlik-Barry. 1996. *Education and Democratic Citizenship in America.* Chicago: University of Chicago Press.

Parker, W. C. 1996. "Advanced" Ideas about Democracy: Toward a Pluralist Conception of Citizen Education. *Teachers College Record,* 98, 104–125.

Parry, L. 1998. "Immigration and Multiculturalism: Issues in Australian Society and Schools." *Social Education* 62, no. 7: 449–53.

Peterson, N., and W. Sanders. 1998. "Introduction." In N. Peterson and W. Sanders, *Citizenship and Indigenous Australians: Changing Conceptions and Possibilities.* Cambridge: Cambridge University Press.

Print, M. 1996. "Renaissance in Citizenship Education: An Australian Perspective." *International Journal of Social Education* 11, no. 2: 37–52.

Print, M., and M. Gray. 2000. "Civics and Citizenship Education: An Australian Perspective." www.abc.net.au/civics/democracy/ccanded.htm.

Print, M., K. Kennedy, and J. Hughes. 1999. "Reconstructing Civic and Citizenship Education in Australia." In *Civic Education across Countries: Twenty-four National Case Studies from the IEA Civic Education Project,* ed. ed. J. Torney-Purta, J. Schwille, and J. Amadeo. Amsterdam: International Association for the Evaluation of Educational Achievement.

Przeworksi, A. 1995. *Sustainable Democracy.* Cambridge: Cambridge University Press.

Read, P. 1998. "Whose Citizens? Whose Country?" In *Citizenship and Indigenous Australians,* ed. N. P. W. Sanders. Cambridge: Cambridge University Press.

Ross, A. 2002. "Citizenship Education and Curriculum Theory." In *Citizenship Education and the Curriculum,* ed. D. Scott and H. Lawson. Westport, Conn.: Ablex.

Said, E. W. 1978. *Orientalism.* New York: Random House.

Senate Standing Committee on Employment, Education, and Training. 1989. *Active Participation in Citizenship Education.* Canberra: Australian Government Printing Service.

State of Queensland. 2000. *Studies of Society and Environment, Years 1 to 10 Syllabus.* Brisbane: Queensland School Curriculum Council.

State of Victoria. 2000. *Studies of Society and Environment Curriculum and Standards II.* CD-ROM. Melbourne: Department of Education, Employment, and Training, Victoria, School Programmes and Student Welfare Division.

Thomas, J. 1994. "How Civics Education Was Taught in the Past." In Civics Expert Group, *Whereas the People: Civics and Citizenship Education.* Canberra: Australian Government Publishing Service.

Torney-Purta, J., L. Rainer, O. Hans, and W. Schulz. 2001. *Citizenship and Education in Twenty-eight Countries: Civic Knowledge and Engagement at Age Fourteen.* Amsterdam: International Association for the Evaluation of Educational Achievement.

Torney-Purta, J., J. Schwille, and J. Amadeo, eds. 1999. *Civic Education across Countries: Twenty-four National Case Studies from the IEA Civic Education Project.* Amsterdam: International Association for the Evaluation of Educational Achievement.

Warhurst, J. 1999. *From Constitutional Convention to Republic Referendum: A Guide to the Primary Participants.* June 29. www.aph.gov.au/library/pubs/rp/1998–99/99rp25.htm.

Welch, A. 1997. *Class, Culture and the State in Australian Education: Reform or Crisis?* Frankfurt am Main: Lang.

Westheimer, J., and J. Kahne. 2004. "What Kind of Citizen? The Politics of Educating for Democracy." *American Educational Research Journal* 41, no. 2: 237–69.

Final Commentary: Democracy Is Not Only for Politicians; Citizenship Education Is Not Only for Schools

Judith Torney-Purta

Everybody likes a story, and the field of civic education has many elements of a good story. There have been crises (perceived and real) and visionaries, beginning with the founding fathers of many countries who believed that the purpose of schooling was to prepare young people for citizenship. In the early 1960s, a small number of scholars working in long-standing democracies established the field of political socialization research. They gathered evidence showing that interest in politics or voting didn't spring up on one's twenty-first birthday, which was the voting age in the United States at that time. There were even unintended villains in this story—those in the 1970s in the United States who used poorly designed studies of small and nonrepresentative samples to argue that education has no impact on young people's citizenship or participation. This stunted a field that was beginning to build evidence on which to base more effective programs. It was nearly two decades before concerns about declining civic and political engagement among young people took scholars back to the study of political socialization and preparation for citizenship in democracy.

In the 1970s, there was also cross-national research. For example, the first civic education study was undertaken in ten countries by the International Association for the Evaluation of Educational Achievement, usually known as IEA (Torney, Oppenheim, and Farnen 1975). Over the last forty years, a number of quantitative survey studies have been done in this field with international participation, while the number of studies incorporating qualitative methods or sociocultural perspectives has been small. To take some recent examples, Hahn (1998) interviewed and surveyed young people in Denmark, Germany, the Netherlands, and the United States; Gordon, Holland, and Lahelma (2000) observed schools in England and Finland; Torney-Purta, Schwille, and Amadeo (1999) prepared a book of twenty-four case studies for the IEA Civic Education Project (primarily from European or English-speaking countries and based on triangulated documentary analysis rather than observations or interviews). A series of chapters synthesized these case studies, identified themes, and included a more critical perspective from comparative education (Steiner-Khamsi, Torney-Purta, and Schwille 2002). Most recently, Schiffauer and colleagues (2004) published ethnographies relating to the civil enculturation of immigrants in Britain, France, Germany, and the Netherlands. The narratives from all these studies enrich the understanding of civic education, but they primarily deal with Europe and North America. There have been few efforts to synthesize material to address common questions across a broad range of countries or identify what can be learned from multimethod and interdisciplinary research.

This volume brings together researchers who enrich the discourse about citizenship education in several ways. They cross disciplines, expand pedagogical models, encompass adults as well as the young, and report on a wide range of countries. This chapter synthesizes the material provided by these anthropologists and qualitative educational researchers and has two major sections. In the first major section, the positioning of the chapter authors will be described, distinguishing in broad strokes between two groups according to the way they relate as outsiders to the insiders in the cultural settings in which they work. The first group is those who rely primarily on ethnographic observational techniques, positioning themselves to learn from insiders by immersing themselves in settings where thinking about civic education and associated action can be observed in classrooms or other educational settings. The second group seeks advice from insiders but focuses on examining several sources of information, often with a critical perspective, to illuminate civic education policy or practice in a broad context. I will also describe my own positioning as a quantitative researcher with a longtime interest in qualitative studies.

The second major section will draw together material across chapters to address two questions. The first question concerns what can be learned by conceptualizing civic education as goals stated in a curriculum in contrast to what can be learned from sociocultural immersion in educational settings. The second question asks how critical perspectives add to the debate about citizenship and education. In answering these questions, data from the surveys of adolescents in the IEA Study of Civic Education conducted from 1994 to 2004 in nearly thirty countries will be related to material found in the chapters of this volume.

THE POSITIONING OF THE CONTRIBUTORS AND THEIR DATA SOURCES

Thirteen authors contributed to this volume, the large majority of them either anthropologists or specialists in educational policy using a qualitative research approach. The authors of four chapters position themselves as outsiders who immerse themselves in the perspectives of insiders in different contexts (Gaylord on Indonesia, this volume; Huff on El Salvador, this volume; Souto-Manning on Brazil, this volume; Whitman on the Spokane, this volume). They give unforgettable ethnographic portraits based on narratives of teachers' activities in the field and observations of artifacts and their use. The teachers described are taking risks in order to develop students' ability to think critically about what they are learning in Indonesia, or challenging a curriculum that does not allow students to partake of the richness of their local identities among the Spokane, or aligning a Christian identity with a civic and national identity that is in the process of rapid evolution in El Salvador. In Brazil, adults are shown struggling to survive economically as street peddlers, and their narratives are submitted to a critical analysis. All these contributions are rich in material about everyday practice and local meaning systems; they make clear that it is not the curriculum or policies written on paper but actions negotiated and enacted by teachers and other adults in their everyday lives that matter for civic education and empowerment. These examples also challenge us to think about how anthropologists can contribute to an international dialogue without threatening their local informants, especially where challenges to governmental authority are explicit or implicit.

The authors of eight of the chapters position themselves as outsiders with access to insider perspectives (through documentary evidence, interviews or observations, or a combination). They observe the structures of a society and try to place civic education in a broadened context by using multiple sources of information (DeJaeghere on Australia, this volume; Foley and Putu on South Africa, this volume; Levinson on Mexico, this volume; Motani on Japan, this volume; Phillippou on Cyprus, this volume; Reed-Danahay on France, this volume; Skukauskaite on Lithuania, this volume; Stevick on Estonia, this volume).

Three of the authors examine broadened national identities with either global perspectives (in Japan) or European perspectives (in Cyprus and in

France). In the case of France, this involves ethnographic portraits summarized from observations at several schools and at a shopping mall during a Europe Day celebration. The author adds an analysis of artifacts (maps of France, a website meant for use in forming pupils' European identity, and two commercial films portraying the contrasting experiences of upper-middle-class students participating in an EU exchange and immigrant hotel workers).

In the chapter on Greek Cyprus, the author uses observations, interviews, and a curricular intervention framed as action research. The interviews with students include a hypothetical scenario about an Algerian worker in France. Cyprus is an especially interesting place to study European identity formation. It is located at the geographic margins of Europe (and an EU member only since 2004); it is known for vigorous nationalism; it is more likely to associate itself with Greece and Greek culture than with broader European institutions.

In Japan, there is considerable resistance to a global orientation (unless it can be shown to promote economic aims). This chapter portrays the roles of several nongovernmental organizations using interviews developed in a separate cross-national project on global citizenship.

The author of the Estonian chapter looks at attempts to broaden views of the nature of tolerance with the establishment of a public commemoration of the Holocaust, primarily using interviews and the juxtaposition of statements from differing perspectives about the meaning of this commemoration. The focus of this research emerged from a broader ethnographic study when it became clear that the discourse about establishing a Holocaust Day provided an example of new educational directives embedded in the longstanding cultural and historical background of a country.

Authors of chapters on Mexico and South Africa use data collection techniques including interviews with leaders of organizations working on civic education in and out of school, along with evaluations of interventions and the analysis of annotated programs of studies or guidelines for teachers. Discursive analysis of interviews with Lithuanian teachers from three generations and hermeneutic interpretations of new meanings of citizenship found in governmental policies and interviews with educators from five states in Australia round out the volume.

Even these brief characterizations of the authors' approaches, sources of data, and positioning suggest the breadth and richness of information available for synthesis from this volume.

My positioning is as a quantitative researcher who has studied political socialization from a background in developmental, educational, and social psychology, but often working in collaboration with political scientists. My first book, in 1967 (Hess and Torney 2005 [reissue]), used interviews with children aged seven to twelve as an important source of information in formulating questions that could be answered by elementary school students in a survey. I grounded a recent rigorous survey of 150,000 adolescents from twenty-nine countries (Torney-Purta et al. 2001) in extensive country-level case study material (Torney-Purta et al. 1999; LeTendre 2002). We used Lave and Wenger's ideas about communities of practice in framing this study (Wenger 1998). My experience as an insider to a program was with the ICONS Computer-Assisted International Simulation. This involved exploring adolescents' meaning systems about international politics through observations of the construction of knowledge during face-to-face meetings to plan computer conferences and through think-aloud protocols gathered from individuals about solutions to hypothetical political problems (Torney-Purta 1992).

My work has been done almost exclusively in Europe and the United States, while the authors in this volume represent three Pacific Rim countries (Australia, Indonesia, and Japan), three Latin American countries (Brazil, Mexico, and El Salvador), two postcommunist Baltic states that are now EU members (Estonia and Lithuania), two other EU members (France and Cyprus), South Africa, and the Spokane (a Native American group in the northwestern United States). The countries that are represented both in this volume and in national samples tested in the IEA survey are Australia, Cyprus, and Lithuania (where both case studies and survey data are available) and Estonia (where there are survey data but no case study material).

The remainder of this commentary will deal with two issues in the form of two questions. For each issue I will include what has been learned from quantitative research particularly the IEA Civic Education Study, augmenting that discussion with insights from the qualitative research in this volume.

TWO QUESTIONS TRACING THEMES ACROSS QUANTITATIVE AND QUALITATIVE STUDIES

Question 1: How Does Sociocultural Immersion in the Everyday Life of Educational Settings Enrich What Can Be Learned about Civic Education from Survey Research or the Examination of Policy Documents?

A shortcoming of quantitative research on democratic political socialization is that it is often necessary to arrive at a single definition and operationalization of each variable, and this definition often misses the nuances of important concepts. For example, civic knowledge tests usually are based on curricular knowledge standards (often linked to examinations). Attitudes of support for the rights of different ethnic groups or immigrants are measured using scales found in the participating countries for measuring adolescents' or adults' attitudes. Even when a study is conducted in a single country, the formulation of these definitions and measures can lead to distortions in the results. For example, the absence of an expected result may be due to the fact that approved textbooks are not available in some schools or the fact that teachers lack confidence in dealing with certain topics or using certain pedagogical techniques. Some attitudes may be left out of research instruments because they are perceived as sensitive issues. When several countries are involved in a piece of research, as was the case in the IEA Civic Education Study, the process of negotiation to decide on measures for a test or survey requires compromises.

In spite of differences of approach, however, many insights found in this volume correspond to data from the IEA civic education test and survey. In that study the results from students did not place countries into simple classifications (e.g., new vs. old democracies, or groupings by region). For example, there was enormous variation among the postcommunist countries. Fourteen-year-olds in Poland, the Czech Republic, and the Slovak Republic had total civic knowledge scores that were above the international mean and higher than a number of Western European countries like England and Portugal (Torney-Purta et al. 2001). In contrast, postcommunist countries like Estonia, Lithuania, Romania, and Latvia had civic knowledge scores that were significantly below the international mean. Students in the Russian Federation scored about as high on the subscale of content/ conceptual knowledge of citizenship as did students in the United States. To take an attitudinal example, the fourteen-year-old respondents in Denmark, Norway, Switzerland, Greece, and Cyprus all expressed high levels of trust in governmental institutions, but there was considerable variation in trust levels among other Western European countries.

When one looks at the broad set of countries in this volume, one appreciates even more subtle dimensions of variation. Many of these variations could not have been predicted from an examination of curricular or policy statements but can be illuminated by observational data and interviews. Three areas are of particular interest—nationalism (including attitudes toward Europe and toward immigrants), teachers' sense of confidence (or powerlessness), and the role of debate and discussion in the classroom. In these areas everyday experience in classrooms is often more informative than statements of policy or curriculum.

Nationalism, Attitudes toward Europe, and the Understanding of Immigration

The IEA data and information found in this volume approach the issue of nationalism from different perspectives. Students in Greece and Cyprus had the most positive sense of national pride and patriotism on the IEA survey. The interviews quoted in the chapter in this volume on Cyprus provide rich detail and make clear the ways in which strong national feeling in Cyprus shapes the construction of immigrants in xenophobic and threatening terms. A curricular intervention with ten-year-olds succeeded in moving this construction toward the discourse of human rights in the context of European identity, but only for some students. Attitudes toward immigrants settling in Cyprus remained more negative than attitudes toward immigrants more generally. This was in part because the students saw similarities between Turks (traditional foes) and immigrants, viewing them both as threats to Greek Cypriot identity.

In Japan, there was a similar national focus on love of country, tradition, and culture in civic-related classes. The 1974 UNESCO Recommendation on Education for International Understanding was meant to mobilize educators to foster a more global identity among young people. However, its implementation consisted largely of enhancing student exchanges and instruction in English, not a broader attempt to teach children to respect those in Japan who were culturally different from the majority.

The chapter on France deals with European identity among rural working-class children. It will take a great deal more than curriculum pronouncements, an EU website, and a yearly Europe Day to make European identity equal in importance to identities based in the local or national community. The author also notes that enhancing European identity is likely to be problematic for French children from farm families, because they hear about Europe primarily when they hear their parents complain about the restrictive agricultural policies of the EU. These children are also likely to be party to conversations suggesting that their families see immigration as a threat.

Historical factors and cultural institutions influence the ability of educators to adopt policies or practices. In Estonia, attempts to establish a day commemorating the Holocaust revealed hidden societal fault lines and continuing enmities from the past that even stood in the way of discourse on the issue. Many Estonian adults believe that their country's suffering under the Russian occupation during the Soviet era is what deserves commemoration and that Nazi atrocities, although horrific, are not as important an issue for Estonians. Furthermore, the continuing presence in the country of Russian-speaking minorities who refuse to learn Estonian mobilizes anger. Resentment that the initiative came from outside the country exacerbated the apathetic or negative attitudes toward the Holocaust commemoration. Consulting general prescriptions about education for tolerance would be an inadequate way for an outsider to learn about the realities of teaching about intergroup relations in Estonia.

The Everyday Lives of Teachers in Classrooms and Their Sense of Confidence

The IEA data from teachers also address an issue that emerges in this volume: the role of teachers' sense of confidence in teaching political topics (such as the constitution or the judicial system). Teachers responding to IEA's 1999 survey in countries like the United States and Finland (where in-service training is widespread and learning about these topics well established in the curriculum) felt empowered to teach about these subjects, and students' results on civic knowledge and skills were also high (Torney-Purta, Richardson, and Barber 2005). The list of IEA countries where teachers lacked confidence in teaching political topics included the postcommunist countries such as the Czech Republic, Estonia, Hungary, and Lithuania (where massive changes to meet the demands of educating for democracy were recently instituted), England (where new provisions for citizenship as a statutory subject were about to be implemented, creating considerable uncertainly among teachers), and countries such as Belgium, Norway, and Portugal (where both pre- and in-service education were historically weak). In Hungary, students who had been taught by more confident teachers performed better on the IEA civic knowledge test, while variations within the country in teachers' confidence did not make a difference in countries such as Finland and the United States. This suggests that a certain threshold level of confidence in teaching about political topics may be a necessary attribute of teachers in a country before strong and effective civic education in democracy can take place. Several of the chapters in this volume address teachers' sense of confidence in a broader sense, but they are nevertheless instructive.

The Lithuanian chapter in this volume provides detailed information about what a lack of confidence or sense of powerlessness means for teachers and some of its sources in the everyday life of schools. Policies of educational reform are "complex social practices, written, read, heard, interpreted, resisted, or appropriated by various actors in varied ways . . . over time" (Skukauskaitė, this volume: p. 147). Policies shaped by the logic of economic efficiency often have unintended negative educational or social consequences. In Lithuania, the "student basket" initiative, in which resources migrated from school to school when students changed their registration, as well as the reduced socioeconomic security of educators in the 1990s worked together to make teachers feel less valued than students. Many teachers saw themselves as easily replaced and more powerless than they had been during the Soviet era. They felt excluded from educational planning and deeply ambivalent about prospects for teaching democracy or implementing new educational initiatives.

The scenarios in which the Indonesian teachers were observed and interviewed also illustrated their lack of confidence and power. Their everyday lives in classrooms diverged radically from high-sounding guidelines at the national or regional levels that emphasized decentralized decision making and education to promote students' interest and participation. The introduction of a validated civic curriculum package (originating outside the country) was intended to provide opportunities for students to become civically engaged and to develop their own views, but lack of democracy in the school environment produced quite different results. When a teacher decided to encourage students to read the textbook primarily to support or defend an argument and to engage in a discussion where she would not judge their opinions as right or wrong, the consequences increased her sense of powerlessness. She was warned against this approach to the text and discussion (both by her husband and by other teachers). They reminded her that only prescribed correct answers would be acceptable on the centrally formulated examinations for which students were being prepared. Reciting definitions and learning slogans were the keys to students' success. She was also advised against holding student debates, as this might lead to unwelcome vigilance about the actions of government (which could have a negative impact on activist students' acceptance for future education).

Teachers in Mexico were presented with a new national curriculum that included teaching about values and human rights, along with a specific time period of three hours a week for a class called "Formación Cívica y Etica." The problems observed were similar to those in Indonesia. The term *human rights* served as a kind of projective test, onto which individual educators and other groups read their own prescriptions for the schools. For some groups, the new course's objectives were to reinstate a sense of traditional values; for some, it meant that schools could be held more accountable; only for a few did it mean creating an engaging or critical approach to analyzing government policies through dialogic pedagogy. In many cases, the chart or questions that were designed for students to discuss became assignments copied into notebooks. Even if there had been more common understanding about what was intended in the new course, the author anticipated that there would have been severe difficulties because of the poorly trained teacher force (consisting of substantial numbers of individuals trained in the law but unable to find employment as lawyers), the difficulty of recruiting new teachers to receive training to teach this class, and widespread suspicion of educational authorities. This course became quite different from what its initiators had envisioned, and teachers did not feel empowered to take positive action.

Debate and Discourse

Several of the examples in the previous section dealt with processes of activity and discussion in the classroom, and the issues of debate and discourse are of primary importance in two other chapters in this volume. The IEA Civic Education Study's results again provide an introduction.

The value of open and respectful exchange of opinion in the classroom has emerged in all the analyses of the Civic Education Study's data. Beginning with the IEA study of the 1970s and emphatically reinforced by the large survey of the 1990s, the perception of a classroom in which the open exchange of opinions is valued has been found to be a potent predictor of students' civic knowledge, of their intention to vote and engage in other kinds of political activities, and of their sense of political efficacy (Torney-Purta et al. 2001; Torney-Purta and Richardson 2004). The *absence* of an open climate for discussion explains some of the gaps between U.S. Latino and non-Latino students in civic knowledge and participation (Torney-Purta, Barber, and Wilkenfeld 2007). In fact, an open climate for discussing knowledge in the classroom turned out to be more important than the possession of factual knowledge itself in a number of analyses (Torney-Purta and Richardson 2004), corroborating a theme in this volume that knowledge by itself is insufficient to maintain involvement among citizens.

The importance of discourse and narratives that link the classroom with the community is a potent theme of the chapter about the Spokane, a group of Native Americans resident in the Northwest of the United States. This group has a civic culture that emphasizes the importance of the group gathering together to make decisions, of close listening by all members to the views of others in the group, and of recognizing abilities that are distributed among group members. Much of the political socialization that takes place within this community is implicit apprenticeship as part of an experience of a democracy of discourse. This looks quite different from the usual course in civic education. According to the author of this chapter, when the school uses standardized curricula emphasizing concepts like global competitiveness and individualized learning, the strong preparation for adulthood found in the local culture of democracy is likely to be lost and replaced with a weak textbook version of civic life that students find less meaningful.

A tension between transmitting factual material and engaging students in discourse also characterizes the classrooms of a Pentecostal Christian school observed in El Salvador. Some teachers try to link formative processes of civic identity and participatory discourse with the provision of information to students, while other teachers have students memorize definitions in order to pass tests. Some of the instructional strategies that were employed struck the observer as participatory in name but not in fact. They were interactive activities whose purpose was to motivate better memorization.

Throughout the quantitative and qualitative studies, from the IEA research through the observations in this volume, a constant theme is that open and respectful discussion of differing views is valuable but that teachers require preparation and support in order to do it well.

Summary

The question posed at the start of this section concerns the ways in which sociocultural studies can enrich quantitative survey research or the examination of policies. The quantitative and qualitative data generally agree about the importance of various dimensions and about the continuing dynamic tensions existing between curriculum pronouncements or policies, administrators' behavior, teachers' practice, and the community context for democracy. It is clear that most existing models in the field fail to go beyond the simple transmission of information. Freire (cited in the Brazilian chapter) called this the banking model of depositing information in children's minds, and I have referred to it as the accumulation model (Hess and Torney 2005). The EU, with its emphasis on active citizenship, the open climate for discussion found to be so powerful in the IEA study's analysis, approaches taken in study circles such as those described in the Brazilian chapter, and pedagogies of action such as those described for young adults in the Political Engagement Project (PEP) in the United States (Beaumont et al. 2006) have a great deal in common and a great deal to offer. They also require a distinct break from the past along with extensive preparation of instructors, leaders, or mentors. And they are not always easy to study as a researcher. In-depth classroom observations are the most satisfying evidence, but both follow-ups to the IEA study and the PEP have shown that it is possible to triangulate evidence from more than one source and thereby to take a significant research step.

The second question is less about what can be learned to enhance the existing situation by an incremental process than it is about more far-reaching changes.

Question 2: To What Extent Is a Critical Perspective on Knowledge (as Contested or Problematized) a Potentially Valuable Part of Civic Education?

A defining characteristic of many of the qualitative researchers writing in this volume is that they have a more critical perspective on civic education processes than do most quantitative or survey researchers. They look beyond existing assumptions about what constitutes useful preparation for citizenship.

However, the IEA survey data showed that a critical point of view is uncomfortable for most teachers. Furthermore, only about half of the students surveyed in the IEA study seemed to feel welcome in classrooms where participating in discussions of controversial issues with other students was expected.

For several of the authors in this volume, the critical view was an important subtheme. In El Salvador, the author believes that teachers need to recognize how the privatization of schooling problematizes the conditions and substance of their work. Among the Spokane, collisions between the local cultural milieu and the economic goals of education are highlighted. In discussing Japan, the author points out that themes of global responsibility, such as protecting the environment or understanding other cultures, are most acceptable when they are not seen in a critical framework but can be justified as contributing to the preparation of future leaders of business in a competitive global economy. The authors of the chapters on Cyprus and France refer to problematizing the European dimension; they use several sources to critically examine the disproportionate benefits for cultural and socioeconomic elites and ways in which minimalist or passive views of citizenship protect the status quo. The chapter on Cyprus proposes critical analysis as a dimension of democratic practice that should permeate the organization, presentation, and use of information.

In three of the chapters, this critical perspective was a major theme: those considering Australia, Brazil, and South Africa.

In discussing Australia, the author distinguishes between "minimal" and "critical" citizenship. Minimal citizenship is focused on imparting what is believed to be uncontested knowledge without recognizing tensions between the interests of different groups who may have different perspectives. Those who practice minimal citizenship emphasize activities such as voting and tend to give little attention to problems experienced in democracy, especially the existence of substantial inequalities or marginalized groups who hold little power (aboriginals, refugees, or immigrants). Viewing citizenship and society through the lens of differential power and needed social change is essential for the critical citizen, according to this point of view. Helping students take personal responsibility for action to solve problems related to social injustice is important. The author of this chapter found this perspective largely absent in the recent standards for school-based civic education in Australia. Most teachers seemed willing to accept this approach, asking how to do what was required in citizenship education more effectively and not whether this might be a limited view.

The Brazilian description of adults' culture circles, tracking discussion with street sellers over time, shows an emergent curriculum of problematizing dilemmas experienced in the present, discourses leading to critical meta-awareness of assumptions, the telling of personal stories illustrating these issues to more fully grasp their meaning, and attempts to formulate shared action to solve problem. For example, problematizing slogans about working hard to succeed and what the minimum wage is designed to support are ways to raise issues of elite privilege or gender inequality. The purpose is to go beyond widely accepted definitions to link the personal with the political in a way that leads to a sense of mastering an underlying problem.

Because many South African citizens participated in boycotts, civil disobedience, and even violence to successfully abolish apartheid, the new concept of citizenship has to be more than a minimalist version. Many of the most successful leaders of this fight were recruited for positions in local or national government, so new leaders have to be developed. At the same time, new channels are needed for citizens to communicate to government when policies fail to meet human needs. Critical skills are needed, such as how to frame a local political problem, how to think strategically about the contributions of different groups, and how to share power. Active citizenship could have two meanings: the more minimal one involving a sense of solidarity and social obligation, and the maximal one meaning an obligation to participate in transforming social structures. These authors prefer the maximal or critical approach.

CONCLUSION

Several things are surprising when looking across these chapters. The ways in which the qualitative studies involving observations, interviews, and close reading of policy documents and guidelines fit with survey results from the 1999 IEA Civic Education Study is somewhat unexpected. There is convergence about a number of topics: nationalism, attitudes toward immigrants and minorities, discomfort with controversy, the extent to which teachers feel powerless along with the impact this has on their students, and the difficulty of enacting dialogic pedagogies. All of these topic areas are rich with possibilities for further research in which anthropologists might collaborate with other social scientists and educational researchers.

The two questions focused our attention on the contribution of sociocultural research and critical analysis, both of which have a substantial role to play in future research. It is refreshing to see that the field has outgrown the question that guided so much of the early research: Which agent of socialization is most important? Is it the family, the school, the community, or the peer group? Researchers not only are recognizing all of these but are looking at their interaction and their place in a broader cultural and historical context.

Looking to the future, many of the conceptual and methodological approaches illustrated here show promise. These include establishing or maintaining communities of practice to form civil society, increasing the sense of power and confidence among teachers, moving from minimal to critical citizenship, using hypothetical situations in interviewing young people, and using linguistic analysis. All of them recognize the importance of situation-specific and reciprocal approaches both in creating citizens who can contribute to democracy and in formulating research to study that process.

It is surprising but encouraging to see the extent to which citizenship education in this wide range of countries is recognized as extending beyond a single course about government structure in upper secondary school. Younger students are often involved. Dialogue about social and political problems can take place with ten-year-olds and with adult street peddlers. Individuals can become part of discourses on human rights and begin to see the world through a new set of lenses.

Awareness is spreading that eloquent words are insufficient to ensure a democratic approach at the point when a teacher meets his or her class. Awareness is also increasing that educators who transmit simple civic-related messages to be copied into notebooks or repeated verbatim on examinations are providing insufficient preparation for democratic thinking or behavior. The story of civic education will continue to develop as it becomes more and more clear that democracy as it is envisioned and enacted in dialogue is not solely the province of politicians, nor is citizenship education solely the province of schools.

REFERENCES

Beaumont, E., A. Colby, T. Ehrlich, and J. Torney-Purta. 2006. "Promoting Political Competence and Engagement in College Students: An Empirical Study." *Journal of Political Science Education* 2.

Gordon, T., J. Holland, and E. Lahelma. 2000. *Making Spaces: Citizenship and Differences in Schools*. New York: St. Martin's.

Hahn, C. 1998. *Becoming Political: Comparative Perspectives on Citizenship*. Albany: State University of New York Press.

Hess, R., and J. Torney. 2005. *The Development of Political Attitudes in Children*. New Brunswick, N.J.: AldineTransaction. (Originally published in 1967.)

LeTendre, G. 2002. "Advancements in Conceptualizing and Analyzing Cultural Effects in Cross-National Studies of Educational Achievement." In *Methodological Advances in Cross-National Surveys of Educational Achievement*, ed. A. C. Porter and A. Gamoran. Washington, D.C.: National Academy Press.

Schiffauer, W., G. Baumann, R. Kastoryano, and S. Vertovec, eds. 2004. *Civil Enculturation: Nation-state, Schools and Ethnic Difference in Four European Countries*. New York: Berghahn Books.

Steiner-Khamsi, G., J. Torney-Purta, and J. Schwille, eds. 2002. *New Paradigms and Recurring Paradoxes in Education for Citizenship*. Vol. 5. Oxford: Elsevier Science.